The Supreme Court

Rulings on American Government and Society

Second Edition

A LANAHAN CASEBOOK

The Supreme Court

Rulings on American Government and Society

Second Edition

A LANAHAN CASEBOOK

Jack Fruchtman Jr.

LANAHAN PUBLISHERS, INC. *Baltimore*

The text of this book was composed in Baskerville with
display type set in Caslon.
Composition by Bytheway Publishing Services
Manufacturing by Victor Graphics, Inc.

ISBN-10 1-930398-18-2
ISBN-13 978-1-930398-18-4

LANAHAN PUBLISHERS, INC.
324 Hawthorne Road, Baltimore, MD 21210
1-866-345-1949 (toll free)
WWW.LANAHANPUBLISHERS.COM

1 2 3 4 5 6 7 8 9 0

To Clara, Juliette, Sophia, Elsa,
and my students, past, present, and future

CONTENTS

PREFACE

The federal judiciary is supreme in the exposition of the law of the Constitution, and that principle has ever since been respected by this Court and the Country as a permanent and indispensable feature of our constitutional system.
—Chief Justice Earl Warren, *Cooper v. Aaron*, 358 U.S. 1 (1958), commenting on Chief Justice John Marshall's 1803 opinion in *Marbury v. Madison*, 5 U.S. 137.

This new second edition, as with the first, is intended to offer students a basic introduction to the work and the words of the Supreme Court. It is both a *primer* on the workings of the Court—its place among the three branches of government, how it comes to hear certain cases, the rules by which it operates—and a *casebook* of its rulings, concurrences, and dissents on such diverse issues as federalism, religious expression, free speech, equal protection, due process, rights of the accused, and privacy.

Although both Democrats and Republicans, liberals and conservatives have criticized the Court because they disagree with some decisions, one thing is settled: we accept the fact that the federal judiciary, especially the Supreme Court of the United States, as the court of last resort, is the final arbiter of the meaning of the Constitution. Court rulings have had a major impact on how our federal and state governments act—for example, whether states may discriminate on the basis of race or sex—and they have had an enormous impact on how we live—for example, whether a woman has a constitutional right to an abortion.

The Supreme Court offers the final authoritative analysis of the Constitution. As Justice John Marshall Harlan wrote in his famous 1896 dissent in *Plessy v. Ferguson*, 163 U.S. 537, the Supreme Court is "the final expositor of the fundamental law of the land" (Case 4.1), a remark echoed by Justice William Brennan in 1962 when he said that the Court has the responsibility to resolve constitutional issues "as ultimate interpreter of the Constitution" (*Baker v. Carr*, 369 U.S. 186) (Case 1.3). Chief Justice William H. Rehnquist repeated this thought in his 1989 dissent in *Texas v. Johnson*, 491 U.S. 397, when he held that the Court is "the final expositor of the Constitution" (Case 3.3).

Eleven years later, Chief Justice Rehnquist noted that even "Congress may not legislatively supersede our decisions interpreting and applying the Constitution" (*Dickerson v. United States*, 530 U.S. 428 [2000]). With the justices' reasoned defense of their positions, whether in writing the Court's opinion, concurring, or dissenting, we can see how they arrive at their conclusions.

Most important, they present their interpretation of the meaning of the various clauses of the Constitution in terms of what it says and does not say. After all, the document is quite specific in some areas: for example, to be the President of the United States, one must be at least 35 years old and born in the United States. At the same time, the Constitution is often so silent that the justices literally read into the document their ideas about its meaning or what they believe the framers might have meant: for example, whether the Second Amendment protects an individual or community right to gun ownership or whether the Bill of Rights includes the right to privacy, the right to be left alone.

Of course, Court decisions depend on a majority of the nine justices, meaning that its rulings depend on who serves on the Court. All federal justices are appointed for life (though they may be impeached), and most contemporary justices tend to remain on the bench for a very long time. Justice Sandra Day O'Connor served on the Court for twenty-four years, eleven of which with the same group of justices (1994–2005), before she announced at the end of the 2004–05 term that she planned to retire. President Ronald Reagan had nominated her as the first woman Supreme Court Justice back in 1981. Then in August of 2005, Chief Justice William H. Rehnquist, himself on the Court since 1972, suddenly died after suffering from cancer for almost a year. These two developments allowed President George W. Bush to send, within a very short time, two nominations for the Court to the U.S. Senate, which has the authority to confirm (or not confirm) the president's nominees. Rather than elevate an existing justice to chief justice, President Bush nominated and the Senate confirmed Judge John G. Roberts Jr. as the new chief justice to begin the 2005–06 term. President Barack Obama added two individuals to the Court: Sandra Sotomayor joined the Court in 2009, succeeding David Souter, and Elena Kagan in 2010, succeeding John Paul Stevens. As the Court's personnel changes, so will its decisions.

The Second Edition

As both a primer on the Court and anthology of case rulings, the first edition has been assigned in courses on American government and politics, the Supreme Court, Constitutional Law, the judicial process, and American history.

This second edition has benefited from instructors of these courses who have suggested the inclusion of more landmark and foundation cases. The first edition contained many such cases—*Marbury v. Madison* (1803), *McCulloch v. Maryland* (1819), *Plessy v. Ferguson* (1896), and *Brown v. Board of Education of Topeka, Kansas* (1954). *Korematsu v. United States* (1944). For the second edition, these landmark and foundation cases have been added:

Ex Parte Milliken (1866)
Gibbons v. Ogden (1824)
National Labor Relations Board v. Jones & Laughlin Steel Corp. (1937)
Heart of Atlanta Motel v. United States (1964)
Katzenbach v. McClung (1964)
Schenck v. United States (1919)
Brandenburg v. Ohio (1969)
New York Times v. Sullivan (1964)
New York Times Co. v. United States (1971)
Everson v. Board of Education of Ewing Township (1947)
Regents of the University of California v. Bakke (1978)
Gideon v. Wainwright (1963)
Miranda v. Arizona (1968)
Lochner v. New York (1905)
Roe v. Wade (1973)

Of course, the Court has not stood still since the publication of the first edition. The second edition includes several more recent rulings: the First Amendment case concerning campaign financing, *Citizens United v. Federal Election Commission* (2010) (Case 3.4); the Second Amendment decision on gun ownership, *McDonald v. City of Chicago* (2010) (Case 5.8); the upholding of most provisions of the Patient Protection and Affordable Care Act, *National Federation of Business v. Sebelius* (2012) (Case

2.7); the challenge to affirmative action, *Parents Involved in Community Schools v. Seattle School District No. 1* (2007) (Case 4.3); and the right-to-die case, *Gonzales v. Oregon* (2006) (Case 6.4). Finally, the Court handed down two important decisions from the October Term 2012 in June of 2013: *Shelby County v. Holder* (Case 1.5), which invalidated a major portion of the Voting Rights Act of 1965 and *United States v. Windsor* (Case 6.6), which overturned the section of the Defense of Marriage Act of 1996 barring federal benefits to married same-sex couples.

As in the first edition, each chapter contains a brief introduction designed to present a coherent perspective of each topic covered in the chapter. Every case is preceded by a brief introduction setting forth the background of the dispute involved and the manner in which the case finally moved to the Supreme Court. The Court's opinion, usually a majority or plurality, then follows along with one or two concurrences or dissents of particular note. Each topic area concludes with a section called "Rulings in Context," which briefly takes students case-by-case through the development of a particular area of constitutional law.

Many people were instrumental in the original formation of this book, although final responsibility for the first, and now second edition, rests with me alone. I appreciated the insightful observations and suggestions I received from my Towson University colleague Cynthia L. Cates, Daniel Devitt at the Menlo School, Joel B. Grossman at Johns Hopkins University, F. Graham Lee at St. Joseph's University in Philadelphia, Frederick P. Lewis at the University of Massachusetts, Lowell, Lewis Ringel at CSU—Long Beach, Paul Weizer at Fitchburg State College, and Amy L. Tenney of the law firm of Jenner & Block. More recently, Bruce Stinebrickner at DePauw University provided a very helpful critique. Many years ago, J. Woodford Howard Jr. at Johns Hopkins first stimulated my interest in the Supreme Court and how its members decide constitutional issues, and I have been deeply indebted to him since that time. As always, JoAnn Fruchtman has been an invaluable source of support and inspiration. Finally, working with Don Fusting at LANAHAN PUBLISHERS has been a most delightful experience, and I deeply appreciate his wise counsel and guidance.

The Supreme Court

Rulings on American Government and Society

Second Edition

A LANAHAN CASEBOOK

CHAPTER I

The Constitution, American Democracy, and the Supreme Court

Far too often, Americans take the Constitution for granted for a number of reasons. First, it has lasted a very long time, since 1789, when the first Federal Congress and the first President were elected under its authority. Sometimes this very fact makes us think it will last forever. Second, it has provided us with a structure of government that has changed very little since it began—we still have three branches, consisting of an executive (a President), a legislative (two houses of Congress, the Senate and the House of Representatives), and a judiciary (the federal courts with the Supreme Court as the court of last resort). Finally, the Constitution does not appear to have changed very much. The basic structure has remained the same, and it has been amended only 27 times (see Appendix).

But if the Constitution has lasted so long mostly unchanged, that it exists at all is remarkable. While we might take it for granted as the foundation of "the American way of liberty and democracy," one thing is clear: it might very well not have existed at all. As you read about the Supreme Court and its rulings, bear in mind that one of the major goals of drafting and ratifying the Constitution was, as the Preamble states, "to form a more perfect Union," where we might place an emphasis on the word *more*. From 1781 until the ratification of the Constitution seven years later, the nation lived precariously under the authority of the Articles of Confederation, a document that was America's first attempt at constitution making. The Articles created what was really a military alliance among the states, a device to unite the country to fight a common enemy, Great Britain. The emphasis in the Articles was to maintain the power of the states, not the national or, as it would later be called, the federal government.

The Development of the Constitution

The Declaration of Independence ends with the resounding words that "these United Colonies are, and of Right ought to be Free and Independent States . . . and that as Free and Independent States, they have full Power to levy War, conclude Peace, contract Alliances, establish commerce, and to do all other Acts and Things which Independent States may of right do." The use of the term, *states*, in this context is significant. A *state*, as we know it today and as the founders of our nation understood it, signifies a nation of people organized under one government in a defined territory. Leaders in the new thirteen states, emerging from their colonial status under the British Crown, believed they were independent, not only of Britain, but of each other. With the exception of a few states that simply adopted their existing colonial charters as their new constitutions, most states immediately drafted new documents for internal, independent governance because the old charters were irrelevant.

When George Washington undertook the task of raising the Continental Army to fight the British soldiers and the German mercenaries that accompanied them, he asked each state to send a number of troops based on the state's population (the Confederation Congress did not have the authority to raise an army). Most did, but at the same time, these soldiers' allegiance was openly to their home state, not to the new United States or to General Washington. When, for example, the troops arrived from New Jersey, and Washington asked them to pledge their loyalty to the United States, they agreed only on the condition that they first pledge their allegiance to their "nation" of New Jersey. This was typical of other regiments as well.

Rhode Island, the smallest of the states, contributed troops to the revolutionary effort, but was very wary of sending money to support it (the Confederation Congress also could not levy taxes). When the war ended and independence won, that state, with a history of border disputes with both Connecticut and Massachusetts, refused to cooperate with the monetary policy that the government established to raise revenues. To protect its independence from these states and even from the United States, Rhode Island refused to support a national import duty. When the Constitutional Convention convened in Philadelphia in 1787, it declined to send any delegates, and it was the last state to ratify the new Constitution. It finally did so in 1790, after the first national elections, and even then, ratification passed by only two votes.

American historians rightly call the years of the Confederation government (1781-1788) "the Critical Period." The nation was in danger of breaking apart. Only through the perseverance and dedication of the founding generation were we able to form that "more perfect Union." The United States could have just as easily wound up as a collection of fragile independent states, vulnerable to outside influence and force. They could well have been subject to fierce interstate competition, even warfare, over such disputes as water rights, mineral rights, and so on.

If the Articles of Confederation proved unworkable, especially after the end of hostilities with Britain—the Treaty of Paris was signed in 1783—the Constitution was designed to overcome its predecessor's economic and political deficiencies. The framers designed the new document to balance the authority of the state and federal governments, but at the same time, to allow the federal government to raise revenue, a military force, and enforce its laws. The first three articles comprise bundles of power. They set forth the structure and authority of the executive, legislative, and judicial branches with strong commanding words. Look how each begins:

> Article I: "All legislative Powers granted herein shall be vested in a Congress. . . ."

> Article II: "The executive Power shall be vested in a President. . . ."

> Article III: "The judicial Power of the United States shall be vested in one supreme Court, and in such inferior Courts as the congress may from time to time ordain and establish."

Two observations immediately come to mind when reading these opening lines. First, Article I refers to "all" legislative powers, not a few, not some, not most. And second, each article uses the imperative form of the verb "to be," *shall*: the Constitution therefore commands that all legislative powers or the executive power or the judicial power shall (not may or might) be vested in these branches of government. They, in short, must be so empowered, leaving far more limited authority to state governments when compared to what they had under the Articles of Confederation.

For some Americans at the time, these words were frightening and bewildering. They were far too reminiscent of the British government from which they had just won their independence. The new government was too powerful because it centralized authority and depleted the hard-won power of the individual states. Because of these suspicions, ratification of the new document was never a certainty.

One group, largely based in New York, the Anti-Federalists, opposed the new Constitution and wanted the Articles only to be amended. Led by their governor, George Clinton, they thought that it constituted a far-too centralized government with broad powers undermining state authority. Because of the critical position that New York State held in the new nation, Alexander Hamilton recruited fellow New Yorker John Jay and Virginian James Madison to address these and many other issues in a series of essays to convince New York to accept the new document. As signers of the new document, these three men were very prominent and highly respected statesmen. Madison, universally known as the Father of the Constitution, was later elected the fourth President of the United States, while Hamilton served as the first Secretary of the Treasury. Jay, an eminent lawyer and diplomat, became the first Chief Justice of the United States.

Publius, the collective pseudonym for the entire series, signed all the essays, five by Jay, the other 80 split between Hamilton, who wrote 51, and Madison. Soon, 85 essays, known collectively as *The Federalist Papers*, appeared periodically in several New York newspapers, analyzing the virtues of the Constitution. Madison's fellow Virginian Thomas Jefferson later called the *Papers* "the best commentary on the principles of government which ever was written," and twentieth-century commentator, Clinton Rossiter, declared that the papers collectively comprised "the one product of the American mind that is rightly counted among the classics of political theory."

While Hamilton's project was successful in gaining New York's ratification (though only after the requisite number of nine states had already ratified it), the Anti-Federalists continued to argue that with the Constitution's emphasis only on powers, it must include something about freedom and rights. In fact, many states conditioned their ratification on the requirement that the first Congress amend the document to provide for an expression of the people's rights and liberties. Many colonists had suffered greatly under British rule when their rights and liberties were threatened or abridged. The result was the passage in the first Federal Congress of the first ten amendments, known collectively as the Bill of Rights, which the states ratified on December 15, 1791.

The Place of the Judiciary

In terms of length and placement, it seems almost as if Article III were an afterthought when we consider the amount of time the framers in 1787 devoted to the Congress and the President. In the document itself, the legislative and executive branches account for more than half of its words. In addition, when we finally arrive at Article III, we see that it addresses only a Supreme Court and its powers. It says nothing about lower federal courts, leaving it to Congress to decide from time to time whether additional courts are necessary.

Unlike members of Congress or the President, federal judges, including the justices of the Supreme Court, do not have to campaign for office, they do not raise money, they do not advertise, they do not engage in political debates, and their names do not appear on the ballot. The President has the authority to nominate federal judges, and the Senate must then decide whether the nominees should be confirmed.

Because the framers wanted to create an independent judiciary unrelated to the executive or legislative branches, they inserted two provisions to ensure federal judges' independence. First, they all have lifetime tenure. This means that once they are confirmed, they "shall hold their Offices during good Behavior": they do not have to resign or retire unless they want to or unless they are impeached. Second, Congress may not reduce their salaries while they are in office, though it may raise them. This means that Congress has no authority to pressure the judges to force them to bend their will to that of the Congress by threatening to lower or eliminate their compensation.

The federal courts possess two basic tasks: First, they are to ensure that each branch of government does not unconstitutionally delegate its powers to another branch. Article I, Section 8, sets forth the powers of Congress, which may not pass a law that gives any of those powers to the President. Congress, for example, has the power to declare war, and it may not constitutionally delegate that power to the President.

Second, the courts must ensure that the President, the Congress, *and* the state governments do not infringe on our individual rights and liberties. No right or liberty is absolute, even those basic ones outlined in the First Amendment, which, among other things, ensures freedom of religion, speech, press, and assembly. But we have a right to talk about our political opinions and write them down, and neither Congress nor any state government may come along and deprive us of them without a pretty good justification. Should a dispute arise over whether the government may limit our speech, that dispute would go to a court of law for a final determination. The judges, perhaps even the Supreme Court justices, would ultimately decide the matter.

The Constitution, Constitutional Law, and the Supreme Court

If the Constitution as a document has not changed significantly in well over 200 years, the judges, especially the justices of the Supreme Court, have transformed its meaning and even its significance.

There is, after all, a major difference between the *Constitution*, which has remained virtually the same over time, and *constitutional law*, which is how the judges have interpreted and thus changed the document. While members of Congress have proposed tens of thousands of amendments over the years, very few have ever passed the stringent requirements set forth in Article V. In recent years, several amendments have failed: among them are those that guaranteed equal rights to women, balanced budgets, term limits, prayer in the public schools or those that would have permanently outlawed abortion and flag desecration. Meantime, the Supreme Court has dealt with all of these issues, and its pronouncements have changed the Constitution and its meaning.

The Constitution is therefore very different today from when it was ratified in 1788 because the judges have made it so. While they are not legislators, that is, representatives elected by the people to make laws on their behalf, judges do make policy when they decide cases on constitutional principles. They focus on "state action," that is when the government or some agency of the government, national or state, has allegedly wronged an individual or group of individuals, and that person or group seeks redress or damages. When the board of education in Topeka, Kansas, for example, denied Linda Brown, an African-American child, the right to attend school with white children, her father sued the school board to force it to change its policy. The Supreme Court ruled in her favor in *Brown v. Board of Education of Topeka, Kansas*, 347 U.S. 483 (1954) (Case 4.2).

Throughout history, Court decisions have had enormous authority in terms of their political impact on our lives. The twentieth-century Court, in particular, faced major social questions: whether schools shall be integrated; whether a woman shall have the right to make decisions concerning her body; whether prayers shall be said in a public school; whether homosexuals shall enjoy the right to privacy in their homes; and on and on. Today's Court will likely rule on even more such issues.

The Court's decisions affect public policy in ways that are very different from how a legislature decides an issue. Legislators must stand for re-election and are accountable to the people; federal judges do not and are not. Legislators have the authority to change the laws; rulings by Supreme Court justices stand and can only be changed if another case on the same issue initiated in a lower court eventually reaches the Supreme Court or if an amendment added to the Constitution overturns the ruling.

The judges on the United States Circuit Courts of Appeal, the intermediate appellate court just below the Supreme Court, do the same for most matters of federal law. Their decisions are, however, effective only in their circuits, that is, the clusters of states that make up each circuit. The exception is the District of Columbia Circuit, which has jurisdiction in Washington, D. C., and the federal agencies there, and the Federal Circuit, which has jurisdiction mainly over tax, patent, and international trade matters. Circuit courts usually hear cases in multi-judge panels of three, but if the case is important enough or if a losing party whose case was heard by those three judges wishes the entire court to rehear the case, the resulting court is said to sit *en banc*, literally "on the bench," but more to the point, "the full bench." The one exception is the Ninth Circuit on the West Coast, which has so many judges that *en banc* hearings consist of only 11 judges of a total of 47.

Box I.I

Appealing a Case to the Supreme Court

One of the goals that William H. Rehnquist had when he became Chief Justice in 1986 was to reduce the size of the Supreme Court's docket, that is, the number of cases the Court hears each year. Thirty years ago, the Court was asked to review around 5,000 cases. At that time, it annually issued almost 150 opinions. Today, the Court accepts less than one percent of the more than 9,000 cases appealed to it each year. The Court decided its lowest number of signed opinions during 2011–2012 term: 64 compared to 75 from the year before. In its 2012–2013 term, it decided 73 signed cases. Some are decided with no opinion: called summary decisions, they may include a simple blunt order or an unsigned or *per curiam*, that is "for the Court," opinions. The Court has said that summary decisions do not serve as precedent, but they are binding on lower courts until the Supreme Court rules otherwise.

Cases appealed to the Supreme Court may come from lower federal courts or from state supreme courts if they raise a constitutional question. Most cases—around 65 percent—arrive from the federal courts, while 30 percent from the state courts. The rest come from the United States Court of Military Appeals or fall within the Court's original jurisdiction. The latter primarily involve disputes between two state governments, such as in 1998 in *New Jersey v. New York*, 523 U.S. 767, when a controversy arose over which of these two states owned Ellis Island, which lies in the Hudson River. The Court ruled that New York owned the original island, which had once consisted of a mere three acres. However, the Court went on, New Jersey owned most of the additional 24.5 acres that the United States had added to the original island because it needed more room to receive and process immigrants to the United States.

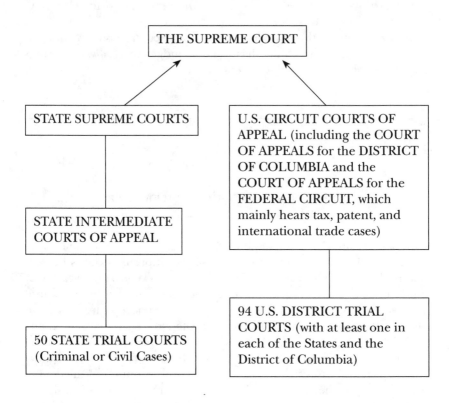

One major power that the Supreme Court justices have, unlike other federal judges, is their discretionary jurisdiction: since the passage of the Judiciary Act of 1925, they have had the broad authority to select the cases they want to review. This means that they can either reject a case or grant what is called a "writ of *certiorari*," thus certifying a case for argument before the Court. For a case to be accepted, at least four justices must agree to hear it. This is informally called the Rule of Four, which is neither a hard nor fast rule.

There are exceptions to the Rule of Four, especially involving the death penalty when *habeas corpus* cases are appealed to the Court. The term *habeas corpus*, which literally translates as "you have the body," refers to due process issues requiring judges to determine whether law enforcement officers have legally detained prisoners, stated the charges against them, provided them with legal counsel, and brought them to trial within a reasonable time. In the event of a *habeas* case, five justices must vote to hear an appeal. In death penalty cases, this holds when a judge has already set an execution date. Justice Lewis Powell often joined four of his colleagues who always wanted to hear these cases. He simply believed that if four of his colleagues agreed to a review, the full Court should hear it as it ordinarily would under the Rule of Four. After Justice Powell's retirement in 1987, several executions have taken place without prior review from the Court because only four justices agreed to hear the appeals.

The Court rarely informs the public why it decides not to accept a case. One well-established reason for a denial to review is known as the "political question" doctrine. This means that the Court decides that one of the political branches of the government, that is, the executive or legislature, could best resolve a dispute. They are called "elected" branches because those who occupy these offices are accountable to the people after they have campaigned for election. This includes the President who is ultimately elected by Electors.

The cases the Supreme Court accepts are those that the Court believes raise a federal question in light of constitutional requirements. The Court is sometimes urged to resolve a statutory rather than a constitutional dispute. Statutory questions do not involve interpreting the Constitution, but rather the meaning of a law as it has been enforced. In fact, just less than 50 percent of the Court's docket focuses on constitutional cases, while about 35 percent deals with congressional legislation. The rest consists of taxation, administrative law, practices and procedure, and patents and claims. An example of the Court's statutory interpretation is its rulings on allegations of racial and sex discrimination in employment practices under Title VII the Civil Rights Act of 1964: see *Griggs v. Duke Power Co.*, 401 U.S. 424 (1971), *Wards Cove Packing Co. v. Atonio*, 490 U.S. 642 (1989), and *Ledbetter v. Goodyear Tire and Rubber Co.*, 550 U.S. 618 (2007). In these cases, rather than appeal to provisions in the Constitution, the justices focused on the precise words of the title and the legislative record to discern legislators' understanding and intentions at the time of the law's passage.

In adjudicating cases like these, judges, including those on the Supreme Court, engage in third-party conflict resolution and judicial "realism" in the sense that their goal is to resolve disputes in pragmatic, practical ways. Congress designed Title VII of the Civil Rights Act of 1964 to ensure fair employment practices so that employers did not discriminate in hiring, promotion, and working conditions on the basis of five categories: race, color, religion, sex, or national origin. In a recent decision noted above, Lilly Ledbetter challenged the employment practices at Goodyear where she worked for over nineteen years. She claimed that her supervisors consistently gave her low performance ratings and consequently low salary increases because of her sex. A federal court jury found that the evidence supported her allegations and awarded her over $3.5 million, which the judge reduced to $360,000. On appeal, Goodyear argued that Title VII required her to file her complaint within 180 days of the employer's discriminatory conduct: this meant that she could challenge only the very last performance review and salary increase, whereas the jury had reviewed her entire nineteen-year career.

The U.S. Court of Appeals for the Eleventh Circuit reversed—a decision that the Supreme Court upheld in a bare five to four majority ruling. Writing for the Court, Justice Samuel Alito held that the law explicitly time-barred Ledbetter's claim except for the immediate 180 days prior to her initial court filing. He noted that Congress had limited civil actions to 180 days to ensure quick resolutions of pay disputes. Congress had indicated, he said, that these disputes became more difficult to defend against as time passed. In dissent, Justice Ruth Bader Ginsburg argued that the majority presented a "cramped" view of Title VII and misconstrued its true intention to overcome discrimination in employment practices. She suggested that Congress could fix the Court's narrow reading of Title VII, which it did in 2009 when it passed the Lilly Ledbetter Fair Pay Act. That law allowed claims for pay discrimination beyond the 180-day limitation.

The Court has applied the same realist analysis involving third-party conflict resolution to cases involving constitutional interpretation. Most states have the death penalty for those convicted of capital crimes. This is a public policy decision. These states have concluded that capital punishment is necessary because of two main factors: retribution for a heinous crime and deterrence of others from committing those crimes. Opponents of the death penalty claim that it violates the "cruel and unusual" provision of the Eighth Amendment. And yet, no Supreme Court majority has ever held that the Constitution prohibits states or the federal government from executing those guilty of capital crimes. In 1972, the Court did set aside all death penalty laws and invited the states to rewrite them. It found that a person could be put to death for so many different crimes that its implementation was arbitrary and random (*Furman v. Georgia*, 408 U.S. 238). Some justices have contended that the death penalty must remain an option for those states and the federal government if they want to keep it on the books, because those who drafted and supported the Eighth Amendment in the eighteenth century fully understood that it did not undermine capital punishment. Thus, the only way to outlaw executions is through a constitutional amendment. Others have argued that the policy of executing anyone is in fact "cruel and unusual punishment" in today's world because times have changed since the amendment's 1791 ratification.

In *Roper v. Simmons*, 543 U.S. 551 (2005) (Case 5.6), the Court ruled by a bare five to four majority that the execution of those who committed a capital crime when they were minors violates the Cruel and Unusual Punishment Clause of the Eighth Amendment. In his opinion for the Court, Justice Anthony Kennedy held that young people under eighteen have neither the experience nor emotional and mental sophistication to judge whether it was right or wrong to commit a capital crime: in this case, Christopher Simmons committed a particularly gruesome murder in the course of a burglary. Kennedy also noted juveniles may also be subject to peer pressure. He held that a clear national consensus opposed executing people like Simmons by adding the number of states without capital punishment to those that allow it but prohibit death sentences for juveniles when they committed the crime. Finally, Kennedy cited international agreements that prohibit the practice, including the United Nations Convention on the Rights of the Child and the International Covenant on Civil and Political Rights, even though the United States has declined to sign them.

The dissent, led by Justice Antonin Scalia, argued that citing international conventions have no place in American law. Moreover, he said, Kennedy's math was faulty. Scalia declined to count those states without the death penalty at all in coming up with a national "consensus" because legislators or governors had ever specifically commented on the execution of those who were juveniles at the time they committed their crime. He asserted that when the states ratified the Eighth Amendment in 1791, they all had death penalty statutes, and many of these included the execution of those committing capital crimes when they were not yet eighteen years old.

After rendering its decision, the Court has a variety of options. It may affirm the lower court's ruling, which means that the party that won in the lower court is the victor. Or it may *vacate* the lower court's decision, which means that it has set it aside or canceled it. In effect, it nullifies the lower court's decision by overruling it. Or it may *remand* the case to the lower court, that is, send it back to that court for further hearings and action consistent with the Supreme Court's decision. In any event, when the Court finally hands down a decision, its ruling acts as a precedent for future cases raising similar issues or questions of law. When a future ruling upholds a previous one, the Court exercises the doctrine of *stare decisis* by letting "the prior decision stand." Most jurists argue that in this way, consistency in the law offers more stability in government.

The Court operates *via* internal rules and conventions that have developed over the past 225 years. They hear cases and issues opinions, for example, from the first Monday of October each year until the end of the following June. Sometimes, the justices' docket requires them to stay in session into July. The October–June period is generally known as the Court's "October Term" and typically those words are followed by a year. For example, 2012–2013 marked the October Term 2012. Over the summer, the justices and their clerks read requests for *certiorari* from appellants who wish to have the Court review their cases. They may issue orders adding cases to their docket for the following term. The justices typically hand down most of their opinions in the spring but they may do so at any time that the Court has completed all its opinions in a case. They usually complete oral arguments in April and devote the remainder of the term to issuing opinions.

The Court has had to struggle with enforcement of its rulings because it relies on the executive branch to ensure that its decisions are complied with. Over the past 225 years, the Court has generally gained the respect of the American people and the other two branches of government so that even when presidents have disagreed with judicial decisions, they have typically agreed to enforce them. Examples of this include President Dwight D. Eisenhower's vigorous support of the Court's 1954 desegregation decision, *Brown v. Board of Education*, and President George W. Bush's agreement, however reluctant, to accept the Court's decisions concerning the due process rights of prisoners held in Guantanamo Bay, Cuba, after their capture as suspected terrorists. The most prominent cases include *Rasul v. Bush*, 542 U.S. 466 (2004), *Hamdi v. Rumsfeld*, 542 U.S. 507 (2004), *Hamdan v. Rumsfeld*, 548 U.S. 557 (2006), and *Boumediene v. Bush*, 551 U.S. 723 (2008).

In 1803, Chief Justice John Marshall stated that "it is emphatically the province and duty of the judicial department to say what the law is" (*Marbury v. Madison*, 5 US. 137) (Case. 1.1). Since then, the justices of the Supreme Court, no matter whether they were progressive or conservative, have invariably argued that they alone have the last word on the meaning of the Constitution. They do not have any problem in actively overruling earlier Supreme or lower court decisions or declaring congressional legislation or state and local laws unconstitutional. As Chief Justice Earl Warren wrote in 1956 in *Cooper v. Aaron*, 358 U.S. 1, when education officials in Little Rock, Arkansas, wanted to delay desegregation of its schools, "the federal judiciary is supreme in the exposition of the law of the Constitution." This principle has "been respected by this Court and the Country as a permanent and indispensable feature of our constitutional system." He concluded with these powerful words: "No state legislator or executive or judicial officer can war against the Constitution without violating his undertaking to support it," that is, war against the Constitution as the Court alone interprets it.

Opinions of the Court

As you read these opinions, you should be mindful of several things. First, they may appear to be written in a difficult style, but the more opinions you read, the easier they are to understand and follow. Judges are not taught to be great writing stylists; they are taught to be lawyers, and their legal training teaches them sophisticated logical and analytical reasoning skills. This also makes for good thinking skills, but not necessarily good or interesting writing ability. Having said that, some justices, like Justice Oliver Wendell Holmes in the last century and Justice Antonin Scalia more recently, developed engaging and intriguing styles, making their opinions especially accessible to readers who are not trained in a law school.

Second, the justices write their decisions in the form of opinions, and that is exactly what they are. They embody the *opinion* of its author and the other justices who sign it. Justices who agree with the outcome of a case, but disagree with the Court's reasoning, write concurring opinions, and justices who disagree with the outcome write dissenting opinions.

Third, decisions result from the justices engaging in debate with one another, sometimes even furious debate. When and if a majority is formed, which may be as few as five justices, the opinion of this group becomes the opinion of the Court. And yet, there are some occasions when the Court is so divided that the justices cannot come up with a majority opinion. We may find that as many as eight or nine opinions come out of a single case. Usually, the opinion with a plurality of justices becomes the opinion of the Court. On rare occasions, as noted above, the Court will release an unsigned or *per curiam* opinion, which again means "by the court." An unsigned opinion usually includes only the facts of the case and its outcome. Several signed opinions, both concurring and dissenting, typically accompany it.

Finally and perhaps most interestingly, some opinions do not read like legal commentary at all. They may well appear to be more historical or even polemical. Justice Harry Blackmun's opinion in the 1973 landmark abortion case of *Roe v. Wade*, 410 U.S. 113, for example, often reads like a medical tract rather than a legal treatise (Case 6.1). When Chief Justice Rehnquist disagreed completely with the majority in the 1989 flag burning case, *Texas v. Johnson*, 491 U.S. 397 (Case 3.3), his dissent reviewed American history and contained very little law. When Justice Scalia dissented in the gay rights case of *Romer v. Evans*, 517 U.S. 620, in 1996, he focused not on the law so much as on what he called the politics of the contemporary "Culture War."

In any event, the cases in this book are designed to introduce students to the ways different members of the Supreme Court have interpreted the Constitution in light of the conflicts that brought these cases to them.

Box 1.2

Locating Judicial Opinions

Each Supreme Court decision has a title, indicating an appellant (the one who has appealed the lower court's decision) and an appellee (the one who has won at the lower court level). Cases are adversarial in that someone is against (or versus, abbreviated as *v.*) someone else. In 1954, along with several other similar cases, the Court decided *Brown v. Board of Education of Topeka, Kansas*, 347 U.S. 483 (see Case 4.2). Linda Brown's father had sued the Topeka school board because his daughter, who was African American, was prohibited from attending a nearby white school. The case evolved into the major question of state-required school segregation. Sometimes cases take on a descriptive title: these are often called the School Desegregation Cases.

A series of abbreviations and numbers follows the title of each case. These refer to where the cases may be found in the major collections. *Brown v. Board*, as it is often called, includes this string: 347 U.S. 483, 74 S.Ct. 686 (1954). The first set (347 U.S. 483) refers to *United States Reports*, which is published by the United States Government Printing Office. The numbers on either side of "U.S." refer to the volume number where the case may be found and the page number on which the case begins. The year indicates when the Court handed down the decision.

In cases decided before 1874, another name may appear instead of "U.S." In those days, a court reporter was assigned to report decisions so a case would be cited by the reporter's name. Prior to 1816 when the Office of the Reporter was officially created, A. J. Dallas (cited as Dall.) and then, William Cranch, reported Supreme Court opinions. *Marbury v. Madison* [see Case 1.1], for example, is properly cited as 5 U.S. (1 Cranch) 137 (1803). The reporters after Cranch included:

Dates	Reporter	Citation
1816–27	Wheaton	Wh.
1828–43	Peters	Pet.
1843–60	Howard	How.
1861–62	Black	Bl.
1863–74	Wallace	Wall.

"S.Ct." refers to *Supreme Court Reporter*, which is a commercial collection. It, too, contains the same source citations, but the volumes and page numbers are different from *U.S. Reports*.

Several internet sources are now available for students who wish to locate Supreme Court opinions, including FindLaw (www.findlaw. com/casecode/) and the Legal Information Institute (www.law.cornell. edu) at the Cornell University School of Law.

The Court and the Issues of the Day

The justices are deeply engaged in a number of constitutional issues, among them, the ongoing struggle to protect American rights and liberties, and at the same time to ensure that American society evolves as a safe, stable, fair, and just community. While the Bill of Rights protects the first of these, the Court must judge when and whether a state law or executive order oversteps what is known by the omnibus term as the government's "police power." According to Justice Rufus W. Peckham in *Lochner v. New York*, 198 U.S. 45 (1905), police powers "relate to the safety, health, morals and general welfare of the public." (The federal government does not possess police powers; only state and local governments do (Case 5.1).)

Without this power, it is conceivable that society would fall into the dangerous abyss of anarchy and decadence. There is a fine line that the Court has to draw that government must not cross when laws interfere with the rights of individuals who wish to do as they please when their actions do not bring harm to anyone else. The ramifications of the right to privacy, for example, raises this very question in the realm of marital rights in *Griswold v. Connecticut*, 391 U.S. 145 (1965) (Case 1.4), or of gay rights in *Lawrence v. Texas*, 539 U.S. 558 (2003) (Case 6.5). More recently, the issue of gay marriage or civil unions has poignantly addressed the very same issues. See *U.S. v. Windsor*, 570 U.S. _____ (2013) (Case 6.6).

The justices have also set the limits of the powers conferred on the President and Congress as well as on the states. Like all government officials, justices wield great authority when they hand down decisions that affect our daily lives about how we live and how we want to live. In the end, we have come to agree that when the Supreme Court speaks, it speaks to and for the nation. For that reason alone, it is important for us to see how, in limiting the power of government, it also draws boundaries on the power of the people.

The contemporary Court has become engaged in the most divisive, most passionate issues of our day. We need to understand how it works and what it says about these issues because we accept the principle, as the Chief Justice noted above, that it is the final expositor of the meaning of the Constitution. What follows are samples of the Court's interpretation. While not all concurring or dissenting opinions for each of the cases are reprinted here, the reader will find that an ongoing and unending debate continues among the justices about the proper meaning of the most important document in American history.

Judicial Review, Judicial Restraint, Judicial Activism: Cases

The Supreme Court of the United States as the court of last resort is rooted in the English common-law tradition of having rules set forth by judges—rather than having statutes brought into being by legislators or decrees issued by the executive. The common law also heavily relies on judicial precedent, the doctrine of *stare decisis*. As previously indicated, the doctrine means that the prior decision will usually stand. The common law as set forth by judges is embodied in one of the Court's earliest decisions acknowledging the power of judicial review in the United States: Chief Justice John Marshall's famous opinion in the 1803 case of *Marbury v. Madison*, 5 U.S. 137 (Case 1.1). In this case, the Chief Justice wrote his famous statement that "it is emphatically the province and duty of the judicial department to say what the law is." Judicial review in terms of the Supreme Court's authority is its duty to review and overturn any state or federal legislation or action that it deems to be in conflict with any provision of the United States Constitution.

When the Court speaks, therefore, it speaks the law, giving it the same binding force as if a legislature had passed a bill and an executive enacted it by signing it. If the Court is the final interpreter of the laws, its decisions become the supreme law of the land. In addition to *Marbury*, you will see in *Korematsu v. U.S.*, 323 U.S. 214 (1944), that the Court confirmed a military order during World War II that led to the deprivation of the civil rights and economic liberties of a single class of citizens, Japanese Americans. Over one hundred thousand of them were sent to internment camps far from their homes (Case 1.2). In *Baker v. Carr*, 369 U.S. 186 (1962), the Court tackled the problem of a political question (Case 1.3). *Baker* shows how the Court used its authority to wield greater authority by ruling that the courts could enter into the political thicket of electoral redistricting.

The Court took a major step in declaring in *Griswold v. Connecticut*,

391 U.S. 145 (1965), that the Constitution was broad enough to include rights that were not specifically listed in the Bill of Rights (Case 1.4). This case, like many of those the Court handed down in the 1960s, was subject to criticism by those who opposed an activist court that overturned laws passed by a democratically elected legislature when that law violated no explicit provision of the Constitution. The Court's majority, however, ruled that many phrases in the Bill of Rights, especially in the First, Third, Fourth, Fifth, and Ninth Amendments could be construed to include what Justice William O. Douglas called "penumbras" or shadings (or hints) of a right to privacy, which includes the right of a married couple to decide when and whether they would have children.

Justice Harlan concurred but explained that he believed that the right to privacy lay embedded in the liberty component of the Due Process Clause. Most justices have accepted the Harlan view.

Finally, in 2013, the Court decided a major voting rights case. By a bare majority, the justices ruled unconstitutional a major section of the Voting Rights Act of 1965, which was designed to overcome discrimination in voting. In *Shelby County v. Holder*, 570 U.S. _____, Chief Justice John Roberts held that Section 4 of the act violated the Constitution's requirement of "equal sovereignty" among the states (Case 1.5). When Congress renewed the act in 2006, it singled out the same nine states, 12 cities, and 57 counties that the act had identified 40 years earlier as having discriminated on the basis of race or ethnicity in voting procedures. These jurisdictions had to submit all proposed electoral changes to the federal government before they went into effect. Roberts suggested that Congress could develop a new formula to determine which jurisdictions currently discriminated in its voting procedures rather than use data that was four decades old. In reading the opinions, note how both the Chief Justice and Justice Ginsburg address "first-generation" discriminatory acts through literacy tests and "second-generation" acts such as redistricting and voter identification laws.

Case I.I

Marbury v. Madison
5 U.S. (I Cranch) 137 (1803)

In February, 1801, in the waning days of his term, President John Adams, a Federalist, nominated an eminent Maryland landowner and banker, William Marbury, along with forty-one others, to serve as justices of the peace in the District of Columbia. Congress had left it to the President to decide whether he wanted to reduce that number as he saw fit, and in fact his successor, Thomas Jefferson, did just that when he took office.

The Senate confirmed all the nominees, including Marbury, and Adams signed their commissions. Most soon took office, but four did not: one was Marbury whose commission was not yet delivered to him. While it was the duty of the Secretary of State to deliver the commissions, he had failed to do so. Adams had nominated his Secretary of State, John Marshall who was Thomas Jefferson's distant cousin, to be Chief Justice of the United States. In fact, for a time, Marshall simultaneously served in both positions and apparently neither he nor Adams ever saw a conflict of interest. In any case, before he took office as Chief Justice, Marshall had affixed the Great Seal of the United States on the commissions, and left it to his clerk, who happened to be his brother James, to deliver them. James, however, had the misfortune of misplacing and thus never delivering Marbury's commission.

After Jefferson took office in March of 1801, he ordered his Acting Secretary of State, Levi Lincoln—and later Jefferson's Attorney General—not to deliver the commissions. Jefferson probably had the commissions destroyed because they have never been found.

By the time Jefferson's permanent Secretary of State, James Madison, arrived in Washington to take office, Marbury filed a petition in the Supreme Court asking it to issue a writ of *mandamus*, an order requiring an official to carry out his duty, to force Madison to deliver Marbury's commission. Marbury had taken advantage of Section 13 of the Judiciary Act of 1789, which was one of the first bills Congress passed in an effort to create the lower federal courts.

Article III of the Constitution specifies only one Supreme Court, but grants to Congress the authority to create lower courts. The article also defines and gives examples of the Court's jurisdiction. The Court is mainly an appellate court, that is, it hears appeals in cases that have a constitutional issue at its core. But in very specific areas, the Court also has original jurisdiction, which means that it may hear a case in its first instance, that is, without a lower court trial first ruling on an issue before it. These include disputes between states and those involving ambassadors, public ministers, and consuls. All of these may begin litigation in the Supreme Court.

While Article III does not address writs of *mandamus*, it is clear from the language of the Constitution that issuing them does not fall within the original jurisdiction of the Supreme Court. Section

13 of the Judiciary Act, however, included a provision expanding the Court's original jurisdiction to issue these writs, and Marbury filed his suit directly in the high court.

Historians and judicial commentators have long analyzed this case in three ways. First, they contend it emphasized the intense ideological and party divisions setting the nationalist and conservative Federalists, led by John Adams and Alexander Hamilton, against the states' rights-oriented and liberal Republicans, led by Thomas Jefferson and James Madison. The Federalists believed that America's future lay with a close alliance, both military and economic, with Britain, whereas the Republicans thought France, especially because French military and financial aid during the American Revolution, was the key to America's future prosperity.

Second, the Federalists held that the new nation would only survive if a strong central government passed laws that effectively bound all Americans, whereas the Republicans preferred local government in the states themselves because they thought that the greatest infringements on citizens' rights would take place at the local not national level. Third and finally, the Federalists believed that a strong nation demanded a sound economy with a national financial system. The Republicans were agrarian in their outlook, holding that the key to the development of civic virtue, that is, the characteristics that go into the making of a true public-spirited citizen, was when a person was close to the land and engaged in agricultural enterprises.

The case also had a greater impact, and this was in the realm of judicial review. With its origins in the English common-law tradition, the American legal system is rooted in the doctrine of judge-made law, but *Marbury* raised the question of whether this tradition gave judges the authority, either in law or precedent, to invalidate acts of a legislature, like the Congress, or the executive, like the President, if the judges determined that these acts conflicted with some provision of the Constitution. The common-law tradition argued in the affirmative in the sense that judges found laws to be void when they restricted judicial power.

The case of *Marbury v. Madison*, with all its historic political intrigue setting Chief Justice Marshall against President Jefferson, was in many ways a case about Congress's attempt in the Judiciary Act of 1789, while establishing the lower federal trial courts, to redefine the Supreme Court's jurisdiction. Marshall's decision in part halted the action.

The decision has generated a great deal of debate over just what Marshall was trying to achieve. Clearly, he wanted to avoid a direct confrontation with Jefferson because he knew that he could not win. Moreover, the Court stood to lose prestige and authority if the President simply disregarded any order requiring Madison to deliver Marbury's commission. But Marshall probably had no real concept of judicial review as we know it today, and he certainly did not advocate judicial superiority over the other branches, which is what judicial review developed into in the second half of the twentieth century.

On the one hand, Marshall may have been saying in his long, detailed opinion that only the Court had final authority to interpret the constitutional provisions involving the judiciary. After all, Jefferson himself once said that the President ought to be the interpreter of laws having to do with the executive branch just as Congress interprets laws concerning the legislative. This is known as "departmentalism" or "coordinate review."

Over time, the doctrine of judicial review—the authority of the Supreme Court to invalidate state and federal laws and action that it considers to be in violation of the Constitution—has been almost universally accepted, though not always particularly preferred or appreciated. As many commentators have long pointed out, the Court's invalidation of a law enacted by a popularly elected legislature is undemocratic and anti-majoritarian. On the other hand, others have argued that the role of the Court is limited to ensure only that those laws literally in conflict with the Constitution should not stand. Still others hold that the role of the Court is to make certain that a freewheeling democratic body may not eliminate the individual's rights and liberties.

Some historians have said that Marshall should have only engaged in statutory construction, which would have meant that he would determine whether Section 13 was an enhancement of Supreme Court authority. He could have found that it did not extend the Court's Article III original jurisdiction because Section 13 merely clarified the Court's original jurisdiction: if one state, for example, sued another state, under Article III it could ask for a writ of *mandamus* directly from the Court.

Others have argued, as Marbury's attorneys did, that the case was actually brought via the Court's appellate jurisdiction because Marbury was in effect appealing Madison's reluctance to deliver the commission to him. An "appeal," as we know it today, was quite different from appeal in the eighteenth century. Alexander Hamilton, in Federalist 81, explained that the members of the Constitutional Convention defined the term "appellate" in its broadest sense: an appeal to the Supreme Court might then well be based on a ministerial decision, not only a judicial one.

Even more, Madison as Secretary of State was "a public minister," and the Court's original jurisdiction extended to public ministers. If that were the case, then Marshall would have had to grant the writ as Marbury requested it, and he would have had to order Madison to deliver the commission. The consequences would have been far graver if, as Marshall suspected, Jefferson would simply have ordered Madison to ignore the Court's order. What was Marshall then to do? He could not force the President to do anything.

In the end, for a unanimous Court, Chief Justice Marshall took the political way out: by ruling that while Marbury did deserve his commission, Section 13 was unconstitutional. In this way, he managed to avoid a direct confrontation with the President while at the same time enhancing the strategic power of the Court for the next 200 years.

Chief Justice MARSHALL delivered the opinion of the Court.

. . . The question, whether an act, repugnant to the Constitution, can become the law of the land, is a question deeply interesting to the United States; but, happily, not of an intricacy proportioned to its interest. It seems only necessary to recognise certain principles . . . to decide it. . . .

The Constitution is either a superior, paramount law, unchangeable by ordinary means, or it is on a level with ordinary legislative acts, and like other acts, is alterable when the legislature shall please to alter it. . . .

If an act of the legislature, repugnant to the Constitution, is void, does it, notwithstanding its invalidity, bind the courts and oblige them to give it effect? Or, in other words, though it be not law, does it constitute a rule as operative as if it was a law? This would be to overthrow in fact what was established in theory; and would seem, at first view, an absurdity too gross to be insisted on. It shall, however, receive a more attentive consideration.

It is emphatically the province and duty of the judicial department to say what the law is. Those who apply the rule to particular cases, must of necessity expound and interpret that rule. If two laws conflict with each other, the courts must decide on the operation of each. So if a law be in opposition to the Constitution: if both the law and the Constitution apply to a particular case, so that the court must either decide that case conformably to the law, disregarding the Constitution; or conformably to the Constitution, disregarding the law: the court must determine which of these conflicting rules governs the case. This is of the very essence of judicial duty.

If then the courts are to regard the Constitution; and the Constitution is superior to any ordinary act of the legislature; the Constitution, and not such ordinary act, must govern the case to which they both apply.

Those then who controvert the principle that the Constitution is to be considered, in court, as a paramount law, are reduced to the necessity of maintaining that courts must close their eyes on the Constitution, and see only the law.

This doctrine would subvert the very foundation of all written Constitutions. . . .

The judicial power of the United States is extended to all cases arising under the Constitution. Could it be the intention of those who gave this power, to say that, in using it, the Constitution should not be looked into? That a case arising under the Constitution should be decided without examining the instrument under which it arises?

This is too extravagant to be maintained.

In some cases then, the Constitution must be looked into by the judges. And if they can open it at all, what part of it are they forbidden to read, or to obey?

There are many other parts of the Constitution which serve to illustrate this subject.

It is declared that "no tax or duty shall be laid on articles exported from any state." Suppose a duty on the export of cotton, of tobacco, or of flour; and a suit instituted to recover it. Ought judgment to be rendered in such a case? Ought the judges to close their eyes on the Constitution, and only see the law.

The Constitution declares that "no bill of attainder or *ex post facto* law shall be passed."

If, however, such a bill should be passed and a person should be prosecuted under it, must the court condemn to death those victims whom the Constitution endeavours to preserve? . . .

From these and many other selections which might be made, it is apparent, that the framers of the Constitution contemplated that instrument as a rule for the government of courts, as well as of the legislature.

Why otherwise does it direct the judges to take an oath to support it? . . . How immoral to impose it on them, if they were to be used as the instruments, and the knowing instruments, for violating what they swear to support! . . .

Why does a judge swear to discharge his duties agreeably to the Constitution of the United States, if that Constitution forms no rule for his government? If it is closed upon him and cannot be inspected by him.

If such be the real state of things, this is worse than solemn mockery. To prescribe, or to take this oath, becomes equally a crime.

It is also not entirely unworthy of observation, that in declaring what shall be the supreme law of the land, the Constitution itself is first mentioned; and not the laws of the United States generally, but those only which shall be made in pursuance of the Constitution, have that rank.

Thus, the particular phraseology of the Constitution of the United States confirms and strengthens the principle, supposed to be essential to all written Constitutions, that a law repugnant to the Constitution is void, and that courts, as well as other departments, are bound by that instrument.

The rule must be discharged.

Case I.2

Korematsu v. United States
323 U.S. 214, 65 S.Ct. 93 (1944)

Justice Robert Jackson tells us in his dissent in this case that the Japanese American Fred Korematsu was as American as he could be. Because he was born in the United States, "the Constitution makes him a citizen of the United States by nativity and a citizen of California by residence." Although his Japanese-born parents gave him a Japanese name, he preferred to be called Fred because it was easier for his friends not only to remember, but for them to pronounce, than his formal name, "Toyosaburo."

But Americans of Japanese descent were suspected of potentially carrying out espionage and sabotage after Japan's surprise attack on the American naval base at Pearl Harbor, Hawaii, on December 6, 1941. Most Americans were not just horrified by the total destruction of the American Pacific fleet; they were so angered that their deepest prejudices against the Japanese living in the U.S. immediately emerged. Congress passed into law an extraordinary presidential executive order that in effect denied Japanese Americans both access to and departure from any military installation designated by the president or secretary of state. The law allowed military commanders, at their discretion, to identify military areas and prohibit anyone from entering or leaving them. Moreover, the commander in charge of the area possessed the authority to impose his discretion in any way he saw fit.

Unrelenting fear spread among many Americans that the 112,000 Japanese Americans residing on the West Coast were all "potential enemies," a Fifth Column of enemies representing a direct threat to the United States in its war with Japan. The commander of the West Coast, Lt. Gen. J. L. DeWitt, declared the entire region a military area (about one quarter of the entire United States). Specifically, it included California, Washington, Oregon, Idaho, Montana, Nevada and Utah, and the southern portion of Arizona. He ordered an 8:00 p.m. to 6:00 a.m. curfew for all those of Japanese ancestry. As Justice Frank Murphy says in his dissent, DeWitt was well known for his prejudices against Japanese. He testified to Congress on April 13, 1943, that he did not "want any of [persons of Japanese ancestry] here. They are a dangerous element. There is no way to determine their loyalty. . . . It makes no difference whether he is an American citizen, he is still a Japanese. American citizenship does not necessarily determine loyalty. . . . But we must worry about the Japanese all the time until he is wiped off the map."

On May 9, 1942, DeWitt ordered all persons of Japanese ancestry to report to relocation centers for transportation to internment camps for the remainder of the war. Even though the United States was at war with Germany and Italy, there was no movement to isolate those of German and Italian descent. DeWitt reasoned that because the entire West Coast was a military area, it was off limits to the Japanese. Now tens of thousands of people of Japanese ancestry—of these, 70,000 were born in the United States—were transported to relocation centers. Suddenly, tens of thousands lost their homes, businesses and, not the least, their dignity and liberty. None of them had been accused or convicted of disloyalty or espionage or sabotage.

In the first challenge to these orders, the Supreme Court dealt only with the curfew issue, even though Kiyoshi Hirabayashi had been sentenced to two three-month prison sentences for violating both the curfew and the relocation order, *Hirabayashi v. United States*, 320 U.S.91 (1943). But the Court upheld only the curfew and refused to confront the issues of relocation and the internment camps. The Court unanimously decided that the emergency created by war was a compelling reason for the government to restrict individual rights, just as the police might stop people from crossing a police line when firefighters are dousing a blazing building.

After California authorities ordered Fred Korematsu to go to a relocation or assembly center, he refused to leave his house. He argued that the orders were contradictory. As Justice Owen Roberts put it in his dissent, "the predicament in which the petitioner thus found himself was this: He was forbidden, by Military Order, to leave the zone in which he lived; he was forbidden, by Military

Order, after a date fixed, to be found within that zone unless he were in an Assembly Center located in that zone. General DeWitt's report to the Secretary of War concerning the programme of evacuation and relocation of Japanese makes it entirely clear, if it were necessary to refer to that document . . . that an Assembly Center was a euphemism for a prison. No person within such a center was permitted to leave except by Military Order."

Korematsu's conviction in federal district court was upheld by the United States Court of Appeals for the Ninth Circuit. He appealed to the Supreme Court on the grounds that the relocation order violated his constitutional rights on the grounds that removing a man from his home was a far greater deprivation than what the curfew imposed. Korematsu's loyalty was not a question before the Supreme Court. On the very same day the Court issued its decision, it ruled that Mitsuye Endo had to be released from a detention center because no court had proved she was disloyal *Ex Parte Endo*, 323 U.S. 283 (1944).

The Court, by a vote of six to three, upheld Korematsu's conviction with Justice Black writing the Court's opinion. Justice Frankfurter concurred, while Justices Roberts, Murphy, and Jackson dissented.

Justice BLACK delivered the opinion of the Court.

It should be noted . . . that all legal restrictions which curtail the civil rights of a single racial group are immediately suspect. That is not to say that all such restrictions are unconstitutional. It is to say that courts must subject them to the most rigid scrutiny. Pressing public necessity may sometimes justify the existence of such restrictions; racial antagonism never can. . . .

Here, as in the *Hirabayashi* case, "we cannot reject as unfounded the judgment of the military authorities and of Congress that there were disloyal members of that population . . . ." It was because we could not reject the finding of the military authorities that it was impossible to bring about an immediate segregation of the disloyal from the loyal that we sustained the validity of the curfew order as applying to the whole group. In the instant case, temporary exclusion of the entire group was rested by the military on the same ground. . . .

We are not unmindful of the hardships imposed by it upon a large group of American citizens. . . . But hardships are part of war, and war is an aggregation of hardships. All citizens alike, both in and out of uniform, feel the impact of war in greater or lesser measure. Citizenship has its responsibilities as well as its privileges, and in time of war the burden is always heavier. Compulsory exclusion of large groups of citizens from their homes, except under circumstances of direst emergency and peril, is inconsistent with our basic governmental institutions. But when under conditions of modern warfare our shores are threatened by hostile forces, the power to protect must be commensurate with the threatened danger. . . .

It is said that we are dealing here with the case of imprisonment of a citizen in a concentration camp solely because of his ancestry. . . . Our task would be simple, our duty clear, were this a case involving the imprisonment of a loyal citizen in a concentration camp because of racial prejudice. Regardless of the true nature of the assembly and relocation centers—and we deem it unjustifiable to call them concentration camps with all the ugly connotations that term implies—we are dealing specifically with nothing but an exclusion order. To cast this case into outlines of racial prejudice, without reference to the real military dangers which were presented, merely confuses the issue. Korematsu was not excluded from the Military Area because of hostility to him or his race. He *was* excluded because we are at war with the Japanese Empire, because the properly constituted military authorities feared an invasion of our West Coast and felt constrained to take proper security measures, because they decided that the military urgency of the situation demanded that all citizens of Japanese ancestry be segregated from the West Coast temporarily, and finally, because Congress, reposing its confidence in this time of war in our military leaders—as inevitably it must—determined that they should have the power to do just this. There was evidence of disloyalty on the part of some, the military authorities considered that the need for action was great, and time was short. We cannot—by availing ourselves of the calm perspective of hindsight—now say that at that time these actions were unjustified. Affirmed.

Justice MURPHY, dissenting.

This exclusion . . . goes over "the very brink of constitutional power" and falls into the ugly abyss of racism.

The main reasons . . . appear . . . to be largely an accumulation of much of the misinformation, half-truths and insinuations that for years have been directed against Japanese Americans by people with racial and economic prejudices—the same people who have been among the foremost advocates of the evacuation. A military judgment based upon such racial and sociological considerations is not entitled to the great weight ordinarily given the judgments based upon strictly military considerations. Especially is this so when every charge relative to race, religion, culture, geographical location, and legal and economic status has been substantially discredited by independent studies made by experts in these matters. . . . I dissent, therefore, from this legalization of racism.

Justice JACKSON, dissenting.

Korematsu was born on our soil, of parents born in Japan. The Constitution makes him a citizen of the United States by nativity and a citizen of California by residence. No claim is made that he is not loyal to this country. There is no suggestion that apart from the matter involved here he is not law-abiding and well disposed. Korematsu, however, has been convicted of an act not commonly a crime. It consists merely of being present in the state whereof he is a citizen, near the place where he was born, and where all his life he has lived. . . .

My duties as a justice . . . do not require me to make a military judgment as to whether General DeWitt's evacuation and detention program was a reasonable military necessity. I do not suggest that the courts should have attempted to interfere with the Army in carrying out its task. But I do not think they may be asked to execute a military expedient that has no place in law under the Constitution. I would reverse the judgment and discharge the prisoner.

Case I.3

Baker v. Carr
369 U.S. 186, 82 S.Ct. 691 (1962)

This case came to the Supreme Court as an equal protection claim under the Fourteenth Amendment. Charles Baker and several other Tennessee citizens believed that their votes had become diluted because of the unequal size of the state electoral districts.

Tennessee, like many other states, provided for the reapportionment of the seats in both the lower and upper house of its state legislature. In 1901, the law required the assembly to reapportion the number of seats according to the national census, which was taken every 10 years. Over a period of 60 years, the population dramatically shifted, as it had in many states, from overwhelmingly rural to overwhelmingly urban. Representation from the counties, however, remained the same, even though there were more people residing in the urban districts than in the rural ones. Every time a reapportionment bill, which might have corrected the imbalance, came before the legislature, it failed.

In his suit against the assembly in federal district court, Baker asked the court to require the state to hold an at-large election or an election based on the 1960 federal census. The court agreed that Baker and the others were aggrieved and had a legitimate complaint. The district court quickly added, however, that it could offer, on jurisdictional grounds, no remedy because his case raised a "political question," an issue that by its nature must be resolved by one of the political branches of the government, those like the executive or legislative that is elected by the people. Hence, it was declared to be a "nonjusticiable" issue, that is, one that could not be resolved by a court of law.

Because of the divisive nature of this question before the Supreme Court, the case was reargued the year after it was first accepted for review. Justices Felix Frankfurter and John Marshall Harlan were hesitant about entering into a political battle that ought, in their minds, be resolved at the state level through the political process. Others like Justices Thomas C. Clark and Charles E. Whittaker agreed. But more progressive justices like Chief Justice Earl Warren and Justices Hugo Black and William O. Douglas believed that not only was the issue justiciable, that is, the courts did have jurisdiction to decide these kinds of cases, but went farther and wanted the Court to declare the Tennessee districts in violation of the Fourteenth Amendment's Equal Protection Clause.

In the end, with Justice Potter Stewart's as the swing vote, Justice William Brennan's opinion for the Court only reached the jurisdictional question. It was left to later cases to decide the merits. Here the Court set forth the principle that the litigants had "standing to sue," that is, they had sustained a personal and direct injury when the state declined to redraw its electoral districts over a period of 60 years. In other words, they had a legally protected interest in having their votes counted equally to all the other votes in Tennessee.

The final vote was six to two with Chief Justice Warren and Justices White, Douglas, Clark, and Stewart joining Justice Brennan's majority opinion. Justices Douglas, Clark, and Stewart wrote concurring opinions. Justices Frankfurter and Harlan dissented. Justice Whittaker did not take part in the proceeding.

Justice BRENNAN delivered the opinion of the Court.

. . . We hold today only (a) that the court possessed jurisdiction of the subject matter; (b) that a justiciable cause of action is stated upon which appellants would be entitled to appropriate relief; and (c) because appellees raise the issue before this Court, that the appellants have standing to challenge the Tennessee apportionment statutes. Beyond noting that we have no cause at this stage to doubt the District Court will be able to fashion relief if violations of constitutional rights are found, it is improper now to consider what remedy would be most appropriate if appellants prevail at the trial.

Jurisdiction of the Subject Matter

. . . The appellees refer to *Colegrove v. Green,* 328 U.S. 549 [1946], as authority that the District Court lacked jurisdiction of the subject matter. Appellees misconceive the holding of that case. The holding was precisely contrary to their reading of it. Seven members of the Court participated in the decision. Unlike many other cases in this field which have assumed without discussion that there was jurisdiction, all three opinions filed in *Colegrove* discussed the question. Two of the opinions expressing the views of four of the Justices, a majority, flatly held that there was jurisdiction of the subject matter. . . .

Justiciability

In holding that the subject matter of this suit was not justiciable, the District Court relied on *Colegrove v. Green* and subsequent *per curiam* cases. . . .

We hold that the claim pleaded here neither rests upon nor implicates the Guaranty Clause [in Article IV that guarantees that every state shall have a republican form of government] and that its justiciability is therefore not foreclosed by our decisions of cases involving that clause. . . . To show why we reject the argument based on the Guaranty Clause, we must examine the authorities under it. But because there appears to be some uncertainty as to why those cases did present political questions, and specifically as to whether this apportionment case is like those cases, we deem it necessary first to consider the contours of the "political question" doctrine. . . .

We have said that "In determining whether a question falls within [the political question] category, the appropriateness under our system of government of attributing finality to the action of the political departments and also the lack of satisfactory criteria for a judicial determination are dominant considerations." *Coleman v. Miller,* 307 U.S. 433 [1939]. The nonjusticiability of a political question is primarily a function of the separation of powers. Much confusion results from the capacity of the "political question" label to obscure the need for case-by-case inquiry. Deciding whether a matter has in any measure been committed by the Constitution to another branch of government, or whether the action of that branch exceeds whatever authority has been committed, is itself a delicate exercise in constitutional interpretation, and is a responsibility of this Court as ultimate interpreter of the Constitution. To demonstrate this requires no less than to analyze representative cases and to infer from them the analytical threads that make up the political question doctrine. We shall then show that none of those threads catches this case.

> [NOTE: Justice Brennan then cites examples of the Court's intervention in political questions involving foreign relations, the dates of duration of hostilities, the validity of enactments, and the status of the Indian tribes.]

But it is argued that this case shares the characteristics of decisions that constitute a category not yet considered, cases concerning the Constitution's guaranty, in Art. IV, Section 4, of a republican form of government. A conclusion as to whether the case at bar does present a political question cannot be confidently reached until we have considered those cases with special care. We shall discover that Guaranty Clause claims involve those elements which define a "political question," and for that reason and no other, they are nonjusticiable. In particular, we shall discover that the nonjusticiability of such claims has nothing to do with their touching upon matters of state governmental organization. . . .

We come, finally, to the ultimate inquiry whether our precedents as to what constitutes a nonjusticiable "political question" bring the case before us under the umbrella of that doctrine. A natural beginning is to note whether any of the common characteristics which we have been able to identify and label descriptively are present. We find none: The question here is the consistency of state action with the Federal Constitution. We have no question decided, or to be decided, by a political branch of government coequal with this Court. Nor do we risk embarrassment of our government abroad, or grave disturbance at home if we take issue with Tennessee as to the constitutionality of her action here challenged. Nor need the appellants, in order to succeed in this action, ask the Court to enter upon policy determinations for which judicially manageable standards are lacking. Judicial standards under the Equal Protection Clause are well developed and familiar, and it has been open to courts since the enactment of the Fourteenth Amendment to determine, if on the particular facts they must, that a discrimination reflects no policy, but simply arbitrary and capricious action.

This case does, in one sense, involve the allocation of political power within a State, and the appellants might conceivably have added a claim under the Guaranty Clause. Of course, as we have seen, any reliance on that clause would be futile. But because any reliance on the Guaranty Clause could not have succeeded it does not follow that appellants may not be heard on the equal protection claim which in fact they tender. True, it must be clear that the Fourteenth Amendment claim is not so enmeshed with those political question elements which render Guaranty Clause claims nonjusticiable as actually to present a political question itself. But we have found that not to be the case here. . . .

We conclude that the complaint's allegations of a denial of equal protection present a justiciable constitutional cause of action upon which appellants are entitled to a trial and a decision. The right asserted is within the reach of judicial protection under the Fourteenth Amendment.

The judgment of the District Court is reversed and the cause is remanded for further proceedings consistent with this opinion.

Reversed and remanded.

Justice FRANKFURTER, whom Justice HARLAN joins, dissenting.

. . . Appellants invoke the right to vote and to have their votes counted. But they are permitted to vote and their votes are counted. They go to the polls, they cast their ballots, they send their representatives to the state councils. Their complaint is simply that the representatives are not sufficiently numerous or powerful—in short, that Tennessee has adopted a basis of representation with which they are dissatisfied. Talk of "debasement" or "dilution" is circular talk. One cannot speak of "debasement" or "dilution" of the value of a vote until there is first defined a standard of reference as to what a vote should be worth. What is actually asked of the Court in this case is to choose among competing bases of representation—ultimately, really, among competing theories of political philosophy—in order to establish an appropriate frame of government for the State of Tennessee and thereby for all the States of the Union. . . .

To find such a political conception legally enforceable in the broad and unspecific guarantee of equal protection is to rewrite the Constitution. Certainly, "equal protection" is no more secure a foundation for judicial judgment of the permissibility of varying forms of representative government than is "Republican Form." . . .

Case I.4

Griswold v. Connecticut
391 U.S. 145, 85 S.Ct. 1678 (1965)

Victorian values pervaded American society throughout the nineteenth century with an emphasis on sexual restraint, crime reduction, and a strict code of personal conduct. The name derives from Queen Victoria who ruled Britain from 1837 to 1901. Connecticut law, after 1879, prohibited the distribution of information about and the use of contraceptives in an effort to ensure that sexual activity was not for pleasure, but only produced children. At the same time, feminists began the battle to achieve equal rights, including the right to vote and hold office and the right to control their own bodies. The birth control movement began in earnest in the United States when Margaret Sanger in 1914 advocated contraception. Following in her footsteps, Dr. C. Lee Buxton with two of his patients, whose pregnancies had been very difficult, challenged the law, but in 1961, the Supreme Court held in *Poe v. Ullman*, 367 U.S. 497, that they lacked standing: the Court said that Connecticut had not enforced the law since the late-nineteenth century, and that therefore Buxton's patients had sustained no direct or person injury. In that case, four justices dissented, and soon two of those in the majority, Justices Felix Frankfurter and Charles E. Whittaker, retired.

Estelle Griswold, the director of Planned Parenthood in Connecticut, along with Dr. Buxton then challenged the law after the legislature refused to repeal it. To assure standing, Griswold and Buxton opened a birth control clinic in violation of the law, and they were soon arrested and convicted. The Supreme Court granted *certiorari* on their appeal.

Justice William O. Douglas wrote the opinion of the Court for a seven to two majority. Justice Arthur J. Goldberg concurred in an opinion joined by Chief Justice Earl Warren. Justices John Marshall Harlan and Byron R. White filed two additional concurrences. Justices Hugo Black and Potter Stewart dissented.

Justice DOUGLAS delivered the opinion of the Court.

. . . We do not sit as a super-legislature to determine the wisdom, need, and propriety of laws that touch economic problems, business affairs, or social conditions. This law, however, operates directly on an intimate relation of husband and wife and their physician's role in one aspect of that relation.

The association of people is not mentioned in the Constitution nor in the Bill of Rights. The right to educate a child in a school of the parents' choice—whether public or private or parochial—is also not mentioned. Nor is the right to study any particular subject or any foreign language. Yet the First Amendment has been construed to include certain of those rights.

By *Pierce v. Society of Sisters* [268 U.S. 510 (1925)], the right to educate one's children as one chooses is made applicable to the States by the force of the First and Fourteenth Amendments. By *Meyer v. Nebraska* [262 U.S. 390 (1923)], the same dignity is given the right to study the German language in a private school. In other words, the State may not, consistently with the spirit of the First Amendment, contract the spectrum of available knowledge. The right of freedom of speech and press includes not only the right to utter or to print, but the right to distribute, the right to receive, the right to read and freedom of inquiry, freedom of thought, and freedom to teach—indeed the freedom of the entire university community. Without those peripheral rights the specific rights would be less secure. And so we reaffirm the principle of the *Pierce* and the *Meyer* cases.

In *NAACP v. Alabama*, 357 U.S. 449 [(1958)], we protected the "freedom to associate and privacy in one's associations," noting that freedom of association was a peripheral First Amendment right. Disclosure of membership lists of a constitutionally valid association, we held, was invalid "as entailing the likelihood of a substantial restraint upon the exercise by petitioner's members of their right to freedom of association." In other words, the First Amendment has a penumbra where privacy is protected from governmental intrusion. . . .

Those cases involved more than the "right of assembly"—a right that extends to all irrespective of their race or ideology. *De Jonge v. Oregon*, 299 U.S. 353 [(1937)]. The right of "association," like the right of belief (*West Virginia Board of Education v. Barnette*, 319 U.S. 624 [1943]), is more than the right to attend a meeting; it includes the right to express one's attitudes or philosophies by membership in a group or by affiliation with it or by other lawful means. Association in that context is a form of expression of opinion; and while it is not expressly included in the First Amendment its existence is necessary in making the express guarantees fully meaningful.

The foregoing cases suggest that specific guarantees in the Bill of Rights have penumbras, formed by emanations from those guarantees that help give them life and substance. See *Poe v. Ullman*, 367 U.S. 497 [(1961)] (dissenting opinion). Various guarantees create zones of privacy. The right of association contained in the penumbra of the First Amendment is one, as we have seen. The Third Amendment in its prohibition against the quartering of soldiers "in any house" in time of peace without the consent of the owner is another facet of that privacy. The Fourth Amendment explicitly affirms the "right of the people to be secure in their persons, houses, papers, and effects, against unreasonable searches and seizures." The Fifth Amendment in its Self-Incrimination Clause enables the citizen to create a zone of privacy which government may not force him to surrender to his detriment. The Ninth Amendment provides: "The enumeration in the Constitution, of certain rights, shall not be construed to deny or disparage others retained by the people."

The Fourth and Fifth Amendments were described in *Boyd v. United States*, 116 U.S. 616 [(1886)], as protection against all governmental invasions "of the sanctity of a man's home and the privacies of life." We recently referred in *Mapp v. Ohio*, 367 U.S. 643 [(1961)], to the Fourth Amendment as creating a "right to privacy, no less important than any other right carefully and particularly reserved to the people." . . . We have had many controversies over these penumbral rights of "privacy and repose." . . .

These cases bear witness that the right of privacy which presses for recognition here is a legitimate one.

The present case, then, concerns a relationship lying within the zone of privacy created by several fundamental constitutional guarantees. And it concerns a law which, in forbidding the *use* of contraceptives rather than regulating their manufacture or sale, seeks to achieve its goals by means having a maximum destructive impact upon that relationship. Such a law cannot stand in light of the familiar principle, so often applied by this Court, that a "governmental purpose to control or prevent activities constitutionally subject to state regulation may not be achieved by means which sweep unnecessarily broadly and thereby invade the area of protected freedoms." *NAACP v. Alabama*. . . .

Would we allow the police to search the sacred precincts of marital bedrooms for telltale signs of the use of contraceptives? The very idea is repulsive to the notions of privacy surrounding the marriage relationship.

We deal with a right of privacy older than the Bill of Rights—older than our political parties, older than our school system. Marriage is a coming together for better or for worse, hopefully enduring, and intimate to the degree of being sacred. It is an association that promotes a way of life, not causes; a harmony in living, not political faiths; a bilateral loyalty, not commercial or social projects. Yet it is an association for as noble a purpose as any involved in our prior decisions.

Reversed.

Justice HARLAN, concurring.

In my view, the proper constitution inquiry in this case is whether this Connecticut statute infringes the Due Process Clause of the Fourteenth Amendment because the enactment violates the basic values "implicit in he concept of order liberty," *Palko v. Connecticut* 302 U.S. 319 (1937). . . . The Due Process Clause stands, in my opinion, on its own bottom.

Justice BLACK, with whom Justice STEWART joins, dissenting.

. . . I get nowhere in this case by talk about a constitutional "right of privacy" as an emanation from one or more constitutional provisions. I like my privacy as well as the next one, but I am nevertheless compelled to admit that government has a right to invade it unless prohibited by some specific constitutional provision. For these reasons I cannot agree with the Court's judgment and the reasons it gives for holding this Connecticut law unconstitutional. . . .

Case I.5

Shelby County v. Holder
570 U.S. ___ (2013)

Congress passed the Voting Rights Act (VRA) in 1965 at the height of the civil rights movement. The Fifteenth Amendment provided that "the right of citizens of the United States to vote shall not be denied or abridged by the United States or by any state on account of race, color, or previous condition of servitude." The VRA implemented Section 2 of the amendment, which empowered Congress "to enforce this article by appropriate legislation."

The VRA addressed entrenched racial discrimination in voting procedures in several states, cities, and counties throughout the nation but mainly in the South. Its section 2 banned any "standard, practice, or procedure" that "results in a denial or abridgement of the right of any citizen . . . to vote on account of race or color." Section 3 empowered the United States government with a "bail-in" and "bail-out" mechanism: states not covered by the act could be subject to it if the Department of Justice, with the approval of a federal court, determined that its officials engaged in racial discrimination in voting procedures; and states covered could be freed from it if state officials abided by the act's terms for at least ten years.

Section 4 laid out the formula to determine which states and localities discriminated in their voting procedures. In the late 1960s and early 1970s, Congress revised the list of states and localities covered under the act. It failed to do so after 1975. That list identified nine states, 12 cities, and 57 counties subject to the VRA because they maintained discriminatory procedures. These included literacy tests and low minority voter registration and turnout. All had very low minority turnouts for voting in the 1960s and 1970s.

Section 5 of the act provided that the identified states and local jurisdictions must seek advance permission from a federal judge or the Department of Justice before they could make any changes to their voting procedures. This permission, known as preclearance, allowed federal authorities to determine the discriminatory impact of any change in voting procedures, such as proposals to move the location of a polling place or to reconfigure electoral districts.

Although the VRA was set to expire in five years, Congress reauthorized it several times. Congress last renewed it in 2006 for 25 years. The measure overwhelmingly passed both houses of Congress with bipartisan majorities. In 2008, a Texas utility district challenged its constitutionality because it claimed the coverage formula was outdated. The Supreme Court resolved the challenge on statutory grounds only but Chief Justice John Roberts in *Northwest Austin Municipal Utility District No. 1 v. Holder* (2009) expressed doubts about the VRA: "Things have changed in the South. Voter turnout and registration rates now approach parity. Blatantly discriminatory evasions of federal decrees are rare. And minority candidates hold office at unprecedented levels."

The very next year, officials in Shelby County, Alabama, claimed that Sections 4 and 5 were facially unconstitutional. The district court for Washington, D.C., upheld the act in a decision affirmed by the United States Court of Appeals for the District of Columbia. Shelby County appealed to the Supreme Court, which by a vote of five to four overruled that decision. Chief Justice Roberts, joined by Justices Scalia, Kennedy, Thomas, and Alito, wrote the opinion of the Court overturning Section 4 but leaving Section 5 intact. He invited Congress to rewrite the coverage formula identifying states and jurisdictions subject to preclearance according to "current conditions." Justice Ginsburg filed a dissent that Justices Breyer, Sotomayor, and Kagan joined.

Chief Justice ROBERTS delivered the opinion of the Court.

The Voting Rights Act of 1965 employed extraordinary measures to address an extraordinary problem. Section 5 of the Act required states to obtain federal permission before enacting any law related to voting—a drastic departure from basic principles of federalism. And Section 4 of the Act applied that requirement only to some states—an equally dramatic departure from the principle that all states enjoy equal sovereignty. This was strong medicine, but Congress determined it was needed to address entrenched racial discrimination in voting, "an insidious and pervasive evil which had been perpetuated in certain parts of our country through unremitting and ingenious defiance of the Constitution." *South Carolina v. Katzenbach*, 383 U.S. 301 (1966).

As we explained in upholding the law, "exceptional conditions can justify legislative measures not otherwise appropriate." *Katzenbach.* Reflecting the unprecedented nature of these measures, they were scheduled to expire after five years.

Nearly 50 years later, they are still in effect; indeed, they have been made more stringent, and are now scheduled to last until 2031. There is no denying, however, that the conditions that originally justified these measures no longer characterize voting in the covered jurisdictions. By 2009, "the racial gap in voter registration and turnout was lower in the states originally covered by Section 5 than it was nationwide." *Northwest Austin Municipal Util. Dist. No. One v. Holder* (2009). Since that time, Census Bureau data indicate that African-American voter turnout has come to exceed white voter turnout in five of the six states originally covered by Section 5, with a gap in the sixth state of less than one half of one percent.

At the same time, voting discrimination still exists; no one doubts that. The question is whether the Act's extraordinary measures, including its disparate treatment of the states, continue to satisfy constitutional requirements. As we put it a short time ago, "the Act imposes current burdens and must be justified by current needs." *Northwest Austin.* . . .

In 1970, Congress reauthorized the Act for another five years, and extended the coverage formula in Section 4(b) to jurisdictions that had a voting test and less than 50 percent voter registration or turnout as of 1968. That swept in several counties in California, New Hampshire, and New York. Congress also extended the ban in Section 4(a) on tests and devices nationwide.

In 1975, Congress reauthorized the Act for seven more years, and extended its coverage to jurisdictions that had a voting test and less than 50 percent voter registration or turnout as of 1972. . . . As a result of these amendments, the States of Alaska, Arizona, and Texas, as well as several counties in California, Florida, Michigan, New York, North Carolina, and South Dakota, became covered jurisdictions. . . .

In 1982, Congress reauthorized the Act for 25 years, but did not alter its coverage formula. . . . In 2006, Congress again reauthorized the Voting Rights Act for 25 years, again without change to its coverage formula. . . . Shortly after this reauthorization, a Texas utility district brought suit, seeking to bail out from the Act's coverage and, in the alternative, challenging the Act's constitutionality. See *Northwest Austin*. A three-judge District Court explained that only a state or political subdivision was eligible to seek bailout under the statute, and concluded that the utility district was not a political subdivision, a term that encompassed only "counties, parishes, and voter-registering subunits." The District Court also rejected the constitutional challenge.

We reversed. We explained that " 'normally the Court will not decide a constitutional question if there is some other ground upon which to dispose of the case.' " Concluding that "underlying constitutional concerns," among other things, "compelled a broader reading of the bailout provision," we construed the statute to allow the utility district to seek bailout. In doing so we expressed serious doubts about the Act's continued constitutionality. . . .

Eight Members of the Court subscribed to these views, and the remaining Member would have held the Act unconstitutional. Ultimately, however, the Court's construction of the bailout provision left the constitutional issues for another day.

Shelby County is located in Alabama, a covered jurisdiction. It has not sought bailout, as the Attorney General has recently objected to voting changes proposed from within the county. Instead, in 2010, the county sued the Attorney General in Federal District Court in Washington, D. C., seeking a declaratory judgment that Sections 4(b) and 5 of the Voting Rights Act are facially unconstitutional, as well as a permanent injunction against their enforcement. The District Court ruled against the county and upheld the Act. The court found that the evidence before Congress in 2006 was sufficient to justify reauthorizing Section 5 and continuing the Section 4(b) coverage formula. The Court of Appeals for the D.C. Circuit affirmed. . . .

States retain broad autonomy in structuring their governments and pursuing legislative objectives. Indeed, the Constitution provides that all powers not specifically granted to the Federal Government are reserved to the States or citizens. Amendment 10. . . . Not only do states retain sovereignty under the Constitution, there is also a "fundamental principle of equal sovereignty" among the states. *Northwest Austin*. . . .

The Voting Rights Act sharply departs from these basic principles. It suspends "*all* changes to state election law—however innocuous— until they have been precleared by federal authorities in Washington, D. C." States must beseech the Federal Government for permission to implement laws that they would otherwise have the right to enact and execute on their own, subject of course to any injunction in a Section 2 action. The Attorney General has 60 days to object to a preclearance request, longer if he requests more information. If a state seeks preclearance from a three-judge court, the process can take years.

And despite the tradition of equal sovereignty, the Act applies to only nine states (and several additional counties). While one state waits months or years and expends funds to implement a validly enacted law, its neighbor can typically put the same law into effect immediately, through the normal legislative process. . . .

In 1966, we found these departures from the basic features of our system of government justified. The "blight of racial discrimination in voting" had "infected the electoral process in parts of our country for nearly a century." *Katzenbach*. Several states had enacted a variety of requirements and tests "specifically designed to prevent" African-Americans from voting. . . . Shortly before enactment of the Voting Rights Act, only 19.4 percent of African-Americans of voting age were registered to vote in Alabama, only 31.8 percent in Louisiana, and only 6.4 percent in Mississippi. Those figures were roughly 50 percentage points or more below the figures for whites. . . .

Nearly 50 years later, things have changed dramatically. Shelby County contends that the preclearance requirement, even without regard to its disparate coverage, is now unconstitutional. Its arguments have a good deal of force. In the covered jurisdictions, "voter turnout and registration rates now approach parity. Blatantly discriminatory evasions of federal decrees are rare. And minority candidates hold office at unprecedented levels." *Northwest Austin.* The tests and devices that blocked access to the ballot have been forbidden nationwide for over 40 years.

Those conclusions are not ours alone. Congress said the same when it reauthorized the Act in 2006, writing that "significant progress has been made in eliminating first generation barriers experienced by minority voters, including increased numbers of registered minority voters, minority voter turnout, and minority representation in Congress, State legislatures, and local elected offices." . . .

Census Bureau data from the most recent election indicate that African-American voter turnout exceeded white voter turnout in five of the six states originally covered by Section 5, with a gap in the sixth state of less than one half of one percent. The preclearance statistics are also illuminating. In the first decade after enactment of Section 5, the Attorney General objected to 14.2 percent of proposed voting changes. In the last decade before reenactment, the Attorney General objected to a mere 0.16 percent.

There is no doubt that these improvements are in large part *because* of the Voting Rights Act. The Act has proved immensely successful at redressing racial discrimination and integrating the voting process.

During the "Freedom Summer" of 1964, in Philadelphia, Mississippi, three men were murdered while working in the area to register African-American voters. On "Bloody Sunday" in 1965, in Selma, Alabama, police beat and used tear gas against hundreds marching in support of African-American enfranchisement. Today both of those towns are governed by African-American mayors. Problems remain in these States and others, but there is no denying that, due to the Voting Rights Act, our Nation has made great strides.

Yet the Act has not eased the restrictions in Section 5 or narrowed the scope of the coverage formula in Section 4(b) along the way. Those extraordinary and unprecedented features were reauthorized–as if nothing had changed. In fact, the Act's unusual remedies have grown even stronger. . . .

Coverage today is based on decades-old data and eradicated practices. The formula captures States by reference to literacy tests and low voter registration and turnout in the 1960s and early 1970s. But such tests have been banned nationwide for over 40 years. And voter registration and turnout numbers in the covered States have risen dramatically in the years since. Racial disparity in those numbers was compelling evidence justifying the preclearance remedy and the coverage formula. There is no longer such a disparity.

In 1965, the States could be divided into two groups: those with a recent history of voting tests and low voter registration and turnout, and those without those characteristics. Congress based its coverage formula on that distinction. Today the Nation is no longer divided along those lines, yet the Voting Rights Act continues to treat it as if it were. . . .

Here, by contrast, the Government's reverse-engineering argument does not even attempt to demonstrate the continued relevance of the formula to the problem it targets. And in the context of a decision as significant as this one—subjecting a disfavored subset of states to "extraordinary legislation otherwise unfamiliar to our federal system," *Northwest Austin*—that failure to establish even relevance is fatal.

The Government falls back to the argument that because the formula was relevant in 1965, its continued use is permissible so long as any discrimination remains in the states Congress identified back then—regardless of how that discrimination compares to discrimination in states unburdened by coverage. This argument does not look to "current political conditions," *Northwest Austin*, but instead relies on a comparison between the states in 1965. That comparison reflected the different histories of the North and South. It was in the South that slavery was upheld by law until uprooted by the Civil War, that the reign of Jim Crow denied African-Americans the most basic freedoms, and that state and local governments worked tirelessly to disenfranchise citizens on the basis of race. The Court invoked that history—rightly so—in sustaining the disparate coverage of the Voting Rights Act in 1966.

But history did not end in 1965. By the time the Act was reauthorized in 2006, there had been 40 more years of it. In assessing the "current need" for a preclearance system that treats states differently from one another today, that history cannot be ignored. During that time, largely because of the Voting Rights Act, voting tests were abolished, disparities in voter registration and turnout due to race were erased, and African-Americans attained political office in record numbers. And yet the coverage formula that Congress reauthorized in 2006 ignores these developments, keeping the focus on decades-old data relevant to decades-old problems, rather than current data reflecting current needs. . . .

Congress compiled thousands of pages of evidence before reauthorizing the Voting Rights Act. . . . But . . . Congress did not use the record it compiled to shape a coverage formula grounded in current conditions. It instead reenacted a formula based on 40-year-old facts having no logical relation to the present day. . . .

There is no valid reason to insulate the coverage formula from review merely because it was previously enacted 40 years ago. If Congress had started from scratch in 2006, it plainly could not have enacted the present coverage formula. It would have been irrational for Congress to distinguish between states in such a fundamental way based on 40-year-old data, when today's statistics tell an entirely different story. And it would have been irrational to base coverage on the use of voting tests 40 years ago, when such tests have been illegal since that time. But that is exactly what Congress has done.

Striking down an Act of Congress "is the gravest and most delicate duty that this Court is called on to perform." We do not do so lightly. That is why, in 2009, we took care to avoid ruling on the constitutionality of the Voting Rights Act when asked to do so, and instead resolved the case then before us on statutory grounds. But in issuing that decision, we expressed our broader concerns about the constitutionality of the Act. Congress could have updated the coverage formula at that time, but did not do so. Its failure to act leaves us today with no choice but to declare Section 4(b) unconstitutional. The formula in that section can no longer be used as a basis for subjecting jurisdictions to preclearance.

Our decision in no way affects the permanent, nationwide ban on racial discrimination in voting found in Section 2. We issue no holding on Section 5 itself, only on the coverage formula. Congress may draft another formula based on current conditions. Such a formula is an initial prerequisite to a determination that exceptional conditions still exist justifying such an "extraordinary departure from the traditional course of relations between the States and the Federal Government."

Our country has changed, and while any racial discrimination in voting is too much, Congress must ensure that the legislation it passes to remedy that problem speaks to current conditions. The judgment of the Court of Appeals is reversed. It is so ordered.

Justice GINSBURG, with whom Justices BREYER, SOTOMAYOR, and KAGAN join, dissenting.

In the Court's view, the very success of Section 5 of the Voting Rights Act demands its dormancy. Congress was of another mind. Recognizing that large progress has been made, Congress determined, based on a voluminous record, that the scourge of discrimination was not yet extirpated. The question this case presents is who decides whether, as currently operative, Section 5 remains justifiable, this Court, or a Congress charged with the obligation to enforce the post-Civil War Amendments "by appropriate legislation." With overwhelming support in both Houses, Congress concluded that, for two prime reasons, Section 5 should continue in force, unabated. First, continuance would facilitate completion of the impressive gains thus far made; and second, continuance would guard against backsliding. Those assessments were well within Congress' province to make and should elicit this Court's unstinting approbation. . . .

Congress . . . found that as "registration and voting of minority citizens increased, other measures may be resorted to which would dilute increasing minority voting strength." Efforts to reduce the impact of minority votes, in contrast to direct attempts to block access to the ballot, are aptly described as "second-generation barriers" to minority voting.

Second-generation barriers come in various forms. One of the blockages is racial gerrymandering, the redrawing of legislative districts in an "effort to segregate the races for purposes of voting." Another is adoption of a system of at-large voting in lieu of district-by-district voting in a city with a sizable black minority. By switching to at-large voting, the overall majority could control the election of each city council member, effectively eliminating the potency of the minority's votes. A similar effect could be achieved if the city engaged in discriminatory annexation by incorporating majority-white areas into city limits, thereby decreasing the effect of VRA-occasioned increases in black voting. Whatever the device employed, this Court has long recognized that vote dilution, when adopted with a discriminatory purpose, cuts down the right to vote as certainly as denial of access to the ballot. . . .

Congress did not take this task lightly. Quite the opposite. The 109th Congress that took responsibility for the renewal started early and conscientiously. . . .

The Court holds Section 4(b) invalid on the ground that it is "irrational to base coverage on the use of voting tests 40 years ago, when such tests have been illegal since that time." But the Court disregards what Congress set about to do in enacting the VRA. That extraordinary legislation scarcely stopped at the particular tests and devices that happened to exist in 1965. The grand aim of the Act is to secure to all in our polity equal citizenship stature, a voice in our democracy undiluted by race. As the record for the 2006 reauthorization makes abundantly clear, second-generation barriers to minority voting rights have emerged in the covered jurisdictions as attempted *substitutes* for the first-generation barriers that originally triggered preclearance in those jurisdictions.

The sad irony of today's decision lies in its utter failure to grasp why the VRA has proven effective. The Court appears to believe that the VRA's success in eliminating the specific devices extant in 1965 means that preclearance is no longer needed. With that belief, and the argument derived from it, history repeats itself. The same assumption—that the problem could be solved when particular methods of voting discrimination are identified and eliminated—was indulged and proved wrong repeatedly prior to the VRA's enactment. Unlike prior statutes, which singled out particular tests or devices, the VRA is grounded in Congress' recognition of the "variety and persistence" of measures designed to impair minority voting rights. *Katzenbach.* In truth, the evolution of voting discrimination into more subtle second-generation barriers is powerful evidence that a remedy as effective as preclearance remains vital to protect minority voting rights and prevent backsliding. . . .

It was the judgment of Congress that "40 years has not been a sufficient amount of time to eliminate the vestiges of discrimination following nearly 100 years of disregard for the dictates of the 15th amendment and to ensure that the right of all citizens to vote is protected as guaranteed by the Constitution." That determination of the body empowered to enforce the Civil War Amendments "by appropriate legislation" merits this Court's utmost respect. In my judgment, the Court errs egregiously by overriding Congress' decision. For the reasons stated, I would affirm the judgment of the Court of Appeals.

Rulings in Context

The Constitution, American Democracy, and the Supreme Court

Missouri v. Holland, 252 U.S. 416 (1920)   7-2

Justice Holmes wrote for the Court that a federal treaty trumps local or state licensing, in this case, a license issued by Missouri regulating, in effect allowing, the hunting of wild, migratory birds, some of which were protected by an international agreement between the United States and Britain. Of particular interest here is Holmes's comments, echoing Chief Justice Marshall's in *McCulloch v. Maryland,* 17 U.S. 316 (1819), that the Constitution was a living document, calling it "an organism," in that "the case before us must be considered in the light of our whole experience and not merely in that of what was said a hundred years ago."

United States v. Nixon, 418 U.S. 683 (1974)   8-0

The Court held that President Nixon's claim of absolute executive privilege in withholding taped conversations in the Oval Office was trumped by the necessity of criminal defendants having a fair trial under Article III and the Fifth Amendment. The President had sought to maintain sole control of the audiotapes on the grounds of confidentiality, asserting that the President needs to have complete candor and objectivity at all times from his staff and counselors. The decision led to President Nixon's resignation when the tapes revealed his involvement in actions he had taken to stonewall the Watergate investigation.

Zadvydas v. Davis, 533 U.S. 678 (2001)   5-4

The Court ruled that the Immigration and Naturalization Service denied resident aliens *habeas corpus* rights under the Due Process Clause of the Fifth Amendment when they are held for deportation because of their criminal records and not deported within the specified 90-day holding period or released under supervision. Zadvydas, who had been in the United States since the end of World War II, was stateless to the extent that no country recognized his nationality. He thus faced permanent detention, as did a potential deportee in a companion case. Justice Breyer wrote for the Court that "once an alien enters the country, the legal circumstance changes, for the Due Process Clause applies to all 'persons' within the United States, including aliens, whether their presence here is lawful, unlawful, temporary, or permanent."

Caperton v. A.T. Massey Coal Co., 129 S.Ct. 2252 (2009)   5-4

The Court ruled that under the Due Process Clause of the Fourteenth Amendment a West Virginia Supreme Court justice should have recused himself in an appeal of a civil damage suit when one of the parties contributed to his reelection campaign. A trial court had awarded Hugh Caperton $50 million in an action against Massey Coal for fraudulent misrepresentation and fraudulent concealment. Brent Benjamin was chief justice of the Supreme Court of Appeals when it overturned the award, despite a $3 million contribution to Chief Justice Benjamin's reelection campaign by Massey's chief executive officer, Donald Blankenship. Justice Kennedy held that the Court did not have to determine whether Chief Justice Benjamin was biased but only that the relationship with Blankenship posed "a risk of actual bias." This risk exists, he argued, when a judge has "a direct, personal, substantial, pecuniary interest" in the outcome, and here Chief Justice Benjamin did.

CHAPTER 2

Organizing Government
and Sharing Powers

We must never forget that it is a Constitution
we are expounding.
—Chief Justice John Marshall, *McCulloch
v. Maryland*, 17 U.S. 316 (1819)

The words that serve as the epigraph for this chapter are from the famous case of *McCulloch v. Maryland* (Case 2.1). Chief Justice Marshall tells us in this case that there is a difference between statutory and constitutional law: statutory law is law made by a legislature; constitutional law is law written into the Constitution by the Supreme Court when it upholds or invalidates statutes in its interpretation of the Articles of and Amendments to the Constitution. He also tells us that the framers designed the Constitution to create a new national government and that its provisions bind the national and state governments.

The Science of Federalism

Political scientists always like to point out that in the United States we have 52 judicial systems: one for the United States and one for each of the 50 states and the District of Columbia. The same is true for the other branches of government in general. Each state has its own executive, a governor, and each state has a legislature. With one exception, today all state assemblies are bicameral, that is, they have two houses, which makes them similar to the United States Congress. Only Nebraska has a single-house legislature.

The Constitution focuses primarily on the national government, but also briefly addresses the states. Article I outlines the states' responsibilities for the apportionment and election of their representatives and the election of their senators to Congress. Article II declares that during the election of the President, the states have certain duties concerning the Electoral College. Article I also places limitations on the states to achieve a stronger central government. Under Congress's Section 8 powers, the states were specifically forbidden to do many of the things they previously did under the old Articles of Confederation, which was ratified in 1781. These included coining their own money and engaging in independent foreign relations with other nations.

In Article IV, the Constitution requires the states, among other things, to acknowledge as genuine the laws passed by all other states (the Full Faith and Credit Clause) and to guarantee to their citizens a republican form of government (the Guaranty Clause). Inherent in the Guaranty Clause is the right to vote; otherwise a republic could not exist. Article IV also indicates how new states are to be admitted to the Union.

Briefly stated, the Constitution provides for government to operate on two levels, state and national. This is the science of federalism that the framers envisioned for the new nation. It has become the organizing feature and a major asset of the American government.

The Supremacy Clause (Article VI, paragraph two) made clear, however, that the laws of the national government would prevail should a conflict arise between it and the states: "This Constitution, and the Laws of the United States . . . and all Treaties made, or which shall be made, under the Authority of the United States, shall be the supreme Law of the Land." Many eighteenth-century state officials were frightened at what they considered to be the dilution of state power as described in the new document. They were angered with the centralization of so much authority, and the absence of a bill of rights troubled them. They were especially afraid of the so-called Necessary and Proper clause, stating that Congress shall have the power "to make all Laws which shall be necessary and proper for carrying into Execution" the powers laid out in Article I, Section 8. Some people thought the clause authorized Congress to do anything to carry out those powers.

As a result, many states ratified the Constitution on the condition that the first Federal Congress amend the document concerning both of these matters. The first 10 amendments was one change, with its declaration of First Amendment rights along with the safeguards and guarantees of the others.

Concerning federalism, the Tenth Amendment spoke directly to their fears and anger concerning declining state power. It reads simply that "the powers not delegated to the United States by the Constitution, nor prohibited by it to the States, are reserved to the States, respectively, or to the people." How these words were to work out in practice is the history of constitutional law from the founding to our own era. It is a process in time and action.

One of the first pronouncements on the Tenth Amendment is Chief Justice Marshall's argument in *McCulloch* when he drew a distinction between the powers of the states and the national government. There, he was candid about the supremacy of the United States over Maryland's attempt to impose a state tax on the national bank. If Maryland prevailed in its argument that it could force the bank to pay a state tax, he said, that principle "would transfer the supremacy" of the United States, "in fact, to the states." The result would have, he thought, destroyed the new national government. And this he was unwilling to do. It is no wonder that historians have called Marshall "the great nationalist."

According to Article I, Section 8, Congress possesses the power to regulate interstate commerce. The Commerce Clause simply reads that "Congress shall have the power . . . to regulate Commerce with Foreign Nations, and among the several States, and with the Indian tribes." In 1824 in *Gibbons v. Ogden*, 22 U.S. (9 Wheat.) 1, Chief Justice John Marshall set the limits of state authority when it collided with federal power (Case 2.2). At issue were two laws—one state, the other federal—that regulated steamboats across the Hudson River from New York to New Jersey. In his unanimous opinion for the Court, Marshall explained his view that Congress's commerce power was complete, absolute, and unlimited.

As the nineteenth century progressed, the Court began to shift away from Marshall's desire to use the Court to empower the new national government. Economic regulation, for many members of the Court, became a matter of individual, not governmental, concern. By the end of the nineteenth century, the Court was handing down decisions declaring that intervention in the economic life of the nation was beyond the power of either federal or state regulation. In *Lochner v. New York*, 198 U.S. 45, the Court developed the doctrine of the liberty of contract to prevent states from passing wage and hour laws (Case 5.1). A bare majority ruled that such laws interfered with workers and owners' freedom to negotiate agreements or contracts concerning the number of hours they worked per day and the wages their employers paid them.

Thirteen years later, in *Hammer v. Dagenhart*, 247 U.S. 251, the Court held that Congress overstepped its commerce power by prohibiting the interstate shipment of goods produced by child labor. With the Great Depression of 1929 and the election of President Franklin D.

Roosevelt in 1932, the Court, often by narrow five to four votes, struck down the most radical New Deal laws as an interference with free market capitalism. When one justice changed his mind, the Court again took up Marshall's broad definition of commerce to uphold laws having an impact on the economy, such as those striking down minimum wages and maximum work hours.

The New Deal Court in 1941 held unanimously, for example, that the 1938 Fair Labor Standards Act, by which Congress as against the states set forth a national standard for minimum wages, was constitutional under the Congress's power to regulate interstate commerce. In upholding the act's provisions in *United States v. Darby Lumber Co.*, 312 U.S. 100 (Case 2.4), Justice Harlan Fiske Stone overruled *Hammer*. The following year, in *Wickard v. Filburn*, 317 U.S. 111, Justice Robert H. Jackson, writing again for a unanimous Court, ruled that when Congress used its broad Commerce Clause authority in setting wheat production limits, it did so because the growing of wheat was not a "local" activity, but one that had far-reaching national effects (Case 2.5).

Congress has used its commerce power authority to pass civil rights legislation, including the Civil Rights Act of 1964. In that same year, the Court affirmed this practice in two companion cases, *Heart of Atlanta Motel v. United States*, 379 U.S. 241, and *Katzenbach v. McClung*, 379 U.S. 274. In both, the Court held that when private businesses like hotels, restaurants, taverns, barbershops, gasoline stations, and so on open their doors to the public, their owners may not exclude people based on their race. The Court once again agreed that Congress had appropriately relied on its broad commerce authority.

Beginning in 1995, the Rehnquist Court most of the time reversed course when state versus national government, or federalism, cases came before it. Often with narrow five to four majorities, it ruled in favor of state authority. It overturned many federal laws because a slim majority of the Court held that Congress lacks Commerce Clause authority to step into the areas where the states are constitutionally prepared to act. When Congress passed a law making it a crime for anyone to carry a gun within 1,000 feet of a school, the Court ruled in *United States v. Lopez*, 514 U.S. 549 (1995) that only the states could make this law (Case 2.6). In 2012, the Court ruled that the Patient Protection and Affordable Health Care Act of 2010 was constitutional by a narrow five to four vote (Case 2.7). The key question in the case known as *National Federation of Business v. Sebelius* was whether the individual mandate, effective in 2014 requiring all Americans to purchase health insurance, violated Congress's commerce and/or taxing power. In an opinion by Chief Justice John G. Roberts Jr., the Court with a bare majority ruled that it did violate the commerce, but not the taxing, power—in effect, upholding the Act.

Federalism is a continuously developing "science," as Madison called it. Its changing nature depends, as it always does, on who sits on the Court. In the nineteenth-century, the idea of "states' rights" focused on the debate and ensuing Civil War over slavery. The segregationist Southern states wanted the right to maintain slavery in the face of opposition led by the abolitionist North. Until 2005, federalism was a vehicle for a majority of the Court to return power to the states so that the most important decisions that government makes, those that affect our day-to-day lives, are made closer to home, by state or local governments.

The Roberts Court's vision of the proper relationship between the federal and state governments may shift yet again.

Separation of Powers

In addition to power divided between the federal government and the states, power is also divided among the branches of the government. Writing in *The Federalist Papers*, Madison was adamant that no single branch of government should ever be in a position to control the other ones. Nor, for the same reason, should two of the branches be able to join together to dominate the third. Each was to be independent and separate, but not totally so. As Justice Louis D. Brandeis so eloquently put it in 1926: "The doctrine of the separation of powers was adopted by [the Constitutional Convention] of 1787, not to promote efficiency, but to preclude the exercise of arbitrary power. The purpose was not to avoid friction, but, by means of the inevitable friction incident to the distribution of governmental powers among three departments, to save the people from autocracy." (*Meyers v. United States*, 272 U.S. 52.)

Beyond inevitable friction, the Constitution also demands cooperation among the branches, especially the executive and legislative. While Congress with its two houses enjoys "*all* legislative Powers" (emphasis added), the President too has some legislative authority when he issues executive orders. In addition, the President has the power to nullify or veto laws that Congress has passed. Then again, Congress may override his veto as long as two-thirds of both houses, the Senate and the House of Representatives, vote to do so.

The president has the sole authority to enforce the laws Congress has passed. Congress has no way to ensure that the laws will be carried out. This is why executive branches at all levels of government control law enforcement officers, including the prosecution of those who allegedly commit crimes against the state. Presidents have also made law when they prepare explanatory documents called "signing statements." President George W. Bush (2001–09), more than any other president, used these statements to comment on over 1,000 provisions of various laws passed by Congress. At times, he declared he would not enforce a law if he believed it interfered with his constitutional duties to keep American safe from terrorist attacks.

Justice Robert H. Jackson eloquently articulated a genuinely Madisonian view in the famous 1952 steel seizure case, *Youngstown Sheet and Tube v. Sawyer*, 343 U.S. 579 (1952) (Case 2.9). Fearing a work stoppage because of a labor dispute during the Korean War, President Harry Truman ordered the Army to take over the operations but not the ownership of steel plants to ensure that they would continue to produce steel for the war effort. The Court denied the President the right to seize the plants, and Jackson concurred with these famous words: "While the Constitution diffuses power the better to secure liberty, it also contemplates that practice will integrate the dispersed powers into a workable government. It enjoins upon its branches separateness but interdependence, autonomy but reciprocity."

In the October Term 2013, the Court heard a case involving the President's authority to make recess appointments without Senate confirmation when Congress is not in session: *National Labor Relations Board v. Noel Canning*. Presidents of both parties have long followed this practice, but a challenge arose when President Obama in January 2012 made three recess appointments to the National Labor Relations Board during Congress' Christmas and New Year's break. The United States Court of Appeals for the District of Columbia ruled in January 2013 that a President may make such appointments only when formal breaks occur between congressional sessions. This happens only about once per year.

Lastly, the judiciary enjoys its own authority to make law, but like legislatures it is wholly dependent upon the executive branch to enforce its decisions.

Federalism and the Commerce Clause: Foundation Cases

We now review how the Court has interpreted the "powers" clauses in the Constitution pertaining to the relationship of the national government to the states.

Two opinions by John Marshall—*McCulloch v. Maryland* (1819) and *Gibbons v. Ogden* (1824)—promote federal authority over the states in near absolutist terms. By the end of the nineteenth century, however, several justices thought that the economy would be most productive with little or no government regulation. Many of them, who made their careers as corporate lawyers, found the free market ideal or *laissez-faire* economics as the best way to enhance American prosperity. Often a bare majority overturned many regulations because they interfered with free market capitalism. By a narrow five to four vote, the Court a ruled as unconstitutional a federal law prohibiting the passage through inter-state commerce of products made by child labor (*Hammer v. Dagenhart*). The Court invalidated many of the first radical New Deal laws Congress passed until 1937, the year after Franklin D. Roosevelt was re-elected President of the United States. Roosevelt was angry at the Court for overturning legislation that he believed would help the nation emerge from the Great Depression. He subsequently submitted to Congress a "court-packing" plan to allow him to nominate an additional justice up to fifteen for every one sitting justice who was above the age of seventy. The plan failed, but first, Chief Justice Charles Evans Hughes and then Justice Owen Roberts changed their minds and switched sides, and the Court began to approve New Deal legislation.

Case 2.1

McCulloch v. Maryland
17 U.S. (4 Wh.) 316 (1819)

James W. McCulloch, the cashier for the Baltimore branch of the Bank of the United States, was hardly a loyal servant of the American government. While in charge of managing the Bank, he spent most of his time looting its resources and later was jailed. As low as his moral character was, however, his name is attached to one of the most important Supreme Court cases in the Court's early history, perhaps as important as *Marbury v. Madison*. Its power was perhaps even more far-reaching than *Marbury*. Judicial review was a known concept long before *Marbury*, and the framers of the Constitution understood that the new federal courts would be engaged in reviewing state and national law as well as governmental action that conflicted with the Constitution.

McCulloch v. Maryland raises the issue that the ratification of the Constitution did not definitively settle: where does state sovereignty begin and end, and what does it mean when Article VI proclaims that the Constitution and laws of the United States are the supreme law of the land? While this question was not resolved with finality in 1819 when *McCulloch* was decided, Chief Justice John Marshall's opinion it established that in a contest between national and state governments, the national government usually wins. The debate itself continued until the end of the Civil War when it was finally, but not conclusively, settled, even though today Americans still hear demands for "states' rights."

The *McCulloch* case focused on the Bank of the United States, a highly controversial institution from the moment it was first incorporated in 1791 during George Washington's first administration. The primary mover behind the Bank was Secretary of the Treasury Alexander Hamilton who, as a nationalist and Federalist, believed in a strong central government and who advocated fiscal soundness in the government's financial dealings. One way he thought that good planning could be achieved was to establish a national bank just as the English had done 100 years earlier when the Bank of England was created. A bank was necessary for a variety of good, sound economic reasons: it provided a foundation for the new national government's right, duty, and ability to tax; it was a place to store the revenue; it gave the government credibility to secure loans from foreign countries; and it allowed the Treasury Department to manage the government's finances in a rational, fiscally sound manner.

Hamilton argued that just because a bank was not explicitly listed in the Constitution as one of the new institutions of the United States, the government could establish one anyway because it was only a means for the government to carry out its new administrative functions. In this way, he argued that the creation of a bank was an implied, rather than an express, power of the government. In other words, government had the power to do whatever was necessary within the authority granted to it by the Constitution. The creation of a bank certainly fit into the Necessary and Proper Clause of Article I, Section 8.

Opposing Federalists Hamilton, George Washington and John Adams, who, as President and Vice President respectively, favored the idea, were the Jeffersonians: James Madison, then serving in the House of Representatives, and Thomas Jefferson himself, the new Secretary of State. Madison could speak freely because he was a legislator, and the bill incorporating the new Bank, once it unanimously passed the Senate, was before the House for consideration. Jefferson, as a member of Washington's cabinet, could only write the President a private memorandum arguing against it.

Meantime, Madison argued that the Bank was not the means itself to create fiscal soundness: it was rather the act of incorporating the Bank that constituted the means. The Bank, he said, was an end in itself, an institution, once established, that would set a precedent to allow the national government to do just about anything it wanted to do. As an alternative, Madison suggested that the federal government use the existing banks or none at all. Jefferson, in his note to Washington, feared that the new Bank would intrude directly on the states' authority and thus radically increase the power of the national government.

In other words, we have here a classic case of a struggle between the new central government of the United States and the state governments.

The bill establishing the Bank passed the House, and the President signed it into law. When its twenty-year charter expired in 1811 during James Madison's first presidential administration, Congress did not renew it because of a combined effort by the Republicans and the owners of private banks and state officials who thought it was too competitive with state-chartered financial institutions. Four years later, however, even Madison and the retired Jefferson advocated the re-establishment of the Bank largely because of the huge debts the United States had incurred during the War of 1812 against Britain. This became the Second Bank of the United States, and the institution under consideration in *McCulloch*.

Many states opposed this Second Bank because it allowed private citizens to deposit their money in it, thus directly competing with local banks. As a result, many states, including Maryland, figured out a way to levy a tax on it: Maryland required the Bank to issue its notes on special stamped paper that Maryland itself sold to it at an annual cost of $15,000; the state then added an additional amount for each note printed. James McCulloch, as the Maryland cashier for the Second Bank, refused to pay the tax. Maryland sued him in Baltimore County Court, and he lost, whereupon he then appealed to the state's Court of Appeals, where he lost yet again. At that point, McCulloch appealed to the Supreme Court.

Madison and Jefferson actually supported the Court's unanimous ruling for *McCulloch*, while they continued to be skeptical of Chief Justice Marshall's expansive view of the national government's power. They were convinced that if the Chief Justice continued to rule as broadly as he did, Congress and the national government would eventually sop up all the political power in the nation, leaving very little for state governments.

Chief Justice MARSHALL delivered the opinion of the Court.

The first question made in the cause is—has Congress power to incorporate a bank? . . .

. . . The Government of the United States . . . though limited in its powers, is supreme, and its laws, when made in pursuance of the Constitution, form the supreme law of the land, "anything in the Constitution or laws of any State to the contrary notwithstanding."

Among the enumerated powers, we do not find that of establishing a bank or creating a corporation. But there is no phrase in the instrument which, like the Articles of Confederation, excludes incidental or implied powers and which requires that everything granted shall be expressly and minutely described. . . .

. . . A Constitution, to contain an accurate detail of all the subdivisions of which its great powers will admit, and of all the means by which they may be carried into execution, would partake of the prolixity of a legal code, and could scarcely be embraced by the human mind. It would probably never be understood by the public. Its nature, therefore, requires that only its great outlines should be marked, its important objects designated, and the minor ingredients which compose those objects be deduced from the nature of the objects themselves. That this idea was entertained by the framers of the American Constitution is not only to be inferred from the nature of the instrument, but from the language. Why else were some of the limitations found in the 9th section of the 1st article introduced? It is also in some degree warranted by their having omitted to use any restrictive term which might prevent its receiving a fair and just interpretation. In considering this question, then, we must never forget that it is *a Constitution* we are expounding.

Although, among the enumerated powers of Government, we do not find the word "bank" or "incorporation," we find the great powers, to lay and collect taxes; to borrow money; to regulate commerce; to declare and conduct a war; and to raise and support armies and navies. The sword and the purse, all the external relations, and no inconsiderable portion of the industry of the nation are intrusted to its Government. . . . But it may with great reason be contended that a Government intrusted with such ample powers, on the due execution of which the happiness and prosperity of the Nation so vitally depends, must also be intrusted with ample means for their execution. The power being given, it is the interest of the Nation to facilitate its execution. . . .

. . . [T]he Constitution of the United States has not left the right of Congress to employ the necessary means for the execution of the powers conferred on the Government to general reasoning. To its enumeration of powers is added that of making "all laws which shall be necessary and proper for carrying into execution the foregoing powers, and all other powers vested by this Constitution in the Government of the United States or in any department thereof." . . .

. . . [T]he argument on which most reliance is placed is drawn from that peculiar language of this clause. Congress is not empowered by it to make all laws which may have relation to the powers conferred on the Government, but such only as may be "necessary and proper" for carrying them into execution. The word "necessary" is considered as controlling the whole sentence, and as limiting the right to pass laws for the execution of the granted powers to such as are indispensable, and without which the power would be nugatory. That it excludes the choice of means, and leaves to Congress in each case that only which is most direct and simple. . . .

Let this be done in the case under consideration. The subject is the execution of those great powers on which the welfare of a Nation essentially depends. It must have been the intention of those who gave these powers to ensure, so far as human prudence could ensure, their beneficial execution. This could not be done by confiding the choice of means to such narrow limits as not to leave it in the power of Congress to adopt any which might be appropriate, and which were conducive to the end. This provision is made in a Constitution intended to endure for ages to come, and consequently to be adapted to the various *crises* of human affairs. To have prescribed the means by which Government should, in all future time, execute its powers would have been to change entirely the character of the instrument and give it the properties of a legal code. It would have been an unwise attempt to provide by immutable rules for exigencies which, if foreseen at all, must have been seen dimly, and which can be best provided for as they occur. To have declared that the best means shall not be used, but those alone without which the power given would be nugatory, would have been to deprive the legislature of the capacity to avail itself of experience, to exercise its reason, and to accommodate its legislation to circumstances. . . .

. . . [T]he argument which most conclusively demonstrates the error of the construction contended for by the counsel for the State of Maryland is founded on the intention of the convention as manifested in the whole clause. To waste time and argument in proving that, without it, Congress might carry its powers into execution would be not much less idle than to hold a lighted taper to the sun. As little can it be required to prove that, in the absence of this clause, Congress would have some choice of means. That it might employ those which, in its judgment, would most advantageously effect the object to be accomplished. That any means adapted to the end, any means which tended directly to the execution of the Constitutional powers of the Government, were in themselves Constitutional. This clause, as construed by the State of Maryland, would abridge, and almost annihilate, this useful and necessary right of the legislature to select its means. That this could not be intended is, we should think, had it not been already controverted, too apparent for controversy.

We think so for the following reasons:

1st. The clause is placed among the powers of Congress, not among the limitations on those powers.

2d. Its terms purport to enlarge, not to diminish, the powers vested in the Government. It purports to be an additional power, not a restriction on those already granted. . . .

We admit, as all must admit, that the powers of the Government are limited, and that its limits are not to be transcended. But we think the sound construction of the Constitution must allow to the national legislature that discretion with respect to the means by which the powers it confers are to be carried into execution which will enable that body to perform the high duties assigned to it in the manner most beneficial to the people. Let the end be legitimate, let it be within the scope of the Constitution, and all means which are appropriate, which are plainly adapted to that end, which are not prohibited, but consist with the letter and spirit of the Constitution, are Constitutional. . . .

It being the opinion of the Court that the act incorporating the bank is constitutional, and that the power of establishing a branch in the State of Maryland might be properly exercised by the bank itself, we proceed to inquire:

2. Whether the State of Maryland may, without violating the Constitution, tax that branch? . . .

This great principle is that the Constitution and the laws made in pursuance thereof are supreme; that they control the Constitution and laws of the respective States, and cannot be controlled by them. From this, which may be almost termed an axiom, other propositions are deduced as corollaries. . . . These are, 1st. That a power to create implies a power to preserve; 2d. That a power to destroy, if wielded by a different hand, is hostile to, and incompatible with these powers to create and to preserve; 3d. That, where this repugnancy exists, that authority which is supreme must control, not yield to that over which it is supreme. . . .

That the power of taxing it by the States may be exercised so as to destroy it is too obvious to be denied. But taxation is said to be an absolute power which acknowledges no other limits than those expressly prescribed in the Constitution, and, like sovereign power of every other description, is intrusted to the discretion of those who use it. But the very terms of this argument admit that the sovereignty of the State, in the article of taxation itself, is subordinate to, and may be controlled by, the Constitution of the United States. How far it has been controlled by that instrument must be a question of construction. In making this construction, no principle, not declared, can be admissible which would defeat the legitimate operations of a supreme Government. It is of the very essence of supremacy to remove all obstacles to its action within its own sphere, and so to modify every power vested in subordinate governments as to exempt its own operations from their own influence. This effect need not be stated in terms. It is so involved in the declaration of supremacy, so necessarily implied in it, that the expression of it could not make it more certain. We must, therefore, keep it in view while construing the Constitution. . . .

The people of a State . . . give to their Government a right of taxing themselves and their property, and as the exigencies of Government cannot be limited, they prescribe no limits to the exercise of this right, resting confidently on the interest of the legislator and on the influence of the constituent over their representative to guard them against its abuse. But the means employed by the Government of the Union have no such security, nor is the right of a State to tax them sustained by the same theory. Those means are not given by the people of a particular State, not given by the constituents of the legislature which claim the right to tax them, but by the people of all the States. They are given by all, for the benefit of all—and, upon theory, should be subjected to that Government only which belongs to all. . . .

That the power to tax involves the power to destroy; that the power to destroy may defeat and render useless the power to create; that there is a plain repugnance in conferring on one Government a power to control the constitutional measures of another, which other, with respect to those very measures, is declared to be supreme over that which exerts the control, are propositions not to be denied. But all inconsistencies are to be reconciled by the magic of the word CONFIDENCE. Taxation, it is said, does not necessarily and unavoidably destroy. To carry it to the excess of destruction would be an abuse, to presume which would banish that confidence which is essential to all Government. . . .

If the States may tax one instrument, employed by the Government in the execution of its powers, they may tax any and every other instrument. They may tax the mail; they may tax the mint; they may tax patent rights; they may tax the papers of the custom house; they may tax judicial process; they may tax all the means employed by the Government to an excess which would defeat all the ends of Government. This was not intended by the American people. They did not design to make their Government dependent on the States. . . .

We are unanimously of opinion that the law passed by the Legislature of Maryland, imposing a tax on the Bank of the United States is unconstitutional and void. . . .

Case 2.2

Gibbons v. Ogden
22 U.S. (9 Wheat.) 1 (1824)

This dispute involved a matter of state vs. federal law, which arose when the New York State legislature granted a monopoly to Robert Livingston and Robert Fulton to operate passenger steamboats across the Hudson River. The two men, in turn, licensed Aaron Ogden to provide exclusive ferry service on steamboats from New York to New Jersey. Thomas Gibbons, in the meantime, also transported passengers on steamboats from New York to Elizabethtown, New Jersey, under a 1793 federal law that had regulated boats "employed in the coasting trade and fisheries."

When Ogden sued Gibbons for interfering with his monopoly, the New York courts agreed with him that the 1798 federal law did not cover steamboats, but only coasting or sailing vessels, and that Congress had passed no law regulating steamboats. Gibbons appealed to the Supreme Court, which, in an opinion by Chief Justice Marshall, unanimously agreed that the New York law interfered with Congress's authority to regulate interstate commerce under its Article I, Section 8, power. The 1798 federal law, in short, superseded New York State's grant of the monopoly to Ogden.

Chief Justice MARSHALL delivered the opinion of the Court.

The subject to be regulated is commerce; and our constitution being, as was aptly said at the bar, one of enumeration, and not of definition, to ascertain the extent of the power, it becomes necessary to settle the meaning of the word. The counsel for the appellee would limit it to traffic, to buying and selling, or the interchange of commodities, and do not admit that it comprehends navigation. This would restrict a general term, applicable to many objects, to one of its significations. Commerce, undoubtedly, is traffic, but it is something more: it is intercourse. It describes the commercial intercourse between nations, and parts of nations, in all its branches, and is regulated by prescribing rules for carrying on that intercourse. The mind can scarcely conceive a system for regulating commerce between nations, which shall exclude all laws concerning navigation, which shall be silent on the admission of the vessels of the one nation into the ports of the other, and be confined to prescribing rules for the conduct of individuals, in the actual employment of buying and selling, or of barter. . . .

All America understands, and has uniformly understood, the word "commerce," to comprehend navigation. It was so understood, and must have been so understood, when the constitution was framed. The power over commerce, including navigation, was one of the primary objects for which the people of America adopted their government, and must have been contemplated in forming it. The convention must have used the word in that sense, because all have understood it in that sense; and the attempt to restrict it comes too late. . . .

To what commerce does this power extend? The constitution informs us, to commerce "with foreign nations, and among the several States, and with the Indian tribes."

It has, we believe, been universally admitted, that these words comprehend every species of commercial intercourse between the United States and foreign nations. . . .

What is this power?

It is the power to regulate; that is, to prescribe the rule by which commerce is to be governed. This power, like all others vested in Congress, is complete in itself, may be exercised to its utmost extent, and acknowledges no limitations, other than are prescribed in the constitution. These are expressed in plain terms, and do not affect the questions which arise in this case, or which have been discussed at the bar. If, as has always been understood, the sovereignty of Congress, though limited to specified objects, is plenary as to those objects, the power over commerce with foreign nations, and among the several States, is vested in Congress as absolutely as it would be in a single government, having in its constitution the same restrictions on the exercise of the power as are found in the constitution of the United States. The wisdom and the discretion of Congress, their identity with the people, and the influence which their constituents possess at elections, are, in this, as in many other instances, as that, for example, of declaring war, the sole restraints on which they have relied, to secure them from its abuse . . .

The power of Congress, then, comprehends navigation, within the limits of every State in the Union; so far as that navigation may be, in any manner, connected with "commerce with foreign nations, or among the several States, or with the Indian tribes." It may, of consequence, pass the jurisdictional line of New York, and act upon the very waters to which the prohibition now under consideration applies.

But it has been urged with great earnestness, that, although the power of Congress to regulate commerce with foreign nations, and among the several States, be co-extensive with the subject itself, and have no other limits than are prescribed in the constitution, yet the States may severally exercise the same power, within their respective jurisdictions. In support of this argument, it is said, that they possessed it as an inseparable attribute of sovereignty, before the formation of the constitution, and still retain it, except so far as they have surrendered it by that instrument; that this principle results from the nature of the government, and is secured by the tenth amendment; that an affirmative grant of power is not exclusive, unless in its own nature it be such that the continued exercise of it by the former possessor is inconsistent with the grant, and that this is not of that description. . . .

But the two grants are not, it is conceived, similar in their terms or their nature. Although many of the powers formerly exercised by the States, are transferred to the government of the Union, yet the State governments remain, and constitute a most important part of our system. The power of taxation is indispensable to their existence, and is a power which, in its own nature, is capable of residing in, and being exercised by, different authorities at the same time. We are accustomed to see it placed, for different purposes, in different hands. Taxation is the simple operation of taking small portions from a perpetually accumulating mass, susceptible of almost infinite division; and a power in one to take what is necessary for certain purposes, is not, in its nature, incompatible with a power in another to take what is necessary for other purposes. Congress is authorized to lay and collect taxes, &c. to pay the debts, and provide for the common defence and general welfare of the United States. This does not interfere with the power of the States to tax for the support of their own governments. . . . But, when a State proceeds to regulate commerce with foreign nations, or among the several States, it is exercising the very power that is granted to Congress, and is doing the very thing which Congress is authorized to do. There is no analogy, then, between the power of taxation and the power of regulating commerce. . . .

[The Act of 1793, licensing coasting vessels] demonstrates the opinion of Congress, that steamboats may be enrolled and licensed, in common with vessels using sails. They are, of course, entitled to the same privileges, and can no more be restrained from navigating waters, and entering ports which are free to such vessels, than if they were wafted on their voyage by the winds, instead of being propelled by the agency of fire. The one element may be as legitimately used as the other, for every commercial purpose authorized by the laws of the Union; and the act of a State inhibiting the use of either to any vessel having a license under the act of Congress, comes, we think, in direct collision with that act.

Federalism and the Commerce Clause:
New Deal and Civil Rights Cases

One of the first cases approving New Deal legislation under the Commerce Clause was the 1937 *Jones & Laughlin* decision, written by Chief Justice Hughes. By 1941, in *U.S. v. Darby* (1941), the Court unanimously upheld a federal law regulating the wages and hours of a local enterprise. In 1964, the Court ruled that the Civil Rights Act was constitutional as a federal regulation of interstate commerce (*Heart of Atlanta Motel v. U.S.* and *Katzenbach v. McClung*).

Case 2.3

National Labor Relations Board v. Jones & Laughlin Steel Corporation
301 U.S. 1, 57 S.Ct. 615 (1937)

This landmark case is generally viewed as one of the first in which the Court reversed itself when reviewing New Deal legislation; the first was actually decided just a week earlier. The National Labor Relations Act created a board to deal with disputes between unions and management in an effort to avoid strikes when organized labor believed a company engaged in unfair labor practices. Also known as the Wagner Act, the law went into effect when an affiliate of the Amalgamated Association of Iron, Tin, and Steel Workers of America filed a petition against the Jones & Laughlin Steel Corporation with the National Labor Relations Board (N.L.R.B.). The workers alleged that the company openly discouraged its workers from joining the union and then fired ten of them when the workers attempted to organize.

The N.L.R.B. ordered the company to allow union organizing, engage in collective bargaining, and reinstate the ten workers. The company declined, claiming that the Wagner Act was a labor, and not an interstate commerce, law. Congress, its lawyers argued, exceeded its power in passing the law. The union appealed to a federal court of appeals, as the act allowed. When that court declined to order the company to comply with the law, the union appealed to the Supreme Court.

With Chief Justice Hughes writing for a bare five to four majority, the Court ordered the company to comply. Hughes ruled that Jones & Laughlin engaged in interstate commerce and was thus covered by the act. Justice McReynolds' dissent was joined by Justices Van Devanter, Sutherland, and Butler (the so-called Four Horsemen). In his opinion, Hughes describes the octopus-like tentacles of the corporation, stretching throughout the United States to prove that it was engaged in interstate commerce.

Chief Justice HUGHES delivered the opinion of the Court.

In a proceeding under the National Labor Relations Act of 1935, the National Labor Relations Board found that the respondent, Jones & Laughlin Steel Corporation, had violated the act by engaging in unfair labor practices affecting commerce. . . . The unfair labor practices charged were that the corporation was discriminating against members of the union with regard to hire and tenure of employment, and was coercing and intimidating its employees in order to interfere with their self-organization. . . .

Jones & Laughlin Steel Corporation . . . is engaged in the business of manufacturing iron and steel in plants situated in Pittsburgh and nearby Aliquippa, Pa. It manufactures and distributes a widely diversified line of steel and pig iron, being the fourth largest producer of steel in the United States. With its subsidiaries—nineteen in number—it is a completely integrated enterprise, owning and operating ore, coal and limestone properties, lake and river transportation facilities and terminal railroads located at its manufacturing plants. It owns or controls mines in Michigan and Minnesota. It operates four ore steamships on the Great Lakes, used in the transportation of ore to its factories. It owns coal mines in Pennsylvania. It operates towboats and steam barges used in carrying coal to its factories. It owns limestone properties in various places in Pennsylvania and West Virginia. It owns the Monongahela connecting railroad which connects the plants of the Pittsburgh works and forms an interconnection with the Pennsylvania, New York Central and Baltimore & Ohio Railroad systems. It owns the Aliquippa & Southern Railroad Company, which connects the Aliquippa works with the Pittsburgh & Lake Erie, part of the New York Central system. Much of its product is shipped to its warehouses in Chicago, Detroit, Cincinnati and Memphis,—to the last two places by means of its own barges and transportation equipment. In Long Island City, New York, and in New

Orleans it operates structural steel fabricating shops in connection with the warehousing of semifinished materials sent from its works. Through one of its wholly-owned subsidiaries it owns, leases, and operates stores, warehouses, and yards for the distribution of equipment and supplies for drilling and operating oil and gas wells and for pipe lines, refineries and pumping stations. It has sales offices in twenty cities in the United States and a wholly-owned subsidiary which is devoted exclusively to distributing its product in Canada. Approximately 75 percent of its product is shipped out of Pennsylvania.

Summarizing these operations, the Labor Board concluded that the works in Pittsburgh and Aliquippa "might be likened to the heart of a self-contained, highly integrated body. They draw in the raw materials from Michigan, Minnesota, West Virginia, Pennsylvania in part through arteries and by means controlled by the respondent; they transform the materials and then pump them out to all parts of the nation through the vast mechanism which the respondent has elaborated."

To carry on the activities of the entire steel industry, 33,000 men mine ore, 44,000 men mine coal, 4,000 men quarry limestone, 16,000 men manufacture coke, 343,000 men manufacture steel, and 83,000 men transport its product. Respondent has about 10,000 employees in its Aliquippa plant, which is located in a community of about 30,000 persons.

Respondent points to evidence that the Aliquippa plant, in which the discharged men were employed, contains complete facilities for the production of finished and semifinished iron and steel products from raw materials. . . .

Practically all the factual evidence in the case . . . supports the findings of the Board that respondent discharged these men "because of their union activity and for the purpose of discouraging membership in the union." We turn to the questions of law which respondent urges in contesting the validity and application of the act.

First. The Scope of the Act.—The act is challenged in its entirety as an attempt to regulate all industry, thus invading the reserved powers of the States over their local concerns. It is asserted that the references in the act to interstate and foreign commerce are colorable at best; that the act is not a true regulation of such commerce or of matters which directly affect it, but on the contrary has the fundamental object of placing under the compulsory supervision of the federal government all industrial labor relations within the nation. . . . The critical words of . . . the Board's authority in dealing with the labor practices, are "affecting commerce." The act specifically defines "affecting commerce" [as] "burdening or obstructing commerce or the free flow of commerce, or having led or tending to lead to a labor dispute burdening or obstructing commerce or the free flow of commerce."

This definition is one of exclusion as well as inclusion. The grant of authority to the Board does not purport to extend to the relationship between all industrial employees and employers. Its terms do not impose collective bargaining upon all industry regardless of effects upon interstate or foreign commerce. It purports to reach only what may be deemed to burden or obstruct that commerce and, thus qualified, it must be construed as contemplating the exercise of control within constitutional bounds. It is a familiar principle that acts which directly burden or obstruct interstate or foreign commerce, or its free flow, are within the reach of the congressional power. Acts having that effect are not rendered immune because they grow out of labor disputes. It is the effect upon commerce, not the source of the injury, which is the criterion. Whether or not particular action does affect commerce in such a close and intimate fashion as to be subject to federal control, and hence to lie within the authority conferred upon the Board, is left by the statute to be determined as individual cases arise. We are thus to inquire whether in the instant case the constitutional boundary has been passed.

Second. . . . In its present application, the statute goes no further than to safeguard the right of employees to self-organization and to select representatives of their own choosing for collective bargaining or other mutual protection without restraint or coercion by their employer.

That is a fundamental right. Employees have as clear a right to organize and select their representatives for lawful purposes as the respondent has to organize its business and select its own officers and agents. Discrimination and coercion to prevent the free exercise of the right of employees to self-organization and representation is a proper subject for condemnation by competent legislative authority. Long ago we stated the reason for labor organizations. We said that they were organized out of the necessities of the situation; that a single employee was helpless in dealing with an employer; that he was dependent ordinarily on his daily wage for the maintenance of himself and family; that, if the employer refused to pay him the wages that he thought fair, he was nevertheless unable to leave the employ and resist arbitrary and unfair treatment; that union was essential to give laborers opportunity to deal on an equality with their employer. . . .

Third. The application of the Act to Employees Engaged in Production.—The Principle Involved.—Respondent says that, whatever may be said of employees engaged in interstate commerce, the industrial relations and activities in the manufacturing department of respondent's enterprise are not subject to federal regulation. The argument rests upon the proposition that manufacturing in itself is not commerce.

The government distinguishes these cases. The various parts of respondent's enterprise are described as interdependent and as thus involving "a great movement of iron ore, coal and limestone along well-defined paths to the steel mills, thence through them, and thence in the form of steel products into the consuming centers of the country—a definite and well-understood course of business." It is urged that these activities constitute a "stream" or "flow" of commerce, of which the Aliquippa manufacturing plant is the focal point, and that industrial strife at that point would cripple the entire movement. . . .

We do not find it necessary to determine whether these features of defendant's business dispose of the asserted analogy to the "stream of commerce" cases. The instances in which that metaphor has been used are but particular, and not exclusive, illustrations of the protective power which the government invokes in support of the present act. The congressional authority to protect interstate commerce from burdens and obstructions is not limited to transactions which can be deemed to be an essential part of a "flow" of interstate or foreign commerce. Burdens and obstructions may be due to injurious action springing from other sources. . . . Although activities may be intrastate in character when separately considered, if they have such a close and substantial relation to interstate commerce that their control is essential or appropriate to protect that commerce from burdens and obstructions, Congress cannot be denied the power to exercise that control. *Schechter Corporation v. United States* [295 U.S.495 (1935)]. Undoubtedly the scope of this power must be considered in the light of our dual system of government and may not be extended so as to embrace effects upon interstate commerce so indirect and remote that to embrace them, in view of our complex society, would effectually obliterate the distinction between what is national and what is local and create a completely centralized government. The question is necessarily one of degree. . . .

It is thus apparent that the fact that the employees here concerned were engaged in production is not determinative. The question remains as to the effect upon interstate commerce of the labor practice involved. . . .

Fourth. Effects of the Unfair Labor Practice in Respondent's Enterprise.—Giving full weight to respondent's contention with respect to a break in the complete continuity of the "stream of commerce" by reason of respondent's manufacturing operations, the fact remains that the stoppage of those operations by industrial strife would have a most serious effect upon interstate commerce. In view of respondent's far-flung activities, it is idle to say that the effect would be indirect or remote. It is obvious that it would be immediate and might be catastrophic. We are asked to shut our eyes to the plainest facts of our national life and to deal with the question of direct and indirect effects in an intellectual vacuum. Because there may be but indirect and remote effects upon interstate commerce in connection with a host of local enterprises throughout the country, it does not follow that other industrial activities do not have such a close and intimate relation to interstate commerce as to make the presence of industrial strife a matter of the most urgent national concern. When industries organize themselves on a national scale, making their relation to interstate commerce the dominant factor in their activities, how can it be maintained that their industrial labor relations constitute a forbidden field into which Congress may not enter when it is necessary to protect interstate commerce from the paralyzing consequences of industrial war? We have often said that interstate commerce itself is a practical conception. It is equally true that interferences with that commerce must be appraised by a judgment that does not ignore actual experience. . . .

The steel industry is one of the great basic industries of the United States, with ramifying activities affecting interstate commerce at every point. The Government aptly refers to the steel strike of 1919–1920 with its far-reaching consequences. The fact that there appears to have been no major disturbance in that industry in the more recent period did not dispose of the possibilities of future and like dangers to interstate commerce which Congress was entitled to foresee and to exercise its protective power to forestall. It is not necessary again to detail the facts as to respondent's enterprise.

Instead of being beyond the pale, we think that it presents in a most striking way the close and intimate relation which a manufacturing industry may have to interstate commerce and we have no doubt that Congress had constitutional authority to safeguard the right of respondent's employees to self-organization and freedom in the choice of representatives for collective bargaining.

Case 2.4

United States v. Darby Lumber Co.
312 U.S. 100, 61 S.Ct. 451 (1941)

Fred Darby, the owner of a lumber and sawmill company in Georgia, was indicted for shipping goods through interstate commerce in violation of the 1938 Fair Labor Standards Act (FLSA). That act required him to pay his workers 25 cents an hour and to pay overtime to anyone who worked more than 40 hours per week. Moreover, the act also specified that all employers maintain complete wage and hour records of their employees.

A federal district judge dismissed the charges against Darby and ruled the act unconstitutional on Tenth Amendment grounds, holding that *Hammer v. Dagenhart*, 247 U.S. 251 (1916) prohibited Congress from regulating production and manufacturing under the Commerce Clause.

The United States appealed to the Supreme Court, which in a unanimous decision in an opinion by Justice Harlan Fiske Stone, upheld the constitutionality of the act and overturned *Hammer*.

Justice STONE delivered the opinion of the Court.

. . . The Fair Labor Standards Act set up a comprehensive legislative scheme for preventing the shipment in interstate commerce of certain products and commodities produced in the United States under labor conditions as respects wages and hours which fail to conform to standards set up by the Act. Its purpose . . . is to exclude from interstate commerce goods produced for the commerce and to prevent their production for interstate commerce, under conditions detrimental to the maintenance of the minimum standards of living necessary for health and general well-being; and to prevent the use of interstate commerce as the means of competition in the distribution of goods so produced, and as the means of spreading and perpetuating such substandard labor conditions among the workers of the several states. . . .

The Prohibition of Shipment of the Proscribed Goods in Interstate Commerce.
While manufacture is not of itself interstate commerce the shipment of manufactured goods interstate is such commerce and the prohibition of such shipment by Congress is indubitably a regulation of the commerce. The power to regulate commerce is the power "to prescribe the rule by which commerce is to be governed." *Gibbons v. Ogden*, 9 Wheat. [22 U.S.] 1 [(1824)]. It extends not only to those regulations which aid, foster and protect the commerce, but embraces those which prohibit it. It is conceded that the power of Congress to prohibit transportation in interstate commerce includes noxious articles, stolen articles, kidnapped persons, and articles such as intoxicating liquor or convict made goods, traffic in which is forbidden or restricted by the laws of the state of destination.

But it is said that the present prohibition falls within the scope of none of these categories; that while the prohibition is nominally a regulation of the commerce its motive or purpose is regulation of wages and hours of persons engaged in manufacture, the control of which has been reserved to the states and upon which Georgia and some of the states of destination have placed no restriction; that the effect of the present statute is not to exclude the prescribed articles from interstate commerce in aid of state regulation . . . but instead, under the guise of a regulation of interstate commerce, it undertakes to regulate wages and hours within the state contrary to the policy of the state which has elected to leave them unregulated.

The power of Congress over interstate commerce "is complete in itself, may be exercised to its utmost extent, and acknowledges no limitations, other than are prescribed by the constitution." *Gibbons v. Ogden.* That power can neither be enlarged nor diminished by the exercise or non-exercise of state power. Congress, following its own conception of public policy concerning the restrictions which may appropriately be imposed on interstate commerce, is free to exclude from the commerce articles whose use in the states for which they are destined it may conceive to be injurious to the public health, morals or welfare, even though the state has not sought to regulate their use.

Such regulation is not a forbidden invasion of state power merely because either its motive or its consequence is to restrict the use of articles of commerce within the states of destination and is not prohibited unless by other Constitutional provisions. It is no objection to the assertion of the power to regulate interstate commerce that its exercise is attended by the same incidents which attend the exercise of the police power of the states. . . .

The motive and purpose of the present regulation are plainly to make effective the Congressional conception of public policy that interstate commerce should not be made the instrument of competition in the distribution of goods produced under substandard labor conditions, which competition is injurious to the commerce and to the states from and to which the commerce flows. The motive and purpose of a regulation of interstate commerce are matters for the legislative judgment upon the exercise of which the Constitution places no restriction and over which the courts are given no control. . . .

In the more than a century which has elapsed since the decision of *Gibbons v. Ogden,* these principles of constitutional interpretation have been so long and repeatedly recognized by this Court as applicable to the Commerce Clause, that there would be little occasion for repeating them now were it not for the decision of this Court twenty-two years ago in *Hammer v. Dagenhart,* 247 U.S. 251 [1916]. In that case it was held by a bare majority of the Court over the powerful and now classic dissent of Mr. Justice Holmes setting forth the fundamental issues involved, that Congress was without power to exclude the products of child labor from interstate commerce. The reasoning and conclusion of the Court's opinion there cannot be reconciled with the conclusion which we have reached, that the power of Congress under the Commerce Clause is plenary to exclude any article from interstate commerce subject only to the specific prohibitions of the Constitution.

Hammer v. Dagenhart has not been followed. The distinction on which the decision was rested that Congressional power to prohibit interstate commerce is limited to articles which in themselves have some harmful or deleterious property—a distinction which was novel when made and unsupported by any provision of the Constitution—has long since been abandoned. . . .

The conclusion is inescapable that *Hammer v. Dagenhart* was a departure from the principles which have prevailed in the interpretation of the commerce clause both before and since the decision and that such vitality, as a precedent, as it then had has long since been exhausted. It should be and now is overruled.

Validity of the Wage and Hour Requirements.
[The FLSA requires] employers to conform to the wage and hour provisions with respect to all employees engaged in the production of goods for interstate commerce. As appellee's employees are not alleged to be "engaged in interstate commerce" the validity of the prohibition turns on the question whether the employment, under other than the prescribed labor standards, of employees engaged in the production of goods for interstate commerce is so related to the commerce and so affects it as to be within the reach of the power of Congress to regulate it.

To answer this question we must at the outset determine whether the particular acts charged . . . constitute "production for commerce" within the meaning of the statute. As the Government seeks to apply the statute in the indictment, and as the court below construed the phrase "produced for interstate commerce," it embraces at least the case where an employer engaged, as are appellees, in the manufacture and shipment of goods in filling orders of extrastate customers, manufactures his product with the intent or expectation that according to the normal course of his business all or some part of it will be selected for shipment to those customers.

Without attempting to define the precise limits of the phrase, we think the acts alleged in the indictment are within the sweep of the statute. The obvious purpose of the Act was not only to prevent the interstate transportation of the proscribed product, but to stop the initial step toward transportation, production with the purpose of so transporting it. Congress was not unaware that most manufacturing businesses shipping their product in interstate commerce make it in their shops without reference to its ultimate destination and then after manufacture select some of it for shipment interstate and some intrastate according to the daily demands of their business, and that it would be practically impossible, without disrupting manufacturing businesses, to restrict the prohibited kind of production to the particular pieces of lumber, cloth, furniture or the like which later move in interstate rather than intrastate commerce. . . .

There remains the question whether such restriction on the production of goods for commerce is a permissible exercise of the commerce power. The power of Congress over interstate commerce is not confined to the regulation of commerce among the states. It extends to those activities intrastate which so affect interstate commerce or the exercise of the power of Congress over it as to make regulation of them appropriate means to the attainment of a legitimate end, the exercise of the granted power of Congress to regulate interstate commerce. . . .

Our conclusion is unaffected by the Tenth Amendment which provides: "The powers not delegated to the United States by the Constitution, nor prohibited by it to the States, are reserved to the States respectively, or to the people." The amendment states but a truism that all is retained which has not been surrendered. There is nothing in the history of its adoption to suggest that it was more than declaratory of the relationship between the national and state governments as it had been established by the Constitution before the amendment or that its purpose was other than to allay fears that the new national government might seek to exercise powers not granted, and that the states might not be able to exercise fully their reserved powers. . . .

Validity of the Wage and Hour Provisions under the Fifth Amendment. Both provisions are minimum wage requirements compelling the payment of a minimum standard wage with a prescribed increased wage for overtime of "not less than one and one-half times the regular rate" at which the worker is employed. Since our decision in *West Coast Hotel Co. v. Parrish*, 300 U.S. 379 [1937], it is no longer open to question that the fixing of a minimum wage is within the legislative power and that the bare fact of its exercise is not a denial of due process under the Fifth more than under the Fourteenth Amendment. Nor is it any longer open to question that it is within the legislative power to fix maximum hours. Similarly the statute is not objectionable because applied alike to both men and women.

The Act is sufficiently definite to meet constitutional demands. One who employs persons, without conforming to the prescribed wage and hour conditions, to work on goods which he ships or expects to ship across state lines, is warned that he may be subject to the criminal penalties of the Act. No more is required.

We have considered, but find it unnecessary to discuss other contentions.

Reversed.

Case 2.5

Heart of Atlanta Motel v. United States
379 U.S. 241, 85 S.Ct. 348 (1964)

and

Katzenbach v. McClung
379 U.S. 294, 85 S.Ct. 377 (1964)

In 1883, the Court invalidated a federal public accommodations law that Congress had passed in 1875 in an effort to implement the Equal Protection Clause of the Fourteenth Amendment. The law required that private enterprises that opened their doors to the public—hotels, restaurants, taverns, theaters, and so on—must not discriminate on the basis of race. The Court overturned the 1875 law in *The Civil Rights Cases*, holding that unless state action sanctioned private discrimination in some way, owners of these establishments could determine whom they would and would not serve. The Civil Rights Act of 1964, also known as the Public Accommodations Law, like the earlier 1875 Act, prohibited racial discrimination and segregation in places open to the public.

The owners of the Heart of Atlanta Motel and the proprietors, Ollie McClung, Jr. and Sr., of Ollie's Barbecue in Birmingham, Alabama, refused to serve black patrons. They challenged the law as overstepping Congress's commerce power, claiming that no state action was involved. The motel owners advertised in national magazines and at least seventy-five percent of their guests, as did its equipment, arrived from out of state. The same was true of Ollie's Barbecue. More than half of the food served there moved through interstate commerce.

Justice Tom Clark, writing for a unanimous Court, upheld the Civil Rights Act of 1964 solely on the basis of Congress's interstate commerce power under Article I, Section 8.

Justice CLARK delivered the opinion of the Court.

Congress first evidenced its interest in civil rights legislation in the Civil Rights or Enforcement Act of April 9, 1866. There followed four Acts, with a fifth, the Civil Rights Act of March 1, 1875, culminating the series.

In 1883 this Court struck down the public accommodations sections of the 1875 Act in the Civil Rights Cases. No major legislation in this field had been enacted by Congress for 82 years when the Civil Rights Act of 1957 became law. It was followed by the Civil Rights Act of 1960. Three years later, on June 19, 1963, the late President Kennedy called for civil rights legislation in a message to Congress to which he attached a proposed bill. Its stated purpose was "to promote the general welfare by eliminating discrimination based on race, color, religion, or national origin in . . . public accommodations through the exercise by Congress of the powers conferred upon it . . . to enforce the provisions of the fourteenth and fifteenth amendments, to regulate commerce among the several States, and to make laws necessary and proper to execute the powers conferred upon it by the Constitution."

Bills were introduced in each House of the Congress, embodying the President's suggestion. . . . However, it was not until July 2, 1964, upon the recommendation of President Johnson, that the Civil Rights Act of 1964, here under attack, was finally passed.

The Act as finally adopted was most comprehensive, undertaking to prevent through peaceful and voluntary settlement discrimination in voting, as well as in places of accommodation and public facilities, federally secured programs and in employment. Since Title II is the only portion under attack here, we confine our consideration to those public accommodation provisions.

Title II of the Act.
This Title is divided into seven sections beginning with 201 (a) which provides that: All persons shall be entitled to the full and equal enjoyment of the goods, services, facilities, privileges, advantages, and accommodations of any place of public accommodation, as defined in this section, without discrimination or segregation on the ground of race, color, religion, or national origin.

There are listed in 201 (b) four classes of business establishments, each of which "serves the public" and "is a place of public accommodation" within the meaning of 201 (a) "if its operations affect commerce, or if discrimination or segregation by it is supported by State action." The covered establishments are: "(1) any inn, hotel, motel, or other establishment which provides lodging to transient guests, other than an establishment located within a building which contains not more than five rooms for rent or hire and which is actually occupied by the proprietor of such establishment as his residence . . . ."

Section 201 (c) defines the phrase "affect commerce" as applied to the above establishments. It first declares that "any inn, hotel, motel, or other establishment which provides lodging to transient guests" affects commerce per se. . . .

The Civil Rights Cases (1883) and their Application.
In light of our ground for decision, it might be well at the outset to discuss the *Civil Rights Cases*, which declared provisions of the Civil Rights
Act of 1875 unconstitutional. We think that decision inapposite, and
without precedential value in determining the constitutionality of the
present Act. Unlike Title II of the present legislation, the 1875 Act
broadly proscribed discrimination in "inns, public conveyances on land
or water, theaters, and other places of public amusement," without limiting the categories of affected businesses to those impinging upon interstate commerce. In contrast, the applicability of Title II is carefully
limited to enterprises having a direct and substantial relation to the interstate flow of goods and people, except where state action is involved.
Further, the fact that certain kinds of businesses may not in 1875 have
been sufficiently involved in interstate commerce to warrant bringing
them within the ambit of the commerce power is not necessarily dispositive of the same question today. Our populace had not reached its present mobility, nor were facilities, goods and services circulating as readily
in interstate commerce as they are today. Although the principles which
we apply today are those first formulated by Chief Justice Marshall in
Gibbons v. Ogden, the conditions of transportation and commerce have
changed dramatically, and we must apply those principles to the present
state of commerce. The sheer increase in volume of interstate traffic
alone would give discriminatory practices which inhibit travel a far
larger impact upon the Nation's commerce than such practices had on
the economy of another day. Finally, there is language in the *Civil Rights
Cases* which indicates that the Court did not fully consider whether the
1875 Act could be sustained as an exercise of the commerce power.
Though the Court observed that "no one will contend that the power to
pass it was contained in the Constitution before the adoption of the last
three amendments [Thirteenth, Fourteenth, and Fifteenth]," the Court
went on specifically to note that the Act was not "conceived" in terms of
the commerce power. . . .

The Basis of Congressional Action.
While the Act as adopted carried no congressional findings the record
of its passage through each house is replete with evidence of the burdens that discrimination by race or color places upon interstate commerce. This testimony included the fact that our people have become
increasingly mobile with millions of people of all races traveling from
State to State; that Negroes in particular have been the subject of discrimination in transient accommodations, having to travel great dis-
tances to secure the same; that often they have been unable to obtain
accommodations and have had to call upon friends to put them up
overnight; and that these conditions had become so acute as to require

the listing of available lodging for Negroes in a special guidebook which was itself "dramatic testimony to the difficulties" Negroes encounter in travel. . . .

The Power of Congress Over Interstate Travel.
The power of Congress to deal with these obstructions depends on the meaning of the Commerce Clause. Its meaning was first enunciated 140 years ago by the great Chief Justice John Marshall in Gibbons v. Ogden. . . .

The same interest in protecting interstate commerce which led Congress to deal with segregation in interstate carriers and the white-slave traffic has prompted it to extend the exercise of its power to gambling, *Lottery Case*, 188 U.S. 321 (1903); to criminal enterprises, *Brooks v. United States*, 267 U.S. 432 (1925); to deceptive practices in the sale of products, *Federal Trade Comm v. Mandel Bros., Inc.*, 359 U.S. 385 (1959); to fraudulent security transactions, *Securities & Exchange Comm'n v. Ralston Purina Co.*, 346 U.S. 119 (1953); to misbranding of drugs, *Weeks v. United States*, 245 U.S. 618 (1918); to wages and hours, *United States, v. Darby*, 312 U.S. 100 (1941); to members of labor unions, *National Labor Relations Board v. Jones & Laughlin Steel Corp.*, 301 U.S. 1 (1937); to crop control, *Wickard v. Filburn*, 317 U.S. 111 (1942); to discrimination against shippers, *United States v. Baltimore & Ohio R. Co.*, 333 U.S. 169 (1948); to the protection of small business from injurious price cutting, *Moore v. Mead's Fine Bread Co.*, 348 U.S. 115 (1954); to resale price maintenance, *Hudson Distributors, Inc. v. Eli Lilly & Co.*, 377 U.S. 386 (1964), *Schwegmann v. Calvert Distillers Corp.*, 341 U.S. 384 (1951); to professional football, *Radovich v. National Football League*, 352 U.S. 445 (1957); and to racial discrimination by owners and managers of terminal restaurants. *Boynton v. Virginia*, 364 US. 454 (1960).

That Congress was legislating against moral wrongs in many of these areas rendered its enactments no less valid. In framing Title II of this Act Congress was also dealing with what it considered a moral problem. But that fact does not detract from the overwhelming evidence of the disruptive effect that racial discrimination has had on commercial intercourse. It was this burden which empowered Congress to enact appropriate legislation, and, given this basis for the exercise of its power, Congress was not restricted by the fact that the particular obstruction to interstate commerce with which it was dealing was also deemed a moral and social wrong. . . .

We, therefore, conclude that the action of the Congress in the adoption of the Act as applied here to a motel which concededly serves interstate travelers is within the power granted it by the Commerce Clause of the Constitution, as interpreted by this Court for 140 years. It may be argued that Congress could have pursued other methods to eliminate the obstructions it found in interstate commerce caused by racial discrimination. But this is a matter of policy that rests entirely with the Congress not with the courts. How obstructions in commerce may be removed—what means are to be employed—is within the sound and exclusive discretion of the Congress. It is subject only to one caveat—that the means chosen by it must be reasonably adapted to the end permitted by the Constitution. We cannot say that its choice here was not so adapted. The Constitution requires no more.

Justice CLARK also delivered the unanimous opinion of the Court in *Katzenbach v. McClung.*

[NOTE: this ruling also upheld Congress's 1964 Civil Rights Act under the commerce clause.]

Federalism and the Commerce Clause: Contemporary Cases

One of the cases that follows, *United States v. Lopez*, was decided more than thirty years after the Court's broad reading of Congress's commerce power in *Heart of Atlanta Motel* and *McClung*. It represented a reversal by a bare majority of justices. One of William Rehnquist's goals when he became Chief Justice in 1986, having served previously as an associate justice since 1972, was to review federal laws that duplicated what the states were already doing, especially in regard to criminal offenses, punishment, and education. He looked skeptically on those laws that he thought were unrelated to interstate commerce: those without, in the words of Chief Justice Hughes, a "close and substantial relation to" interstate commerce. In this way, Rehnquist attracted a bare majority to overturn several federal laws. This case represented the first time he was successful. By the time of Rehnquist's death in 2005, the Court had invalided nearly thirty-five such laws. But in the second case here, *National Association of Business v. Sebelius* (2012), the Court held that while Congress could not create interstate commerce in order to regulate it, it could legitimately require individuals to pay a tax under the Taxing and Spending Clause of Article I if they declined to purchase health insurance.

Case **2.6**

United States v. Lopez
514 U.S. 549, 115 S.Ct. 1624 (1995)

Alphonso Lopez was in the twelfth grade when, on March 10, 1992, he brought a .38 caliber pistol loaded with five bullets to school. He did not know that in 1990 Congress had passed the Gun-Free School Zones Act in an effort to cut down on school violence by making it illegal for anyone to possess a firearm within 1,000 feet of a public or private school: he had committed a federal offense. And yet, when he walked into Edison High School in San Antonio, Texas, local law enforcement officers, acting on an anonymous tip, arrested him and initially charged him with violating the Texas law that prohibited gun possession in a school. These charges were dismissed the next day when federal authorities pressed charges under the Gun-Free School Zones Act.

Before long, this situation developed not into a gun-in-the-school case, but into a classic federal vs. state case. Counsel for Lopez moved to have the federal charges dismissed on the grounds that Congress had no authority under the Commerce Clause to control local public schools. The district court denied his motion, claiming that Supreme Court precedent has shown that public education in fact did have an impact on interstate commerce. Lopez was subsequently sentenced to six months imprisonment and two years probation. The Court of Appeals for the Fifth Circuit reversed, holding that Congress lacked authority under the Commerce Clause to pass the Gun-Free School Zones Act. The United States appealed to the Supreme Court.

In upholding the Court of Appeals decision, the Court agreed that Congress had exceeded its authority under the Commerce Clause. Chief Justice William H. Rehnquist wrote the opinion for the five to four majority. Justices Anthony M. Kennedy and Clarence Thomas wrote concurring opinions. Justices John Paul Stevens, David H. Souter, and Stephen G. Breyer wrote dissenting opinions with which Justice Ruth Bader Ginsburg joined. Note particularly the Chief Justice's rehearsal of the history of the Court's Commerce Clause jurisprudence.

Chief Justice REHNQUIST delivered the opinion of the Court.

. . . We start with first principles. . . . The commerce power "is the power to regulate; that is, to prescribe the rule by which commerce is to be governed. This power, like all others vested in Congress, is complete in itself, may be exercised to its utmost extent, and acknowledges no limitations, other than are prescribed in the constitution." [*Gibbons v. Ogden,* 22 U.S. 1 (1824)]. The *Gibbons* Court, however, acknowledged that limitations on the commerce power are inherent in the very language of the Commerce Clause. "It is not intended to say that these words comprehend that commerce, which is completely internal, which is carried on between man and man in a State, or between different parts of the same State, and which does not extend to or affect other States. Such a power would be inconvenient, and is certainly unnecessary." "Comprehensive as the word 'among' is, it may very properly be restricted to that commerce which concerns more States than one. . . . The enumeration presupposes something not enumerated; and that something, if we regard the language or the subject of the sentence, must be the exclusively internal commerce of a State." [*Gibbons*]

For nearly a century thereafter, the Court's Commerce Clause decisions dealt but rarely with the extent of Congress' power, and almost entirely with the Commerce Clause as a limit on state legislation that discriminated against interstate commerce. Under this line of precedent, the Court held that certain categories of activity such as "production," "manufacturing," and "mining" were within the province of state governments, and thus were beyond the power of Congress under the Commerce Clause. . . .

In 1887, Congress enacted the Interstate Commerce Act, and in 1890, Congress enacted the Sherman Antitrust Act. These laws ushered in a new era of federal regulation under the commerce power. When cases involving these laws first reached this Court, we imported from our negative Commerce Clause cases the approach that Congress could not regulate activities such as "production," "manufacturing," and "mining." See, e.g., *United States v. EC Knight Co.,* 156 U.S. 1 (1895); *Carter v. Carter Coal Co.,* 298 U.S. 238 (1936). Simultaneously, however, the Court held that, where the interstate and intrastate aspects of commerce were so mingled together that full regulation of interstate commerce required incidental regulation of intrastate commerce, the Commerce Clause authorized such regulation.

In *ALA Schechter Poultry Corp. v. United States,* 295 U.S. 495 (1935), the Court struck down regulations that fixed the hours and wages of individuals employed by an intrastate business because the activity being regulated related to interstate commerce only indirectly. In doing so, the Court characterized the distinction between direct and indirect effects of intrastate transactions upon interstate commerce as "a fundamental one, essential to the maintenance of our constitutional system." . . .

Two years later, in the watershed case of *NLRB v. Jones & Laughlin Steel Corp.*, 301 U.S. 1 (1937), the Court upheld the National Labor Relations Act against a Commerce Clause challenge, and in the process, departed from the distinction between "direct" and "indirect" effects on interstate commerce. The Court held that intrastate activities that "have such a close and substantial relation to interstate commerce that their control is essential or appropriate to protect that commerce from burdens and obstructions" are within Congress' power to regulate.

In *United States v. Darby*, 312 U.S. 100 (1941), the Court upheld the Fair Labor Standards Act. . . .

In *Wickard v. Filburn* [317 U.S. 111 (1942)] the Court upheld the application of amendments to the Agricultural Adjustment Act of 1938 to the production and consumption of home-grown wheat. The *Wickard* Court explicitly rejected earlier distinctions between direct and indirect effects on interstate commerce, stating: "Even if appellee's activity be local and though it may not be regarded as commerce, it may still, whatever its nature, be reached by Congress if it exerts a substantial economic effect on interstate commerce, and this irrespective of whether such effect is what might at some earlier time have been defined as 'direct' or 'indirect.' " . . .

Jones & Laughlin Steel, *Darby*, and *Wickard* ushered in an era of Commerce Clause jurisprudence that greatly expanded the previously defined authority of Congress under that Clause. In part, this was a recognition of the great changes that had occurred in the way business was carried on in this country. Enterprises that had once been local or at most regional in nature had become national in scope. But the doctrinal change also reflected a view that earlier Commerce Clause cases artificially had constrained the authority of Congress to regulate interstate commerce.

But even these modern-era precedents which have expanded congressional power under the Commerce Clause confirm that this power is subject to outer limits. In *Jones & Laughlin Steel*, the Court warned that the scope of the interstate commerce power "must be considered in the light of our dual system of government and may not be extended so as to embrace effects upon interstate commerce so indirect and remote that to embrace them, in view of our complex society, would effectually obliterate the distinction between what is national and what is local and create a completely centralized government." Since that time, the Court has heeded that warning and undertaken to decide whether a rational basis existed for concluding that a regulated activity sufficiently affected interstate commerce.

Similarly, in *Maryland v. Wirtz*, 392 U.S. 183 (1968), the Court reaffirmed that "the power to regulate commerce, though broad indeed, has limits" that "the Court has ample power" to enforce. In response to the dissent's warnings that the Court was powerless to enforce the limitations on Congress' commerce powers because "all activities affecting commerce, even in the minutest degree, [*Wickard*], may be regulated and controlled by Congress," (Justice Douglas, dissenting), the *Wirtz* Court replied that the dissent had misread precedent as "neither here nor in *Wickard* has the Court declared that Congress may use a relatively trivial impact on commerce as an excuse for broad general regulation of state or private activities." Rather, "the Court has said only that where a general regulatory statute bears a substantial relation to commerce, the *de minimis* character of individual instances arising under that statute is of no consequence."

Consistent with this structure, we have identified three broad categories of activity that Congress may regulate under its commerce power. First, Congress may regulate the use of the channels of interstate commerce. Second, Congress is empowered to regulate and protect the instrumentalities of interstate commerce, or persons or things in interstate commerce, even though the threat may come only from intrastate activities. Finally, Congress' commerce authority includes the power to regulate those activities having a substantial relation to interstate commerce.

Within this final category, admittedly, our case law has not been clear whether an activity must "affect" or "substantially affect" interstate commerce in order to be within Congress' power to regulate it under the Commerce Clause. We conclude, consistent with the great weight of our case law, that the proper test requires an analysis of whether the regulated activity "substantially affects" interstate commerce.

We now turn to consider the power of Congress, in the light of this framework, to enact 922(q). The first two categories of authority may be quickly disposed of: 922(q) is not a regulation of the use of the channels of interstate commerce, nor is it an attempt to prohibit the interstate transportation of a commodity through the channels of commerce; nor can 922(q) be justified as a regulation by which Congress has sought to protect an instrumentality of interstate commerce or a thing in interstate commerce. Thus, if 922(q) is to be sustained, it must be under the third category as a regulation of an activity that substantially affects interstate commerce.

First, we have upheld a wide variety of congressional Acts regulating intrastate economic activity where we have concluded that the activity substantially affected interstate commerce. Examples include the regulation of intrastate coal mining; intrastate extortionate credit transactions, restaurants utilizing substantial interstate supplies, inns and hotels catering to interstate guests, and production and consumption of home-grown wheat. These examples are by no means exhaustive, but the pattern is clear. Where economic activity substantially affects interstate commerce, legislation regulating that activity will be sustained. . . .

Section 922(q) is a criminal statute that by its terms has nothing to do with "commerce" or any sort of economic enterprise, however broadly one might define those terms. Section 922(q) is not an essential part of a larger regulation of economic activity, in which the regulatory scheme could be undercut unless the intrastate activity were regulated. It cannot, therefore, be sustained under our cases upholding regulations of activities that arise out of or are connected with a commercial transaction, which viewed in the aggregate, substantially affects interstate commerce. . . .

The Government's essential contention, in fine, is that . . . possession of a firearm in a school zone may result in violent crime and that violent crime can be expected to affect the functioning of the national economy in two ways. First, the costs of violent crime are substantial, and, through the mechanism of insurance, those costs are spread throughout the population. Second, violent crime reduces the willingness of individuals to travel to areas within the country that are perceived to be unsafe. The Government also argues that the presence of guns in schools poses a substantial threat to the educational process by threatening the learning environment. A handicapped educational process, in turn, will result in a less productive citizenry. That, in turn, would have an adverse effect on the Nation's economic well-being. As a result, the Government argues that Congress could rationally have concluded that 922(q) substantially affects interstate commerce. . . .

To uphold the Government's contentions here, we would have to pile inference upon inference in a manner that would bid fair to convert congressional authority under the Commerce Clause to a general police power of the sort retained by the States. Admittedly, some of our prior cases have taken long steps down that road, giving great deference to congressional action. The broad language in these opinions has suggested the possibility of additional expansion, but we decline here to proceed any further. To do so would require us to conclude that the Constitution's enumeration of powers does not presuppose something not enumerated, and that there never will be a distinction between what is truly national and what is truly local. This we are unwilling to do.

For the foregoing reasons the judgment of the Court of Appeals is Affirmed.

Justice BREYER, with whom Justices STEVENS, SOUTER, and GINSBURG join, dissenting.

The majority's holding—that Section 922 falls outside the scope of the Commerce Clause—creates three serious legal problems. First, the majority's holding runs contrary to modern Supreme Court cases that have upheld congressional actions despite connections to interstate or foreign commerce that are less significant than the effect of school violence. . . .

In *Katzenbach v. McClung*, 379 U.S. 294 (1964), this Court upheld, as within the commerce power, a statute prohibiting racial discrimination at local restaurants, in part because that discrimination discouraged travel by African Americans and in part because that discrimination affected purchases of food and restaurant supplies from other States. In *Daniel v. Paul*, 395 U.S. 298 (1969), this Court found an effect on commerce caused by an amusement park located several miles down a country road in the middle of Alabama—because some customers (the Court assumed), some food, 15 paddleboats, and a juke box had come from out of State. In both of these cases, the Court understood that the specific instance of discrimination (at a local place of accommodation) was part of a general practice that, considered as a whole, caused not only the most serious human and social harm, but had nationally significant economic dimensions as well. It is difficult to distinguish the case before us, for the same critical elements are present. . . . Most importantly, like the local racial discrimination at issue in *McClung* and *Daniel*, the local instances here, taken together and considered as a whole, create a problem that causes serious human and social harm, but also has nationally significant economic dimensions.

The second legal problem the Court creates comes from its apparent belief that it can reconcile its holding with earlier cases by making a critical distinction between "commercial" and noncommercial "transactions." That is to say, the Court believes the Constitution would distinguish between two local activities, each of which has an identical effect upon interstate commerce, if one, but not the other, is "commercial" in nature. As a general matter, this approach fails to heed this Court's earlier warning not to turn "questions of the power of Congress" upon "formulas" that would give "controlling force to nomenclature such as 'production' and 'indirect' and foreclose consideration of the actual effects of the activity in question upon interstate commerce." *Wickard* [*v. Filburn*, 317 U.S. 111 (1942)]. . . .

. . . The business of schooling requires expenditure of these funds on student transportation, food and custodial services, books, and teachers' salaries. And, these expenditures enable schools to provide a valuable service—namely, to equip students with the skills they need to survive in life and, more specifically, in the workplace. Certainly, Congress has often analyzed school expenditure as if it were a commercial investment, closely analyzing whether schools are efficient, whether they justify the significant resources they spend, and whether they can be restructured to achieve greater returns. Why could Congress, for Commerce Clause purposes, not consider schools as roughly analogous to commercial investments from which the Nation derives the benefit of an educated work force?

The third legal problem created by the Court's holding is that it threatens legal uncertainty in an area of law that, until this case, seemed reasonably well settled. Congress has enacted many statutes (more than 100 sections of the United States Code), including criminal statutes (at least 25 sections), that use the words "affecting commerce" to define their scope. Do these, or similar, statutes regulate noncommercial activities? If so, would that alter the meaning of "affecting commerce" in a jurisdictional element? More importantly, in the absence of a jurisdictional element, are the courts nevertheless to take *Wickard* (and later similar cases) as inapplicable, and to judge the effect of a single non-commercial activity on interstate commerce without considering similar instances of the forbidden conduct? However these questions are eventually resolved, the legal uncertainty now created will restrict Congress' ability to enact criminal laws aimed at criminal behavior that, considered problem by problem rather than instance by instance, seriously threatens the economic, as well as social, well-being of Americans. . . .

Case 2.7

National Federation of Independent Business v. Sebelius
567 U.S. ___ (2012)

Following World War II, most European nations developed universal health care plans. President Harry Truman in November of 1945 proposed a national health care program to ensure that all Americans had access to doctors and hospitals. His proposal failed to pass Congress after conservatives and the American Medical Association attacked it as Communist and "socialized" medicine. The debate continued to surface through the years with leading proponents like Democratic Senator Edward M. Kennedy of Massachusetts advocating its adoption.

In 1993, President Bill Clinton appointed a special task force, led by his wife, First Lady Hillary Rodham Clinton, to propose universal health care legislation. The task force's plan would have required all employers to provide health care for their workers. In response, the Heritage Foundation, a conservative think tank in

Washington, D.C., originated the idea of "the individual mandate," which would require individual citizens to purchase health insurance by a certain date. Many Republican senators led by John Chafee of Rhode Island prepared legislation based on this alternative, though it too failed to pass. The individual mandate, originally a conservative and Republican idea, promoted personal responsibility and placed all citizens on health care.

Responding to the failure or inability of millions of Americans to obtain health insurance, Congress in 2010 finally passed the Patient Protection and Affordable Care Act (the A.C.A.). The goal was to open a pathway for all Americans to acquire health insurance. It also restricted the insurance industry in several ways. It could not exclude preexisting conditions from coverage, and most children may remain on their parents' insurance policy until age 26. In addition, the law expanded the eligibility threshold that states must adopt to remain qualified to remain in Medicaid, the federal program that provides health care funding for the poor. Most controversially, the A.C.A. mandated that in 2014, all Americans must obtain health insurance or face a financial penalty or tax based on their income. This was the individual mandate that the Heritage Foundation and several Republican senators originally proposed in 1993. An individual subject to this penalty or tax, if imposed, must pay it to the Internal Revenue Service when federal taxes are due.

After President Obama signed the bill into law, twenty-six state attorneys general, the National Federation of Independent Business, and several individuals challenged the constitutionality of the act, especially the individual mandate. They claimed that it exceeded Congress's interstate commerce power in that it forced individuals to purchase health care or pay a penalty—in other words, compelling, not regulating, commerce. They also argued that the Medicaid expansion was too broad because if a state did not meet all the new requirements, they could lose all of their Medicaid funding.

The challenged law was eventually heard in twelve U.S. Circuit Courts of Appeal. The Obama administration persuaded nine that the individual mandate was constitutional based on the Commerce Clause, but failed in the three others. In Florida, the United States Court of Appeals for the Eleventh Circuit held that the individual mandate violated Congress's commerce power, but did not rule on its severability, that is, whether the rest of the act could stand without the mandate. At the same time, the court upheld the Medicaid requirements. Both the U.S. government and Florida appealed: the U.S., concerning the mandate, and Florida concerning Medicaid. The National Federation of Independent Business argued that the entire law must fail.

Meantime, the Eleventh Circuit also did not consider whether the law violated the 1793 Anti-Injunction Act, which stated that a tax is not enforceable until it is actually paid. The U.S. Court of Appeals for the Fourth Circuit had, however, ruled that the A.C.A. case was not ripe until someone actually paid the penalty to the Internal Revenue Service.

The Supreme Court agreed to hear the case on four grounds: whether the case was premature as a violation of the Anti-Injunction Act of 1793 because no individual faced having to pay the penalty or tax until 2014; whether the individual mandate exceeded Congress's power under the Commerce, Taxing, and Necessary and Proper Clauses of Article I, Section 8; whether the rest of the act could be salvaged if the Court invalidated the individual mandate; and whether the Medicaid requirements could withstand judicial scrutiny. The Court scheduled an extraordinary three-day session in March of 2012 to hear oral arguments.

The Court's decision was split. Four justices—Ruth Bader Ginsburg, Stephen Breyer, Sonia Sotomayor, and Elena Kagan—joined Chief Justice John G. Roberts's opinion for the Court that Congress, under its Taxing power, possessed the authority to impose a tax on those who failed to purchase health insurance. Roberts, joined by four other justices, rejected the government's argument that it could impose the individual mandate under Congress's commerce power or under the Necessary and Proper Clause. The Court did not reach the severability question. He also ruled that the Anti-Injunction Act did not apply because Congress referred to the tax in the A.C.A. as a penalty. The Chief Justice also upheld the Medicaid extension, but struck down the requirement that a state would lose all of its Medicaid funding if it rejected the expansion.

Justice Ginsburg, joined by Justices Sotomayor and Breyer, filed an opinion, concurring and dissenting in part. She agreed that Congress had the power to tax those who declined to buy health insurance, but added that Congress could also use its commerce power to create the individual mandate. In terms of the Medicaid expansion, she argued that Congress could force the states to accept it or lose all of their federal funding under the program.

The four dissenters—Justices Antonin Scalia, Anthony Kennedy, Clarence Thomas, and Samuel Alito—filed an extraordinary joint opinion. They argued that Congress had no authority under its Article I, Section 8, power to pass the A.C.A. and Medicaid expansion. They argued that each of these areas fell within the realm of the states' police power.

Chief Justice ROBERTS delivered the opinion of the Court.

This case concerns two powers that the Constitution does grant the Federal Government, but which must be read carefully to avoid creating a general federal authority akin to [state] police power. The Constitution authorizes Congress to "regulate Commerce with foreign Nations, and among the several States, and with the Indian Tribes." Our precedents read that to mean that Congress may regulate "the channels of interstate commerce," "persons or things in interstate commerce," and "those activities that substantially affect interstate commerce." The power over activities that substantially affect interstate commerce can be expansive. That power has been held to authorize federal regulation of such seemingly local matters as a farmer's decision to grow wheat for himself and his livestock, and a loan shark's extortionate collections from a neighborhood butcher shop. See *Wickard v. Filburn*, 317 U.S. 111 (1942); *Perez v. United States*, 402 U.S. 146 (1971).

Congress may also "lay and collect Taxes, Duties, Imposts and Excises, to pay the Debts and provide for the common Defence and general Welfare of the United States." Put simply, Congress may tax and spend. This grant gives the Federal Government considerable influence even in areas where it cannot directly regulate. The Federal Government may enact a tax on an activity that it cannot authorize, forbid, or otherwise control. And in exercising its spending power, Congress may offer funds to the States, and may condition those offers on compliance with specified conditions. See, e.g., *College Savings Bank v. Florida Prepaid Postsecondary Ed. Expense Bd.*, 527 U.S. 666 (1999). These offers may well induce the States to adopt policies that the Federal Government itself could not impose. See, e.g., *South Dakota v. Dole*, 483 U.S. 203 (1987) (conditioning federal highway funds on States raising their drinking age to 21).

The reach of the Federal Government's enumerated powers is broader still because the Constitution authorizes Congress to "make all Laws which shall be necessary and proper for carrying into Execution the foregoing Powers." We have long read this provision to give Congress great latitude in exercising its powers. . . .

Our permissive reading of these powers is explained in part by a general reticence to invalidate the acts of the Nation's elected leaders. "Proper respect for a co-ordinate branch of the government" requires that we strike down an Act of Congress only if "the lack of constitutional authority to pass [the] act in question is clearly demonstrated." *United*

States v. Harris, 106 U.S. 629 (1883). Members of this Court are vested with the authority to interpret the law; we possess neither the expertise nor the prerogative to make policy judgments. Those decisions are entrusted to our Nation's elected leaders, who can be thrown out of office if the people disagree with them. It is not our job to protect the people from the consequences of their political choices.

Our deference in matters of policy cannot, however, become abdication in matters of law. "The powers of the legislature are defined and limited; and that those limits may not be mistaken, or forgotten, the constitution is written." *Marbury v. Madison*, 1 Cranch 137 (1803). Our respect for Congress's policy judgments thus can never extend so far as to disavow restraints on federal power that the Constitution carefully constructed. . . . And there can be no question that it is the responsibility of this Court to enforce the limits on federal power by striking down acts of Congress that transgress those limits. *Marbury v. Madison*. . . .

The second provision of the Affordable Care Act directly challenged here is the Medicaid expansion. . . . The Affordable Care Act expands the scope of the Medicaid program and increases the number of individuals the States must cover. For example, the Act requires state programs to provide Medicaid coverage to adults with incomes up to 133 percent of the federal poverty level, whereas many States now cover adults with children only if their income is considerably lower, and do not cover childless adults at all. The Act increases federal funding to cover the States' costs in expanding Medicaid coverage, although States will bear a portion of the costs on their own. If a State does not comply with the Act's new coverage requirements, it may lose not only the federal funding for those requirements, but all of its federal Medicaid funds. . . .

Before turning to the merits, we need to be sure we have the authority to do so. The Anti-Injunction Act [of 1793] provides that "no suit for the purpose of restraining the assessment or collection of any tax shall be maintained in any court by any person, whether or not such person is the person against whom such tax was assessed." This statute protects the Government's ability to collect a consistent stream of revenue, by barring litigation to enjoin or otherwise obstruct the collection of taxes. Because of the Anti-Injunction Act, taxes can ordinarily be challenged only after they are paid, by suing for a refund. See *Enochs v. Williams Packing & Nav. Co.*, 370 U.S. 1 (1962).

The penalty for not complying with the Affordable Care Act's individual mandate first becomes enforceable in 2014. The present challenge to the mandate thus seeks to restrain the penalty's future collection. . . . The Affordable Care Act does not require that the penalty for failing to comply with the individual mandate be treated as a tax for purposes of the Anti-Injunction Act. The Anti-Injunction Act therefore does not apply to this suit, and we may proceed to the merits. . . .

The Government contends that the individual mandate is within Congress's power because the failure to purchase insurance "has a substantial and deleterious effect on interstate commerce" by creating the cost-shifting problem. The path of our Commerce Clause decisions has not always run smooth, see *United States v. Lopez*, 514 U.S. 549 (1995), but it is now well established that Congress has broad authority under the Clause. We have recognized, for example, that "[t]he power of Congress over interstate commerce is not confined to the regulation of commerce among the states," but extends to activities that "have a substantial effect on interstate commerce." *United States v. Darby*, 312 U.S. 100 (1941). Congress's power, moreover, is not limited to regulation of an activity that by itself substantially affects interstate commerce, but also extends to activities that do so only when aggregated with similar activities of others. See *Wickard*.

The individual mandate, however, does not regulate existing commercial activity. It instead compels individuals to *become* active in commerce by purchasing a product, on the ground that their failure to do so affects interstate commerce. Construing the Commerce Clause to permit Congress to regulate individuals precisely *because* they are doing nothing would open a new and potentially vast do-main to congressional authority. . . . Congress addressed the insurance problem by ordering everyone to buy insurance. Under the Government's theory, Congress could address the diet problem by ordering everyone to buy vegetables. People, for reasons of their own, often fail to do things that would be good for them or good for society. Those failures—joined with the similar failures of others—can readily have a substantial effect on interstate commerce. Under the Government's logic, that authorizes Congress to use its commerce power to compel citizens to act as the Government would have them act.

[NOTE: The CHIEF JUSTICE then rejected the argument that the Court could sustain the individual mandate as a matter of Congress's power to make all Laws which shall be necessary and proper for carrying into Execution" the powers enumerated in the Constitution. The commerce power does not authorize Congress to pass such a law. Even if the individual mandate is "necessary" to the Act's insurance reforms, such an expansion of federal power is not a "proper" means for making those reforms effective.]

Because the Commerce Clause does not support the individual mandate, it is necessary to turn to the Government's second argument: that the mandate may be upheld as within Congress's enumerated power to "lay and collect Taxes." . . . Under the mandate, if an individual does not maintain health insurance, the only consequence is that he must make an additional payment to the IRS when he pays his taxes. That, according to the Government, means the mandate can be regarded as establishing a condition—not owning health insurance—that triggers a tax—the required payment to the IRS. Under that theory, the mandate is not a legal command to buy insurance. Rather, it makes going without insurance just another thing the Government taxes, like buying gasoline or earning income. And if the mandate is in effect just a tax hike on certain taxpayers who do not have health insurance, it may be within Congress's constitutional power to tax. . . .

The exaction the Affordable Care Act imposes on those without health insurance looks like a tax in many respects. . . . It is of course true that the Act describes the payment as a "penalty," not a "tax." But while that label is fatal to the application of the Anti-Injunction Act, it does not determine whether the payment may be viewed as an exercise of Congress's taxing power. It is up to Congress whether to apply the Anti-Injunction Act to any particular statute, so it makes sense to be guided by Congress's choice of label on that question. That choice does not, however, control whether an exaction is within Congress's constitutional power to tax. . . .

The joint dissenters argue that we cannot uphold [the law] as a tax because Congress did not "frame" it as such. In effect, they contend that even if the Constitution permits Congress to do exactly what we interpret this statute to do, the law must be struck down because Congress used the wrong labels. An example may help illustrate why labels should not control here. Suppose Congress enacted a statute providing that every taxpayer who owns a house without energy efficient windows must pay $50 to the IRS. The amount due is adjusted based on factors such as taxable income and joint filing status, and is paid along with the taxpayer's income tax return. Those whose income is below the filing threshold need not pay. The required payment is not called a "tax," a "penalty," or anything else. No one would doubt that this law imposed a tax, and was within Congress's power to tax. That conclusion should not change simply because Congress used the word "penalty" to describe the payment. Interpreting such a law to be a tax would hardly "impose a tax through judicial legislation." Rather, it would give practical effect to the Legislature's enactment. . . .

Whether the mandate can be upheld under the Commerce Clause is a question about the scope of federal authority. Its answer depends on whether Congress can exercise what all acknowledge to be the novel course of directing individuals to purchase insurance. Congress's use of the Taxing Clause to encourage buying something is, by contrast, not new. Tax incentives already promote, for example, purchasing homes and professional educations. Sustaining the mandate as a tax depends only on whether Congress *has* properly exercised its taxing power to encourage purchasing health insurance, not whether it *can*. Upholding the individual mandate under the Taxing Clause thus does not recognize any new federal power. It determines that Congress has used an existing one. . . . The Affordable Care Act's requirement that certain individuals pay a financial penalty for not obtaining health insurance may reasonably be characterized as a tax. Because the Constitution permits such a tax, it is not our role to forbid it, or to pass upon its wisdom or fairness. . . .

The States also contend that the Medicaid expansion exceeds Congress's authority under the Spending Clause. They claim that Congress is coercing the States to adopt the changes it wants by threatening to withhold all of a State's Medicaid grants, unless the State accepts the new expanded funding and complies with the conditions that come with it. . . . We have upheld Congress's authority to condition the receipt of funds on the States' complying with restrictions on the use of those funds, because that is the means by which Congress ensures that the funds are spent according to its view of the "general Welfare." Conditions that do not here govern the use of the funds, however, cannot be justified on that basis. When, for example, such conditions take the form of threats to terminate other significant independent grants, the conditions are properly viewed as a means of pressuring the States to accept policy changes. *South Dakota v. Dole*, 483 U.S. 203 (1987). . . .

The Affordable Care Act is constitutional in part and unconstitutional in part. The individual mandate cannot be upheld as an exercise of Congress's power under the Commerce Clause. That Clause authorizes Congress to regulate interstate commerce, not to order individuals to engage in it. In this case, however, it is reasonable to construe what Congress has done as increasing taxes on those who have a certain amount of income, but choose to go without health insurance. Such legislation is within Congress's power to tax.

As for the Medicaid expansion, that portion of the Affordable Care Act violates the Constitution by threatening existing Medicaid funding. Congress has no authority to order the States to regulate according to its instructions. Congress may offer the States grants and require the States to comply with accompanying conditions, but the States must have a genuine choice whether to accept the offer. The States are given no such choice in this case: They must either accept a basic change in the nature of Medicaid, or risk losing all Medicaid funding. The remedy for that constitutional violation is to preclude the Federal Government from imposing such a sanction. That remedy does not require striking down other portions of the Affordable Care Act.

The Framers created a Federal Government of limited powers, and assigned to this Court the duty of enforcing those limits. The Court does so today. But the Court does not express any opinion on the wisdom of the Affordable Care Act. Under the Constitution, that judgment is reserved to the people. The judgment of the Court of Appeals for the Eleventh Circuit is affirmed in part and reversed in part.

Justice GINSBURG, concurring in part, dissenting in part.

The provision of health care is today a concern of national dimension, just as the provision of old-age and survivors' benefits was in the 1930's. In the Social Security Act, Congress installed a federal system to provide monthly benefits to retired wage earners and, eventually, to their survivors. Beyond question, Congress could have adopted a similar scheme for health care. Congress chose, instead, to preserve a central role for private insurers and state governments. According to The CHIEF JUSTICE, the Commerce Clause does not permit that preservation. This rigid reading of the Clause makes scant sense and is stunningly retrogressive.

Since 1937, our precedent has recognized Congress' large authority to set the Nation's course in the economic and social welfare realm. See *United States v. Darby*, 312 U.S. 100 (1941) (overruling *Hammer v. Dagenhart*, 247 U.S. 251 (1918), and recognizing that "regulations of commerce which do not infringe some constitutional prohibition are within the plenary power conferred on Congress by the Commerce Clause"); *NLRB v. Jones & Laughlin Steel Corp.*, 301 U.S. 1 (1937) ("[The commerce] power is plenary and may be exerted to protect interstate commerce no matter what the source of the dangers which threaten it."). The CHIEF JUSTICES's crabbed reading of the Commerce Clause harks back to the era in which the Court routinely thwarted Congress' efforts to regulate the national economy in the interest of those who labor to sustain it. It is a reading that should not have staying power. . . .

Joint opinion signed by Justices SCALIA, KENNEDY, THOMAS, and ALITO.

Congress has set out to remedy the problem that the best health care is beyond the reach of many Americans who cannot afford it. It can assuredly do that, by exercising the powers accorded to it under the Constitution. The question in this case, however, is whether the complex structures and provisions of the Patient Protection and Affordable Care Act (Affordable Care Act or ACA) go beyond those powers. We conclude that they do.

This case is in one respect difficult: it presents two questions of first impression. The first of those is whether failure to engage in economic activity (the purchase of health insurance) is subject to regulation under the Commerce Clause. Failure to act does result in an effect on commerce, and hence might be said to come under this Court's "affecting commerce" criterion of Commerce Clause jurisprudence. But in none of its decisions has this Court extended the Clause that far. The second question is whether the congressional power to tax and spend permits the conditioning of a State's continued receipt of all funds under a massive state-administered federal welfare program upon its acceptance of an expansion to that program. Several of our opinions have suggested that the power to tax and spend cannot be used to coerce state administration of a federal program, but we have never found a law enacted under the spending power to be coercive. Those questions are difficult.

The case is easy and straightforward, however, in another respect. What is absolutely clear, affirmed by the text of the 1789 Constitution, by the Tenth Amendment ratified in 1791, and by innumerable cases of ours in the 220 years since, is that there are structural limits upon federal power—upon what it can prescribe with respect to private conduct, and upon what it can impose upon the sovereign States. Whatever may be the conceptual limits upon the Commerce Clause and upon the power to tax and spend, they cannot be such as will enable the Federal Government to regulate all private conduct and to compel the States to function as administrators of federal programs.

That clear principle carries the day here. The striking case of *Wickard v. Filburn*, 317 U.S. 111 (1942), which held that the economic activity of growing wheat, even for one's own consumption, affected commerce sufficiently that it could be regulated, always has been regarded as the *ne plus ultra* of expansive Commerce Clause jurisprudence. To go beyond that, and to say the *failure* to grow wheat (which is *not* an economic activity, or any activity at all) nonetheless affects commerce and therefore can be federally regulated, is to make mere breathing in and out the basis for federal prescription and to extend federal power to virtually all human activity.

As for the constitutional power to tax and spend for the general welfare: The Court has long since expanded that beyond (what Madison thought it meant) taxing and spending for those aspects of the general welfare that were within the Federal Government's enumerated powers. Thus, we now have sizable federal Departments devoted to subjects not mentioned among Congress' enumerated powers, and only marginally related to commerce: the Department of Education, the Department of Health and Human Services, the Department of Housing and Urban Development. The principal practical obstacle that prevents Congress from using the tax-and-spend power to assume all the general-welfare responsibilities traditionally exercised by the States is the sheer impossibility of managing a Federal Government large enough to administer such a system. That obstacle can be overcome by granting funds to the States, allowing them to administer the program. That is fair and constitutional enough when the States freely agree to have their powers employed and their employees enlisted in the federal scheme. But it is a blatant violation of the constitutional structure when the States have no choice.

The Act before us here exceeds federal power both in mandating the purchase of health insurance and in denying nonconsenting States all Medicaid funding. These parts of the Act are central to its design and operation, and all the Act's other provisions would not have been enacted without them. In our view it must follow that the entire statute is inoperative. . . .

To say that the Individual Mandate merely imposes a tax is not to interpret the statute but to rewrite it. Judicial tax-writing is particularly troubling. Taxes have never been popular, see, e.g., Stamp Act of 1765, and in part for that reason, the Constitution requires tax increases to originate in the House of Representatives. That is to say, they must originate in the legislative body most accountable to the people, where legislators must weigh the need for the tax against the terrible price they might pay at their next election, which is never more than two years off. We have no doubt that Congress knew precisely what it was doing when it rejected an earlier version of this legislation that imposed a tax instead of a requirement-with-penalty. Imposing a tax through judicial legislation inverts the constitutional scheme, and places the power to tax in the branch of government least accountable to the citizenry. . . .

The Government and those who support its position . . . make the remarkable argument that [the Act] is not a tax for purposes of the Anti-Injunction Act, but is a tax for constitutional purposes. The rhetorical device that tries to cloak this argument in superficial plausibility is the same device employed in arguing that for constitutional purposes the minimum-coverage provision is a tax: confusing the question of what Congress *did* with the question of what Congress *could have done.* What qualifies as a tax for purposes of the Anti-Injunction Act, unlike what qualifies as a tax for purposes of the Constitution, is entirely within the control of Congress. Congress could have defined "tax" for purposes of that statute in such fashion as to exclude some exactions that in fact are "taxes." It might have prescribed, for example, that a particular exercise of the taxing power "shall not be regarded as a tax for purposes of the Anti-Injunction Act." But there is no such prescription here. What the Government would have us believe in these cases is that the very same textual indications that show this is *not* a tax under the Anti-Injunction Act show that it *is* a tax under the Constitution. That carries verbal wizardry too far, deep into the forbidden land of the sophists.

Rulings in Context

Federalism

Texas v. White, 7 Wall. (74 U.S.) 700 (1869)   5-3

The Court ruled that the federal Reconstruction-era laws were constitutional because the United States never recognized the legitimacy of the Southern states' secession. At issue was whether the Confederate state of Texas could sell bonds owned by pre-Civil War Texas. Writing for the majority, Chief Justice Salmon Chase held that "the Constitution, in all its provisions, looks to an indestructible Union, composed of indestructible States."

New State Ice Co. v. Liebmann, 285 U.S. 262 (1932)   6-2

The Court held that an Oklahoma law requiring state licensing for a business enterprise was unconstitutional if the company was engaged in a public interest. In dissent, Justice Brandeis wrote his famous dictum that "it is one of the happy incidents of the federal system that a single courageous State may, if its citizens choose, serve as a laboratory and try novel social and economic experiments without risk to the rest of the country."

Wickard v. Filburn, 317 U.S. 111 (1942)   9-0

The Court held that the regulation of agricultural production, in this case by means of the Agricultural Adjustment Act of 1938 limiting the production of wheat, had a national, not a local or state impact. Therefore Congress, under its Commerce Clause powers, may set national acreage allotments for wheat.

Garcia v. San Antonio Metropolitan Transit Authority,
469 U.S. 528 (1985)   5-4

Overturning *National League of Cities v. Usery,* 426 U.S. 833 (1976), decided just nine years earlier, the Court held that the federal government, in setting minimum wage and overtime regulations, required state public employees to be subject to these same regulations.

Tennessee v. Lane, 541 U.S. 509 (2004)   5-4

The Court ruled that the federal Americans With Disabilities Act allowed disabled individuals to sue for damages in their state courts when state courthouses were inaccessible to the disabled. The case marked a departure from earlier Supreme Court decisions that had given the states broad immunity from such suits under federal law.

Gonzales v. Raich, 545 U.S. 1 (2005)   6-3

Distinguishing the facts of this case from *Lopez v. U.S.* and *Morrison v. U.S.,* the Court ruled that the federal Controlled Substances Act of 1970, which listed marijuana as an illegal Schedule I drug, trumped the California Compassionate Use Act of 1996, which allowed those suffering severe illnesses to grow and consume marijuana. The decision found a close and substantial relationship to interstate commerce even when an ill person grew marijuana for home use and it never entered the interstate market.

Gonzales v. Oregon, 546 U.S. 243 (2006)   6-3

After Oregon became the first state in 1994 to legalize physician-assisted suicide for terminally ill patients with its Death with Dignity Act, the U.S. Attorney General in 2002 issued a rule that the law conflicted with the federal Controlled Substances Act. He argued that the use of the drugs by physicians for this purpose was unlawful and threatened to revoke the license of any physician who participated in a suicide by one of their patients. The Court ruled that medical practice was historically a matter of state, not federal, regulation, and the Attorney General's rule was an unconstitutional infringement on state authority.

Arizona v. United States, 567 U.S. ___ (2012)   8-0/split on
some provisions

In 2010, Arizona became the first state to require state and local law enforcement officers to check the immigration status of individuals whom they stop or arrest if they suspect they are illegal immigrants. After the Justice Department challenged the law, the Supreme Court unanimously ruled that this provision was constitutional because the state supported federal law. The Court, however, overturned three other provisions as infringing on federal power:

Arizona may not make it a state crime when immigrants fail to register under federal law (6-2 vote); nor may it make it a crime for illegal immigrants to work or try to find work (5-3 vote); and police may not arrest anyone without a warrant even when they have probable cause to believe that they have committed acts that would make them deportable under federal law (5-3 vote). Justice Kagan recused herself because she had worked on the matter while serving as U.S. Solicitor General in the Obama administration.

Arizona v. Inter Tribal Council of Arizona, 569 U.S. _____ (2013)   7-2

The Court ruled on both constitutional and statutory grounds that the federal National Voter Registration Act (NVRA) of 1993 preempted Arizona's 2004 law requiring prospective voters to prove they were U.S. citizens by providing copies of passports, birth certificates, driver's licenses, or naturalization papers. The NVRA, also known as the "Motor Voter Law" because application forms are available in state department of motor vehicle offices, was designed to increase access to registration. Writing for the Court, Antonin Scalia held that the Elections Clause of Article I, Section

4, empowered Congress to prescribe federal election rules. Under the NVRA , Congress required the states to "accept and use" a federal form to register voters who must declare, under penalty of perjury, that they are U.S. citizens. The state law therefore conflicted with the federal law and was preempted by it.

The Separation of Powers: Cases

Two cases highlight the separation of powers, the division of power between the executive and legislative branches, but also between the executive and judicial branches as well. The first case, *Ex Parte Milligan* (1866), asked whether the executive branch may conduct military tribunals of civilians when civilian courts are open and operating. The second, *Youngstown Sheet and Tube Co. v. Sawyer* (1952), raised the question of whether the President may act in wartime without congressional approval, especially when Congress prohibited him from so acting.

Case 2.8

Ex Parte Milligan
71 U.S. (4 Wall.) 2 (1866)

The Civil War was unquestionably the most divisive moment in American history. Not only did most citizens hold strong views about the issues, but for the first and only time the Union was dramatically split apart when the Southern states seceded to create the Confederate States of America. Even in the farthest western corners of the United States, there were intense feelings on both sides.

Because of the emergency, President Lincoln in 1862 suspended the writ of *habeas corpus* and ordered that anyone, including citizens of the United States, charged with disloyalty to the Union must be tried before military commissions rather than in the civilian courts. Congress confirmed his order at its next session when it enacted a law suspending the writ. A writ of *habeas corpus*, literally "you have the body," is a court order to bring a prisoner before a judge to determine whether there is sufficient evidence and witnesses to detain him. Long part of the English common-law tradition, Parliament passed it into law in 1651 and Congress did so in 1789.

In October of 1864, Lambdin P. Milligan, a lawyer, a citizen of the United States, and a resident of Indiana, was arrested by the military commander of the District of Indiana and held in a military prison. Later that month, he was tried by a military commission in Indianapolis for having conspired against the government of the United States, giving and aid and comfort to rebels, inciting insurrection, engaging in disloyal practices, and violating the laws of war.

The Army commander, Gen. Alvin P. Hovey, testified that Milligan had joined a secret society known as the Order of American Knights or Sons of Liberty whose purpose was to overthrow the government of the United States. He claimed that Milligan had conspired with leaders involved in the rebellion to seize Union war materiel and to liberate Confederate prisoners of war. After the military commission rejected Milligan's claim that the commission had no jurisdiction to try him, he was found guilty and sentenced to death by hanging.

Milligan appealed to the federal circuit court for a writ of *habeas corpus*, claiming that at no time had he ever been in the military service of any state in rebellion against the United States and that he was a resident of Indiana, which was not a state in insurrection. Moreover, he argued that Indiana had functioning civilian courts, and they could not have tried him.

The circuit court was deeply divided and certified several questions for the Supreme Court to address. Among these were whether Milligan had a right to a writ of *habeas corpus* and whether the military commission had jurisdiction over him.

The Court, in an opinion by Justice David Davis, ruled five to four that the President had no authority to try Milligan when the civilian courts were open and that he could use military commissions only with prior congressional authorization. Chief Justice Salmon Chase, along with three other justices, objected to Davis's position that Congress did not have the authority to create military commissions.

Justice DAVIS delivered the opinion of the court.

The controlling question in the case is this: Upon the facts stated in Milligan's petition, and the exhibits filed, had the military commission mentioned in it *jurisdiction*, legally, to try and sentence him? Milligan, not a resident of one of the rebellious states, or a prisoner of war, but a citizen of Indiana for twenty years past, and never in the military or naval service, is, while at his home, arrested by the military power of the United States, imprisoned, and, on certain criminal charges preferred against him, tried, convicted, and sentenced to be hanged by a military commission, organized under the direction of the military commander of the military district of Indiana. Had this tribunal the legal power and authority to try and punish this man?

No graver question was ever considered by this court, nor one which more nearly concerns the rights of the whole people; for it is the birthright of every American citizen when charged with crime, to be tried and punished according to law. . . . The Constitution of the United States is a law for rulers and people, equally in war and in peace, and covers with the shield of its protection all classes of men, at all times, and under all circumstances. No doctrine, involving more pernicious consequences, was ever invented by the wit of man than that any of its provisions can be suspended during any of the great exigencies of government. Such a doctrine leads directly to anarchy or despotism, but the theory of necessity on which it is based is false; for the government, within the Constitution, has all the powers granted to it, which are necessary to preserve its existence; as has been happily proved by the result of the great effort to throw off its just authority. . . .

Every trial involves the exercise of judicial power; and from what source did not military commission that tried him derive their authority? Certainly no part of judicial power of the country was conferred on them; because the Constitution expressly vests it "in one supreme court and such inferior courts as the Congress may from time to time ordain and establish," and it is not pretended that the commission was a court ordained and established by Congress. They cannot justify on the mandate of the President; because he is controlled by law, and has his appropriate sphere of duty, which is to execute, not to make, the laws; and there is "no unwritten criminal code to which resort can be had as a source of jurisdiction."

But it is said that the jurisdiction is complete under the "laws and usages of war."

It can serve no useful purpose to inquire what those laws and usages are, whence they originated, where found, and on whom they operate; they can never be applied to citizens in states which have upheld the authority of the government, and where the courts are open and their process unobstructed. This court has judicial knowledge that in Indiana the Federal authority was always unopposed, and its courts always open to hear criminal accusations and redress grievances; and no usage of war could sanction a military trial there for any offence whatever of a citizen in civil life, in nowise connected with the military service. Congress could grant no such power; and to the honor of our national legislature be it said, it has never been provoked by the state of the country even to attempt its exercise. One of the plainest constitutional provisions was, therefore, infringed when Milligan was tried by a court not ordained and established by Congress, and not composed of judges appointed during good behavior. . . .

Another guarantee of freedom was broken when Milligan was denied a trial by jury. The great minds of the country have differed on the correct interpretation to be given to various provisions of the Federal Constitution; and judicial decision has been often invoked to settle their true meaning; but until recently no one ever doubted that the right of trial by jury was fortified in the organic law against the power of attack. It is now assailed; but if ideas can be expressed in words, and language has any meaning, this right—one of the most valuable in a free country—is preserved to every one accused of crime who is not attached to the army, or navy, or militia in actual service. The Sixth amendment affirms that "in all criminal prosecutions the accused shall enjoy the right to a speedy and public trial by an impartial jury," language broad enough to embrace all persons and cases; but the Fifth, recognizing the necessity of an indictment, or presentment, before any one can be held to answer for high crimes, "excepts cases arising in the land or naval forces, or in the militia, when in actual service, in time of war or public danger;" and the framers of the Constitution, doubtless, meant to limit the right of trial by jury, in the Sixth amendment, to those persons who were subject to indictment or presentment in the Fifth. . . .

It is claimed that martial law covers with its broad mantle the proceedings of this military commission. The proposition is this: that in a time of war the commander of an armed force (if in his opinion the exigencies of the country demand it, and of which he is to judge), has the power, within the lines of his military district, to suspend all civil rights and their remedies, and subject citizens as well as soldiers to the rule of his will; and in the exercise of his lawful authority cannot be restrained, except by his superior officer or the President of the United States.

If this position is sound to the extent claimed, then when war exists, foreign or domestic, and the country is subdivided into military departments for mere convenience, the commander of one of them can, if he chooses, within his limits, on the plea of necessity, with the approval of the Executive, substitute military force for and to the exclusion of the laws, and punish all persons, as he thinks right and proper, without fixed or certain rules.

The statement of this proposition shows its importance; for, if true, republican government is a failure, and there is an end of liberty regulated by law. . . . Civil liberty and this kind of martial law cannot endure together; the antagonism is irreconcilable; and, in the conflict, one or the other must perish.

This nation, as experience has proved, cannot always remain at peace, and has no right to expect that it will always have wise and humane rulers, sincerely attached to the principles of the Constitution. Wicked men, ambitious of power, with hatred of liberty and contempt of law, may fill the place once occupied by Washington and Lincoln; and if this right is conceded, and the calamities of war again befall us, the dangers to human liberty are frightful to contemplate. If our fathers had failed to provide for just such a contingency, they would have been false to the trust reposed in them. . . .

It follows, from what has been said on this subject, that there are occasions when martial rule can be properly applied. If, in foreign invasion or civil war, the courts are actually closed, and it is impossible to administer criminal justice according to law, then, on the theatre of active military operations, where war really prevails, there is a necessity to furnish a substitute for the civil authority, thus overthrown, to preserve the safety of the army and society; and as no power is left but the military, it is allowed to govern by martial rule until the laws can have their free course. As necessity creates the rule, so it limits its duration; for, if this government is continued after the courts are reinstated, it is a gross usurpation of power. Martial rule can never exist where the courts are open, and in the proper and unobstructed exercise of their jurisdiction. It is also confined to the locality of actual war.

Case 2.9

Youngstown Sheet & Tube Co. v. Sawyer
343 U.S. 579, 72 S.Ct. 863 (1952)

In June of 1950, the United States entered the Korean War after North Korea invaded South Korea. Under the authority of the United Nations, President Harry Truman mobilized hundreds of thousands of American troops and ordered the build-up of war materiel. In late 1951, a labor dispute broke out between steel workers and the management of the steel mills. When the negotiations failed, the United Steelworkers of America ordered a strike to begin in December of that year.

The strike was halted with the intervention by the Federal Mediation and Conciliation Service, originally created to mediate disputes between labor and management, and the Federal Wage Stabilization Board, designed to find a middle ground between the sides. After their efforts failed to bring about a settlement, the union again ordered a strike, this time to begin on April 9, 1952.

The President feared that without steel production, the war effort would be seriously hampered and national security jeopardized. Accordingly, a few hours before the strike was to begin, he issued Executive Order 10340 authorizing Secretary of Commerce Charles Sawyer to take possession though not ownership of the steel mills to keep them running. The Secretary appointed the presidents of the steel companies operating managers and ordered them to keep their factories open and to produce steel. President Truman reported his actions to Congress the next morning, and twelve days later sent to it a lengthy report to explain his actions. Congress took no action.

The steel companies, however, filed a request for an injunction in federal district court, arguing that no act of Congress and no provision of the Constitution authorized the President to seize the mills. The United States argued that a strike would disrupt the American war effort because weapons and other war materiel would not be produced. A strike would so endanger national security that the President had "inherent" power to seize the mills to keep them running, and that this power may be found in the Constitution, in historical precedent, and in court decisions. The district court issued a preliminary injunction on April 30 restraining the secretary of commerce from "continuing the seizure and possession of the plants . . . and from acting under the purported authority of Executive Order No. 10340." The same day the United States Court of Appeals for the District of Columbia agreed.

The Supreme Court heard arguments on May 12-13. Less than a month later, by a six to three margin, the Court upheld the appellate court's decision. Writing for the majority was Justice Black. Justices Jackson, Burton, Clark, Douglas, and Frankfurter all submitted separate concurrences. Chief Justice Vinson dissented in an opinion joined by Justices Reed and Minton.

Justice BLACK delivered the opinion of the Court.

The President's power, if any, to issue the order must stem either from an act of Congress or from the Constitution itself. There is no statute that expressly authorizes the President to take possession of property as he did here. Nor is there any act of Congress to which our attention has been directed from which such a power can fairly be implied. Indeed, we do not understand the Government to rely on statutory authorization for this seizure. There are two statutes which do authorize the President to take both personal and real property under certain conditions. However, the Government admits that these conditions were not met and that the President's order was not rooted in either of the statutes. The Government refers to the seizure provisions of one of these statutes (Section 201(b) of the Defense Production Act) as "much too cumbersome, involved, and time-consuming for the crisis which was at hand."

Moreover, the use of the seizure technique to solve labor disputes . . . was not only unauthorized by any congressional enactment; prior to this controversy, Congress had refused to adopt that method of settling labor disputes. When the Taft-Hartley Act was under consideration in 1947, Congress rejected an amendment which would have authorized such governmental seizures in cases of emergency. Apparently it was thought that the technique of seizure, like that of compulsory arbitration, would interfere with the process of collective bargaining. Consequently, the plan Congress adopted in that Act did not provide for seizure under any circumstances. Instead, the plan sought to bring about settlements by use of the customary devices of mediation, conciliation, investigation by boards of inquiry, and public reports. In some instances temporary injunctions were authorized to provide cooling-off periods. All this failing, unions were left free to strike after a secret vote by employees as to whether they wished to accept their employers' final settlement offer.

It is clear that if the President had authority to issue the order he did, it must be found in some provision of the Constitution. And it is not claimed that express constitutional language grants this power to the President. The contention is that presidential power should be implied from the aggregate of his powers under the Constitution. Particular reliance is placed on provisions in Article II which say that "The executive Power shall be vested in a President . . ."; that "he shall take Care that the Laws be faithfully executed"; and that he "shall be Commander in Chief of the Army and Navy of the United States."

The order cannot properly be sustained as an exercise of the President's military power as Commander in Chief of the Armed Forces. The Government attempts to do so by citing a number of cases upholding broad powers in military commanders engaged in day-to-day fighting in a theater of war. Such cases need not concern us here. Even though "theater of war" be an expanding concept, we cannot with faithfulness to our constitutional system hold that the Commander in Chief of the Armed Forces has the ultimate power as such to take possession of private property in order to keep labor disputes from stopping production. This is a job for the Nation's lawmakers, not for its military authorities.

Nor can the seizure order be sustained because of the several constitutional provisions that grant executive power to the President. In the framework of our Constitution, the President's power to see that the laws are faithfully executed refutes the idea that he is to be a lawmaker. The Constitution limits his functions in the lawmaking process to the recommending of laws he thinks wise and the vetoing of laws he thinks bad. And the Constitution is neither silent nor equivocal about who shall make laws which the President is to execute. The first section of the first article says that "All legislative Powers herein granted shall be vested in a Congress of the United States." . . .

The President's order does not direct that a congressional policy be executed in a manner prescribed by Congress—it directs that a presidential policy be executed in a manner prescribed by the President. The preamble of the order itself, like that of many statutes, sets out reasons why the President believes certain policies should be adopted, proclaims these policies as rules of conduct to be followed, and again, like a statute, authorizes a government official to promulgate additional rules and regulations consistent with the policy proclaimed and needed to carry that policy into execution. The power of Congress to adopt such public policies as those proclaimed by the order is beyond question. It can authorize the taking of private property for public use. It can make laws regulating the relationships between employers and employees, prescribing rules designed to settle labor disputes, and fixing wages and working conditions in certain fields of our economy. The Constitution does not subject this lawmaking power of Congress to presidential or military supervision or control.

It is said that other Presidents without congressional authority have taken possession of private business enterprises in order to settle labor disputes. But even if this be true, Congress has not thereby lost its exclusive constitutional authority to make laws necessary and proper to carry out the powers vested by the Constitution "in the Government of the United States, or any Department or Officer thereof."

The Founders of this Nation entrusted the lawmaking power to the Congress alone in both good and bad times. It would do no good to recall the historical events, the fears of power and the hopes for freedom that lay behind their choice. Such a review would but confirm our holding that this seizure order cannot stand.

The judgment of the District Court is Affirmed.

**Justice JACKSON, concurring in the judgment and opinion
of the Court.**

. . . A judge, like an executive adviser, may be surprised at the poverty of
really useful and unambiguous authority applicable to concrete problems of executive power as they actually present themselves. Just what
our forefathers did envision, or would have envisioned had they foreseen modern conditions, must be divined from materials almost as enig-
matic as the dreams Joseph was called upon to interpret for Pharaoh. A
century and a half of partisan debate and scholarly speculation yields no
net result but only supplies more or less apt quotations respected
sources on each side of any question. They largely cancel each other.
And court decisions are indecisive because of the judicial practice of
dealing with the largest questions in the most narrow way.

The actual art of governing under our Constitution does not and
cannot conform to judicial definitions of the power of any of its branches
based on isolated clauses or even single Articles torn from context.
While the Constitution diffuses power the better to secure liberty, it also
contemplates that practice will integrate the dispersed powers into a
workable government. It enjoins upon its branches separateness but
interdependence, autonomy but reciprocity. Presidential powers are not
fixed but fluctuate, depending upon their disjunction or conjunction
with those of Congress. We may well begin by a somewhat over-simplified
grouping of practical situations in which a President may doubt, or others may challenge, his powers, and by distinguishing roughly the legal
consequences of this factor of relativity.

1. When the President acts pursuant to an express or implied authorization of Congress, his authority is at its maximum, for it
   includes all that he possesses in his own right plus all that Congress can delegate. . . . A seizure executed by the President
   pursuant to an Act of Congress would be supported by the
   strongest of presumptions. . . .

2. When the President acts in absence of either a congressional
   grant or denial of authority, he can only rely upon his own independent powers, but there is a zone of twilight in which he and
   Congress may have concurrent authority, or in which its distribution is uncertain. . . . In this area, any actual test of power is
   likely to depend on the imperatives of events and contemporary
   imponderables rather than on abstract theories of law.

3. When the President takes measures incompatible with the expressed or implied will of Congress, his power is at its lowest

ebb, for then he can rely only upon his own constitutional powers minus any constitutional powers of Congress over the matter. Courts can sustain exclusive presidential control in such a case only by disabling the Congress from acting upon the subject. Presidential claim to a power at once so conclusive and preclusive must be scrutinized with caution, for what is at stake is the equilibrium established by our constitutional system.

Into which of these classifications does this executive seizure of the steel industry fit? It is eliminated from the first by admission, for it is conceded that no congressional authorization exists for this seizure. . . .

Can it then be defended under flexible tests available to the second category? It seems clearly eliminated from that class because Congress has not left seizure of private property an open field but has covered it by three statutory policies inconsistent with this seizure. . . .

This leaves the current seizure to be justified only by the severe tests under the third grouping, where it can be supported only by any remainder of executive power after subtraction of such powers as Congress may have over the subject. In short, we can sustain the President only by holding that seizure of such strike-bound industries is within his domain and beyond control by Congress. . . .

Chief Justice VINSON, with whom Justices REED and MINTON join, dissenting.

. . . Those who suggest that this is a case involving extraordinary powers should be mindful that these are extraordinary times. A world not yet recovered from the devastation of World War II has been forced to face the threat of another and more terrifying global conflict. . . .

. . . As an illustration of the magnitude of the over-all program, Congress has appropriated $130 billion for our own defense and for military assistance to our allies since the June, 1950, attack in Korea. . . .

Even before Korea, steel production at levels above theoretical 100% capacity was not capable of supplying civilian needs alone. Since Korea, the tremendous military demand for steel has far exceeded the increases in productive capacity. . . .

The President has the duty to execute the foregoing legislative programs. Their successful execution depends upon continued production of steel and stabilized prices for steel. . . .

. . . The Union and the steel companies may well engage in a lengthy struggle. Plaintiffs' counsel tells us that "sooner or later" the mills will operate again. That may satisfy the steel companies and, perhaps, the Union. But our soldiers and our allies will hardly be cheered with the assurance that the ammunition upon which their lives depend will be forthcoming—"sooner or later," or, in other words, "too little and too late."

Accordingly, if the President has any power under the Constitution to meet a critical situation in the absence of express statutory authorization, there is no basis whatever for criticizing the exercise of such power in this case.

The steel mills were seized for a public use. . . . Plaintiffs cannot complain that any provision in the Constitution prohibits the exercise of the power of eminent domain in this case. The Fifth Amendment provides: "nor shall private property be taken for public use, without just compensation." It is no bar to this seizure for, if the taking is not otherwise unlawful, plaintiffs are assured of receiving the required just compensation. . . .

Admitting that the Government could seize the mills, plaintiffs claim that the implied power of eminent domain can be exercised only under an Act of Congress. . . . Under this view, the President is left powerless at the very moment when the need for action may be most pressing and when no one, other than he, is immediately capable of action. Under this view, he is left powerless because a power not expressly given to Congress is nevertheless found to rest exclusively with Congress. . . .

. . . In this case, we need only look to history and time-honored principles of constitutional law—principles that have been applied consistently by all branches of the Government throughout our history. It is those who assert the invalidity of the Executive Order who seek to amend the Constitution in this case.

A review of executive action demonstrates that our Presidents have on many occasions exhibited the leadership contemplated by the Framers when they made the President Commander in Chief, and imposed upon him the trust to "take Care that the Laws be faithfully executed." With or without explicit statutory authorization, Presidents have at such times dealt with national emergencies by acting promptly and resolutely to enforce legislative programs, at least to save those programs until Congress could act. Congress and the courts have responded to such executive initiative with consistent approval. . . .

[NOTE: The chief justice reviewed several moments in American history when Presidents had acted without congressional authority when he alone determined the best interests of the country. These included Washington's use of the military during the 1794 Whiskey Rebellion, Jefferson's 1803 purchase of Louisiana, Lincoln's blockade of Spanish ports during the Civil War, Hayes and Cleveland's use of military force during railroad strikes, and Franklin Roosevelt's seizure of an airplane factory just before Pearl Harbor, a move then Attorney General, now Justice Jackson had enthusiastically supported.]

Focusing now on the situation confronting the President on the night of April 8, 1952, we cannot but conclude that the President was performing his duty under the Constitution to "take Care that the Laws be faithfully executed"—a duty described by President Benjamin Harrison as "the central idea of the office." The President reported to Congress the morning after the seizure that he acted because a work stoppage in steel production would immediately imperil the safety of the Nation by preventing execution of the legislative programs for procurement of military equipment. . . .

. . . The President's action served the same purposes as a judicial stay entered to maintain the status quo in order to preserve the jurisdiction of a court. . . .

The broad executive power granted by Article II to an officer on duty 365 days a year cannot, it is said, be invoked to avert disaster. Instead, the President must confine himself to sending a message to Congress recommending action. Under this messenger-boy concept of the Office, the President cannot even act to preserve legislative programs from destruction so that Congress will have something left to act upon. . . .

As the District Judge stated, this is no time for "timorous" judicial action. But neither is this a time for timorous executive action. . . . The President immediately informed Congress of his action and clearly stated his intention to abide by the legislative will. No basis for claims of arbitrary action, unlimited powers or dictatorial usurpation of congressional power appears from the facts of this case. . . .

Rulings in Context

The Separation of Powers

United States v. Curtiss-Wright Corporation, 299 U.S. 304 (1936)   7-1
The Court held that the President is supreme in deciding foreign and military policy and that Congress did not unconstitutionally delegate its authority to the President when it authorized him to prohibit the sale of military material to Paraguay and Bolivia, two South American countries at war with each other.

Immigration and Naturalization Service v. Chadha,
> 462 U.S. 919 (1983)   7-2
> The Court ruled that the Constitution did not provide for a legislative one-house veto of an executive branch decision, but left open the possibility that a two-house veto may be constitutionally valid.

Morrison v. Olson, 487 U.S. 654 (1988)   7-1
> The Court ruled as constitutional the provision in the Ethics in Government Act of 1978, establishing the office of the independent counsel to investigate wrongdoing in the executive branch of the federal government. The act provided that when necessary, the Attorney General must request the appointment of an independent counsel from a Special Division of the U.S. Court of Appeals for the District of Columbia. The question was whether the appointment by the judiciary was a violation of the separation of powers doctrine.

CHAPTER 3

Expression and the Religion Clauses

*If there is any fixed star in our constitutional constellation,
it is that no official, high or petty, can prescribe what
shall be orthodox in politics, nationalism, religion, or other
matters of opinion or force citizens to confess by word or act
their faith therein.*
—Robert Jackson, *West Virginia State Board
of Education v. Barnette*, 319 U.S. 624 (1943)

The First Amendment outlines our basic or, as some say, our fundamental rights and liberties concerning expression and faith.

The Religion Clauses

The First Amendment opens with the two religion clauses: one asserts that the United States may not establish an official religion, and to further that goal, the other guarantees religious liberty to the people. Like all the amendments, it has been left to the Court to decide just what constitutes "a religious establishment" and how to define "religious liberty."

While many people regard the two religion clauses as separate, they often intertwine and even conflict with one another. In interpreting the phrase "religious establishment," for example, the Court ruled in a series of cases after 1962 that public school officials may not require students to attend religious services, write prayers for them to recite, or organize or lead students in prayers or in readings from the Bible or any other religious text. For some, this prohibition violates the second clause because it infringes on their religious freedom to pray when they wish or to read from the Bible or the Koran, the holy book of Islam, or the Talmud, the Jewish commentaries on Hebrew scripture.

The challenge of the two in conflict is deeply interesting and perplexing. First, the amendment asks just how far may a person go to exercise religious liberty. Mainstream religions like all the sects of Christianity, the three main branches of Judaism, and the two major streams of Islam are typically left alone. However, difficult constitutional questions arise involving unusual religions or those that have few adherents in the United States.

For example, in the 1993 case of *Church of the Lukumi Babalu Aye v. City of Hialeah*, 508 U.S. 502, the Court faced the challenge to an ordinance that on its face appeared to be directed at closing down a non-mainstream religion that posed no dangers to anyone. In that case, a group that practiced a religious faith known as Santeria opened a church in Hialeah, Florida. The public protested when it learned that one of the rituals involved animal sacrifice, even though the members cooked and then consumed the animals. In response, the city passed several ordinances outlawing the practice. The Supreme Court unanimously struck down the ordinance as a violation of religious liberty guarantees in the First Amendment. If, however, a religious practice involved human sacrifice or forced its adherents to engage in lawless activities, the Court would agree that it had crossed the limits of religious freedom.

Second, the amendment also asks how far government, and this could be federal, state, or local government, may go in supporting religion without becoming involved, or "entangled," as the Court now puts it, in religious affairs. May a state, for example, provide public funds for parochial education? May government officials place on public property religious symbols such as a crèche (a manger scene) during Christmas depicting Jesus, Mary, and Joseph surrounded by sheep and the three wise men, a Chanukah menorah (an eight-candle Jewish symbol), or even the Ten Commandments? May the local fire department erect a cross on top of the engine house before Easter or during Christmastime? Is the phrase, "under God," in the Pledge of Allegiance or the phrase "In God We Trust" on U.S. currency merely expressions of "ceremonial deism," as Dean Walter Rostow of the Yale Law School once wrote, or do they violate the Establishment Clause? The Court has had to deal with these difficult questions particularly over the past 30 years and will continue to do so in the future.

While these provisions encompass rights regarding religion, other clauses of the amendment address speech, press, and assembly.

The Rights of Free Speech, Free Press, Free Assembly

The First Amendment also encompasses our rights of free speech and press and our right to gather together and to submit our complaints to the government. In this way, it helps fulfill the promise of the first two Articles, which, as we have explained, set forth the republican structure of a representative democracy.

The framers of the Constitution made a number of assumptions concerning this structure. They assumed that the people were not naturally civic-minded, that they were mostly selfish and self-interested. Therefore, if they were to vote, even if the right was not expressly set forth anywhere in the document, as pointed out earlier, most elections were to be indirect.

The framers also assumed that if the people were to vote, they must be informed about the candidates and the issues of the day. They ought to engage in debate and discussion, and candidates for public office ought to let the people know where they stand: in short, the people need to have the freedom of speech. Otherwise, they would know nothing, having heard and debated nothing.

At the same time, the framers assumed that the people would have to have a free press. If they could not travel to where the candidates were speaking or debating, they would want to read about them in their newspapers, journals, pamphlets, and penny numbers. At the same time, the framers assumed that the people might want to associate freely: they would want to join forces with others if they had a grievance against the government or if they simply wanted to create a political organization or party, as the term was just then coming into common use, to support a particular candidate.

We would say then that these three freedoms are fundamental because the democratic republic, a representative democracy, cannot work without them. Of all the different kinds speech, political speech clearly ranks the highest, but even political speech has its limits, giving credence to the idea that no right or liberty is absolute.

The first major free speech cases came to the Court as a result of protests against the United States's entry into World War I. How far might demonstrators go in demanding American withdrawal from the war or in trying to convince young men not to enlist in the armed forces? It was at that time that the Court developed its "clear and present danger" test to come to grips with the reach of the First Amendment.

In 1919, Justice Oliver Wendell Holmes first articulated the test in *Schenck v. United States*, 249 U.S. 47 (Case 3.1). In giving the government the right to stop anti-war demonstrators from mailing leaflets to draft inductees, he noted that "the question in every case is whether the words used are used in such circumstances and are of such a nature as to create a clear and present danger that they will bring about the substantive evils that Congress has a right to prevent."

Several cases followed on the heels of *Schenck*. The Court used the clear and present danger test many times in the aftermath of World War I and into the 1920s during the first "Red Scare" just after the success of the 1917 Bolshevik or Communist Revolution in Russia. The Court also used it throughout the mid-twentieth century during the Cold War (the second "Red Scare") in the 1950s when many governmental officials were frightened of Communist infiltration in the United States, especially in the government itself. While it has not been used since the end of the Cold War, the test may well revive in the face of threats of international terrorism.

Not all speech is equal in the sense that the Court regards all forms of speech to equal political speech. In fact, over time, the justices have worked out a hierarchy of speech. At the top and the most protected is, as noted above, political speech, which merits the highest protection of all.

In the second tier, we will find commercial speech such as advertisements. In recent years, some justices would like commercial speech to receive the same protection as political speech, but that is still evolving doctrine. In addition, we will also find cases involving libel, that is, a printed attack on an individual that results in the defamation of character. The burden to prove libel of a public figure is on the victim to show that the attack was written with "actual malice"—or, in terms of the Court's meaning, "with knowledge that it was false or with reckless disregard of whether it was false or not." *New York Times v. Sullivan*, 376 U.S. 254 (1964) (Case 3.5).

Last and unprotected by the First Amendment are fighting words, pornography, obscenity, and other offensive speech. The Court has argued that these categories deserve no protection at all. Defining pornography and obscenity with precision has posed a major difficulty for the justices, and for everyone else as well. Perhaps out of frustration, in 1964 Justice Potter Stewart noted in *Jacobellis v. Ohio*, 378 U.S. 476, "I know it [pornography] when I see it." In 1973, the Court tried to develop a test concerning pornography and obscenity. It took its name (the *Miller* test) from the case of *Miller v. California*, 413 U.S. 15, but like the clear and present danger test, it too has failed to be a reliable measure.

The most difficult category, even in view of pornography and obscenity, is symbolic speech, especially when words are neither spoken nor printed. In 1984, Greg Johnson was arrested for violating an anti-flag desecration law in Texas when he burned an American flag to protest the re-nomination of President Reagan at the Republican National Convention (Case 3.3). He claimed he had a First Amendment right of free speech, even though he was not arrested for uttering anything. The Court struggled with how to define unspoken speech, or speech acts, and this too is evolving law.

Box 3.1

A Note on Incorporation

The rights and liberties guaranteed and protected by the Constitution are all binding on the federal government (it is after all a *federal* document). For many years after the document's ratification, a person with a grievance against his state or local government would have no basis for an appeal to the Supreme Court by citing any of the provisions of the Constitution. Chief Justice Marshall John Marshall codified this concept in *Barron v. Baltimore,* 7 Peters (32 U.S.) 243 (1833), when he wrote that the Fifth Amendment, like the rest of the Constitution, "must be understood as restraining the power of the general [the federal] government, not as applicable to the states."

For long afterward, the Court consistently held that the Bill of Rights was binding only on the federal government. With the addition of the Fourteenth Amendment in 1868 however, the states became subject to many of the same restrictions. This was not an immediate process, but one that has evolved over many years. This process has historically been known as "the doctrine of incorporation." It is another example of judge-made law.

Throughout the twentieth century, the Court gradually incorporated most of the Bill of Rights and applied them to actions by state and local governments. For example, Case 3.5 shows Justice Scalia's reference to the incorporation of the Free Exercise Clause as applied to the states through *Cantwell v. Connecticut,* 310 U.S. 296 (1940). Today, the Court has not yet incorporated the following few rights.

The Third Amendment's prohibition against quartering troops in private homes

The Fifth Amendment's right to an indictment by a grand jury

The Seventh Amendment's right to a trial by jury in civil cases

The Eighth Amendment's prohibition against excessive fines and bail

At the same time, a long divisive debate has taken place among many judges and justices over whether the Court has the authority to incorporate rights at all, and, if so, into which jurisdictions its authority extends.

How the incorporation doctrine will continue to evolve in the future is anyone's guess. Just as the justices have gradually incorporated most rights over the past seventy-five years, they also possess the authority to undo their incorporation.

Free Expression: Cases

The first two cases concerning free speech focus on the rise and development of the Clear and Present Danger Test. Justice Oliver Wendell Holmes first articulated this test in 1919 in *Schenck v. United States*. The Court modified it over the years when the government feared Communist and other subversive activities in the United States until it undermined it in 1969 in *Brandenburg v. Ohio*. The third case, *Texas v. Johnson*, raises the question of whether the First Amendment protects symbolic speech when a person burns the American flag as an act of political protest. Finally, *Citizens United v. the Federal Election Commission* (2010), involving campaign financing, asks whether corporations, like individual people, are subject to the guarantees of the First Amendment when they contribute funds to federal political campaigns.

Case 3.1

Schenck v. United States
249 U.S. 47, 39 S.Ct. 247 (1919)

During World War I, Charles T. Schenck, the secretary of the Socialist Party in America, printed, distributed, and mailed to draft-eligible men leaflets advocating opposition to U.S. involvement in the war. The leaflets argued that the war had nothing to do with workingmen, because it was one between the great capitalist or imperialist powers. Workingmen would only become cannon fodder for those who owned the great industries, and the benefits of the war would never filter down to those who worked in the factories or on the farms.

The leaflets ultimately urged them to resist the draft. Schenck was arrested, tried, and convicted of violating the Espionage Act of 1917, which was passed during the so-called Red Scare after the Bolshevik Revolution in Russia. It was also a response to growing economic dislocations due to the war and the growing number of aliens and foreign-born radicals coming to the United States to advocate a Communist revolution along the lines of the one in Russia. The act made it a crime for an individual to interfere with the war effort, specifically military recruitment, by encouraging insubordination, disloyalty, or refusal of duty in the military service.

Schenck's appeal was the first of many to challenge the Espionage Act. The Court's decision was unanimous with the opinion announced by Justice Oliver Wendell Holmes who laid out for the first time the Clear and Present Doctrine as a limitation on the First Amendment during wartime. In addition, he raised the old common law doctrine known as the Bad Tendency Test, when he confounded it with a clear and present danger. Speech with a "bad tendency" occurred when it possessed a natural tendency to bring about a result that may have forbidden consequences.

Justice HOLMES delivered the opinion of the Court.

The document in question . . . said that . . . a conscript is little better than a convict. In impassioned language it intimated that conscription was despotism in its worst form and a monstrous wrong against humanity in the interest of Wall Street's chosen few. It said, "Do not submit to intimidation," but in form at least confined itself to peaceful measures such as a petition for the repeal of the act. The other and later printed side of the sheet was headed "Assert Your Rights." It stated reasons for alleging that any one violated the Constitution when he refused to recognize "your right to assert your opposition to the draft," and went on, "If you do not assert and support your rights, you are helping to deny or disparage rights which it is the solemn duty of all citizens and residents of the United States to retain." It described the arguments on the other side as coming from cunning politicians and a mercenary capitalist press, and even silent consent to the conscription law as helping to support an infamous conspiracy. It denied the power to send our citizens away to foreign shores to shoot up the people of other lands, and added that words could not express the condemnation such cold-blooded ruthlessness deserves , &c., &c., winding up, "You must do your share to maintain, support and uphold the rights of the people of this country."

Of course the document would not have been sent unless it had been intended to have some effect, and we do not see what effect it could be expected to have upon persons subject to the draft except to influence them to obstruct the carrying of it out. The defendants do not deny that the jury might find against them on this point.

But it is said, suppose that that was the tendency of this circular, it is protected by the First Amendment to the Constitution. Two of the strongest expressions are said to be quoted respectively from well-known public men. It well may be that the prohibition of laws abridging the freedom of speech is not confined to previous restraints, although to prevent them may have been the main purpose.

We admit that in many places and in ordinary times the defendants in saying all that was said in the circular would have been within their constitutional rights. But the character of every act depends upon the circumstances in which it is done. The most stringent protection of free speech would not protect a man in falsely shouting fire in a theatre and causing a panic. It does not even protect a man from an injunction against uttering words that may have all the effect of force. The question in every case is whether the words used are used in such circumstances and are of such a nature as to create a clear and present danger that they will bring about the substantive evils that Congress has a right to prevent. It is a question of proximity and degree.

When a nation is at war many things that might be said in time of peace are such a hindrance to its effort that their utterance will not be endured so long as men fight and that no Court could regard them as protected by any constitutional right. It seems to be admitted that if an actual obstruction of the recruiting service were proved, liability for words that produced that effect might be enforced. The statute of 1917 . . . punishes conspiracies to obstruct as well as actual obstruction. If the act, (speaking, or circulating a paper,) its tendency and the intent with which it is done are the same, we perceive no ground for saying that success alone warrants making the act a crime.

Case 3.2

Brandenburg v. Ohio
395 U.S. 444, 89 S.Ct. 1827 (1969)

Ohio's Criminal Syndicalism Act of 1919 made it a crime to "advocate . . . the duty, necessity, or propriety of crime, sabotage, violence, or unlawful methods of terrorism as a means of accomplishing industrial or political reform" or to "voluntarily assemble with any society, group, or assemblage of persons to teach or advocate the doctrines of political syndicalism."

Clarence Brandenburg, a leader of the Ku Klux Klan, was convicted under this statute for organizing Klan meetings and arranging for their filming and broadcasting. All of the participants were hooded, but only some were armed and some burned crosses. Included in the speeches were such remarks as, "Personally, I believe the nigger should be returned to Africa, the Jew to Israel" and "We're not a revengent [sic] organization, but if our President, our Congress, our Supreme Court continues to suppress the white, Caucasian race, it's possible that there might have to be some revengeance taken." He was fined $1,000 and sentenced to imprison for a term of one to ten years.

The Ohio appellate courts sustained the conviction, and Brandenburg appealed to the Supreme Court, which unanimously overturned his conviction. Chief Justice Warren assigned Justice Abe Fortas to write the opinion, but Fortas was forced to resign in May before he completed the assignment. Consequently, the Court released a *per curiam* opinion.

Per Curiam

The Ohio Criminal Syndicalism Statute was enacted in 1919. From 1917 to 1920, identical or quite similar laws were adopted by 20 States and two territories. In 1927, this Court sustained the constitutionality of California's Criminal Syndicalism Act, the text of which is quite similar to that of the laws of Ohio. *Whitney v. California*, 274 U.S. 357 (1927). The Court upheld the statute on the ground that, without more, "advocating" violent means to effect political and economic change involves such danger to the security of the State that the State may outlaw it. But *Whitney* has been thoroughly discredited by later decisions. These later decisions have fashioned the principle that the constitutional guarantees of free speech and free press do not permit a State to forbid or proscribe advocacy of the use of force or of law violation except where such advocacy is directed to inciting or producing imminent lawless action and is likely to incite or produce such action. . . .

Measured by this test, Ohio's Criminal Syndicalism Act cannot be sustained. . . . Neither the indictment nor the trial judge's instructions to the jury in any way refined the statute's bald definition of the crime in terms of mere advocacy not distinguished from incitement to imminent lawless action.

Case 3.3

Texas v. Johnson
491 U.S. 397, 109 S.Ct. 2533 (1989)

Ronald Reagan's first administration was outwardly conservative in its support for corporations through tax reductions and for anti-Communist dictatorships in Latin America and other regions. During the 1984 Republican National Convention in Dallas, Texas, when President Reagan was re-nominated, Gregory Johnson joined a political demonstration protesting the policies of the Reagan administration and the actions of some Dallas-based corporations. After a march through the city streets, Johnson burned an American flag while fellow protesters chanted. Although no one was physically injured or threatened with injury, several witnesses were deeply offended by the flag burning. Johnson was convicted of desecration of a venerated object in violation of Texas law and disturbing the peace, and the state's Court of Appeals affirmed.

The Texas Court of Criminal Appeals reversed his conviction, holding that the law violated the First Amendment. Johnson's act of burning the flag was expressive conduct that the Constitution protected. Texas then appealed to the Supreme Court, which upheld the Criminal Appeals court's ruling.

In a five to four decision, Justice William J. Brennan delivered the opinion of the Court, in which Justices Thurgood Marshall, Harry A. Blackmun, Antonin Scalia, and Anthony M. Kennedy joined. Justice Kennedy filed a concurring opinion. Chief Justice William H. Rehnquist dissented in an opinion joined by Justices Byron R. White and Sandra Day O'Connor.

The Court majority explicitly distinguished this case from *United States v. O'Brien*, 391 U.S. 367. In that 1971 case, the Court held that the government did not infringe on David O'Brien's First Amendment free expression rights when it prosecuted him for burning his draft card to protest the Vietnam War. The Court ruled that O'Brien's expressive conduct did not trump the government's compelling interest in raising the armed forces under its Article I, Section 8, power. Under that authority, the government made it a crime for anyone to knowingly mutilate a draft card.

Justice BRENNAN delivered the opinion of the Court.

. . . We must first determine whether Johnson's burning of the flag constituted expressive conduct, permitting him to invoke the First Amendment in challenging his conviction. If his conduct was expressive, we next decide whether the State's regulation is related to the suppression of free expression. See, e.g., *United States v. O'Brien*, 391 U.S. 367 (1968). If the State's regulation is not related to expression, then the less stringent standard we announced in *United States v. O'Brien* for regulations of non-communicative conduct controls. If it is, then we are outside of *O'Brien*'s test, and we must ask whether this interest justifies Johnson's conviction under a more demanding standard. A third possibility is that the State's asserted interest is simply not implicated on these facts, and in that event the interest drops out of the picture.

The First Amendment literally forbids the abridgment only of "speech," but we have long recognized that its protection does not end at the spoken or written word. While we have rejected "the view that an apparently limitless variety of conduct can be labeled 'speech' whenever the person engaging in the conduct intends thereby to express an idea," *United States v. O'Brien*, we have acknowledged that conduct may be "sufficiently imbued with elements of communication to fall within the scope of the First and Fourteenth Amendments." . . .

Especially pertinent to this case are our decisions recognizing the communicative nature of conduct relating to flags. Attaching a peace sign to the flag, *Spence* [*v. Washington*, 418 U.S. 405 (1974)]; refusing to salute the flag, [*West Virginia Board of Education v. Barnette*, 319 U.S. 624 (1943)]; and displaying a red flag, *Stromberg v. California*, 283 U.S. 359 (1931), we have held, all may find shelter under the First Amendment. That we have had little difficulty identifying an expressive element in conduct relating to flags should not be surprising. The very purpose of a national flag is to serve as a symbol of our country; it is, one might say, "the one visible manifestation of two hundred years of nationhood." . . .

We have not automatically concluded, however, that any action taken with respect to our flag is expressive. Instead, in characterizing such action for First Amendment purposes, we have considered the context in which it occurred. . . .

The State of Texas conceded for purposes of its oral argument in this case that Johnson's conduct was expressive conduct. . . . Johnson burned an American flag as part—indeed, as the culmination—of a political demonstration that coincided with the convening of the Republican Party and its renomination of Ronald Reagan for President. The expressive, overtly political nature of this conduct was both intentional and overwhelmingly apparent. . . . In these circumstances, Johnson's burning of the flag was conduct "sufficiently imbued with elements of communication," to implicate the First Amendment.

The government generally has a freer hand in restricting expressive conduct than it has in restricting the written or spoken word. . . . It may not, however, proscribe particular conduct because it has expressive elements. . . . It is, in short, not simply the verbal or nonverbal nature of the expression, but the governmental interest at stake, that helps to determine whether a restriction on that expression is valid.

Thus, although we have recognized that where " 'speech' and 'nonspeech' elements are combined in the same course of conduct, a sufficiently important governmental interest in regulating the nonspeech element can justify incidental limitations on First Amendment freedoms," we have limited the applicability of *O'Brien*'s relatively lenient standard to those cases in which "the governmental interest is unrelated to the suppression of free expression." . . .

In order to decide whether *O'Brien*'s test applies here, therefore, we must decide whether Texas has asserted an interest in support of Johnson's conviction that is unrelated to the suppression of expression. If we find that an interest asserted by the State is simply not implicated on the facts before us, we need not ask whether *O'Brien*'s test applies. The State offers two separate interests to justify this conviction: preventing breaches of the peace and preserving the flag as a symbol of nationhood and national unity. We hold that the first interest is not implicated on this record and that the second is related to the suppression of expression.

Texas claims that its interest in preventing breaches of the peace justifies Johnson's conviction for flag desecration. However, no disturbance of the peace actually occurred or threatened to occur because of Johnson's burning of the flag. . . .

The State also asserts an interest in preserving the flag as a symbol of nationhood and national unity. In *Spence*, we acknowledged that the government's interest in preserving the flag's special symbolic value "is directly related to expression in the context of activity" such as affixing a peace symbol to a flag. We are equally persuaded that this interest is related to expression in the case of Johnson's burning of the flag. The State, apparently, is concerned that such conduct will lead people to believe either that the flag does not stand for nationhood and national unity, but instead reflects other, less positive concepts, or that the concepts reflected in the flag do not in fact exist, that is, that we do not enjoy unity as a Nation. These concerns blossom only when a person's treatment of the flag communicates some message, and thus are related "to the suppression of free expression" within the meaning of *O'Brien*. We are thus outside of *O'Brien*'s test altogether.

It remains to consider whether the State's interest in preserving the flag as a symbol of nationhood and national unity justifies Johnson's conviction.

As in *Spence*, "we are confronted with a case of prosecution for the expression of an idea through activity," and "accordingly, we must examine with particular care the interests advanced by [petitioner] to support its prosecution." Johnson was not, we add, prosecuted for the expression of just any idea; he was prosecuted for his expression of dissatisfaction with the policies of this country, expression situated at the core of our First Amendment values.

Moreover, Johnson was prosecuted because he knew that his politically charged expression would cause "serious offense." If he had burned the flag as a means of disposing of it because it was dirty or torn, he would not have been convicted of flag desecration under this Texas law: federal law designates burning as the preferred means of disposing of a flag "when it is in such condition that it is no longer a fitting emblem for display," and Texas has no quarrel with this means of disposal. The Texas law is thus not aimed at protecting the physical integrity of the flag in all circumstances, but is designed instead to protect it only against impairments that would cause serious offense to others. Texas concedes as much. . . .

Whether Johnson's treatment of the flag violated Texas law thus depended on the likely communicative impact of his expressive conduct. Our decision in *Boos v. Barry*, 485 U.S. 312, (1988), tells us that this restriction on Johnson's expression is content based. In *Boos*, we considered the constitutionality of a law prohibiting "the display of any sign within 500 feet of a foreign embassy if that sign tends to bring that foreign government into 'public odium' or 'public disrepute.'" Rejecting the argument that the law was content neutral because it was justified by "our international law obligation to shield diplomats from speech that offends their dignity," we held that "the emotive impact of speech on its audience is not a 'secondary effect'" unrelated to the content of the expression itself.

According to the principles announced in *Boos*, Johnson's political expression was restricted because of the content of the message he conveyed. We must therefore subject the State's asserted interest in preserving the special symbolic character of the flag to "the most exacting scrutiny." *Boos*. . . .

The State's argument is not that it has an interest simply in maintaining the flag as a symbol of something, no matter what it symbolizes; indeed, if that were the State's position, it would be difficult to see how that interest is endangered by highly symbolic conduct such as Johnson's. Rather, the State's claim is that it has an interest in preserving the flag as a symbol of nationhood and national unity, a symbol with a determinate range of meanings. According to Texas, if one physically treats the flag in a way that would tend to cast doubt on either the idea that nationhood and national unity are the flag's referents or that national unity actually exists, the message conveyed thereby is a harmful one and therefore may be prohibited.

If there is a bedrock principle underlying the First Amendment, it is that the government may not prohibit the expression of an idea simply because society finds the idea itself offensive or disagreeable. . . .

We have not recognized an exception to this principle even where our flag has been involved. . . .

In short, nothing in our precedents suggests that a State may foster its own view of the flag by prohibiting expressive conduct relating to it. To bring its argument outside our precedents, Texas attempts to convince us that even if its interest in preserving the flag's symbolic role does not allow it to prohibit words or some expressive conduct critical of the flag, it does permit it to forbid the outright destruction of the flag. The State's argument cannot depend here on the distinction between written or spoken words and nonverbal conduct. That distinction, we have shown, is of no moment where the nonverbal conduct is expressive, as it is here, and where the regulation of that conduct is related to expression, as it is here. . . .

There is, moreover, no indication—either in the text of the Constitution or in our cases interpreting it—that a separate juridical category exists for the American flag alone. Indeed, we would not be surprised to learn that the persons who framed our Constitution and wrote the Amendment that we now construe were not known for their reverence for the Union Jack. The First Amendment does not guarantee that other concepts virtually sacred to our Nation as a whole—such as the principle that discrimination on the basis of race is odious and destructive—will go unquestioned in the marketplace of ideas. See *Brandenburg v. Ohio*, 395 U.S. 444 (1969). We decline, therefore, to create for the flag an exception to the joust of principles protected by the First Amendment.

The way to preserve the flag's special role is not to punish those who feel differently about these matters. It is to persuade them that they are wrong. . . .

Johnson was convicted for engaging in expressive conduct. The State's interest in preventing breaches of the peace does not support his conviction because Johnson's conduct did not threaten to disturb the peace. Nor does the State's interest in preserving the flag as a symbol of nationhood and national unity justify his criminal conviction for engaging in political expression. The judgment of the Texas Court of Criminal Appeals is therefore

Affirmed.

Chief Justice REHNQUIST, with whom Justices WHITE and O'CONNOR join, dissenting.

. . . For more than 200 years, the American flag has occupied a unique position as the symbol of our Nation, a uniqueness that justifies a governmental prohibition against flag burning in the way respondent Johnson did here. . . .

No other American symbol has been as universally honored as the flag. In 1931, Congress declared "The Star-Spangled Banner" to be our national anthem. In 1949, Congress declared June 14th to be Flag Day. In 1987, John Philip Sousa's "The Stars and Stripes Forever" was designated as the national march. Congress has also established "The Pledge of Allegiance to the Flag" and the manner of its deliverance. The flag has appeared as the principal symbol on approximately 33 United States postal stamps and in the design of at least 43 more, more times than any other symbol.

Both Congress and the States have enacted numerous laws regulating misuse of the American flag. Until 1967, Congress left the regulation of misuse of the flag up to the States. Now, however, 18 U.S.C. 700(a) provides that:

> Whoever knowingly casts contempt upon any flag of the United States by publicly mutilating, defacing, defiling, burning, or trampling upon it shall be fined not more than $1,000 or imprisoned for not more than one year, or both.

Congress has also prescribed detailed rules for the design of the flag, the time and occasion of flag's display, the position and manner of its display, respect for the flag, and conduct during hoisting, lowering, and passing of the flag. With the exception of Alaska and Wyoming, all of the States now have statutes prohibiting the burning of the flag. . . .

The American flag, then, throughout more than 200 years of our history, has come to be the visible symbol embodying our Nation. It does not represent the views of any particular political party, and it does not represent any particular political philosophy. The flag is not simply another "idea" or "point of view" competing for recognition in the marketplace of ideas. Millions and millions of Americans regard it with an almost mystical reverence regardless of what sort of social, political, or philosophical beliefs they may have. I cannot agree that the First Amendment invalidates the Act of Congress, and the laws of 48 of the 50 States, which make criminal the public burning of the flag. . . .

The result of the Texas statute is obviously to deny one in Johnson's frame of mind one of many means of "symbolic speech." Far from being a case of "one picture being worth a thousand words," flag burning is the equivalent of an inarticulate grunt or roar that, it seems fair to say, is most likely to be indulged in not to express any particular idea, but to antagonize others. . . .

The Court concludes its opinion with a regrettably patronizing civics lecture, presumably addressed to the Members of both Houses of Congress, the members of the 48 state legislatures that enacted prohibitions against flag burning, and the troops fighting under that flag in Vietnam who objected to its being burned: "The way to preserve the flag's special role is not to punish those who feel differently about these matters. It is to persuade them that they are wrong." The Court's role as the final expositor of the Constitution is well established, but its role as a Platonic guardian admonishing those responsible to public opinion as if they were truant schoolchildren has no similar place in our system of government. The cry of "no taxation without representation" animated those who revolted against the English Crown to found our Nation—the idea that those who submitted to government should have some say as to what kind of laws would be passed. Surely one of the high purposes of a democratic society is to legislate against conduct that is regarded as evil and profoundly offensive to the majority of people—whether it be murder, embezzlement, pollution, or flag burning. . . .

Case 3.4

Citizens United v. Federal Elections Commission
558 U.S. 50, 130 S.Ct. 876 (2010)

Congress first restricted corporate contributions in federal elections in 1907 with the passage of the Tillman Act, named for Democratic Senator Benjamin Tillman of South Carolina, who was an avowedly white supremacist. Although President Theodore Roosevelt had accepted corporate contributions for his reelection in 1904, he strongly supported the act: he also advocated prohibiting corporate funding of state elections and the use of corporate money to influence legislation. The Supreme Court upheld such limitations as recently as 2003 when the justices reviewed various provisions of the Bipartisan Campaign Reform Act of 2002, also known as the McCain-Feingold Campaign Reform Act (*McConnell v. Federal Election Commission*, 540 U.S. 93). *McConnell* was largely based on a 1990 decision when the Court outlawed corporate funding of campaign advertisements, *Austin v. Michigan Chamber of Commerce*, 494 U.S. 652.

The Bipartisan Campaign Reform Act, co-sponsored by

Republican Senator John McCain of Arizona and Democratic Senator Russell Feingold of Wisconsin, was designed to regulate so-called "soft money," which is unregulated funding that wealthy contributors and corporations use for advertisements to attack candidates they wished to see defeated. Contributors did not direct money to official campaign organizations, but rather to Political Action Committees or PACs, set up for the purpose of skirting federal limitations on campaign contributions. Some sixty percent of the total amount of soft money spent in the 2000 election—around $500 million—came from 800 individuals, corporations, and labor unions.

The Court concentrated on Sections 203 and 441b of McCain-Feingold, which is how the Act is also known, because those two provisions directly addressed soft money that corporations and labor unions used to finance campaign advertisements. The case focused on the use of money by Citizens United, a conservative, non-profit organization. In 2008, the organization opposed the candidacy of Senator Hillary Rodham Clinton of New York, the wife of former President Bill Clinton, for the Democratic nomination for the presidency. At issue was whether the organization's distribution of a ninety-minute political film called *Hillary: The Movie* violated the McCain-Feingold Act or whether its distribution was protected by the First Amendment.

Fearing that McCain-Feingold prohibited a corporation from directly encouraging citizens to vote against a candidate, Citizens United sought, but failed to receive, declaratory and injunctive relief against the Federal Election Commission in U.S. district court. That court held that the provisions prohibiting *Hillary* from being funded by a corporation were constitutional because it was "susceptible of no other interpretation than to inform the electorate that Senator Clinton is unfit for office, that the United States would be a dangerous place in a President Hillary Clinton world, and that viewers should vote against her." Citizens United appealed to the Supreme Court, and on re-argument, the Court asked the parties to address whether it should overrule the part of *McConnell* that addressed the facial validity of McCain-Feingold.

Voting five to four, the Court overruled the district court's decision. In so doing, it also overruled *Austin* and found the McCain-Feingold Sections 203 and 441b unconstitutional. Justice Kennedy wrote the opinion for the Court. He was joined by Chief Justice Roberts and Justices Scalia, Alito, and Thomas. Justice Stevens dissented in an opinion joined by Justices Ginsburg, Breyer, and Sotomayor.

Justice KENNEDY delivered the opinion of the Court.

The law before us is an outright ban, backed by criminal sanctions. It makes it a felony for all corporations—including nonprofit advocacy corporations—either to expressly advocate the election or defeat of candidates or to broadcast electioneering communications within 30 days of a primary election and 60 days of a general election. Thus, the following acts would all be felonies under 441b: The Sierra Club runs an ad, within the crucial phase of 60 days before the general election, that exhorts the public to disapprove of a Congressman who favors logging in national forests; the National Rifle Association publishes a book urging the public to vote for the challenger because the incumbent U. S. Senator supports a handgun ban; and the American Civil Liberties Union creates a Web site telling the public to vote for a Presidential candidate in light of that candidate's defense of free speech. These prohibitions are classic examples of censorship.

441b is a ban on corporate speech notwithstanding the fact that a PAC [political action committee] created by a corporation can still speak. A PAC is a separate association from the corporation. So the PAC exemption from [the law's] expenditure ban does not allow corporations to speak. Even if a PAC could somehow allow a corporation to speak—and it does not—the option to form PACs does not alleviate the First Amendment problems with 441b. PACs are burdensome alternatives; they are expensive to administer and subject to extensive regulations. For example, every PAC must appoint a treasurer, forward donations to the treasurer promptly, keep detailed records of the identities of the persons making donations, preserve receipts for three years, and file an organization statement and report changes to this information within 10 days. . . .

We find no basis for the proposition that, in the context of political speech, the Government may impose restrictions on certain disfavored speakers. Both history and logic lead us to this conclusion.

The Court has recognized that First Amendment protection extends to corporations. This protection has been extended by explicit holdings to the context of political speech. Under the rationale of these precedents, political speech does not lose First Amendment protection "simply because its source is a corporation." The Court has thus rejected the argument that political speech of corporations or other associations should be treated differently under the First Amendment simply because such associations are not "natural persons." . . .

There is simply no support for the view that the First Amendment, as originally understood, would permit the suppression of political speech by media corporations. The Framers may not have anticipated modern business and media corporations. Yet television networks and major newspapers owned by media corporations have become the most important means of mass communication in modern times. The First Amendment was certainly not understood to condone the suppression of political speech in society's most salient media. It was understood as a response to the repression of speech and the press that had existed in England and the heavy taxes on the press that were imposed in the colonies. The great debates between the Federalists and the Anti-Federalists over our founding document were published and expressed in the most important means of mass communication of that era—newspapers owned by individuals. At the founding, speech was open, comprehensive, and vital to society's definition of itself; there were no limits on the sources of speech and knowledge. The Framers may have been unaware of certain types of speakers or forms of communication, but that does not mean that those speakers and media are entitled to less First Amendment protection than those types of speakers and media that provided the means of communicating political ideas when the Bill of Rights was adopted. . . .

When Government seeks to use its full power, including the criminal law, to command where a person may get his or her information or what distrusted source he or she may not hear, it uses censorship to control thought. This is unlawful. The First Amendment confirms the freedom to think for ourselves. . . . For the reasons explained above, we now conclude that independent expenditures, including those made by corporations, do not give rise to corruption or the appearance of corruption. . . . The appearance of influence or access, furthermore, will not cause the electorate to lose faith in our democracy. By definition, an independent expenditure is political speech presented to the electorate that is not coordinated with a candidate. See *Buckley* [424 U.S. 1 (1976)]. The fact that a corporation, or any other speaker, is willing to spend money to try to persuade voters presupposes that the people have the ultimate influence over elected officials. This is inconsistent with any suggestion that the electorate will refuse "'to take part in democratic governance'" because of additional political speech made by a corporation or any other speaker. *McConnell.*

Austin is overruled, so it provides no basis for allowing the Government to limit corporate independent expenditures. As the Government appears to concede, overruling *Austin* "effectively invalidate[s] not only BCRA Section 203, but also 2 U.S.C. 441b's prohibition on the use of corporate treasury funds for express advocacy." Section 441b's restrictions on corporate independent expenditures are therefore invalid and cannot be applied to *Hillary.*

Given our conclusion we are further required to overrule the part of *McConnell* that upheld BCRA §203's extension of §441b's restrictions on corporate independent expenditures. The *McConnell* Court relied on the antidistortion interest recognized in *Austin* to uphold a greater restriction on speech than the restriction upheld in *Austin*, and we have found this interest unconvincing and insufficient. This part of *McConnell* is now overruled. . . .

When word concerning the plot of the movie *Mr. Smith Goes to Washington* reached the circles of Government, some officials sought, by persuasion, to discourage its distribution. Under *Austin*, though, officials could have done more than discourage its distribution—they could have banned the film. After all, it, like *Hillary*, was speech funded by a corporation that was critical of Members of Congress. *Mr. Smith Goes to Washington* may be fiction and caricature; but fiction and caricature can be a powerful force. . . .

The judgment of the District Court is reversed with respect to the constitutionality of §441b's restrictions on corporate independent expenditures.

Justice STEVENS, concurring in part and dissenting in part.

The majority's approach to corporate electioneering marks a dramatic break from our past. Congress has placed special limitations on campaign spending by corporations ever since the passage of the Tillman Act in 1907. We have unanimously concluded that this "reflects a permissible assessment of the dangers posed by those entities to the electoral process," *FEC v. National Right to Work Comm.*, 459 U.S. 197 (1982), and have accepted the "legislative judgment that the special characteristics of the corporate structure require particularly careful regulation." The Court today rejects a century of history when it treats the distinction between corporate and individual campaign spending as an invidious novelty born of *Austin v. Michigan Chamber of Commerce* (1990). Relying largely on individual dissenting opinions, the majority blazes through our precedents, overruling or disavowing a body of case law. . . .

In a democratic society, the longstanding consensus on the need to limit corporate campaign spending should outweigh the wooden application of judge-made rules. The majority's rejection of this principle "elevates corporations to a level of deference which has not been seen at least since the days when substantive due process was regularly used to invalidate regulatory legislation thought to unfairly impinge upon established economic interests." At bottom, the Court's opinion is thus a rejection of the common sense of the American people, who have recognized a need to prevent corporations from undermining self-government since the founding, and who have fought against the distinctive corrupting potential of corporate electioneering since the days of Theodore Roosevelt. It is a strange time to repudiate that common sense. While American democracy is imperfect, few outside the majority of this Court would have thought its flaws included a dearth of corporate money in politics. I would affirm the judgment of the District Court.

Free Press: Cases

The first case from 1964, *New York Times v. Sullivan,* focuses on whether the First Amendment extends as far as to protect libelous statements; the other, *New York Times v. United States* (1971), raises the issue of whether the federal government, in the interest of national security, may prohibit newspapers from publishing classified material in wartime.

Case 3.5

New York Times v. Sullivan
376 U.S. 254, 84 S.Ct. 710 (1964)

On March 29, 1960, an advertisement appeared in the *New York Times* relating to the mistreatment of civil rights workers by Montgomery, Alabama, officials and law enforcement officers. L. B. Sullivan, a Montgomery commissioner, sued the paper and several people responsible for writing the advertisement for libel, claiming that the misstatements and outright lies were placed in the advertisement, including a charge that "truckloads of police armed with shotguns and tear-gas ringed the Alabama State College Campus" where they locked the doors of a building filled with the workers "in an attempt to starve them into submission." The advertisement also addressed how the police mistreated Dr. Martin Luther King Jr., the leader of the Civil Rights Movement, when they "bombed his home almost killing his wife and child."

Although none of the statements mentioned Sullivan by name, he claimed the ad targeted him because as commissioner

he supervised Montgomery police. In his mind, he was the one accused of "ringing" the campus. The police never at any time could
be found to "ring" the campus, and they did not bomb Dr. King's
home or arrest him.

After Sullivan sued for libel, a state trial judge instructed the
jury that the statements were "libelous per se," which means that
because of untrue statements, for the jury to award compensatory
damages, it needed only to determine the fact of publication. The
judge also said that for punitive damages, negligence was no defense. The jury awarded Sullivan $500,000 and the state supreme
court affirmed.

After the *Times* appealed, the Supreme Court unanimously
overturned the award in an opinion by Justice William Brennan.

Justice BRENNAN delivered the opinion of the Court.

We are required in this case to determine for the first time the extent to
which the constitutional protections for speech and press limit a State's
power to award damages in a libel action brought by a public official
against critics of his official conduct. . . .

We reverse the judgment. We hold that the rule of law applied by
the Alabama courts is constitutionally deficient for failure to provide the
safeguards for freedom of speech and of the press that are required by
the First and Fourteenth Amendments in a libel action brought by a

public official against critics of his official conduct. We further hold
that under the proper safeguards the evidence presented in this case is
constitutionally insufficient to support the judgment for respondent. . . .

We consider this case against the background of a profound national commitment to the principle that debate on public issues should
be uninhibited, robust, and wide-open, and that it may well include ve-
hement, caustic, and sometimes unpleasantly sharp attacks on government and public officials. The present advertisement, as an expression
of grievance and protest on one of the major public issues of our time,
would seem clearly to qualify for the constitutional protection. The
question is whether it forfeits that protection by the falsity of some of its
factual statements and by its alleged defamation of respondent.

Authoritative interpretations of the First Amendment guarantees
have consistently refused to recognize an exception for any test of truth—
whether administered by judges, juries, or administrative officials—and
especially one that puts the burden of proving truth on the speaker. The
constitutional protection does not turn upon "the truth, popularity, or
social utility of the ideas and beliefs which are offered." . . .

Injury to official reputation affords no more warrant for repressing speech that would otherwise be free than does factual error. Where judicial officers are involved, this Court has held that concern for the dignity and reputation of the courts does not justify the punishment as criminal contempt of criticism of the judge or his decision. This is true even though the utterance contains "half-truths" and "misinformation." Such repression can be justified, if at all, only by a clear and present danger of the obstruction of justice. . . .

If neither factual error nor defamatory content suffices to remove the constitutional shield from criticism of official conduct, the combination of the two elements is no less inadequate. This is the lesson to be drawn from the great controversy over the Sedition Act of 1798, which first crystallized a national awareness of the central meaning of the First Amendment. . . .

Although the Sedition Act was never tested in this Court, the attack upon its validity has carried the day in the court of history. Fines levied in its prosecution were repaid by Act of Congress on the ground that it was unconstitutional. . . . Jefferson, as President, pardoned those who had been convicted and sentenced under the Act and remitted their fines. . . .

There is no force in respondent's argument that the constitutional limitations implicit in the history of the Sedition Act apply only to Congress and not to the States. It is true that the First Amendment was originally addressed only to action by the Federal Government. . . . But this distinction was eliminated with the adoption of the Fourteenth Amendment and the application to the States of the First Amendment's restrictions.

What a State may not constitutionally bring about by means of a criminal statute is likewise beyond the reach of its civil law of libel. . . . The judgment awarded in this case—without the need for any proof of actual pecuniary loss—was one thousand times greater than the maximum fine provided by the Alabama criminal statute, and one hundred times greater than that provided by the Sedition Act. And since there is no double-jeopardy limitation applicable to civil lawsuits, this is not the only judgment that may be awarded against petitioners for the same publication. Whether or not a newspaper can survive a succession of such judgments, the pall of fear and timidity imposed upon those who would give voice to public criticism is an atmosphere in which the First Amendment freedoms cannot survive. Plainly the Alabama law of civil libel is "a form of regulation that creates hazards to protected freedoms markedly greater than those that attend reliance upon the criminal law." . . .

The constitutional guarantees require, we think, a federal rule that prohibits a public official from recovering damages for a defamatory falsehood relating to his official conduct unless he proves that the statement was made with "actual malice"—that is, with knowledge that it was false or with reckless disregard of whether it was false or not. . . .

We conclude that such a privilege is required by the First and Fourteenth Amendments.

We hold today that the Constitution delimits a State's power to award damages for libel in actions brought by public officials against critics of their official conduct. Since this is such an action, the rule requiring proof of actual malice is applicable. . . .

[T]he proof presented to show actual malice lacks the convincing clarity which the constitutional standard demands, and hence that it would not constitutionally sustain the judgment for respondent under the proper rule of law. . . .

We also think the evidence was constitutionally defective in another respect: it was incapable of supporting the jury's finding that the allegedly libelous statements were made "of and concerning" respondent. . . . There was no reference to respondent in the advertisement, either by name or official position. A number of the allegedly libelous statements—the charges that the dining hall was padlocked and that Dr. King's home was bombed, his person assaulted, and a perjury prosecution instituted against him—did not even concern the police; despite the ingenuity of the arguments which would attach this significance to the word "They," it is plain that these statements could not reasonably be read as accusing respondent of personal involvement in the acts in question. . . . The judgment of the Supreme Court of Alabama is reversed and the case is remanded to that court for further proceedings not inconsistent with this opinion.

Case 3.6

New York Times Co. v. United States
403 U.S. 713, 91 S.Ct. 2140 (1971)

The Nixon administration, in the midst of growing opposition to the war in Vietnam, sought to enjoin publication in the *New York Times* and the *Washington Post* of certain classified material. The documents originated from a forty-seven volume study known as *History of U.S. Decision Making Process on Viet Nam Policy* that the Defense Department ordered in 1967. The department designated the study as Top Secret "Sensitive" because it might prove embarrassing—"Sensitive" is not an official designation. It showed that the officials knew early on that the United States could not win the war in Southeast Asia and that its continuation would lead to many more casualties. President Nixon feared that the publication of the papers would increase opposition to the war and his presidency.

The *New York Times* received copies of the study from Daniel Ellsberg, a former Pentagon official who was then working for a Washington think tank. After the paper began publication on June 13, 1971, a federal district court issued a temporary restraining order that was upheld by the Second Circuit Court of Appeals. With the *Times* halted from publishing, Ellsberg then sent copies to the *Post*, but a D.C. federal judge denied the injunction, but issued a temporary restraining order until the D.C. Circuit Court of Appeals considered the government's application for an injunction. On June 22, that court remanded the case to the lower court for further consideration.

Meantime, the *Times* appealed its injunction to the Supreme Court, which decided six to three, on June 27, just two weeks after the first installments appeared, that the doctrine of no prior restraint prohibited the government's attempt to shut down publication of what are now known as the Pentagon Papers. The Court decision was announced in a *per curiam* or by the court opinion, but all nine justices also wrote concurrences or dissents, for a total of ten opinions in a single decision. The Court focused on the court-created doctrine of prior restraint, which has its roots in the English common-law principle that government may not prohibit expression on the basis of its content, but may punish the speaker if what he says is unlawful. The Court had first announced the doctrine in constitutional law in the 1931 free press case of *Near v. Minnesota*, 283 U.S. 697. Only Justice Harlan's dissent is reprinted along with the *per curiam* opinion.

Per Curiam

We granted *certiorari* in these cases in which the United States seeks to enjoin the *New York Times* and the *Washington Post* from publishing the contents of a classified study entitled "History of U.S. Decision-Making Process on Viet Nam Policy."

"Any system of prior restraints of expression comes to this Court bearing a heavy presumption against its constitutional validity." *Bantam Books, Inc. v. Sullivan*, 372 U.S. 58 (1963); see also *Near v. Minnesota*, 283 U.S. 697 (1931). The Government "thus carries a heavy burden of showing justification for the imposition of such a restraint." *Organization for a Better Austin v. Keefe*, 402 U.S. 415 (1971). The District Court for the Southern District of New York in the *New York Times* case and the District Court for the District of Columbia and the Court of Appeals for the District of Columbia Circuit in the *Washington Post* case held that the Government had not met that burden. We agree.

The judgment of the Court of Appeals for the District of Columbia Circuit is therefore affirmed. The order of the Court of Appeals for the Second Circuit is reversed and the case is remanded with directions to enter a judgment affirming the judgment of the District Court for the Southern District of New York. The stays entered June 25, 1971, by the Court are vacated. The judgments shall issue forthwith.

Justice HARLAN dissenting.

With all respect, I consider that the Court has been almost irresponsibly feverish in dealing with these cases.

Both the Court of Appeals for the Second Circuit and the Court of Appeals for the District of Columbia Circuit rendered judgment on June 23. The *New York Times'* petition for *certiorari*, its motion for accelerated consideration thereof, and its application for interim relief were filed in this Court on June 24 at about 11 a. m. The application of the United States for interim relief in the *Post* case was also filed here on June 24 at about 7:15 p. m. This Court's order setting a hearing before us on June 26 at 11 a. m., a course which I joined only to avoid the possibility of even more peremptory action by the Court, was issued less than 24 hours before. The record in the *Post* case was filed with the Clerk shortly before 1 p. m. on June 25; the record in the *Times* case did not arrive until 7 or 8 o'clock that same night. The briefs of the parties were received less than two hours before argument on June 26.

This frenzied train of events took place in the name of the presumption against prior restraints created by the First Amendment. Due regard for the extraordinarily important and difficult questions involved in these litigations should have led the Court to shun such a precipitate timetable. [Justice Harlan then listed seven unanswered questions, including the authority of the U.S. Attorney General to raise the issue at all and a determination of the impact of the publication of the documents on the American war effort in Vietnam.]

These are difficult questions of fact, of law, and of judgment; the potential consequences of erroneous decision are enormous. The time which has been available to us, to the lower courts, and to the parties has been wholly inadequate for giving these cases the kind of consideration they deserve. . . . Forced as I am to reach the merits of these cases, I dissent from the opinion and judgments of the Court.

Rulings in Context

Free Speech, Expression, and the Press

Gitlow v. People of the State of New York, 268 U.S. 652 (1925)   7-2

The Court, over Justice Holmes and Brandeis's objection, transformed the clear and present danger test to include the "bad tendency" test in First Amendment jurisprudence. Gitlow's conviction for causing to print his "Left-Wing Manifesto" was upheld because his speech tended to have potentially bad consequences, in this case advocacy of the overthrow of the United States government. In a dissent, joined by Justice Brandeis, Justice Holmes famously noted that "every idea is an incitement," and because there was no indication of imminent danger, Gitlow's words represented no clear and present danger.

Chaplinsky v. New Hampshire, 315 U.S. 568 (1942)   9-0

The Court held that the free speech guaranteed by the First Amendment was not protected when a man is convicted of inciting violence by the use of "fighting words," or "words which by their very utterance inflict injury or tend to incite an immediate breach of peace."

Dennis v. United States, 341 U.S. 494 (1951)   6-2

Several members of the Communist Party appealed their convictions under the 1940 Smith, or Alien Registration, Act, which made it illegal to conspire, teach, or advocate the overthrow of the United States government or to belong to any organization that advocated these goals. In upholding their convictions, Chief Justice Vinson adopted the balancing technique designed by Judge Learned Hand of the Second Circuit, who had first heard the appeal. Judge Hand had written that "in each case courts must ask whether the gravity of the 'evil,' discounted by its probability, justifies such invasion of free speech as is necessary to avoid the danger." Thus, the Court extended the test so that the mere teaching of Marxist-Leninist doctrine posed a "clear and probable" danger.

Tinker v. Des Moines, 393 U.S. 503 (1969)   7-2

The Court ruled that high school students and teachers do not lose their First Amendment rights at the schoolhouse gate after Mary Beth Tinker and her brother John faced suspension when they wore armbands to school to protest the United States's role in the Vietnam War.

Miller v. California, 413 U.S. 15 (1971)   5-4

The Court, in establishing the so-called *Miller* test, held that obscenity was not protected by the First Amendment to the extent that a government ban on any work must satisfy three prongs of the test: the work must "appeal to prurient interest in sex;" it must portray sex "in a patently offensive way;" and, when taken as a whole, does not possess "serious literary, artistic, political, or scientific value."

Ashcroft v. Free Speech Coalition, 535 U.S. 234 (2002)   6½-2½

The Court held that two provisions of the Child Pornography Prevention Act of 1996 were overbroad and therefore unconstitutional. The two major provisions were the production of "virtual," or computer-based, child pornography images and pornographic films using adults acting as children.

Ashcroft v. American Civil Liberties Union, 535 U.S. 564 (2002)   8-1

As the legislation's title suggests, the Child Online Protection Act of 1998 was designed to protect children from pornographic sites on the Internet. Both the district court and the United States Court of Appeals for the Third Circuit overturned the act on the basis of the strict scrutiny test (see the judicial tests outlined in Box 4.1) as applied to the First Amendment. The Supreme Court vacated the lower courts' decision and remanded the case for further hearings, but maintained the stay placed on it by the Third Circuit.

McConnell v. Federal Election Commission, 540 U.S. 93 (2003)   5-4

The Court ruled that most of the provisions in the campaign finance reform law passed by Congress in 2002 posed no burden on the First Amendment. In particular, the Court upheld as constitutional the limitations placed on so-called "soft money" contributions to political action committees and political parties. The Court also found no First Amendment violation in restricting the mention of a federal candidate in an opponent's advertisement thirty days before an election.

Pleasant Grove v. Summum, 555 U.S. 460 (2009)   9-0

In this case, Summum, a religious organization, wanted to place a stone monument of its "Seven Aphorisms" on the grounds of a public park where there were 15 other permanent displays, some of which were placed there by private groups or individuals. These included an historic granary, a wishing well, the City's first fire station, a September 11 monument, and a Ten Commandments monument donated by the Fraternal Order of Eagles in 1971. After the city of Pleasant Grove denied the request and Summum filed suit, the Court unanimously held that government may constitutionally protect its own speech by deciding what messages it wished to convey in public places.

Agency for International Development v. Alliance for Open Society International, 570 U.S. _____ (2013)   6-2

Chief Justice John Roberts ruled for the Court that United States may not, as a condition of funding, require a recipient to have a policy that "regulates speech outside the contours of the program" it supports. The Alliance for Open Society received federal funds to combat HIV/AIDS and other diseases abroad. The money was contingent on the group adopting a policy mirroring the government's opposition to prostitution and sex trafficking. The Court held that the condition conflicted with the First Amendment when it required recipients "to pledge allegiance to the government's policy of eradicating prostitution." The requirement "can result in an unconstitutional burden on First Amendment rights." Justice Elena Kagan did not take part in the case.

Free Exercise of Religion: Case

The following case asks whether the State of Oregon violated the Free Exercise provision of the First Amendment when it denied employment benefits to two Native Americans who were dismissed from their jobs for cause, namely for ingesting an illicit drug. They had done so as part of an ancient religious practices.

Case 3.7

Employment Division, Dept. of Human Resources, Oregon v. Smith
494 U.S. 872, 110 S.Ct. 1595 (1990)

Alfred Smith and Galen Black were employed as counselors at a private drug rehabilitation agency when they were found to have ingested a prohibited Schedule I illegal drug as part of a religious ceremony in their Native American Church. Even though they did not take the drug while they were at work, they were dismissed from their jobs. The Oregon Department of Human Resources denied their claim for unemployment compensation because they were fired for work-related "misconduct." Smith and Black challenged that result, claiming that Oregon infringed on their religious freedom, which is guaranteed by the Constitution's First Amendment Free Exercise Clause.

Native American religious ceremonies predate not only the

Constitution, but also the arrival of the first white people to the Western Hemisphere. Congress recognized this fact when it passed the American Indian Religious Freedom Act: "it shall be the policy of the United States to protect and preserve for American Indians their inherent right of freedom to believe, express, and exercise the traditional religions . . . including but not limited to access to sites, use and possession of sacred objects, and the freedom to worship through ceremonials and traditional rites" (1982 ed.). In 1978, Congress noted that certain substances, such as peyote—the drug ingested by Smith and Black—"have religious significance because they are sacred, they have power, they heal, they are necessary to the exercise of the rites of the religion, they are necessary to the cultural integrity of the tribe, and, therefore, religious survival."

In the meantime, Congress also designated as illegal several drugs and substances and classified them as Schedule I drugs, from which Oregon adopted its policy. Prohibited among Schedule I drugs is the growing, harvesting, and ingesting of peyote, a hallucinogenic narcotic derived from a cactus plant. According to the federal Drug Enforcement Administration (DEA), however, "the listing of peyote as a controlled substance in Schedule I does not apply to the non-drug use of peyote in *bona fide* religious ceremonies of the Native American Church, and members of the Native American Church so using peyote are exempt from registration. Any person who manufactures peyote for or distributes peyote to the Native American Church, however, is required to obtain registration annually and to comply with all other requirements of law."

While the DEA made this determination, the state of Oregon did not. And yet, Oregon's highest court saw otherwise. The Employment Division said that it could deny a claim when a person was fired for committing a crime. The State Supreme Court rejected the Employment Division's argument that benefits had been denied because Smith and Black had committed a crime. The court said that the only reason why the state could ever deny anybody unemployment compensation was because it was legally required to preserve the financial integrity of the compensation fund. And that reason was insufficient to justify the discrimination against their religious practices.

In 1987, Oregon appealed to the U.S. Supreme Court, once again using the argument that the Employment Division could reject a claim on the basis of Smith and Black's criminal use of a controlled substance. The Supreme Court, in what is now *Smith I*, stated that the criminal aspect of the denial may be relevant, but before it ruled finally on that issue, the Court remanded the case. It asked the Oregon Supreme Court to find whether state law prohibited sacramental peyote use. Being "uncertain about the legality of the religious use of peyote in Oregon," the justices said that it would not be "appropriate for us to decide whether the practice is protected by the Federal Constitution." The state supreme court found that Oregon law did in fact prohibit the religious use of peyote because there were no exceptions. The court then concluded that the law violated the Free Exercise Clause. Oregon, a second time, appealed to the U.S. Supreme Court.

The question is how to draw the line between religious rites, especially those that are ancient, on the one hand, and generally applicable laws, on the other. We see here the Court's struggle to find the right balance between a free religious practice that does no community harm and a generally applicable law that is designed to protect the people. The government has long possessed the authority to protect the people through laws known as "police power" that affect our safety, health, welfare, and morals. We see it most effectively, for example, through our traffic laws. We may claim a right of locomotion to go as fast as we want in our cars or a right to keep going and never stop. But the government has determined that traffic laws, like speed limits and red lights, are more important.

When a basic or fundamental freedom like the First Amendment freedoms of speech, the press, religion encounter a law made through the government's police power, the Court has historically used the strict scrutiny test (see the judicial tests in Box 4.1). This test places the burden of proof on the government—in this case Oregon—to show why it has a *compelling* interest to further some government goal or policy while overcoming a fundamental right (in the *Smith* case, the free exercise of religion). The "compelling interest" in this case means that based on public safety there is no alternative to prohibiting the use of peyote. Moreover, the government has the burden to show why its prohibition is "narrowly tailored" to achieve its goal or policy, that is, how the law is limited because it is the least restrictive means it could use.

In matters having nothing to do with fundamental rights (or in the case of Fourteenth Amendment Equal Protection cases, suspect categories like race), the Court will use the rational basis test (see Box 4.1). This test places the burden of proof on the plaintiff and all the government need show is that its law or policy is "reasonable" because the government has a "legitimate" interest in protecting public health, safety, welfare, and so on. The traffic laws fit into this test.

Here we have a generally applicable law—one that prohibits the use of a controlled substance—designed to protect the safety and health of the people. But because it is a case involving the sacramental or religious use of the drug, it raises the free exercise claim. Note how Justice Antonin Scalia in his opinion for the Court raises the issue of whether the "compelling interest" or "strict scrutiny" test should be applied here. In the end, he argues on rational basis grounds that Oregon need only show that the law is "generally applicable" and that it is not directed at any particular religion; certainly not the Native American Church.

So for the first time, the Court removed religious challenges from the lofty strict scrutiny arena to the more easily accessible rational basis ground. And this is what infuriated Justice Harry A. Blackmun in his dissent.

The Court reversed the Oregon Supreme Court by a six to three vote. Justice Sandra Day O'Connor concurred and joined the majority. She disagreed with Justice Scalia that the rational basis test could resolve a constitutional challenge based on a religion question. Her argument was that Oregon did have a compelling interest to prohibit the use of peyote, and that the state had shown why.

Justices William J. Brennan and Thurgood Marshall agreed with her reasoning (that strict scrutiny applied here), but disagreed with her conclusion. Justice Harry A. Blackmun, whose dissent was joined by Justices Brennan and Marshall, argued that Oregon had failed to show a compelling interest that was narrowly tailored to prohibit the sacramental use of peyote.

Justice SCALIA delivered the opinion of the Court.

. . . Respondents' claim for relief rests on our decisions in *Sherbert v. Verner*, [374 U.S. 398 (1963)], *Thomas v. Review Bd. of Indiana Employment Security Div.*, [450 U.S. 707 (1981)], and *Hobbie v. Unemployment Appeals Comm'n of Florida*, 480 U.S. 136 (1987), in which we held that a State could not condition the availability of unemployment insurance on an individual's willingness to forgo conduct required by his religion. As we observed in *Smith I*, however, the conduct at issue in those cases was not prohibited by law. We held that distinction to be critical, for "if Oregon does prohibit the religious use of peyote, and if that prohibition is consistent with the Federal Constitution, there is no federal right to engage in that conduct in Oregon," and "the State is free to withhold unemployment compensation from respondents for engaging in work-related misconduct, despite its religious motivation." Now that the Oregon Supreme Court has confirmed that Oregon does prohibit the religious use of peyote, we proceed to consider whether that prohibition is permissible under the Free Exercise Clause. . . .

The Free Exercise Clause of the First Amendment, which has been made applicable to the States by incorporation into the Fourteenth

Amendment, see *Cantwell v. Connecticut*, 310 U.S. 296 (1940), provides that "Congress shall make no law respecting an establishment of religion, or prohibiting the free exercise thereof. . . ." The free exercise of religion means, first and foremost, the right to believe and profess whatever religious doctrine one desires. Thus, the First Amendment obviously excludes all "governmental regulation of religious *beliefs* as such." *Sherbert v. Verner.*

But the "exercise of religion" often involves not only belief and profession but the performance of (or abstention from) physical acts: assembling with others for a worship service, participating in sacramental use of bread and wine, proselytizing, abstaining from certain foods or certain modes of transportation. It would be true, we think (though no case of ours has involved the point), that a State would be "prohibiting the free exercise [of religion]" if it sought to ban such acts or abstentions only when they are engaged in for religious reasons, or only because of the religious belief that they display. It would doubtless be unconstitutional, for example, to ban the casting of "statues that are to be used for worship purposes," or to prohibit bowing down before a golden calf.

Respondents in the present case, however, seek to carry the meaning of "prohibiting the free exercise [of religion]" one large step further. They contend that their religious motivation for using peyote places them beyond the reach of a criminal law that is not specifically directed at their religious practice, and that is concededly constitutional as applied to those who use the drug for other reasons. . . . As a textual matter, we do not think the words must be given that meaning. It is no more necessary to regard the collection of a general tax, for example, as "prohibiting the free exercise [of religion]" by those citizens who believe support of organized government to be sinful, than it is to regard the same tax as "abridging the freedom . . . of the press" of those publishing companies that must pay the tax as a condition of staying in business. It is a permissible reading of the text, in the one case as in the other, to say that if prohibiting the exercise of religion (or burdening the activity of printing) is not the object of the tax but merely the incidental effect of a generally applicable and otherwise valid provision, the First Amendment has not been offended. . . .

Our decisions reveal that the latter reading is the correct one. We have never held that an individual's religious beliefs excuse him from compliance with an otherwise valid law prohibiting conduct that the State is free to regulate. On the contrary, the record of more than a century of our free exercise jurisprudence contradicts that proposition. [NOTE: Justice Scalia cites the ban on polygamy among members of the Mormon Church and the requirement that Amish employers pay Social Security taxes even though their religion prohibits them from participating in government support programs.]

The only decisions in which we have held that the First Amendment bars application of a neutral, generally applicable law to religiously motivated action have involved not the Free Exercise Clause alone, but the Free Exercise Clause in conjunction with other constitutional protections, such as freedom of speech and of the press, see *Cantwell v. Connecticut*, (invalidating a licensing system for religious and charitable solicitations under which the administrator had discretion to deny a license to any cause he deemed nonreligious); *Murdock v. Pennsylvania*, 319 U.S. 105 (1943) (invalidating a flat tax on solicitation as applied to the dissemination of religious ideas); *Follett v. McCormick*, 321 U.S. 573 (1944) (same), or the right of parents, acknowledged in *Pierce v. Society of Sisters*, 268 U.S. 510 (1925), to direct the education of their children, see *Wisconsin v. Yoder*, 406 U.S. 205 (1972) (invalidating compulsory school-attendance laws as applied to Amish parents who refused on religious grounds to send their children to school). Some of our cases prohibiting compelled expression, decided exclusively upon free speech grounds, have also involved freedom of religion, see *Wooley v. Maynard*, 430 U.S. 705 (1977) (invalidating compelled display of a license plate slogan that offended individual religious beliefs); *West Virginia Bd. of Education v. Barnette*, 319 U.S. 624 (1943) (invalidating compulsory flag salute statute challenged by religious objectors)....

The present case does not present such a hybrid situation, but a free exercise claim unconnected with any communicative activity or parental right. Respondents urge us to hold, quite simply, that when otherwise prohibitable conduct is accompanied by religious convictions, not only the convictions but the conduct itself must be free from governmental regulation. We have never held that, and decline to do so now. There [is] no contention that Oregon's drug law represents an attempt to regulate religious beliefs, the communication of religious beliefs, or the raising of one's children in those beliefs....

Respondents argue that even though exemption from generally applicable criminal laws need not automatically be extended to religiously motivated actors, at least the claim for a religious exemption must be evaluated under the balancing test set forth in *Sherbert v. Verner*. Under the *Sherbert* test, governmental actions that substantially burden a religious practice must be justified by a compelling governmental interest.... Applying that test we have, on three occasions, invalidated state unemployment compensation rules that conditioned the availability of benefits upon an applicant's willingness to work under conditions forbidden by his religion. We have never invalidated any governmental action on the basis of the *Sherbert* test except the denial of unemployment compensation....

Even if we were inclined to breathe into *Sherbert* some life beyond the unemployment compensation field, we would not apply it to require exemptions from a generally applicable criminal law....

We conclude today that the sounder approach, and the approach in accord with the vast majority of our precedents, is to hold the test inapplicable to such challenges. The government's ability to enforce generally applicable prohibitions of socially harmful conduct, like its ability to carry out other aspects of public policy, "cannot depend on measuring the effects of a governmental action on a religious objector's spiritual development." *Lyng v. Northwest Indian Cemetery Association*, [485 U.S. 439 (1988)]. . . .

Values that are protected against government interference through enshrinement in the Bill of Rights are not thereby banished from the political process. Just as a society that believes in the negative protection accorded to the press by the First Amendment is likely to enact laws that affirmatively foster the dissemination of the printed word, so also a society that believes in the negative protection accorded to religious belief can be expected to be solicitous of that value in its legislation as well. It is therefore not surprising that a number of States have made an exception to their drug laws for sacramental peyote use. But to say that a nondiscriminatory religious-practice exemption is permitted, or even that it is desirable, is not to say that it is constitutionally required, and that the appropriate occasions for its creation can be discerned by the courts. It may fairly be said that leaving accommodation to the political process will place at a relative disadvantage those religious practices that are not widely engaged in; but that unavoidable consequence of democratic government must be preferred to a system in which each conscience is a law unto itself or in which judges weigh the social importance of all laws against the centrality of all religious beliefs.

Because respondents' ingestion of peyote was prohibited under Oregon law, and because that prohibition is constitutional, Oregon may, consistent with the Free Exercise Clause, deny respondents unemployment compensation when their dismissal results from use of the drug. The decision of the Oregon Supreme Court is accordingly reversed.

It is so ordered.

Justice O'CONNOR, with whom Justices BRENNAN, MARSHALL, and BLACKMUN join as to Parts I and II, concurring in the judgment.

. . . [T]oday's holding dramatically departs from well-settled First Amendment jurisprudence, appears unnecessary to resolve the question presented, and is incompatible with our Nation's fundamental commitment to individual religious liberty. . . .

. . . The compelling interest test effectuates the First Amendment's command that religious liberty is an independent liberty, that it occupies a preferred position, and that the Court will not permit encroachments upon this liberty, whether direct or indirect, unless required by clear and compelling governmental interests "of the highest order." . . .

I would therefore adhere to our established free exercise jurisprudence and hold that the State in this case has a compelling interest in regulating peyote use by its citizens and that accommodating respondents' religiously motivated conduct "will unduly interfere with fulfillment of the governmental interest."

Justice BLACKMUN, with whom Justices BRENNAN and MARSHALL join, dissenting.

This Court over the years painstakingly has developed a consistent and exacting standard to test the constitutionality of a state statute that burdens the free exercise of religion. Such a statute may stand only if the law in general, and the State's refusal to allow a religious exemption in particular, are justified by a compelling interest that cannot be served by less restrictive means.

Until today, I thought this was a settled and inviolate principle of this Court's First Amendment jurisprudence. The majority, however, perfunctorily dismisses it as a "constitutional anomaly." . . .

The American Indian Religious Freedom Act, in itself, may not create rights enforceable against government action restricting religious freedom, but this Court must scrupulously apply its free exercise analysis to the religious claims of Native Americans, however unorthodox they may be. Otherwise, both the First Amendment and the stated policy of Congress will offer to Native Americans merely an unfulfilled and hollow promise.

For these reasons, I conclude that Oregon's interest in enforcing its drug laws against religious use of peyote is not sufficiently compelling to outweigh respondents' right to the free exercise of their religion. Since the State could not constitutionally enforce its criminal prohibition against respondents, the interests underlying the State's drug laws cannot justify its denial of unemployment benefits. Absent such justification, the State's regulatory interest in denying benefits for religiously motivated "misconduct," is indistinguishable from the state interests this Court has rejected. . . . The State of Oregon cannot, consistently with the Free Exercise Clause, deny respondents unemployment benefits.

I dissent.

Rulings in Context

The Free Exercise of Religion

Sherbert v. Verner, 374 U.S. 398 (1963)   7-2

The Court ruled that, under strict scrutiny analysis (see Box 4.1), a woman must be allowed unemployment compensation when she refused to work on a Saturday because she was a Seventh-Day Adventist (for whom Saturday is always the Sabbath). The Court held that the Free Exercise Clause mandated the state to accommodate her religious observance as a matter of strict scrutiny.

Wisconsin v. Yoder, 406 U.S. 208 (1972)   6½-1½

The Court held that Amish people were exempt from compulsory school attendance because the government may accommodate their religious requirements without endorsing religion or entering into an excessive entanglement with it. The Court held that the Amish might home school their children and not face charges of violating mandatory school attendance laws.

Church of the Lukumi Babalu Aye, Inc. v. Hialeah,
508 U.S. 520 (1993)   9-0

The Court, unlike its ruling in *Employment Division v. Smith,* 494 U.S. 872 (1990) (Case 3.5), struck down a Hialeah, Florida, law banning animal sacrifices for health and sanitary reasons, although it, like the law at issue in *Smith,* was "generally applicable." The Court ruled that the Hialeah law was specially designed to force the followers of Santeria, whose religious ceremony sometimes involves animal sacrifice, to leave the city.

City of Boerne v. Flores, 521 U.S. 507 (1997)   6-3

In light of the 1990 *Smith* decision (Case 3.7) allowing rational basis analysis in free exercise cases, Congress passed the Religious Freedom Restoration Act of 1993. The act was designed to reestablish the strict scrutiny test set forth in *Sherbert v. Verner.* In light of the act, the leaders of a Catholic church in Boerne, Texas, sought to overcome design restrictions imposed on its building, which was in a historic preservation district, by arguing that the town had to show a compelling reason why it could not expand and renovate its building. The Court struck down the act as exceeding Congress's powers, ruling that Congress's future enforcement of Section 5 of the Fourteenth Amendment must meet a standard of "congruence and proportionality" before it may act.

The Establishment Clause: Cases

The following cases consider the Establishment Clause. The first focuses on whether public funding of transportation costs for children attending parochial school crosses the line separating religion and state. The second challenges the Court to determine when it is permissible to display the Ten Commandments on public property.

Case 3.8

Everson v. Board of Education of Ewing Township
330 U.S. 1, 67 S.Ct. 504 (1947)

A New Jersey statute allowed all local school districts to make their own regulations concerning the busing of children. The Board of Education of the Ewing Township provided bus transportation for all children, whether attending public or private school, in order for them to arrive safely at school. Most of the private schools there were Catholic parochial schools. A state court judge ended the program after a parent, Arch Everson, challenged the public funding of busing school children to religious schools. He based his argument on the Establishment Clause of the First Amendment. The New Jersey Court of Errors and Appeals reversed that decision, ruling that the program conflicted with neither the New Jersey constitution nor the U.S. Constitution. The Supreme Court granted review when Everson appealed.

The Court upheld the Court of Errors and Appeals' ruling by a five to four vote with Justice Black writing the Court's opinion. Justice Rutledge filed a dissent.

Justice BLACK delivered the opinion of the Court.

The New Jersey statute is challenged as a "law respecting an establishment of religion." . . . A large proportion of the early settlers of this country came here from Europe to escape the bondage of laws which compelled them to support and attend government favored churches. The centuries immediately before and contemporaneous with the colonization of America had been filled with turmoil, civil strife, and persecutions, generated in large part by established sects determined to maintain their absolute political and religious supremacy. With the power of government supporting them, at various times and places, Catholics had persecuted Protestants, Protestants had persecuted Catholics, Protestant sects had persecuted other Protestant sects, Catholics of one shade of belief had persecuted Catholics of another shade of belief, and all of these had from time to time persecuted Jews. . . .

These practices of the old world were transplanted to and began to thrive in the soil of the new America. The very charters granted by the English Crown to the individuals and companies designated to make the laws which would control the destinies of the colonials authorized these individuals and companies to erect religious establishments which all, whether believers or non-believers, would be required to support and attend. . . . These practices became so commonplace as to shock the freedom-loving colonials into a feeling of abhorrence. The imposition of taxes to pay ministers' salaries and to build and maintain churches and church property aroused their indignation. It was these feelings which found expression in the First Amendment. . . .

This Court has previously recognized that the provisions of the First Amendment, in the drafting and adoption of which Madison and Jefferson played such leading roles, had the same objective and were intended to provide the same protection against governmental intrusion on religious liberty as the[ir] Virginia statute. Prior to the adoption of the Fourteenth Amendment, the First Amendment did not apply as a restraint against the states. Most of them did soon provide similar constitutional protections for religious liberty. But some states persisted for about half a century in imposing restraints upon the free exercise of religion and in discriminating against particular religious groups. In recent years, so far as the provision against the establishment of a religion is concerned, the question has most frequently arisen in connection with proposed state aid to church schools and efforts to carry on religious teachings in the public schools in accordance with the tenets of a particular sect. Some churches have either sought or accepted state financial support for their schools. Here again the efforts to obtain state aid or acceptance of it have not been limited to any one particular faith. The state courts, in the main, have remained faithful to the language of their own constitutional provisions designed to protect religious freedom and to separate religious and governments. Their decisions, however, show the difficulty in drawing the line between tax legislation which provides funds for the welfare of the general public and that which is designed to support institutions which teach religion. . . .

The "establishment of religion" clause of the First Amendment means at least this: Neither a state nor the Federal Government can set up a church. Neither can pass laws which aid one religion, aid all religions, or prefer one religion over another. Neither can force nor influence a person to go to or to remain away from church against his will or force him to profess a belief or disbelief in any religion. No person can be punished for entertaining or professing religious beliefs or disbeliefs, for church attendance or non-attendance. No tax in any amount, large or small, can be levied to support any religious activities or institutions, whatever they may be called, or whatever from they may adopt to teach or practice religion. Neither a state nor the Federal Government can, openly or secretly, participate in the affairs of any religious organizations or groups and vice versa. In the words of Jefferson, the clause against establishment of religion by law was intended to erect "a wall of separation between Church and State."

We must consider the New Jersey statute in accordance with the foregoing limitations imposed by the First Amendment. But we must not strike that state statute down if it is within the state's constitutional power even though it approaches the verge of that power. New Jersey cannot consistently with the "establishment of religion" clause of the First Amendment contribute tax-raised funds to the support of an institution which teaches the tenets and faith of any church. On the other hand, other language of the amendment commands that New Jersey cannot hamper its citizens in the free exercise of their own religion. Consequently, it cannot exclude individual Catholics, Lutherans, Mohammedans, Baptists, Jews, Methodists, Non-believers, Presbyterians, or the members of any other faith, because of their faith, or lack of it, from receiving the benefits of public welfare legislation. While we do not mean to intimate that a state could not provide transportation only to children attending public schools, we must be careful, in protecting the citizens of New Jersey against state-established churches, to be sure that we do not inadvertently prohibit New Jersey from extending its general State law benefits to all its citizens without regard to their religious belief.

Measured by these standards, we cannot say that the First Amendment prohibits New Jersey from spending tax-raised funds to pay the bus fares of parochial school pupils as a part of a general program under which it pays the fares of pupils attending public and other schools. It is undoubtedly true that children are helped to get to church schools. There is even a possibility that some of the children might not be sent to the church schools if the parents were compelled to pay their children's bus fares out of their own pockets when transportation to a public school would have been paid for by the State. The same possibility exists where the state requires a local transit company to provide reduced fares to school children including those attending parochial schools, or where a municipally owned transportation system undertakes to carry all school children free of charge. Moreover, state-paid policemen, detailed to protect children going to and from church schools from the very real hazards of traffic, would serve much the same purpose and accomplish much the same result as state provisions intended to guarantee free transportation of a kind which the state deems to be best for the school children's welfare. And parents might refuse to risk their children to the serious danger of traffic accidents going to and from parochial schools, the approaches to which were not protected by policemen. Similarly, parents might be reluctant to permit their children to attend schools which the state had cut off from such general government services as ordinary police and fire protection, connections for sewage disposal, public highways and sidewalks. Of course, cutting off church schools from these services, so separate and so indisputably marked off from the religious function, would make it far more difficult for the schools to operate. But such is obviously not the purpose of the First Amendment. That Amendment requires the state to be a neutral in its relations with groups of religious believers and non-believers; it does not require the state to be their adversary. State power is no more to be used so as to handicap religions, than it is to favor them. . . .

The First Amendment has erected a wall between church and state. That wall must be kept high and impregnable. We could not approve the slightest breach. New Jersey has not breached it here.

Justice RUTLEDGE, dissenting.

The Amendment's purpose was not to strike merely at the official establishment of a single sect, creed or religion, outlawing only a formal relation such as had prevailed in England and some of the colonies. Necessarily it was to uproot all such relationships. But the object was broader than separating church and state in this narrow sense. It was to create a complete and permanent separation of the spheres of religious activity and civil authority by comprehensively forbidding every form of public aid or support for religion. In proof the Amendment's wording and history unite with this Court's consistent utterances whenever attention has been fixed directly upon the question. . . .

No one conscious of religious values can by unsympathetic toward the burden which our constitutional separation puts on parents who desire religious instruction mixed with secular for their children. They pay taxes for others' children's education, at the same time the added cost of instruction for their own. Nor can one happily see benefits denied to children which others receive, because in conscience they or their parents for them desire a different kind of training others do not demand. . . .

But it does not make the state unneutral to withhold what the Constitution forbids it to give. On the contrary it is only by observing the prohibition rigidly that the state can maintain its neutrality and avoid partisanship in the dissensions inevitable when sect opposes sect over demands for public moneys to further religious education, teaching or training in any form or degree, directly or indirectly. . . .

Now as in Madison's day it is one of principle, to keep separate the separate spheres as the First Amendment drew them; to prevent the first experiment upon our liberties; and to keep the question from becoming entangled in corrosive precedents. We should not be less strict to keep strong and untarnished the one side of the shield of religious freedom than we have been of the other. The judgment should be reversed.

Case 3.9

McCreary v. ACLU
545 U.S. 844, 125 S.Ct. 2772 (2005)

This case, along with one from Texas, announced on the last day of the 2004 term, addressed whether the placement of the Ten Commandments on public property violated the Establishment Clause of the First Amendment.

In the Texas case, *Van Orden v. Perry*, 125 S.Ct. 2854 (2005), the Court ruled five to four in an opinion by the Chief Justice that the religious message of the display of the Ten Commandments at the Texas State Capitol was diluted when it appeared among twenty-one historical markers and seventeen monuments. Specifically, the Court held that while the Commandments are religious, they have an undeniable historical meaning. Simply having religious content or promoting a message consistent with a religious doctrine does not run afoul of the Establishment Clause.

In Kentucky, two county executives in 1999 erected displays of the Ten Commandments in county courthouses. The American Civil Liberties Union asked a federal district court to enjoin the displays, after which both county councils adopted nearly identical resolutions calling for a more extensive exhibit meant to show that the Commandments were Kentucky's "precedent legal code." The resolutions noted several grounds for taking that position, including the state legislature's acknowledgment of Christ as the "Prince of Ethics." The displays around the Commandments were then modified to include eight smaller historical documents containing religious references as their sole common element. Included in these was the Declaration of Independence "endowed by their Creator" passage.

The district court entered a preliminary injunction, citing the test from *Lemon v. Kurtzman*, 403 U.S. 602 (1971), that the original display lacked any secular purpose because the Commandments were a distinctly religious document and that the second version lacked such a purpose because the counties narrowly tailored their selection of foundational documents to those specifically referring to Christianity.

After changing counsel, the counties revised the exhibits a third time. No new resolution authorized the new exhibits, nor did the counties repeal the resolutions that preceded the second one. The new posting, entitled "The Foundations of American Law and Government Display," consisted of nine framed documents of equal size. One set out the Commandments explicitly identified as the "King James Version," quoted them at greater length, and explained that they had profoundly influenced the formation of Western legal thought and this Nation. Included with the Commandments were framed copies of the Star Spangled Banner's lyrics and the Declaration of Independence, accompanied by statements about their historical and legal significance.

On the ACLU's motion, the district court ruled that this third display was unconstitutional despite the counties' professed intent to show that the Commandments were part of the foundation of "American Law and Government" and to educate county citizens about the documents. The court held that the counties had a religious, rather than secular, purpose when it proclaimed that the Commandments were the legal and historical foundation of American law. Under *Stone v. Graham*, 449 U.S. 39 (1980), the court said, this violated the Establishment Clause because *Stone* had overturned a Kentucky law requiring the display of the Ten Commandments in all public school classrooms. The court found that the counties' asserted educational goals crumbled in light of this litigation's history. Affirming, the Sixth Circuit of the United States Court of Appeals stressed that, under *Stone*, displaying the Commandments bespeaks a religious object unless they are integrated with a secular message. The court saw no integration here because of a lack of a demonstrated analytical or historical connection between the Commandments and the other documents.

The counties appealed to the Supreme Court, which granted review and upheld the lower court's ruling by a five to four vote. Justice David H. Souter delivered the opinion of the Court, in which Justices

John Paul Stevens, Sandra Day O'Connor, Ruth Bader Ginsburg, and Stephen G. Breyer joined. Justice O'Connor also filed a concurring opinion. Justice Antonin Scalia filed a dissenting opinion, in which Chief Justice William H. Rehnquist and Clarence Thomas joined, and in which Justice Anthony Kennedy joined in part.

Justice SOUTER delivered the opinion of the Court.

. . . Twenty-five years ago in a case prompted by posting the Ten Commandments in Kentucky's public schools, this Court recognized that the Commandments "are undeniably a sacred text in the Jewish and Christian faiths" and held that their display in public classrooms violated the First Amendment's bar against establishment of religion. *Stone v. Graham*, 449 U.S. 39 (1980). *Stone* found a predominantly religious purpose in the government's posting of the Commandments, given their prominence as " 'an instrument of religion.' " The Counties ask for a different approach here by arguing that official purpose is unknowable and the search for it inherently vain. In the alternative, the Counties would avoid the District Court's conclusion by having us limit the scope of the purpose enquiry so severely that any trivial rationalization would suffice, under a standard oblivious to the history of religious government action like the progression of exhibits in this case.

Ever since *Lemon v. Kurtzman* [403 U.S. 602 (1971)] summarized the three familiar considerations for evaluating Establishment Clause claims, looking to whether government action has "a secular legislative purpose" has been a common, albeit seldom dispositive, element of our cases. Though we have found government action motivated by an illegitimate purpose only four times since *Lemon*, and "the secular purpose requirement alone may rarely be determinative . . . it nevertheless serves an important function." *Wallace v. Jaffree*, 472 U.S. 38 (1985) (O'Connor, J., concurring in judgment).

The touchstone for our analysis is the principle that the "First Amendment mandates governmental neutrality between religion and religion, and between religion and nonreligion." *Epperson v. Arkansas*, 393 U.S. 97 (1968); *Everson v. Board of Ed. of Ewing*, 330 U.S. 1 (1947); *Wallace v. Jaffree*. When the government acts with the ostensible and predominant purpose of advancing religion, it violates that central Establishment Clause value of official religious neutrality, there being no neutrality when the government's ostensible object is to take sides. Manifesting a purpose to favor one faith over another, or adherence to religion generally, clashes with the "understanding, reached . . . after decades of religious war, that liberty and social stability demand a religious tolerance that respects the religious views of all citizens." *Zelman v.*

Simmons-Harris, 536 U.S. 639 (2002) (Breyer, J., dissenting). By showing a purpose to favor religion, the government "sends the . . . message to . . . nonadherents 'that they are outsiders, not full members of the political community, and an accompanying message to adherents that they are insiders, favored members. . . . ' " *Santa Fe Independent School Dist. v. Doe*, 530 U.S. 290 (2000). . . .

Despite the intuitive importance of official purpose to the realization of Establishment Clause values, the Counties ask us to abandon *Lemon*'s purpose test, or at least to truncate any enquiry into purpose here. Their first argument is that the very consideration of purpose is deceptive: according to them, true "purpose" is unknowable, and its search merely an excuse for courts to act selectively and unpredictably in picking out evidence of subjective intent. The assertions are as seismic as they are unconvincing. . . .

. . . [S]crutinizing purpose does make practical sense, as in Establishment Clause analysis, where an understanding of official objective emerges from readily discoverable fact, without any judicial psychoanalysis of a drafter's heart of hearts. The eyes that look to purpose belong to an " 'objective observer,' " one who takes account of the traditional external signs that show up in the " 'text, legislative history, and implementation of the statute,' " or comparable official act. There is, then, nothing hinting at an unpredictable or disingenuous exercise when a court enquires into purpose after a claim is raised under the Establishment Clause.

The cases with findings of a predominantly religious purpose point to the straightforward nature of the test. In *Wallace*, for example, we inferred purpose from a change of wording from an earlier statute to a later one, each dealing with prayer in schools. . . . ; in *Stone*, the Court held that the "posting of religious texts on the wall served no . . . educational function," and found that if "the posted copies of the Ten Commandments [were] to have any effect at all, it [would] be to induce the schoolchildren to read, meditate upon, perhaps to venerate and obey, the Commandments." In each case, the government's action was held unconstitutional only because openly available data supported a common-sense conclusion that a religious objective permeated the government's action. . . .

After declining the invitation to abandon concern with purpose wholesale, we also have to avoid the Counties' alternative tack of trivializing the enquiry into it. The Counties would read the cases as if the purpose enquiry were so naive that any transparent claim to secularity would satisfy it, and they would cut context out of the enquiry, to the point of ignoring history, no matter what bearing it actually had on the significance of current circumstances. There is no precedent for the Counties' arguments, or reason supporting them. . . .

We take *Stone* as the initial legal benchmark, our only case dealing with the constitutionality of displaying the Commandments. *Stone* recognized that the Commandments are an "instrument of religion" and that, at least on the facts before it, the display of their text could presumptively be understood as meant to advance religion: although state law specifically required their posting in public school classrooms, their isolated exhibition did not leave room even for an argument that secular education explained their being there. But *Stone* did not purport to decide the constitutionality of every possible way the Commandments might be set out by the government, and under the Establishment Clause detail is key. Hence, we look to the record of evidence showing the progression leading up to the third display of the Commandments.

The display rejected in *Stone* had two obvious similarities to the first one in the sequence here: both set out a text of the Commandments as distinct from any traditionally symbolic representation, and each stood alone, not part of an arguably secular display. *Stone* stressed the significance of integrating the Commandments into a secular scheme to forestall the broadcast of an otherwise clearly religious message, and for good reason, the Commandments being a central point of reference in the religious and moral history of Jews and Christians. They proclaim the existence of a monotheistic god (no other gods). They regulate details of religious obligation (no graven images, no sabbath breaking, no vain oath swearing). And they unmistakably rest even the universally accepted prohibitions (as against murder, theft, and the like) on the sanction of the divinity proclaimed at the beginning of the text. Displaying that text is thus different from a symbolic depiction, like tablets with 10 roman numerals, which could be seen as alluding to a general notion of law, not a sectarian conception of faith. Where the text is set out, the insistence of the religious message is hard to avoid in the absence of a context plausibly suggesting a message going beyond an excuse to promote the religious point of view. The display in *Stone* had no context that might have indicated an object beyond the religious character of the text, and the Counties' solo exhibit here did nothing more to counter the sectarian implication than the postings at issue in *Stone*. Actually, the posting by the Counties lacked even the *Stone* display's implausible disclaimer that the Commandments were set out to show their effect on the civil law. What is more, at the ceremony for posting the framed Commandments in Pulaski County, the county executive was accompanied by his pastor, who testified to the certainty of the existence of God. The reasonable observer could only think that the Counties meant to emphasize and celebrate the Commandments' religious message.

This is not to deny that the Commandments have had influence on civil or secular law; a major text of a majority religion is bound to be felt. The point is simply that the original text viewed in its entirety is an unmistakably religious statement dealing with religious obligations and with morality subject to religious sanction. When the government initiates an effort to place this statement alone in public view, a religious object is unmistakable. . . .

. . . The display's unstinting focus was on religious passages, showing that the Counties were posting the Commandments precisely because of their sectarian content. That demonstration of the government's objective was enhanced by serial religious references and the accompanying resolution's claim about the embodiment of ethics in Christ. Together, the display and resolution presented an indisputable, and undisputed, showing of an impermissible purpose.

Today, the Counties make no attempt to defend their undeniable objective. . .

The importance of neutrality as an interpretive guide is no less true now than it was when the Court broached the principle in *Everson v. Board of Ed. of Ewing*, 330 U.S. 1 (1947), and a word needs to be said about the different view taken in today's dissent. We all agree, of course, on the need for some interpretative help. The First Amendment contains no textual definition of "establishment," and the term is certainly not self-defining. No one contends that the prohibition of establishment stops at a designation of a national church, but nothing in the text says just how much more it covers. . . .

. . . [T]he dissent's argument for the original understanding is flawed from the outset by its failure to consider the full range of evidence showing what the Framers believed. The dissent is certainly correct in putting forward evidence that some of the Framers thought some endorsement of religion was compatible with the establishment ban; the dissent quotes the first President as stating that "national morality [cannot] prevail in exclusion of religious principle," for example, and it cites his first Thanksgiving proclamation giving thanks to God. Surely if expressions like these from Washington and his contemporaries were all we had to go on, there would be a good case that the neutrality principle has the effect of broadening the ban on establishment beyond the Framers' understanding of it (although there would, of course, still be the question of whether the historical case could overcome some 60 years of precedent taking neutrality as its guiding principle).

But the fact is that we do have more to go on, for there is also evidence supporting the proposition that the Framers intended the Establishment Clause to require governmental neutrality in matters of religion, including neutrality in statements acknowledging religion. The very language of the Establishment Clause represented a significant departure from early drafts that merely prohibited a single national religion, and, the final language instead "extended [the] prohibition to state support for 'religion' in general." See *Lee v. Weisman*,

505 U.S. 577 (1992) (Souter, J., concurring) (tracing development of language). . . .

Historical evidence thus supports no solid argument for changing course (whatever force the argument might have when directed at the existing precedent), whereas public discourse at the present time certainly raises no doubt about the value of the interpretative approach invoked for 60 years now. We are centuries away from the St. Bartholomew's Day massacre and the treatment of heretics in early Massachusetts, but the divisiveness of religion in current public life is inescapable. This is no time to deny the prudence of understanding the Establishment Clause to require the Government to stay neutral on religious belief, which is reserved for the conscience of the individual.

Given the ample support for the District Court's finding of a predominantly religious purpose behind the Counties' third display, we affirm the Sixth Circuit in upholding the preliminary injunction. It is so ordered.

Justice SCALIA, with whom the Chief Justice [REHNQUIST] and Justice THOMAS join, and with whom Justice KENNEDY joins in part, dissenting.

I would uphold McCreary County and Pulaski County, Kentucky's (hereinafter Counties) displays of the Ten Commandments. I shall discuss first, why the Court's oft repeated assertion that the government cannot favor religious practice is false; second, why today's opinion extends the scope of that falsehood even beyond prior cases; and third, why even on the basis of the Court's false assumptions the judgment here is wrong.

On September 11, 2001, I was attending in Rome, Italy, an international conference of judges and lawyers, principally from Europe and the United States. That night and the next morning virtually all of the participants watched, in their hotel rooms, the address to the Nation by the President of the United States concerning the murderous attacks upon the Twin Towers and the Pentagon, in which thousands of Americans had been killed. The address ended, as Presidential addresses often do, with the prayer "God bless America." The next afternoon I was approached by one of the judges from a European country, who, after extending his profound condolences for my country's loss, sadly observed, "How I wish that the Head of State of my country, at a similar time of national tragedy and distress, could conclude his address 'God bless ————.' It is of course absolutely forbidden."

That is one model of the relationship between church and state—a model spread across Europe by the armies of Napoleon, and reflected in the Constitution of France, which begins "France is [a] . . . secular . . . Republic." Religion is to be strictly excluded from the public forum. This is not, and never was, the model adopted by America. George Washington added to the form of Presidential oath prescribed by Art. II, §1, cl. 8, of the Constitution, the concluding words "so help me God." The Supreme Court under John Marshall opened its sessions with the prayer, "God save the United States and this Honorable Court." The First Congress instituted the practice of beginning its legislative sessions with a prayer. The same week that Congress submitted the Establishment Clause as part of the Bill of Rights for ratification by the States, it enacted legislation providing for paid chaplains in the House and Senate. The day after the First Amendment was proposed, the same Congress that had proposed it requested the President to proclaim "a day of public thanksgiving and prayer, to be observed, by acknowledging, with grateful hearts, the many and signal favours of Almighty God." President Washington offered the first Thanksgiving Proclamation shortly thereafter, devoting November 26, 1789, on behalf of the American people "'to the service of that great and glorious Being who is the beneficent author of all the good that is, that was, or that will be,'" thus beginning a tradition of offering gratitude to God that continues today. The same Congress also reenacted the Northwest Territory Ordinance of 1787, of which provided: "Religion, morality, and knowledge, being necessary to good government and the happiness of mankind, schools and the means of education shall forever be encouraged." And of course the First Amendment itself accords religion (and no other manner of belief) special constitutional protection. . . .

With all of this reality (and much more) staring it in the face, how can the Court *possibly* assert that "'the First Amendment mandates governmental neutrality between . . . religion and nonreligion,'" and that "manifesting a purpose to favor . . . adherence to religion generally," is unconstitutional? Who says so? Surely not the words of the Constitution. Surely not the history and traditions that reflect our society's constant understanding of those words. Surely not even the current sense of our society, recently reflected in an Act of Congress adopted *unanimously* by the Senate and with only 5 nays in the House of Representatives, criticizing a Court of Appeals opinion that had held "under God" in the Pledge of Allegiance unconstitutional. Nothing stands behind the Court's assertion that governmental affirmation of the society's belief in God is unconstitutional except the Court's own say-so, citing as support only the unsubstantiated say-so of earlier Courts going back no farther than the mid-20th century. (*Lemon v. Kurtzman*, 403 U.S. 602 [1971]) And it is, moreover, a thoroughly discredited say-so. It is discredited, to begin with, because a majority of the Justices on the current Court (including at least one Member of today's majority) have, in separate opinions, repudiated the brain-spun "*Lemon* test" that embodies the supposed principle of neutrality between religion and irreligion. . . .

What distinguishes the rule of law from the dictatorship of a shifting Supreme Court majority is the absolutely indispensable requirement that judicial opinions be grounded in consistently applied principle. That is what prevents judges from ruling now this way, now that—thumbs up or thumbs down—as their personal preferences dictate. Today's opinion forthrightly (or actually, somewhat less than forthrightly) admits that it does not rest upon consistently applied principle. In a revealing footnote, the Court acknowledges that the "Establishment Clause doctrine" it purports to be applying "lacks the comfort of categorical absolutes." What the Court means by this lovely euphemism is that sometimes the Court chooses to decide cases on the principle that government cannot favor religion, and sometimes it does not. The footnote goes on to say that "in special instances we have found good reason" to dispense with the principle, but "no such reasons present themselves here." It does not identify all of those "special instances," much less identify the "good reason" for their existence.

I have cataloged elsewhere the variety of circumstances in which this Court—even *after* its embrace of *Lemon*'s stated prohibition of such behavior—has approved government action "undertaken with the specific intention of improving the position of religion," *Edwards v. Aguillard,* 482 U.S. 578 (1987) (Scalia, J., dissenting). Suffice it to say here that when the government relieves churches from the obligation to pay property taxes, when it allows students to absent themselves from public school to take religious classes, and when it exempts religious organizations from generally applicable prohibitions of religious discrimination, it surely means to bestow a benefit on religious practice—but we have approved it. See [*Corporation of Presiding Bishop of Church of Jesus Christ of Latter-day Saints v.*] *Amos,* [483 U.S. 327 (1987)], (exemption from federal prohibition of religious discrimination by employers); *Walz v. Tax Comm'n of City of New York,* 397 U.S. 664 (1970) (property tax exemption for church property); *Zorach* [*v. Clauson, 343 U.S. 306 (1952)*], (law permitting students to leave public school for the purpose of receiving religious education). Indeed, we have even approved (post-*Lemon*) government-led prayer to God. In *Marsh v. Chambers,* [463 U.S. 783 (1983)], the Court upheld the Nebraska State Legislature's practice of paying a chaplain to lead it in prayer at the opening of legislative sessions. The Court explained that "to invoke Divine guidance on a public body entrusted with making the laws is not . . . an 'establishment' of religion or a step toward establishment; it is simply a tolerable acknowledgment of beliefs widely held among the people of this country." (Why, one wonders, is not respect for the Ten Commandments a tolerable acknowledgment of beliefs widely held among the people of this country?). . . .

As bad as the *Lemon* test is, it is worse for the fact that, since its inception, its seemingly simple mandates have been manipulated to fit whatever result the Court aimed to achieve. Today's opinion is no different. In two respects it modifies *Lemon* to ratchet up the Court's hostility to religion. First, the Court justifies inquiry into legislative purpose, not as an end itself, but as a means to ascertain the appearance of the government action to an "'objective observer.'" Because in the Court's view the true danger to be guarded against is that the objective observer would feel like an "outsider" or "not a full member of the political community," its inquiry focuses not on the *actual purpose* of government action, but the "purpose apparent from government action." Under this approach, even if a government could show that its actual purpose was not to advance religion, it would presumably violate the Constitution as long as the Court's objective observer would think otherwise. . . .

Acknowledgment of the contribution that religion has made to our Nation's legal and governmental heritage partakes of a centuries-old tradition. Members of this Court have themselves often detailed the degree to which religious belief pervaded the National Government during the founding era. Display of the Ten Commandments is well within the mainstream of this practice of acknowledgment. Federal, State, and local governments across the Nation have engaged in such display. The Supreme Court Building itself includes depictions of Moses with the Ten Commandments in the Courtroom and on the east pediment of the building, and symbols of the Ten Commandments "adorn the metal gates lining the north and south sides of the Courtroom as well as the doors leading into the Courtroom." Similar depictions of the Decalogue appear on public buildings and monuments throughout our Nation's Capital. The frequency of these displays testifies to the popular understanding that the Ten Commandments are a foundation of the rule of law, and a symbol of the role that religion played, and continues to play, in our system of government. . . .

For the foregoing reasons, I would reverse the judgment of the Court of Appeals.

Rulings in Context

The Establishment Clause

Engel v. Vitale, 370 U.S. 421 (1962)   6-1
> The Court declared that a prayer drafted by the Regents of the State of New York that children were to recite aloud each school day violated the Establishment Clause.

Lemon v. Kurtzman, 403 U.S. 602 (1971)   8-0
> The Court, in rejecting direct aid to parochial schools, including teacher

salary supplements and textbooks used in secular subjects, designed a test to examine all future cases involving government aid to religious schools. The *Lemon* test, which over time failed to satisfy the justices' hopes and needs, consisted of three prongs: the government program must have a secular legislative purpose; it must not advance or inhibit religion; and it must not foster an excessive entanglement of religion.

Zobrest v. Catalina Foothills School District, 509 U.S. 1 (1993)   5-4
The Court held that the Establishment Clause was not violated when a school district provided a sign language interpreter for a deaf student attending a parochial school. The Court reasoned that the student, not the school, was the beneficiary, so that the line between church and state had not been crossed.

Agostini v. Felton, 521 U.S. 203 (1997)   5-4
The Court overturned *Aguilar v. Felton,* 473 U.S. 402 (1985) in holding that public schools may send teachers into parochial schools to provide remedial education under Title I of the Elementary and Secondary Education Act of 1965. The Court, with Justice O'Connor writing for a bare majority, held that this practice did not constitute an endorsement of religion.

Santa Fe Independent School District v. Doe, 530 U.S. 290 (2000)   6-3
The Court reaffirmed its rulings concerning prayer in public schools, by holding that state-sponsored school prayer before high school football games violated the Establishment Clause.

Zelman v. Simmons-Harris, 536 U.S. 639 (2002)   5-4
The Court ruled that parents may constitutionally use school vouchers, paid for by the Ohio government, for their children to attend parochial schools. Because the funds went directly to the parents of the children, the Court held, and not to the schools, it was a matter of the parents' free school choice. Thus, the program was therefore neutral and there was no Establishment Clause violation.

Locke v. Davey, 540 U.S. 712 (2004)   7-2
The Court held, with the Chief Justice writing the majority opinion, that Washington State's denial of a scholarship for a student pursuing a devotional theology degree, despite its otherwise inclusive scholarship aid program, does not violate the Free Exercise Clause. The Court rejected the contention of Joshua Davey, who was denied a state scholarship to study for the ministry, that, under *Church of the Lukumi Babalu Aye v. Hialeah,* 508 U.S. 520 (1993), the program was presumptively unconstitutional because it was not facially neutral with respect to religion.

CHAPTER **4**

Equal Protection of the Laws

*In order to get beyond racism, we must first
take account of race.*
—Justice Harry A. Blackmun, dissenting in
part and concurring in part in *Regents of the
University of California v. Bakke,*
438 U.S. 265 (1978)

Ratified in 1868, the Fourteenth Amendment was one of three post-Civil
War amendments. The three were designed to address many of the
causes of that horrible conflict. The Thirteenth (1865) formally ended
the institution of slavery while the Fifteenth (1870) guaranteed to all
people the right to vote no matter their race or previous condition of
servitude. The Fourteenth was the most far-reaching: it bound the states
to three legal concepts, where two of them had until this time bound
only the federal government.

    First, the Privileges and Immunities Clause recognized the dual citi-
zenship of the American people: they were at once citizens of the state
in which they were residing and citizens of the United States; the Clause
thus guaranteed that they would possess in their states the same privileges and immunities that all citizens of the United States enjoyed. Second, the Due Process Clause guaranteed to the citizens of each state due
process of law, whenever they might be accused of a state crime; this

provision mirrored the Fifth Amendment's Due Process Clause, which protected citizens' rights whenever they might be accused of violating federal law.

Moreover, the Fourteenth Amendment added a third protection, notably the equal protection of the laws, as a means to ensure that the newly freed black slaves would be treated like everyone else in American courts.

The Meaning and Intention of the Fourteenth Amendment

Scholars, jurists, and journalists have much debated the intentions of the members of Congress when they launched these amendments. One thing is clear: their history has proven to be rocky and controversial. Today, courts use the Fourteenth Amendment, in particular its Equal Protection Clause, to review matters involving discrimination and affirmative action. Race is the category judges most closely watch over, but other categories like religion, gender, and national origin also come under judges' scrutiny (see Box 4.1, Three Judicial Tests For Deciding Equal Protection and Fundamental Rights Cases).

From a purely historical perspective, the post-Civil War amendments overturned the Court's infamous 1857 *Dred Scott* ruling. In this case Chief Justice Roger Brooke Taney declared that slaves were the property of their masters in ways similar to their wagons and donkeys (*Dred Scott v. Sandford*, 60 U.S. 393).

While the Fourteenth Amendment for the first time wrote the concept of equality into the Constitution, it really addressed only the equal protection of the *laws*, not *social* equality. It would take another hundred years for the Court to sort out the challenges raised by discrimination based on race and integration of black citizens into society. Many white Americans—and these were not exclusively Southerners—took for granted that a segregated way of life was not only natural or traditional, but was also founded on strongly held religious beliefs.

It is clear that Congress intended the amendment to ensure that all people would enjoy the benefits of equality before the law, not that people would be subjected to severe and harsh punishment or held liable in a civil suit just because of their race. Human beings were, in short, to be treated the same before the law because justice demanded the principle of legal equality.

It is also clear that in the first years after the Civil War the beneficiaries of all three amendments were the newly freed black slaves. The Court's decision in the 1873 *Slaughter-House Cases*, decided just five years after the amendment's ratification, was one of the first to interpret the Fourteenth Amendment. In that case, a group of white butchers sued when Louisiana, in an attempt to preserve the purity of the Mississippi

River, granted a monopoly to a single slaughterhouse. Writing for a bare five to four majority, Justice Samuel F. Miller stated that "the one pervading purpose . . . lying at the foundation of [all three post-Civil War amendments], and without which none of them would have been even suggested [is] . . . the freedom of the slave race, the security and firm establishment of that freedom, and the protection of the newly made freemen and citizens from the oppressions of those who had formerly exercised unlimited dominion over him." *Butchers' Benevolent Association v. Cresent City Livestock Landing & Slaughterhouse Co.*, 83 U.S. 36.

One major result of this case was that the Court did not use the Privileges and Immunities Clause again for over a hundred years. Justice Miller decided that the clause did not prohibit states from doing whatever they wished to its own citizens. It was not until 1999, in *Saenz v. Roe*, 526 U.S. 489, that the Court revived the Privileges and Immunities Clause, if only momentarily. The case involved whether California could limit state welfare payments to new residents at the rate paid by their previous state rather than that paid by California; the Court ruled it could not because the Privileges and Immunities Clause of the Fourteenth Amendment guaranteed the right to travel.

A few years after the *Slaughter-House Cases*, the Court was asked whether the Fourteenth Amendment protected a group of Chinese laundry operators in San Francisco after the city passed an ordinance that all laundries had to be housed in buildings made of stone or brick. As it happened, Chinese laundry operators typically housed their facilities in wooden structures. Despite the ordinance's emphasis on safety under the city's police power, the Court ruled the law a violation of the Fourteenth Amendment. For Justice Stanley Matthews, writing for the Court in 1886, the law was not merely designed for health and safety reasons, but really to run the Chinese owners out of business: "Though the law itself be fair on its face and impartial in appearance, yet, if it is applied and administered by a public authority with an evil eye and an unjust hand, so as practically to make unjust and illegal discrimination between persons in similar circumstances, material to their rights, the denial of equal justice is . . . within the prohibition of the Constitution." *Yick Wo v. Hopkins*, 118 U.S. 356.

Having said this, the Court at the time was unwilling to declare that the amendment meant that private discrimination in places of public accommodation like restaurants, hotels, theaters, schools, cemeteries, transportation facilities were now to accommodate all people, no matter their race or color. Despite the Court's extraordinary image of a law that is administered with "an evil eye and an unjust hand," it ruled three years before *Yick Wo* that the Civil Rights Act of 1875 did not address "state action" because the law was directed at private preferences (*The Civil Rights Cases*, 109 U.S. 3). If an owner or operator of a store chose not to serve a black patron, the government may not interfere.

A hearty eight to one majority decided this case with Justice Joseph

P. Bradley, who was originally from New Jersey (and not a Southerner), writing the opinion for the Court. In casting the lone dissent, Justice John Marshall Harlan (I), a former Kentucky slave owner, argued that Section 5 of the Fourteenth Amendment had authorized Congress to enforce the amendment by passing appropriate legislation, and the public accommodations law achieved that goal. (He is often identified as John Marshall Harlan (I) because his grandson with the same name later served on the Court from 1955 until 1971.) Racial discrimination, he said, whether it was by state or private action, constituted "badges of slavery and servitude." He then made the statement, remarkably prescient for its time, that he believed "that no state . . . nor any corporation or individual wielding power . . . for the public benefit or the public convenience, can . . . discriminate against freemen or citizens, in their civil rights, because of their race."

Justice Harlan could hardly have made a stronger statement, although he outdid himself thirteen years later in his famous dissent in *Plessy v. Ferguson*, 163 U.S. 537 (Case 4.1). Here the Court held by a seven to one vote that Jim Crow laws were constitutional when it interpreted the Fourteenth Amendment's Equal Protection Clause as having the plain meaning that as long as public facilities were equal, the people could be kept in separate compartments or areas. Railway cars would separately accommodate white and black people who would also have access to separate drinking fountains. In fact, it was just as much a crime for a white person to sit in a railway car reserved exclusively for black people as it was for the reverse to happen. Dissenting, Justice Harlan famously argued that "our constitution is color-blind, and neither knows nor tolerates classes among citizens."

It was not until fifty-eight years later that the Court finally overturned *Plessy* to travel the long road to reinterpret the meaning of the Fourteenth Amendment in light of changing times and attitudes. Along with its 1954 landmark decision in *Brown v. Board of Education*, 347 U.S. 483, the Court revealed a new world of trying to come to grips with how public school integration was to take place (Case 4.2). Should schools be forced to open their doors to all children, no matter their race? Must public school authorities use buses to transport children to schools to ensure integration? These were the issues that so galvanized American society throughout the 1970s and 1980s.

Integration, Affirmative Action, and the Court

Segregation based on the law is known as *de jure* segregation. Under *Brown*, it was clearly a violation of the Fourteenth Amendment's Equal Protection Clause. But what of those instances when segregated schools were not based on the law, but resulted from the people's conscious choice to live where they wanted? If some black people wanted to live in a black community, one likely result would be that their schools would have mostly black children. The Court held open this possibility in 1971 when it ruled that school busing to achieve racial integration was permissible when segregation was state-imposed (*Swann v. Charlotte-Mecklenberg Board of Education*, 402 U.S. 1).

By the mid-1990s, however, the Court lifted court-ordered desegregation plans when it became clear that segregated schools no longer existed because they were required to do so by state or local law. When schools are segregated by race because people choose to live in certain areas, the government has no role to play. In 1995 in *Missouri v. Jenkins*, 515 U.S. 70, the Court signaled the end of desegregation enforcement by federal courts. Chief Justice William Rehnquist reasoned for a bare majority that the schools in Kansas City were segregated because of the choices individuals made about where they resided (*de facto* segregation) and not by any government action (*de jure* segregation).

In 2007, in the *Seattle School District*, the Court ruled by a bare majority that a student placement program that relied on race violated the Equal Protection Clause of the Fourteenth Amendment (Case 4.3). Chief Justice John Roberts noted that "the way to stop discrimination on the basis of race is to stop discriminating on the basis of race."

Even more difficult has been the Court's attempt to determine whether public institutions have gone too far to try to compensate for past discrimination. Beginning in the 1960s, the policy of the United States government was to take "affirmative action" to assist blacks in gaining access to public higher education, employment opportunities, and government contracts. Almost immediately, critics raged against affirmation action, calling it reverse discrimination or denoting it as set-aside or race preference programs.

These critics argued that affirmative action programs violated not only the Equal Protection Clause of the Fourteenth Amendment, but also Title VI of the Civil Rights Act of 1964 that prohibited racial discrimination generally. Often citing Justice Harlan's "color-blind constitution" argument, they argued that it was outrageous for government to say now that the only way racial and ethnic discrimination could be overcome was to discriminate against white people who were not directly responsible for past discrimination and its effects. Indeed, one longtime observer has called this outcome "the irony of affirmation action."

In 1978, Justice Lewis Powell wrote the opinion in the first affirmation action case the Court decided. The case concerned the medical school admissions program at a public institution, the University of California, Davis. In accepting 100 students each year, the school set aside

16 places for disadvantaged minority students whose grades or board scores were lower than the required minimum. In *Regents of the University of California v. Bakke*, 438 U.S. 265, Justice Powell held that the strict scrutiny test must be used when the Court evaluates the constitutionality of all affirmation programs (Box 4.1). This meant that the government had to demonstrate a "compelling" interest whenever it uses a race-based criterion because as a result of America's history of slavery and racial discrimination, race was a "suspect" class.

In the late 1980s and early 1990s, the Court dealt major blows to both state and federal affirmative action programs. With Justice O'Connor writing for the majority in these cases, the Court demanded, under strict scrutiny, that public authorities show explicitly with data and facts just how government had specifically discriminated in the past against various minority groups. Otherwise, affirmative action programs would not stand even if they supposedly remedied the historic effects of past discrimination.

Two cases concluded that at both the state and federal level, the Court must use the strict scrutiny test, as Justice Powell had in *Bakke*, to review the constitutionality of affirmative action programs: in 1989 *City of Richmond v. J. A. Croson*, 488 U.S. 469, pertained to the states, and six years later *Adarand Constructors, Inc. v. Pena*, 515 U.S. 200, to the federal government (Case 4.5). In both cases, the Court held that it was no longer enough to argue in a general way that the history of slavery and discrimination caused blacks to be held back in construction contract awards or employment opportunities.

For higher education, in the meantime, the argument shifted away from overcoming the effects of past discrimination to a desire to achieve a diverse student body. College and university officials argued that because the United States consisted of so many different kinds of people in a rapidly shrinking world of interdependence and globalism, their schools should reflect this in their student bodies, faculty, and staff. Statistics from the 2000 and 2010 Censuses in particular showed that America had become far more diverse than it ever was in the past. New immigrants to America and an increase in mixed marriages were creating a new society that one commentator now called "transracial America." Social science studies demon- strated that in academic settings, students exposed to people with different backgrounds than their own perform far better academically than those in racially and ethnically homogeneous environments.

In 2003, the Court dealt with two admissions programs involving the University of Michigan, finding one of them constitutionally sound, the other invalid. In the first case, *Gratz v. Bollinger*, 539 U.S. 244, the undergraduate college's admissions office used a "selection index" based on the number of points awarded to an applicant. These included, for the most part, test scores, grades, essays, letters of recommendation, and leadership positions in student organizations. It also reserved 40 points for other factors, including 20 for students coming from underrepresented minorities or economically disadvantaged groups. Writing for a six to three majority, Chief Justice William Rehnquist found that the award of 20 points for minorities constituted an unconstitutional quota under the Equal Protection Clause and Title VI.

In the second case, *Grutter v. Bollinger*, 539 U.S. 306, and decided the same day as *Gratz*, Justice Sandra Day O'Connor wrote for a five to four majority (Case 4.6). Here, however, unlike Chief Justice Rehnquist in *Gratz*, she ruled that the use of race for admission to the University's law school was merely one factor among several. Moreover, race was not counted differently or weighted any heavier than the other factors. She thus found the program was consistent with Powell's *Bakke* decision in that it did not violate either the Equal Protection Clause or Title VI. It was, she said, a program along the lines of the Harvard Plan approved by Justice Powell twenty-five years earlier in *Bakke*.

In fact, the Court had redefined affirmative action in higher education: it no longer encompassed race-preference programs (as in a quota system); it now embraced only race-conscious ones. As Justice O'Connor put it, race consciousness means that admissions offices may consider race and ethnicity a " 'plus' in a particular applicant's file."

In a 2013 case, it appeared that the Court would overturn all affirmative action programs in college and university admissions programs when it ruled on *Fisher v. University of Texas*. Instead, the Court vacated and remanded the case to the United States Court of Appeals for the Fifth Circuit to determine whether the University's race-conscious admissions program complied with the strict scrutiny test (see Box 4.1). For the moment, affirmative action remained intact in admissions programs because the United States Court of Appeals for the Fifth Circuit had upheld the Texas program. The case may well return to the Court at a later time. Meantime, the justices had another opportunity to rule on affirmative action admissions programs in its October Term 2013 in *Schuette v. Coalition to Defend Affirmative Action*. It concerned a Michigan voter initiative banning race-conscious admissions at public universities.

In the meantime, beginning in the 1970s, the Court also began to use the Fourteenth Amendment to combat more than racial discrimination. It also examined discrimination based on age, condition of disability, wealth, sexual orientation (Case 6.5), and other characteristics.

It also devoted a good deal of attention to the investigation of gender discrimination. In the nineteenth century, it was common for the Court routinely to proclaim the patent differences between men and women. Justice Joseph P. Bradley's famous 1873 concurring opinion in *Bradwell v. Illinois*, 83 U.S. 130, which upheld a law denying women the right to practice law, is a good example. He took the view that the God-given role of women was for them to be their husband's helpmate: they were to stay at home, cook the meals, raise the children, and clean the house. Even the passage of the Nineteenth Amendment—women's voting rights—almost 50 years later, in 1920, did not guarantee women's legal and social equality with men.

Not until 1971 did the Court rule that there was no rational basis for women to be treated differently from men in disputes regarding an adjudication of a will (*Reed v. Reed*, 404 U.S. 71). Two years later, Air Force Lieutenant Sharron Frontiero, whose husband was a full-time student, successfully sued the Secretary of Defense after she was denied better quarters, allowances, and medical benefits because she was a woman (*Frontiero v. Richardson*, 411 U.S. 677). The Defense Department, as a matter of policy, offered all of these benefits only to male officers and their families, assuming that female officers could rely on their husbands providing them through their workplace benefits. By an eight to one majority, the Court held that the department had discriminated against Frontiero. However, only four members of the Court argued that sex was a suspect classification so that gender discrimination was not subject to strict scrutiny, but only heightened or intermediate scrutiny.

From the mid-1970s, the Court has used the intermediate scrutiny test in cases involving gender discrimination. In 1996, the Court declared that the Virginia Military Institute, an all-male, public university that trains men for future military service, could no longer continue to deny admission to women (Case 4.7). There, the Court reaffirmed, over Justice Antonin Scalia's blistering dissent, that gender discrimination was still subject to intermediate scrutiny. For the majority, VMI's sex-based classification failed to show that its male-only admissions policy served *important governmental objectives* and that the policy was *substantially* related to the achievement of those objectives.

Box 4.1

Three Judicial Tests For Deciding Equal Protection and Fundamental Rights Cases

In the twentieth century, more than at any other time in its history, the Court directly confronted the problem of equality in America. The Post-Civil War amendments were designed to ensure that everyone would be treated equally before the law. And yet, under certain circumstances, government often classifies people so that some are treated differently from others. Driver's licenses, for example, will only be issued to those who pass a vision test. The physically disabled may be exempt from military service during a draft, or a pacifist may serve in a non-combat role. Taxes may be higher for the wealthy than they are for the poor.

The problem becomes more sharply focused, however, when government classifies people on the basis of race or gender or other qualities. To determine whether classifications are legitimate or illegitimate, the justices began in the 1930s to develop basic judicial tests to help them review legislation under the First Amendment (like political speech or religious liberty) and the Fourteenth Amendment's Equal Protection Clause. At first, there were two tests: the rational basis test, which the Court uses in the vast majority of its cases, including those that involve non-Fourteenth Amendment and non-fundamental rights cases; and then later the Court began to use the strict scrutiny test when it considers laws affecting fundamental rights and "suspect categories," such as race.

In the 1970s, the Court added a third or intermediate tier, known as heightened (or intermediate) scrutiny. The Court uses this test when the challenged law discriminates against quasi-suspect categories, such as sex, or in First Amendment cases involving commercial speech.

The Rational Basis Test

The Court applies the rational basis test to the vast majority of the cases it hears. The outcome usually results in the Court upholding the challenged law. Here, the burden of proof falls on the plaintiffs, that is, on those challenging the law. They must prove that (1) the government has no legitimate interest in enacting the law (2) because it is neither a reasonable nor plausible public policy. Many, but not all, of the Court's decisions using the rational basis test have focused on economic regulations.

In 1996, the Court considered an amendment to the Colorado constitution that prohibited any subdivision from passing laws forbidding discrimination on the basis of sexual orientation (*Romer v. Evans*, 517 U.S. 620). In striking down the amendment, Justice Kennedy wrote that "if a law neither burdens a fundamental right nor targets a suspect class, we will uphold the legislative classification so long as it bears a rational relation to some legitimate end." He found, along with a six to three majority, that there was no rational basis for the amendment because it did not further a legitimate government interest.

The Strict Scrutiny Test

The second test, which the Court applies to cases involving fundamental rights and suspect categories, is of more recent vintage. Its first suggestion appeared buried in a footnote in the 1938 case of *United States v. Carolene Products Co.*, 304 U.S. 144.

If people challenge a law on the grounds that it compromises a fundamental right like free speech or discriminates on the basis of race, they do not bear the burden to prove that they are right. The Court regards race as a "suspect" classification or category. According to the

Court's strict scrutiny test, the burden of proof lies on the government to show that it had (1) a *compelling* interest to pass the law. Moreover, the government must also demonstrate that even if its interest is compelling, (2) it has achieved that interest through the most *narrowly tailored* (or least restrictive) means so that only minimal harm is possible.

In *Adarand Constructors, Inc., v. Pena*, 515 U.S. 200, the Court considered a federal set-aside program in 1995 that highlights how this works in practice (Case 4.5). The program required construction companies with federal contracts to include minority-owned subcontractors in their projects. Adarand Constructors filed a low bid for a sub-contract for guardrail work in Colorado, but lost to the Gonzales Construction Company simply because Gonzales met the minority-owned requirements. Adarand sued and eventually won in the Supreme Court. Writing for a five to four majority, Justice O'Connor noted that "federal racial classifications . . . must serve a *compelling* governmental interest, and must be *narrowly tailored* to further that interest" (emphasis added). The five justices who joined the opinion could find no compelling interest in the government's decision to classify people on the basis of race.

The Intermediate or Heightened Scrutiny Test

Finally, the Court developed the heightened scrutiny test for non-racial classifications, such as sex, and in First Amendment cases involving commercial speech. Here, the burden is still placed on the government, but the standards are far lower than the requirements of the strict scrutiny test. The government need only show that (1) it has an *important* interest in enacting the law. It then must demonstrate that (2) the law achieves that interest in a way that is *substantially related* to the achievement of its objective, and the law or regulation is not more extensive than necessary to reach the interest.

In 1973, four justices wanted to make sex discrimination, like racial classifications, subject to strict scrutiny (*Frontiero v. Richardson*, 411 U.S. 677). But four justices was one short of a majority to transform that desire into precedent.

Three years later, Justice William Brennan clearly described heightened scrutiny in an opinion addressing how a statute did not constitutionally distinguish between young men and women (*Craig v. Boren*, 429 U.S. 190). The Oklahoma law in this case permitted young women to purchase low-alcohol—or 3.2 percent—beer at eighteen, but young men had to wait until they were twenty-one. The state reasoned that the law was constitutionally valid because young men were more susceptible to alcohol-related automobile accidents than young women. Justice Brennan noted that while traffic safety comprised an important government interest, "the relationship between sex and traffic safety becomes far too tenuous to satisfy [the] requirement that the gender-based difference be substantially related to achievement of the statutory objective."

While these tests are important for students studying the Supreme Court to understand, they are often muddled—by the Court itself. Many commentators who oppose affirmative action programs often cite Justice John Marshall Harlan's famous dictum in his dissent in *Plessy v. Ferguson*, 163 U.S. 537 (1896), when he wrote that "our Constitution is color-blind, and neither knows nor tolerates classes among citizens" (Case 4.1).

According to Justice Thurgood Marshall, however, racial classifications are only impermissible when African Americans, the most oppressed race in American history, are excluded. When a racial classification is *compensatory* in the sense that it rights past wrongs, he argued, it is a legitimate classification. Affirmative action, programs designed to help African Americans and other distressed minorities enter the mainstream of American life, are therefore perfectly constitutional. They are no burden on the Equal Protection Clause. Justice Marshall's contention demonstrates the legal and moral difficulties underlying all classifications, especially racial ones.

The table offers a schematic way that differentiates the three tests.

Burden of Proof	Government Interest	Legal Standard
Rational Basis Test (The Court usually upholds legislation when using this test)		
On plaintiff	legitimate	reasonable person standard
Strict Scrutiny Test (The Court uses this test in cases involving suspect classifications and fundamental rights. Legislation is rarely upheld.)		
On government	compelling	law is narrowly tailored to reach that interest with least restrictive means
Intermediate Scrutiny Test (The Court uses this test in matters involving sex discrimination and commercial speech.)		
On government	important	law is substantially related to achieve that objective and not more extensive than necessary

Segregation and Desegregation: Cases

In 1896, *Plessy* upheld the Jim Crow laws and proclaimed that the "separate but equal" doctrine was consonant with the Fourteenth Amendment's Equal Protection Clause. Fifty-eight years later, *Brown* overruled that decision when it declared that "separate educational facilities are inherently unequal." Despite the Court's support of busing to achieve integrated public schools, it determined that it had no authority to oversee segregated facilities when they were a result not of laws passed by subdivisions and states, but of demographic living and housing patterns.

Case 4.1

Plessy v. Ferguson
163 U.S. 537, 3 S.Ct.18 (1896)

This historic case marked the "constitutionalization" of Jim Crow or "separate but equal" laws in the United States. Not until the 1954 school desegregation case of *Brown v. Board of Education* (Case 4.2) was *Plessy* finally overturned. Constitutionalization meant that the Jim Crow laws, which had been on many states' books, were now protected by the Constitution even though no provision in the document expressly addressed these laws. The *Plessy* case marked the first time that a challenged Jim Crow law successfully reached the Supreme Court. The Court, by a seven to one margin, upheld the law with John Marshall Harlan providing the lone impassioned and indignant dissent.

Designed to protect the newly freed black slaves, the Fourteenth Amendment guaranteed several things to them: states could not infringe upon the privileges and immunities of citizens of the United States nor could they deprive any person of the equal protection of the laws. One result of the amendment in the South was the rise of Jim Crow laws, which allowed segregationists to undercut the impact of equal protection. The principle was that if government provided the same facilities for black citizens, but kept them separate, it would satisfy the amendment's guarantee of equality. After all, the amendment did not address integration: as long as black children had their own schools, that was all that mattered; as long as black railway riders had their own train cars to sit in, that too was all that mattered. All children, no matter their race, received an education, and all railroad passengers made it to their destinations.

Such laws were modeled on ones that had been on the books in several Northern states before the Civil War, so it is not surprising that the South would follow suit once the issue of slavery was finally settled, particularly in an area where so many black citizens resided. Political leaders in several Southern states talked openly about the obvious relationship between segregated railway cars and segregated schools. Their argument was if Congress could provide separate schools for black and white children in Washington, D. C., then it was perfectly legitimate for them to segregate the races whenever and wherever they felt that the encounter of white and black citizens was, as they put it, "objectionable," which meant most of the time and in most places. The actual legal basis that the states used to segregate facilities was police power: it was a reasonable way of maintaining the peace and safety of the community. Beyond schools and trains, these included restaurants, theaters, hotels, taverns, hospitals, cemeteries, bathrooms, and drinking fountains. The result was that most facilities were not precisely equal in terms of quality, but white Southern leaders were convinced that equality only meant that the facilities had to exist for blacks, period.

In Louisiana, several citizens, who were mainly Creole in origin—French speakers of mixed blood, often called mulattoes, living in the state for generations—joined together after the passage of an 1890 law requiring the segregation of races on passenger trains. They called themselves the Citizens' Committee to Test the Constitutionality of the Separate Car Law. They challenged the constitutionality of the law as a violation of the Fourteenth Amendment's guarantee of equal protection. Homer Plessy, whose last name was probably of French origin, was a member of this group. A shoemaker who was one-eighth black—he had one black great-grandparent—he lived in an integrated neighborhood in New Orleans. On June 7, 1892, he was arrested for sitting in a first-class railcar reserved for whites only.

Plessy was not the first man to challenge the law. A few months earlier, a man by the name of Daniel Desdunes, who was also one-eighth black, had ridden in a first-class car from New Orleans to an out-of-state destination, but in his case, the judge, a man by the name of John Ferguson, ruled that the law did not apply to out-of-state travel because it came under federal jurisdiction through the Commerce Clause of the Constitution (Article I, Section 8). Plessy's ticket was to take him from New Orleans to Covington, both in Louisiana.

Plessy could easily "pass" for white. But that did not matter for the white citizens of Louisiana. Once they learned of people's racial background, the slightest link to a black heritage damned them in their eyes. In this case, in setting up the case to challenge the law, the citizens group involved the East Louisiana Railway Company itself. Typically, companies did not like Jim Crow laws because it cost them additional money that ate into their profits. The law required railroad companies to add an additional car even if only one black passenger purchased a ticket on a train filled with white people. Moreover, if the white cars were full, white passengers could not simply ride with black passengers. That too the segregation laws prohibited. A white man discovered riding in a car reserved for black passengers faced the same criminal penalties as Plessy. In any case, the conductor was most likely either waiting for Plessy or he announced his racial background to the conductor who then called the police.

After his arrest, Plessy appeared before John Ferguson, the same judge who presided over the Desdunes case. Before going to trial, Plessy asked the Louisiana Supreme Court to prohibit the judge from trying him because the law was unconstitutional on the basis of the prohibition of slavery in the Thirteenth Amendment and the Privileges and Immunities and Equal Protection Clauses of the Fourteenth Amendment. Discrimination, his lawyers argued, was a form of slavery, which the Thirteenth forbade, and Plessy's right to ride in whatever railcar he wished denied him privileges and immunities as a U.S. citizen. Besides, separate cars violated the Equal Protection Clause on its face. One of the arguments that Plessy's chief counsel, Albion Winegar Tourgée, made was that while justice was blind, her daughter, the law, ought to be "color-blind," a metaphor that Justice Harlan later used in his historic dissent.

When the Louisiana Supreme Court refused to grant the writ, Plessy appealed to the U.S. Supreme Court on a writ of error, which was allowed by the chief justice of the Louisiana Supreme Court. The Supreme Court's decision, in an opinion by Justice Henry B. Brown, was seven to one with one justice not participating because he had not heard the oral arguments. Justice John Marshall Harlan wrote the lone dissent, now a classic, often quoted, opinion.

Justice BROWN delivered the opinion of the court.

This case turns upon the constitutionality of an act of the general assembly of the state of Louisiana, passed in 1890, providing for separate railway carriages for the white and colored races. . . .

The constitutionality of this act is attacked upon the ground that it conflicts both with the Thirteenth Amendment of the Constitution, abolishing slavery, and the Fourteenth Amendment, which prohibits certain restrictive legislation on the part of the states.

1. That it does not conflict with the thirteenth amendment, which abolished slavery and involuntary servitude, except a punishment for crime, is too clear for argument. Slavery implies involuntary servitude,— a state of bondage; the ownership of mankind as a chattel, or, at least, the control of the labor and services of one man for the benefit of another, and the absence of a legal right to the disposal of his own person, property, and services. . . .

2. The object of the Fourteenth Amendment was undoubtedly to enforce the absolute equality of the two races before the law, but, in the nature of things, it could not have been intended to abolish distinctions based upon color, or to enforce social, as distinguished from political, equality, or a commingling of the two races upon terms unsatisfactory to either. Laws permitting, and even requiring, their separation, in places where they are liable to be brought into contact, do not necessarily imply the inferiority of either race to the other, and have been generally, if not universally, recognized as within the competency of the state legislatures in the exercise of their police power. The most common instance of this is connected with the establishment of separate schools for white and colored children, which have been held to be a valid exercise of the legislative power even by courts of states where the political rights of the colored race have been longest and most earnestly enforced. . . .

The distinction between laws interfering with the political equality of the negro and those requiring the separation of the two races in schools, theaters, and railway carriages has been frequently drawn by this court. . . .

In this connection, it is also suggested by the learned counsel for the plaintiff in error that the same argument that will justify the state legislature in requiring railways to provide separate accommodations for the two races will also authorize them to require separate cars to be provided for people whose hair is of a certain color, or who are aliens, or who belong to certain nationalities, or to enact laws requiring colored people to walk upon one side of the street, and white people upon the other, or requiring white men's houses to be painted white, and colored men's black, or their vehicles or business signs to be of different colors, upon the theory that one side of the street is as good as the other, or that a house or vehicle of one color is as good as one of another color. The reply to all this is that every exercise of the police power must be reasonable, and extend only to such laws as are enacted in good faith for the promotion of the public good, and not for the annoyance or oppression of a particular class. . . .

So far, then, as a conflict with the Fourteenth Amendment is concerned, the case reduces itself to the question whether the statute of Louisiana is a reasonable regulation, and with respect to this there must necessarily be a large discretion on the part of the legislature. In determining the question of reasonableness, it is at liberty to act with reference to the established usages, customs, and traditions of the people, and with a view to the promotion of their comfort, and the preservation of the public peace and good order. Gauged by this standard, we cannot say that a law which authorizes or even requires the separation of the two races in public conveyances is unreasonable, or more obnoxious to the Fourteenth Amendment than the acts of Congress requiring separate schools for colored children in the District of Columbia, the constitutionality of which does not seem to have been questioned, or the corresponding acts of state legislatures.

We consider the underlying fallacy of the plaintiff's argument to consist in the assumption that the enforced separation of the two races stamps the colored race with a badge of inferiority. If this be so, it is not by reason of anything found in the act, but solely because the colored race chooses to put that construction upon it. The argument necessarily assumes that if, as has been more than once the case, and is not unlikely to be so again, the colored race should become the dominant power in the state legislature, and should enact a law in precisely similar terms, it would thereby relegate the white race to an inferior position. We imagine that the white race, at least, would not acquiesce in this assumption. The argument also assumes that social prejudices may be overcome by legislation. . . . Legislation is powerless to eradicate racial instincts, or to abolish distinctions based upon physical differences, and the attempt to do so can only result in accentuating the difficulties of the present situation. If the civil and political rights of both races be equal, one cannot be inferior to the other civilly or politically. If one race be inferior to the other socially, the Constitution of the United States cannot put them upon the same plane.

The judgment of the court below is therefore affirmed.

Justice HARLAN dissenting.

. . . We have before us a state enactment that compels, under penalties, the separation of the two races in railroad passenger coaches, and makes it a crime for a citizen of either race to enter a coach that has been assigned to citizens of the other race.

Thus, the state regulates the use of a public highway by citizens of the United States solely upon the basis of race.

However apparent the injustice of such legislation may be, we have only to consider whether it is consistent with the Constitution of the United States. . . .

In respect of civil rights, common to all citizens, the Constitution of the United States does not, I think, permit any public authority to know the race of those entitled to be protected in the enjoyment of such rights. Every true man has pride of race, and under appropriate circumstances, when the rights of others, his equals before the law, are not to be affected, it is his privilege to express such pride and to take such action based upon it as to him seems proper. But I deny that any legislative body or judicial tribunal may have regard to the race of citizens when the civil rights of those citizens are involved. Indeed, such legislation as that here in question is inconsistent not only with that equality of rights which pertains to citizenship, national and state, but with the personal liberty enjoyed by every one within the United States. . . .

It was said in argument that the statute of Louisiana does not discriminate against either race, but prescribes a rule applicable alike to white and colored citizens. But this argument does not meet the difficulty. Every one knows that the statute in question had its origin in the purpose, not so much to exclude white persons from railroad cars occupied by blacks, as to exclude colored people from coaches occupied by or assigned to white persons. Railroad corporations of Louisiana did not make discrimination among whites in the matter of accommodation for travelers. The thing to accomplish was, under the guise of giving equal accommodation for whites and blacks, to compel the latter to keep to themselves while traveling in railroad passenger coaches. No one would be so wanting in candor as to assert the contrary. The fundamental objection, therefore, to the statute, is that it interferes with the personal freedom of citizens. "Personal liberty," it has been well said, "consists in the power of locomotion, of changing situation, or removing one's person to whatsoever places one's own inclination may direct, without imprisonment or restraint, unless by due course of law" [Blackstone's *Commentary*]. If a white man and a black man choose to occupy the same public conveyance on a public highway, it is their right to do so; and no government, proceeding alone on grounds of race, can prevent it without infringing the personal liberty of each.

It is one thing for railroad carriers to furnish, or to be required by law to furnish, equal accommodations for all whom they are under a legal duty to carry. It is quite another thing for government to forbid citizens of the white and black races from traveling in the same public conveyance, and to punish officers of railroad companies for permitting persons of the two races to occupy the same passenger coach. If a state can prescribe, as a rule of civil conduct, that whites and blacks shall not travel as passengers in the same railroad coach, why may it not so regulate the use of the streets of its cities and towns as to compel white citizens to keep on one side of a street, and black citizens to keep on the other? Why may it not, upon like grounds, punish whites and blacks who ride together in street cars or in open vehicles on a public road or street? Why may it not require sheriffs to assign whites to one side of a court room, and blacks to the other? And why may it not also prohibit the commingling of the two races in the galleries of legislative halls or in public assemblages convened for the consideration of the political questions of the day? Further, if this statute of Louisiana is consistent with the personal liberty of citizens, why may not the state require the separation in railroad coaches of native and naturalized citizens of the United States, or of Protestants and Roman Catholics? . . .

The white race deems itself to be the dominant race in this country. And so it is, in prestige, in achievements, in education, in wealth, and in power. So, I doubt not, it will continue to be for all time, if it remains true to its great heritage, and holds fast to the principles of constitutional liberty. But in view of the Constitution, in the eye of the law, there is in this country no superior, dominant, ruling class of citizens. There is no caste here. Our Constitution is color-blind, and neither knows nor tolerates classes among citizens. In respect of civil rights, all citizens are equal before the law. The humblest is the peer of the most powerful. The law regards man as man, and takes no account of his surroundings or of his color when his civil rights as guarantied by the supreme law of the land are involved. It is therefore to be regretted that this high tribunal, the final expositor of the fundamental law of the land, has reached the conclusion that it is competent for a state to regulate the enjoyment by citizens of their civil rights solely upon the basis of race.

In my opinion, the judgment this day rendered will, in time, prove to be quite as pernicious as the decision made by this tribunal in the *Dred Scott Case* [*Dred Scott v. Sandford*, 60 U.S. 393 (1857)]. . . .

The present decision, it may well be apprehended, will not only stimulate aggressions, more or less brutal and irritating, upon the admitted rights of colored citizens, but will encourage the belief that it is possible, by means of state enactments, to defeat the beneficent purposes which the people of the United States had in view when they adopted the recent amendments of the Constitution, by one of which the blacks of this country were made citizens of the United States and of the states in which they respectively reside, and whose privileges and immunities, as citizens, the states are forbidden to abridge. Sixty millions of whites are in no danger from the presence here of eight millions of blacks. The destinies of the two races, in this country, are indissolubly linked together, and the interests of both require that the common government of all shall not permit the seeds of race hate to be planted under the sanction of law. What can more certainly arouse race hate, what more certainly create and perpetuate a feeling of distrust between these races, than state enactments which, in fact, proceed on the ground that colored citizens are so inferior and degraded that they cannot be allowed to sit in public coaches occupied by white citizens? That, as all will admit, is the real meaning of such legislation as was enacted in Louisiana. . . .

I am of opinion that the state of Louisiana is inconsistent with the personal liberty of citizens, white and black, in that state, and hostile to both the spirit and letter of the Constitution of the United States. If laws of like character should be enacted in the several states of the Union, the effect would be in the highest degree mischievous. Slavery, as an institution tolerated by law, would, it is true, have disappeared from our country; but there would remain a power in the states, by sinister legislation, to interfere with the full enjoyment of the blessings of freedom, to regulate civil rights, common to all citizens, upon the basis of race, and to place in a condition of legal inferiority a large body of American citizens, now constituting a part of the political community, called the "People of the United States," for whom, and by whom through representatives, our government is administered. Such a system is inconsistent with the guaranty given by the Constitution to each state of a republican form of government, and may be stricken down by congressional action, or by the courts in the discharge of their solemn duty to maintain the supreme law of the land, anything in the Constitution or laws of any state to the contrary notwithstanding.

For the reason stated, I am constrained to withhold my assent from the opinion and judgment of the majority.

Case 4.2

Brown v. Board of Education of Topeka, Kansas
347 U.S. 483, 74 S.Ct. 686 (1954)

Plessy set forth the constitutional doctrine that public facilities everywhere could be legally segregated by race as long as an equivalent one was created for black people. "Separate but equal" became the prevalent doctrine throughout the South, but also in several non-Southern states as well. In 1909, the National Association for the Advancement of Colored People (NAACP), formed in New York City, began to challenge several segregation laws. It was only after 1935 that public education became its main focus when the organization's new legal director, Charles Hamilton Houston, who had served as dean of the Howard University School of Law, hired his former student, Thurgood Marshall, to litigate segregation cases.

The early cases involved segregated law schools and universities. In Missouri, for example, the state paid to send black students out of state because there was no state law school for them, though there was one for white students. In 1938, the Supreme Court ruled that this procedure violated the Fourteenth Amendment's Equal Protection Clause because only black students had to leave the state for a legal education (*Missouri ex rel. Gaines v. Canada*, 305 U.S. 337).

In 1939, Marshall became the director of the NAACP's newly established Legal and Education Defense Fund. In the early 1950s, the organization successfully convinced the Supreme Court that segregation in graduate and professional school violated the Equal Protection Clause. A black college professor in Oklahoma wanted to take education courses toward a Ph.D. degree, but only the segregated white university offered it. Although he was admitted by means of a federal court order, the university forced him to listen to the lectures outside the classroom in the hallway, sit by himself in the library behind a screen, and eat by himself in the lunchroom. By the time, his case reached the Supreme Court, he no longer had to sit outside the classroom, but he sat at a desk behind a rail with the sign that read "reserved for colored." In the 1950 opinion for the Court, Chief Justice Fred M. Vinson wrote that by all measures the state was not treating George W. McLaurin the same as white students (*McLaurin v. Oklahoma*, 339 U.S. 637).

In another case decided the same year, a young black man, Herman Marion Sweatt (his first name is spelled in a variety of ways in the records), applied to the segregated University of Texas School of Law because it was the only law school in the state. The university immediately set up a black law school in two rooms in a downtown Houston office building with no library and only two part-time professors. When it was clear that this facility was unequal, the university increased the space and hired three part-time professors. In his opinion in *Sweatt v. Painter*, 339 U.S. 629, Chief Justice Vinson wrote that by any standard the two schools could not possibly be equal, especially when it was well known that eighty-five percent of the population of Texas was white. Because Sweatt would have had no contact with them, his legal practice would never get off the ground, especially when most of his colleagues in the profession were white.

Curiously, in neither case did Vinson overturn *Plessy*.

Meantime, Marshall began to realize that the NAACP's incremental progress on a case-by-case basis was the wrong strategy. It became clear to him that it would take several years to develop the constitutional and legal doctrine that would substantially change the American culture and society to ensure integration and most important to see the Court overturn *Plessy*. The change in strategy came when the organization shifted its focus to public elementary and secondary schools.

The decision in *Brown v. Board of Education*, 58 years after *Plessy*, encompassed four separate cases on appeal from Kansas, South Carolina, Virginia, and Delaware. In addition, the Court also decided a companion case from the District of Columbia the very same day. In this sense, it was a class action suit that included more than a single person. The four states, along with the District and fourteen other states, at the time prescribed segregated schools for public school children. A court decision in favor of integration could potentially have a monumental impact.

In 1950, when she was eight years old, Linda Brown thought she was going to walk a short 10 minutes to school from her home in a multi-ethnic neighborhood in Topeka, Kansas. When her father took her to the nearby Sumner School to enroll her for the fall term, he found that Linda was ineligible because she was African American. Linda would have to walk six blocks from her community through heavy traffic and then cross some railroad tracks, where she would wait for the bus to take her to the Monroe School on the other side of town where the "black" school was located. If she arrived before 9:00 a.m., even if it were rainy, snowy, or freezing cold, she would have to wait outside for the principal to open the doors.

When her father sued the school district on her behalf in federal district court to allow her to attend school close to home, he lost because the court found that, despite its distance, the Monroe School was roughly "equal" to Sumner. The teachers, facilities, and supplies were all adequate. With the support of the NAACP, Linda Brown's father now appealed on her behalf.

In South Carolina, things were very different. There, the case for a denial of equal protection was stark: black schools were clearly inferior to white ones. Some were so dilapidated they were literally falling down and just unsafe. Others stuffed far too many students into one-room schools, while still others had no cafeterias, playgrounds, or libraries. Their white counterparts had many of these amenities. Nearly 70 percent of the school population in the state was African American. This meant that many black children were growing up unable to read and write. Moreover, the state spent far less per student each year: expenditures were $43

for each black student, but $179 for every white one. The petition-
ers lost when the federal judge decided, based on evidence presented at trial, that the state was about to increase funding for
public education by $75 million.

After the NAACP encouraged an appeal in this case, it became clear that the Supreme Court wanted to hear all four together. Despite the differences within each school district, NAACP
attorneys argued that segregation by itself, despite any differences
in expenses or facilities, violated the Fourteenth Amendment's
Equal Protection Clause.

The Court's decision, written by Chief Justice Earl Warren,
was unanimous in overturning school segregation laws. His opinion rested in part on the literature of social science, in addition to
legal sources, a practice with its origins in the famous written brief
submitted by Louis D. Brandeis for his client in *Muller v. Oregon*,
208 U.S. 412 (1908). His argument is now universally known as a
"Brandeis Brief." Brandeis became a Supreme Court justice in
1916. See the footnote to Chief Justice Warren's opinion.

Chief Justice WARREN delivered the opinion of the Court.

These cases . . . are premised on different facts and different local conditions, but a common legal question justifies their consideration together in this consolidated opinion. . . .

The plaintiffs contend that segregated public schools are not
"equal" and cannot be made "equal," and that hence they are deprived
of the equal protection of the laws. . . . Argument was heard in the 1952
Term, and reargument was heard this Term on certain questions pro-
pounded by the Court.

Reargument was largely devoted to the circumstances surrounding
the adoption of the Fourteenth Amendment in 1868. . . . This discussion and our own investigation convince us that, although these sources
cast some light, it is not enough to resolve the problem with which we
are faced. At best, they are inconclusive. . . .

An additional reason for the inconclusive nature of the Amendment's history, with respect to segregated schools, is the status of public
education at that time. In the South, the movement toward free common schools, supported by general taxation, had not yet taken hold.
Education of white children was largely in the hands of private groups.
Education of Negroes was almost nonexistent, and practically all of the
race were illiterate. In fact, any education of Negroes was forbidden by
law in some states. . . . It is true that public school education at the time
of the Amendment had advanced further in the North, but the effect of

the Amendment on Northern States was generally ignored in the congressional debates. Even in the North, the conditions of public education did not approximate those existing today. . . .

In the first cases in this Court construing the Fourteenth Amendment, decided shortly after its adoption, the Court interpreted it as proscribing all state-imposed discriminations against the Negro race. The doctrine of "separate but equal" did not make its appearance in this Court until 1896 in the case of *Plessy v. Ferguson* [163 U.S. 537 (1896)], involving not education but transportation. American courts have since labored with the doctrine for over half a century. In this Court, there have been six cases involving the "separate but equal" doctrine in the field of public education. In *Cummings v. County Board of Education*, 175 U.S. 528 [(1899)], and *Gong Lum v. Rice*, 275 U.S. 78 [(1927)], the validity of the doctrine itself was not challenged. In more recent cases, all on the graduate school level, inequality was found in that specific benefits enjoyed by white students were denied to Negro students of the same educational qualifications. *Missouri ex rel. Gaines v. Canada*, 305 U.S. 337 [(1938)]; *Sipuel v. Oklahoma*, 332 U.S. 631; *Sweatt v. Painter*, 339 U.S. 629 [(1950)]; *McLaurin v. Oklahoma State Regents*, 339 U.S. 637 [(1950)]. In none of these cases was it necessary to re-examine the doctrine to grant relief to the Negro plaintiff. And in *Sweatt v. Painter*, the Court expressly reserved decision on the question whether *Plessy v. Ferguson* should be held inapplicable to public education.

In the instant cases, that question is directly presented. Here, unlike *Sweatt v. Painter*, there are findings below that the Negro and white schools involved have been equalized, or are being equalized, with respect to buildings, curricula, qualifications and salaries of teachers, and other "tangible" factors. Our decision, therefore, cannot turn on merely a comparison of these tangible factors in the Negro and white schools involved in each of the cases. We must look instead to the effect of segregation itself on public education.

In approaching this problem, we cannot turn the clock back to 1868 when the Amendment was adopted, or even to 1896 when *Plessy v. Ferguson* was written. We must consider public education in the light of its full development and its present place in American life throughout the Nation. . . .

Today, education is perhaps the most important function of state and local governments. Compulsory school attendance laws and the great expenditures for education both demonstrate our recognition of the importance of education to our democratic society. It is required in the performance of our most basic public responsibilities, even service in the armed forces. It is the very foundation of good citizenship. Today it is a principal instrument in awakening the child to cultural values, in preparing him for later professional training, and in helping him to adjust normally to his environment. In these days, it is doubtful that any child may reasonably be expected to succeed in life if he is denied the opportunity of an education. Such an opportunity, where the state has undertaken to provide it, is a right which must be made available to all on equal terms.

We come then to the question presented: Does segregation of children in public schools solely on the basis of race, even though the physical facilities and other "tangible" factors may be equal, deprive the children of the minority group of equal educational opportunities? We believe that it does.

In *Sweatt v. Painter,* in finding that a segregated law school for Negroes could not provide them equal educational opportunities, this Court relied in large part on "those qualities which are incapable of objective measurement but which make for greatness in a law school." In *McLaurin v. Oklahoma State Regents,* the Court, in requiring that a Negro admitted to a white graduate school be treated like all other students, again resorted to intangible considerations: "his ability to study, to engage in discussions and exchange views with other students, and, in general, to learn his profession." Such considerations apply with added force to children in grade and high schools. To separate them from others of similar age and qualifications solely because of their race generates a feeling of inferiority as to their status in the community that may affect their hearts and minds in a way unlikely ever to be undone. . . .

Whatever may have been the extent of psychological knowledge at the time of *Plessy v. Ferguson,* this finding is amply supported by modern authority.* Any language in *Plessy v. Ferguson* contrary to this finding is rejected.

We conclude that in the field of public education the doctrine of "separate but equal" has no place. Separate educational facilities are inherently unequal. . . .

Because these are class actions, because of the wide applicability of this decision, and because of the great variety of local conditions, the formulation of decrees in these cases presents problems of considerable complexity. . . . In order that we may have the full assistance of the par-

---

* [NOTE: Here Chief Justice Warren cites the following authorities.] K.B. Clark, "Effect of Prejudice and Discrimination on Personality Development" (Midcentury White House Conference on Children and Youth, 1950); Witmer and Kotinsky, *Personality in the Making* (1952), c. VI; Deutscher and Chein, "The Psychological Effects of Enforced Segregation: A Survey of Social Science Opinion," 26 *J. Psychol.* 259 (1948); Chein, "What are the Psychological Effects of Segregation Under Conditions of Equal Facilities?," 3 *Int. J. Opinion and Attitude Res.* 229 (1949); Brameld, *Educational Costs, in Discrimination and National Welfare* (MacIver, ed., (1949), 44-48; Frazier, *The Negro in the United States* (1949), 674-681. And see generally Myrdal, *An American Dilemma* (1944).

ties in formulating decrees, the cases will be restored to the docket, and the parties are requested to present further argument on [how they intend to implement this decision]. The Attorney General of the United States is again invited to participate. The Attorneys General of the states requiring or permitting segregation in public education will also be permitted to appear as *amici curiae* upon request to do so by September 15, 1954, and submission of briefs by October 1, 1954.

It is so ordered.

[NOTE: In *Bolling v. Sharpe*, 347 U.S. 497 (1954), the federal companion case from the District of Columbia, decided on the same day as *Brown*, the Court ruled that the same principles apply to the federal government, even though the District of Columbia is not subject to the Fourteenth Amendment, which addresses only the states. The Chief Justice ruled, however, that the Fifth Amendment's Due Process Clause incorporated the Fourteenth's Equal Protection Clause and applied it to actions by the federal government, and thus segregated schools were prohibited there as well. "The Fifth Amendment, which is applicable in the District of Columbia," he said, "does not contain an equal protection clause as does the Fourteenth Amendment which applies only to the states. But the concepts of equal protection and due process, both stemming from our American ideal of fairness, are not mutually exclusive. . . . Segregation in public education is not reasonably related to any proper governmental objective, and thus it imposes on Negro children of the District of Columbia a burden that constitutes an arbitrary deprivation of their liberty in violation of the Due Process Clause."]

Case 4.3

Parents Involved in Community Schools v. Seattle School District No. 1
551 U.S. 701, 127 S.Ct. 2738 (2007)

The *Brown I* and *II* decisions set forth the reasons why public schools must desegregate "with all deliberate speed." From the 1950s to the 1990s, school officials shifted away from desegregation to forced integration, mainly by busing students to schools to achieve racial balance. But busing proved to be hugely unpopular in some school districts. This resulted in numerous challenges to school districts' busing plans. Some parents feared that their children were being forced to attend schools in dangerous neighborhoods far from their home even though there might be a local school just around the corner. They claimed that busing severely undermined their children's education and compromised their personal safety. In some localities, parents challenged the busing plans. In South Boston, the protests became so severe that they turned violent. Some white parents threw rocks at black children. The city government had to summon the police to restore order.

The Court upheld busing in 1971 in *Swann v. Charlotte-Mecklenburg Board of Education.* Many school districts fell under federal court supervision to achieve integration. Soon, however, the Court rejected attempts at racial balancing. This occurred after school boards began sending students across school district lines and attempted to ensure equality not only among students but also in school facilities, books, teachers, salaries, and other areas. Once schools were successfully integrated and federal court supervision lifted, many districts became re-segregated as a result of housing patterns rather than by law. When officials took what the Court eventually called "heroic" measures to integrate the schools by attempting to achieve racial balance in schools, the Court again stepped in.

This case, along with one from Kentucky, questioned the constitutionality of a program in a Seattle, Washington, school district that voluntarily adopted student assignment plans that relied on race to determine which schools certain children may attend. The district had never operated legally segregated schools, as had many in Eastern states, nor had it ever been subject to court-ordered desegregation. Despite these factors, the school board classified children as white or nonwhite and used the racial classifications as a "tiebreaker" to allocate slots in particular high schools.

The petitioners comprised an organization of Seattle parents who claimed that sending children to different public schools based solely on their race violated the Fourteenth Amendment's Equal Protection Clause. The district court upheld the program, finding that its plan survived strict scrutiny on the federal constitutional claim because it was narrowly tailored to serve a compelling government interest, namely a diverse student body. The U. S. Court of Appeals for the Ninth Circuit affirmed. The parents appealed to the Supreme Court. The Court ruled on a companion case from Kentucky's Jefferson County at the same time.

The Court reversed the Ninth Circuit's ruling by a vote of five to four with Chief Justice John Roberts writing the opinion of the Court with concurrences by Justices Anthony Kennedy and Clarence Thomas. Justices Stephen Breyer, Ruth Bader Ginsburg, John Paul Stevens, and David Souter dissented.

Chief Justice ROBERTS delivered the opinion of the Court.

It is well established that when the government distributes burdens or benefits on the basis of individual racial classifications, that action is reviewed under strict scrutiny. *Grutter v. Bollinger*, 539 U.S. 306 (2003). As the Court recently reaffirmed, "'racial classifications are simply too pernicious to permit any but the most exact connection between justification and classification.'" *Gratz v. Bollinger*, 539 U.S. 244 (2003). In order to satisfy this searching standard of review, the school districts must demonstrate that the use of individual racial classifications in the assignment plans here under review is "narrowly tailored" to achieve a "compelling" government interest.

Without attempting in these cases to set forth all the interests a school district might assert, it suffices to note that our prior cases, in evaluating the use of racial classifications in the school context, have recognized two interests that qualify as compelling. The first is the compelling interest of remedying the effects of past intentional discrimination. See *Freeman v. Pitts*, 503 U.S. 467 (1992). Yet the Seattle public schools have not shown that they were ever segregated by law, and were not subject to court-ordered desegregation decrees. The Jefferson County [Kentucky] public schools were previously segregated by law and were subject to a desegregation decree entered in 1975. In 2000, the District Court that entered that decree dissolved it, finding that Jefferson County had "eliminated the vestiges associated with the former policy of segregation and its pernicious effects," and thus had achieved "unitary" status. . . .

The second government interest we have recognized as compelling for purposes of strict scrutiny is the interest in diversity in higher education upheld in *Grutter*. The specific interest found compelling in *Grutter* was student body diversity "in the context of higher education." The diversity interest was not focused on race alone but encompassed "all factors that may contribute to student body diversity." . . .

The entire gist of the analysis in *Grutter* was that the admissions program at issue there focused on each applicant as an individual, and not simply as a member of a particular racial group. The classification of applicants by race upheld in *Grutter* was only as part of a "highly individualized, holistic review." The point of the narrow tailoring analysis in which the *Grutter* Court engaged was to ensure that the use of racial classifications was indeed part of a broader assessment of diversity, and not simply an effort to achieve racial balance, which the Court explained would be "patently unconstitutional."

In the present cases, by contrast, race is not considered as part of a broader effort to achieve "exposure to widely diverse people, cultures, ideas, and viewpoints," race, for some students, is determinative standing alone. . . . Like the University of Michigan undergraduate plan struck down in *Gratz*, the plans here "do not provide for a meaningful individualized review of applicants" but instead rely on racial classifications in a "non-individualized, mechanical" way.

Even when it comes to race, the plans here employ only a limited notion of diversity, viewing race exclusively in white/nonwhite terms in Seattle and black/"other" terms in Jefferson County. The Seattle "Board Statement Reaffirming Diversity Rationale" speaks of the "inherent educational value" in "providing students the opportunity to attend schools with diverse student enrollment." But under the Seattle plan, a school with 50 percent Asian-American students and 50 percent white students but no African-American, Native-American, or Latino students would qualify as balanced, while a school with 30 percent Asian-American, 25 percent African-American, 25 percent Latino, and 20 percent white students would not. It is hard to understand how a plan that could allow these results can be viewed as being concerned with achieving enrollment that is " 'broadly diverse,'". . .

In *Brown v. Board of Education*, 347 U.S. 483 (1954) (*Brown I*), we held that segregation deprived black children of equal educational opportunities regardless of whether school facilities and other tangible factors were equal, because government classification and separation on grounds of race themselves denoted inferiority. It was not the inequality of the facilities but the fact of legally separating children on the basis of race on which the Court relied to find a constitutional violation in 1954. The next Term, we accordingly stated that "full compliance" with *Brown I* required school districts "to achieve a system of determining admission to the public schools on a nonracial basis." *Brown II*, 349 U.S. 294 (1955).

The parties and their *amici* debate which side is more faithful to the heritage of *Brown*, but the position of the plaintiffs in *Brown* was spelled out in their brief and could not have been clearer: "The Fourteenth Amendment prevents states from according differential treatment to American children on the basis of their color or race." What do the racial classifications at issue here do, if not accord differential treatment on the basis of race? As counsel who appeared before this Court for the plaintiffs in *Brown* put it: "We have one fundamental contention which we will seek to develop in the course of this argument, and that contention is that no State has any authority under the equal-protection clause of the Fourteenth Amendment to use race as a factor in affording educational opportunities among its citizens." There is no ambiguity in that statement. And it was that position that prevailed in this Court, which emphasized in its remedial opinion that what was "at stake is the personal interest of the plaintiffs in admission to public schools as soon as practicable on a nondiscriminatory basis," and what was required was "determining admission to the public schools on a nonracial basis." *Brown II*. What do the racial classifications do in these cases, if not determine admission to a public school on a racial basis?

Before *Brown*, schoolchildren were told where they could and could not go to school based on the color of their skin. The school districts in these cases have not carried the heavy burden of demonstrating that we should allow this once again—even for very different reasons. For schools that never segregated on the basis of race, such as Seattle, or that have removed the vestiges of past segregation, such as Jefferson County, the way "to achieve a system of determining admission to the public schools on a nonracial basis," *Brown II*, is to stop assigning students on a racial basis. The way to stop discrimination on the basis of race is to stop discriminating on the basis of race.

The judgments of the Courts of Appeals for the Sixth and Ninth Circuits are reversed, and the cases are remanded for further proceedings.

Justice STEVENS, dissenting

There is a cruel irony in the Chief Justice's reliance on our decision in *Brown v. Board of Education*. The first sentence in the concluding paragraph of his opinion states: "Before *Brown*, schoolchildren were told where they could and could not go to school based on the color of their skin." This sentence reminds me of Anatole France's observation: "The majestic equality of the law forbids rich and poor alike to sleep under bridges, to beg in the streets, and to steal their bread." The Chief Justice fails to note that it was only black schoolchildren who were so ordered; indeed, the history books do not tell stories of white children struggling to attend black schools. In this and other ways, the Chief Justice rewrites the history of one of this Court's most important decisions.

The Chief Justice rejects the conclusion that the racial classifications at issue here should be viewed differently than others, because they do not impose burdens on one race alone and do not stigmatize or exclude. The only justification for refusing to acknowledge the obvious importance of that difference is the citation of a few recent opinions— none of which even approached unanimity—grandly proclaiming that all racial classifications must be analyzed under "strict scrutiny." . . .

It is my firm conviction that no Member of the Court that I joined in 1975 would have agreed with today's decision.

Rulings in Context

Segregation and Desegregation

Dred Scott v. Sandford, 19 How. (60 U.S.) 393 (1857)   7-2

In this historic case, Chief Justice Roger Brooke Taney ruled that slaves were not citizens, but mere property and that Congress had unconstitutionally passed the Missouri Compromise of 1820, which permitted slavery in Missouri, but prohibited it in the new states north of Missouri. According to the Chief Justice, the states carved out of the Louisiana Purchase had the right to determine for themselves whether they would be free states or slave states. The Fourteenth Amendment overturned the ruling.

Cooper v. Aaron, 358 U.S. 1 (1958)   9-0

The Court unanimously rejected a two and a half year delay request by the Little Rock, Arkansas, school board to implement desegregation plans. Chief Justice Earl Warren argued that the Court's decision in *Brown v. Board of Education,* 347 U.S. 483 (1954), was the law of the land and that "no state legislator or executive or judicial officer can war against the Constitution without violating his undertaking to support it."

Keyes v. Denver School District No. 1, 413 U.S. 189 (1973)   7-1

The Court ruled that schools must desegregate even if separate facilities are a result of *de facto* segregation (segregation brought about by housing and other choices individuals make) when the evidence proves that the responsibility for this outcome results from government action. For the first time, the Court clearly distinguished between *de jure* segregation (segregation by law) and *de facto* segregation.

Milliken v. Bradley, 418 U.S. 717 (1974)   5-4

The Court held that busing children to achieve desegregation in Detroit, Michigan, did not mean that the busing program had to cross school district lines. The Court said that the desegregation plan was constitutionally impermissible when it included Detroit and 53 other districts when those districts had not engaged in *de jure* segregation, but had segregated schools only as a result of housing patterns (*de facto* segregation).

Freeman v. Pitts, 503 U.S.467 (1992)   9-0

The Court ruled that once a school district had achieved a unitary status, it no longer had to remain under federal court order to desegregate even if the schools had become re-segregated as a result of housing patterns. It held that *de facto* segregation was not subject to court oversight when the evidence presented in court failed to show government action as the cause of segregated schools; only *de jure* segregated schools were subject to federal court supervision.

U.S. v. Fordice, 505 U.S. 717 (1992)   8½-½

On behalf of this decision, notably odd for the breakdown of the justices, Justice White ruled that public institutions of higher education must de-segregate by relaxing admissions standards because they are "traceable to the *de jure* system and were originally adopted for a discriminatory purpose." Justice White also held that because the duplication of non-core programs at these institutions impeded desegregation efforts, the institutions must halt all "unnecessary duplication." (The Court defined "non-core" programs as all basic non-liberal arts and science courses at the bachelor's level and all programs above the master's level.)

Missouri v. Jenkins, 515 U.S. 70 (1995)   5-4

In this case, the Court signaled the end of desegregation enforcement by federal courts when Chief Justice Rehnquist ruled that Missouri could not constitutionally order the state of Missouri to raise property taxes and construction bonds to pay for new schools, improved facilities, and higher teacher salaries in the predominantly black school districts in order to at-tract white students. He held that schools, once desegregated under court order, that had now become re-segregated as a result of *de facto* housing patterns, precluded federal court oversight because of the absence of state action or *de jure* segregation.

Affirmative Action and Race: Cases

Affirmative action programs, sometimes referred to as racial prefer-ences or reverse discrimination, became highly controversial in Ameri-can society in the last quarter of the twentieth century. In the three cases below, the Court set forth its position on how race may and may not be constitutionally used in federal contracts and in higher education ad-missions programs in light of the requirements of the Equal Protection Clause of the Fourteenth Amendment and Title VI of the Civil Rights Act of 1964.

Case 4.4

Regents of the University of California v. Bakke
438 U.S. 265, 98 S.Ct. 2733 (1978)

Medical school admissions officials at the University of California, Davis, accepted 100 students each year in its regular admissions program. Meantime, the school set aside 16 of those places in its special admissions program for disadvantaged minority students whose grades or board scores were lower than the required minimum. The school denied admission to Allen Bakke, a white applicant, both times he applied, and he filed suit to compel his admission. Bakke claimed that the special admissions program excluded him because of his race in violation of the Equal Protection Clause of the Fourteenth Amendment, a provision of the California Constitution, and 601 of Title VI of the Civil Rights Act of 1964, which provided that no person shall on the ground of race or color be excluded from participating in any program receiving federal financial assistance.

The California trial court found that the special admissions program of UC-Davis was a racial quota. The school rated minority applicants in that program, the court said, only against one another, and 16 places in the class of 100 were reserved for them. The court declined to order Bakke's admission, however, because he failed to show that the school would have admitted him even if there were no special program. The California Supreme Court applied the strict-scrutiny standard and concluded that the special admissions program was not the least restrictive means of achieving the goals of the admittedly compelling state interests of integrating the medical profession and increasing the number of doctors willing to serve minority patients. The court held that Davis's special admissions program violated the Equal Protection Clause and ordered Bakke's admission to the medical school. The Regents of the University appealed to the Supreme Court.

In a decision that mustered a staggering split 1-4-4 vote, Justice Lewis Powell held that the strict scrutiny test must be used when the Court evaluates the constitutionality of all affirmation programs (Box 4.1). This meant that the government had to demonstrate a "compelling" interest whenever it uses a race-based criterion because as a result of America's history of slavery and racial discrimination, race was a "suspect" class.

When reviewing the set aside of 16 out of 100 students admitted to the school, Powell agreed with the lower court that the program was unconstitutional because it was a quota system. In fact, it was not narrowly tailored at all. He did, however, approve an admissions program along the lines of the so-called "Harvard Plan." Here race and ethnicity were used as one factor among many, and not by "the assignment of a fixed number of places to a minority group."

Two groups of justices differed over basic premises. One group of four justices, led by Justice William J. Brennan, agreed with Powell that the Fourteenth Amendment could accommodate affirmative action programs and thought the Davis program was constitutional. A separate group of four justices held that the Davis program was unconstitutional as a violation of the Equal Protection Clause and Title VI of the Civil Rights Act of 1964. This group, led by Justice John Paul Stevens, made no judgment about whether affirmative action programs were constitutional.

The decision worked out along these lines:

	Is Affirmative Action Constitutional?	Is the Davis Program Constitutional?
Lewis Powell	Yes	No
William J. Brennan	Yes	Yes
Byron R. White	Yes	Yes
Thurgood Marshall	Yes	Yes
Harry A. Blackmun	Yes	Yes
John Paul Stevens	No decision	No
Warren Burger	No decision	No
William Rehnquist	No decision	No
Potter Stewart	No decision	No

Justice POWELL delivered the opinion of the Court.

Over the past 30 years, this Court has embarked upon the crucial mission of interpreting the Equal Protection Clause with the view of assuring to all persons "the protection of equal laws" in a Nation confronting a legacy of slavery and racial discrimination. Because the landmark decisions in this area arose in response to the continued exclusion of

Negroes from the mainstream of American society, they could be characterized as involving discrimination by the "majority" white race against the Negro minority. But they need not be read as depending upon that characterization for their results. It suffices to say that "over the years, this Court has consistently repudiated 'distinctions between citizens solely because of their ancestry' as being 'odious to a free people whose institutions are founded upon the doctrine of equality.'" *Loving v. Virginia*, 388 U.S. 1 (1967), quoting *Hirabayashi [v. United States]*, 320 [U.S. 81 (1943)].

Petitioner urges us to adopt for the first time a more restrictive view of the Equal Protection Clause and hold that discrimination against members of the white "majority" cannot be suspect if its purpose can be characterized as "benign." The clock of our liberties, however, cannot be turned back to 1868. It is far too late to argue that the guarantee of equal protection to all persons permits the recognition of special wards entitled to a degree of protection greater than that accorded others. "The Fourteenth Amendment is not directed solely against discrimination due to a 'two-class theory'—that is, based upon differences between 'white' and Negro." *Hernandez [v. Texas]*, 347 U.S. [475 (1954)].

Once the artificial line of a "two-class theory" of the Fourteenth Amendment is put aside, the difficulties entailed in varying the level of judicial review according to a perceived "preferred" status of a particular racial or ethnic minority are intractable. . . .

Moreover, there are serious problems of justice connected with the idea of preference itself. First, it may not always be clear that a so-called preference is in fact benign. Courts may be asked to validate burdens imposed upon individual members of a particular group in order to advance the group's general interest. Nothing in the Constitution supports the notion that individuals may be asked to suffer otherwise impermissible burdens in order to enhance the societal standing of their ethnic groups. Second, preferential programs may only reinforce common stereotypes holding that certain groups are unable to achieve success without special protection based on a factor having no relationship to individual worth. Third, there is a measure of inequity in forcing innocent persons in respondent's position to bear the burdens of redressing grievances not of their making. . . .

If it is the individual who is entitled to judicial protection against classifications based upon his racial or ethnic background because such distinctions impinge upon personal rights, rather than the individual only because of his membership in a particular group, then constitutional standards may be applied consistently. Political judgments regarding the necessity for the particular classification may be weighed in the constitutional balance, *Korematsu v. United States*, 323 U.S. 214 (1944), but the standard of justification will remain constant. This is as it should be, since those political judgments are the product of rough compromise struck by contending groups within the democratic process. When they touch upon an individual's race or ethnic background, he is entitled to a judicial determination that the burden he is asked to bear on that basis is precisely tailored to serve a compelling governmental interest. The Constitution guarantees that right to every person regardless of his background. . . .

In this case . . . there has been no determination by the legislature or a responsible administrative agency that the University engaged in a discriminatory practice requiring remedial efforts. Moreover, the operation of petitioner's special admissions program is quite different from the remedial measures approved in those cases. It prefers the designated minority groups at the expense of other individuals who are totally foreclosed from competition for the 16 special admissions seats in every Medical School class. Because of that foreclosure, some individuals are excluded from enjoyment of a state-provided benefit—admission to the Medical School—they otherwise would receive. When a classification denies an individual opportunities or benefits enjoyed by others solely because of his race or ethnic background, it must be regarded as suspect.

We have held that in "order to justify the use of a suspect classification, a State must show that its purpose or interest is both constitutionally permissible and substantial, and that its use of the classification is 'necessary . . . to the accomplishment' of its purpose or the safeguarding of its interest." The special admissions program purports to serve the purposes of: (i) "reducing the historic deficit of traditionally disfavored minorities in medical schools and in the medical profession," (ii) countering the effects of societal discrimination; (iii) increasing the number of physicians who will practice in communities currently underserved; and (iv) obtaining the educational benefits that flow from an ethnically diverse student body. It is necessary to decide which, if any, of these purposes is substantial enough to support the use of a suspect classification. . . .

The State certainly has a legitimate and substantial interest in ameliorating, or eliminating where feasible, the disabling effects of identified discrimination. The line of school desegregation cases, commencing with Brown, attests to the importance of this state goal and the commitment of the judiciary to affirm all lawful means toward its attainment. In the school cases, the States were required by court order to redress the wrongs worked by specific instances of racial discrimination. That goal was far more focused than the remedying of the effects of "societal discrimination," an amorphous concept of injury that may be ageless in its reach into the past.

We have never approved a classification that aids persons perceived as members of relatively victimized groups at the expense of other innocent individuals in the absence of judicial, legislative, or administrative findings of constitutional or statutory violations. After such findings have been made, the governmental interest in preferring members of the injured groups at the expense of others is substantial, since the legal rights of the victims must be vindicated. In such a case, the extent of the injury and the consequent remedy will have been judicially, legislatively, or administrative defined. Also, the remedial action usually remains subject to continuing oversight to assure that it will work the least harm possible to other innocent persons competing for the benefit. Without such findings of constitutional or statutory violations, it cannot be said that the government has any greater interest in helping one individual than in refraining from harming another. Thus, the government has no compelling justification for inflicting such harm.

Petitioner does not purport to have made, and is in no position to make, such findings. Its broad mission is education, not the formulation of any legislative policy or the adjudication of particular claims of illegality. For reasons similar to those stated [above in] this opinion, isolated segments of our vast governmental structures are not competent to make those decisions, at least in the absence of legislative mandates and legislatively determined criteria. Before relying upon these sorts of findings in establishing a racial classification, a governmental body must have the authority and capability to establish, in the record, that the classification is responsive to identified discrimination. Lacking this capability, petitioner has not carried its burden of justification on this issue.

Hence, the purpose of helping certain groups whom the faculty of the Davis Medical School perceived as victims of "societal discrimination" does not justify a classification that imposes disadvantages upon persons like respondent, who bear no responsibility for whatever harm the beneficiaries of the special admissions program are thought to have suffered. To hold otherwise would be to convert a remedy heretofore reserved for violations of legal rights into a privilege that all institutions throughout the Nation could grant at their pleasure to whatever groups are perceived as victims of societal discrimination. That is a step we have never approved.

Petitioner identifies, as another purpose of its program, improving the delivery of health-care services to communities currently underserved. It may be assumed that in some situations a State's interest in facilitating the health care of its citizens is sufficiently compelling to support the use of a suspect classification. But there is virtually no evidence in the record indicating that petitioner's special admissions program is either needed or geared to promote that goal. . . .

Petitioner simply has not carried its burden of demonstrating that it must prefer members of particular ethnic groups over all other individuals in order to promote better health-care delivery to deprived citizens. Indeed, petitioner has not shown that its preferential classification is likely to have any significant effect on the problem.

The fourth goal asserted by petitioner is the attainment of a diverse student body. This clearly is a constitutionally permissible goal for an institution of higher education. Academic freedom, though not a specifically enumerated constitutional right, long has been viewed as a special concern of the First Amendment. The freedom of a university to make its own judgments as to education includes the selection of its student body. . . . It may be argued that there is greater force to these views at the undergraduate level than in a medical school where the training is centered primarily on professional competency. But even at the graduate level, our tradition and experience lend support to the view that the contribution of diversity is substantial. . . . Physicians serve a heterogeneous population. An otherwise qualified medical student with a particular background—whether it be ethnic, geographic, culturally advantaged or disadvantaged—may bring to a professional school of medicine experiences, outlooks, and ideas that enrich the training of its student body and better equip its graduates to render with understanding their vital service to humanity.

Ethnic diversity, however, is only one element in a range of factors a university properly may consider in attaining the goal of a heterogeneous student body. Although a university must have wide discretion in making the sensitive judgments as to who should be admitted, constitutional limitations protecting individual rights may not be disregarded. Respondent urges—and the courts below have held—that petitioner's dual admissions program is a racial classification that impermissibly infringes his rights under the Fourteenth Amendment. As the interest of diversity is compelling in the context of a university's admissions program, the question remains whether the program's racial classification is necessary to promote this interest.

It may be assumed that the reservation of a specified number of seats in each class for individuals from the preferred ethnic groups would contribute to the attainment of considerable ethnic diversity in the student body. But petitioner's argument that this is the only effective means of serving the interest of diversity is seriously flawed. In a most fundamental sense the argument misconceives the nature of the state interest that would justify consideration of race or ethnic background. It is not an interest in simple ethnic diversity, in which a specified percentage of the student body is in effect guaranteed to be members of selected ethnic groups, with the remaining percentage an undifferentiated aggregation of students. The diversity that furthers a compelling state interest encompasses a far broader array of qualifications and characteristics of which racial or ethnic origin is but a single though important element. Petitioner's special admissions program, focused solely on ethnic diversity, would hinder rather than further attainment of genuine diversity.

Nor would the state interest in genuine diversity be served by expanding petitioner's two-track system into a multitrack program with a prescribed number of seats set aside for each identifiable category of applicants. Indeed, it is inconceivable that a university would thus pursue the logic of petitioner's two-track program to the illogical end of insulating each category of applicants with certain desired qualifications from competition with all other applicants.

The experience of other university admissions programs, which take race into account in achieving the educational diversity valued by the First Amendment, demonstrates that the assignment of a fixed number of places to a minority group is not a necessary means toward that end. An illuminating example is found in the Harvard College program:

> "In recent years Harvard College has expanded the concept of diversity to include students from disadvantaged economic, racial and ethnic groups. Harvard College now recruits not only Californians or Louisianans but also blacks and Chicanos and other minority students. . . .
>
> "In practice, this new definition of diversity has meant that race has been a factor in some admission decisions. When the Committee on Admissions reviews the large middle group of applicants who are 'admissible' and deemed capable of doing good work in their courses, the race of an applicant may tip the balance in his favor just as geographic origin or a life spent on a farm may tip the balance in other candidates' cases. A farm boy from Idaho can bring something to Harvard College that a Bostonian cannot offer. Similarly, a black student can usually bring something that a white person cannot offer. . . .
>
> "In Harvard College admissions the Committee has not set target-quotas for the number of blacks, or of musicians, football players, physicists or Californians to be admitted in a given year. . . . But that awareness [of the necessity of including more than a token number of black students] does not mean that the Committee sets a minimum number of blacks or of people from west of the Mississippi who are to be admitted. It means only that in choosing among thousands of applicants who are not only 'admissible' academically but have other strong qualities, the Committee, with a number of criteria in mind, pays some attention to distribution among many types and categories of students." App. to Brief for Columbia University, Harvard University, Stanford University, and the University of Pennsylvania, as *Amici Curiae* 2-3.

In such an admissions program, race or ethnic background may be deemed a "plus" in a particular applicant's file, yet it does not insulate the individual from comparison with all other candidates for the available seats. The file of a particular black applicant may be examined for his potential contribution to diversity without the factor of race being decisive when compared, for example, with that of an applicant identified as an Italian-American if the latter is thought to exhibit qualities more likely to promote beneficial educational pluralism. Such qualities could include exceptional personal talents, unique work or service experience, leadership potential, maturity, demonstrated compassion, a history of overcoming disadvantage, ability to communicate with the poor, or other qualifications deemed important. In short, an admissions program operated in this way is flexible enough to consider all pertinent elements of diversity in light of the particular qualifications of each applicant, and to place them on the same footing for consideration, although not necessarily according them the same weight. Indeed, the weight attributed to a particular quality may vary from year to year depending upon the "mix" both of the student body and the applicants for the incoming class.

This kind of program treats each applicant as an individual in the admissions process. The applicant who loses out on the last available seat to another candidate receiving a "plus" on the basis of ethnic background will not have been foreclosed from all consideration for that seat simply because he was not the right color or had the wrong surname. It would mean only that his combined qualifications, which may have included similar nonobjective factors, did not outweigh those of the other applicant. His qualifications would have been weighed fairly and competitively, and he would have no basis to complain of unequal treatment under the Fourteenth Amendment. . . .

In summary, it is evident that the Davis special admissions program involves the use of an explicit racial classification never before countenanced by this Court. It tells applicants who are not Negro, Asian, or Chicano that they are totally excluded from a specific percentage of the seats in an entering class. No matter how strong their qualifications, quantitative and extracurricular, including their own potential for contribution to educational diversity, they are never afforded the chance to compete with applicants from the preferred groups for the special admissions seats. At the same time, the preferred applicants have the opportunity to compete for every seat in the class.

The fatal flaw in petitioner's preferential program is its disregard of individual rights as guaranteed by the Fourteenth Amendment. Such rights are not absolute. But when a State's distribution of benefits or imposition of burdens hinges on ancestry or the color of a person's skin, that individual is entitled to a demonstration that the challenged classification is necessary to promote a substantial state interest. Petitioner has failed to carry this burden. For this reason, that portion of the California court's judgment holding petitioner's special admissions program invalid under the Fourteenth Amendment must be affirmed.

In enjoining petitioner from ever considering the race of any applicant, however, the courts below failed to recognize that the State has a substantial interest that legitimately may be served by a properly devised admissions program involving the competitive consideration of race and ethnic origin. For this reason, so much of the California court's judgment as enjoins petitioner from any consideration of the race of any applicant must be reversed.

Case 4.5

Adarand Constructors, Inc., v. Pena
515 U.S. 200, 115 S.Ct. 2097 (1995)

To stimulate the growth of minority-owned businesses, the Small Business Administration encouraged the award of subcontracts on federal projects to companies that the federal government certified "as small businesses owned and controlled by socially and economically disadvantaged individuals." The Small Business Act (SBA) defined "socially and economically disadvantaged individuals" as those "who have been subject to racial or ethnic prejudice or cultural bias." Moreover, another federal law, the Surface Transportation and Uniform Relocation Assistance Act (STURAA), required that at least 10 percent of such federal contracts be awarded to companies owned by socially and economically disadvantaged individuals.

Adarand Constructors was not such a business. Primarily engaged in erecting guardrails along highways, it placed a low bid on a sub-contract for work on a project undertaken by a company that had a contract from the U.S. Department of Transportation. When the sub-contract was awarded to a minority-owned enterprise, the Gonzales Construction Co., Adarand sued the Department of Transportation in federal district court, which granted the respondent's motion for summary judgment.

Adarand appealed to the U.S. Court of Appeals for the Tenth Circuit, which upheld the lower court's ruling. The court based its ruling on the Supreme Court's decisions in *Fullilove v. Klutznick*, 448 U.S. 448 (1980), and *Metro Broadcasting v. Federal Communications Commission*, 497 U.S. 547 (1990), upholding such procedures. Adarand appealed to the Supreme Court, which granted *certiorari*.

Writing the judgment of the Court for a five to four majority, Justice Sandra Day O'Connor overturned *Metro Broadcasting*, and held that the strict scrutiny test must be used in federal affirmative action cases. She thus argued that actions by the United States government must conform to a 1989 ruling that set forth the same strict scrutiny requirement for constitutional challenges of state and local laws (*City of Richmond v. J. A. Croson*, 488 U.S. 469). Justices Clarence Thomas and Antonin Scalia filed opinions concurring in part and concurring in the judgment.

Justice John Paul Stevens filed a dissenting opinion, in which Justice Ruth Bader Ginsburg joined. Justice David H. Souter filed a dissenting opinion, in which Justices Rith Bader Ginsburg and Stephen G. Breyer joined. Justice Ginsburg filed a dissenting opinion, in which Justice Breyer joined.

Justice O'CONNOR announced the judgment of the Court.

. . . Adarand's claim arises under the Fifth Amendment to the Constitution, which provides that "No person shall . . . be deprived of life, liberty, or property, without due process of law." Although this Court has always understood that Clause to provide some measure of protection against arbitrary treatment by the Federal Government, it is not as explicit a guarantee of equal treatment as the Fourteenth Amendment, which provides that "No State shall . . . deny to any person within its jurisdiction the equal protection of the laws." Our cases have accorded varying degrees of significance to the difference in the language of those two Clauses. We think it necessary to revisit the issue here. . . .

In *Bolling v. Sharpe*, 347 U.S. 497 (1954), the Court for the first time explicitly questioned the existence of any difference between the obligations of the Federal Government and the States to avoid racial classifications. *Bolling* did note that "the 'equal protection of the laws' is a more explicit safeguard of prohibited unfairness than 'due process of law.'" But *Bolling* then concluded that, "in view of [the] decision that the Constitution prohibits the states from maintaining racially segregated public schools, it would be unthinkable that the same Constitution would impose a lesser duty on the Federal Government."

Bolling's facts concerned school desegregation, but its reasoning was not so limited. The Court's observations that "distinctions between citizens solely because of their ancestry are by their very nature odious," *Hirabayashi* [*v. United States*], 320 U.S. [81 (1943)], and that "all legal restrictions which curtail the civil rights of a single racial group are immediately suspect," *Korematsu* [*v. United States*], 323 U.S. [214 (1944)], carry no less force in the context of federal action than in the context of action by the States—indeed, they first appeared in cases concerning action by the Federal Government. . . .

Most of the cases discussed above involved classifications burdening groups that have suffered discrimination in our society. In 1978, the Court confronted the question whether race-based governmental action designed to benefit such groups should also be subject to "the most rigid scrutiny." *Regents of Univ. of California v. Bakke*, 438 U.S. 265 [1978], involved an equal protection challenge to a state-run medical school's practice of reserving a number of spaces in its entering class for minority students. . . . In a passage joined by Justice White, Justice Powell wrote [for the Court] that "the guarantee of equal protection cannot mean one thing when applied to one individual and something else when applied to a person of another color." He concluded that "racial and ethnic distinctions of any sort are inherently suspect and thus call for the most exacting judicial examination." . . .

Two years after *Bakke*, the Court faced another challenge to remedial race-based action, this time involving action undertaken by the Federal Government. In *Fullilove v. Klutznick*, 448 U.S. 448 (1980), the Court upheld Congress' inclusion of a 10% set-aside for minority-owned businesses in the Public Works Employment Act of 1977. As in *Bakke*, there was no opinion for the Court. Chief Justice Burger, in an opinion joined by Justices White and Powell, observed that "any preference based on racial or ethnic criteria must necessarily receive a most searching examination to make sure that it does not conflict with constitutional guarantees." That opinion, however, "did not adopt, either expressly or implicitly, the formulas of analysis articulated in such cases as [*Bakke*]." It employed instead a two-part test which asked, first, "whether the objectives of the legislation are within the power of Congress," and second, "whether the limited use of racial and ethnic criteria, in the context presented, is a constitutionally permissible means for achieving the congressional objectives." It then upheld the program under that test, adding at the end of the opinion that the program also "would survive judicial review under either 'test' articulated in the several *Bakke* opinions." . . .

In *Wygant v. Jackson Board of Ed.*, 476 U.S. 267 (1986), the Court considered . . . whether a school board could adopt race-based preferences in determining which teachers to lay off. Justice Powell's plurality opinion observed that "the level of scrutiny does not change merely because the challenged classification operates against a group that historically has not been subject to governmental discrimination," and stated the two-part inquiry as "whether the layoff provision is supported by a compelling state purpose and whether the means chosen to accomplish that purpose are narrowly tailored." In other words, "racial classifications of any sort must be subjected to 'strict scrutiny.' " . . .

The Court's failure to produce a majority opinion in *Bakke*, *Fullilove*, and *Wygant* left unresolved the proper analysis for remedial race-based governmental action. . . .

The Court resolved the issue, at least in part, in 1989. [*City of*]

Richmond v. J. A. Croson Co., 488 U.S. 469 (1989), concerned a city's determination that 30% of its contracting work should go to minority-owned businesses. A majority of the Court in *Croson* held that "the standard of review under the Equal Protection Clause is not dependent on the race of those burdened or benefited by a particular classification," and that the single standard of review for racial classifications should be "strict scrutiny." . . . The Court also thought it "obvious that [the] program is not narrowly tailored to remedy the effects of prior discrimination."

With *Croson*, the Court finally agreed that the Fourteenth Amendment requires strict scrutiny of all race-based action by state and local governments. But *Croson* of course had no occasion to declare what standard of review the Fifth Amendment requires for such action taken by the Federal Government. . . .

Despite lingering uncertainty in the details, however, the Court's cases through *Croson* had established three general propositions with respect to governmental racial classifications. First, skepticism: " 'any preference based on racial or ethnic criteria must necessarily receive a most searching examination,' " *Wygant*. Second, consistency: "the standard of review under the Equal Protection Clause is not dependent on the race of those burdened or benefited by a particular classification," *Croson*. And third, congruence: "equal protection analysis in the Fifth Amendment area is the same as that under the Fourteenth Amendment," *Buckley v. Valeo*, 424 U.S. [1 (1976)]. Taken together, these three propositions lead to the conclusion that any person, of whatever race, has the right to demand that any governmental actor subject to the Constitution justify any racial classification subjecting that person to unequal treatment under the strictest judicial scrutiny. . . .

A year later, however, the Court took a surprising turn. *Metro Broadcasting, Inc. v. FCC*, 497 U.S. 547 (1990), involved a Fifth Amendment challenge to two race-based policies of the Federal Communications Commission. . . . It did so by holding that "benign" federal racial classifications need only satisfy intermediate scrutiny, even though *Croson* had recently concluded that such classifications enacted by a State must satisfy strict scrutiny. . . .

By adopting intermediate scrutiny as the standard of review for congressionally mandated "benign" racial classifications, *Metro Broadcasting* departed from prior cases in two significant respects. First, it turned its back on *Croson*'s explanation of why strict scrutiny of all governmental racial classifications is essential. . . .

Second, *Metro Broadcasting* squarely rejected one of the three propositions established by the Court's earlier equal protection cases, namely, congruence between the standards applicable to federal and state racial classifications, and in so doing also undermined the other two—skepticism of all racial classifications, and consistency of treatment irrespective of the race of the burdened or benefited group. Under *Metro Broadcasting*, certain racial classifications ("benign" ones enacted by the Federal Government) should be treated less skeptically than others; and the race of the benefited group is critical to the determination of which standard of review to apply. *Metro Broadcasting* was thus a significant departure from much of what had come before it. . . .

Accordingly, we hold today that all racial classifications, imposed by whatever federal, state, or local governmental actor, must be analyzed by a reviewing court under strict scrutiny. In other words, such classifications are constitutional only if they are narrowly tailored measures that further compelling governmental interests. To the extent that *Metro Broadcasting* is inconsistent with that holding, it is overruled. . . .

It is worth pointing out the difference between the applications of *stare decisis* in this case and in *Planned Parenthood of Southeastern Pa. v. Casey*, 505 U.S. 833 (1992). *Casey* explained how considerations of *stare decisis* inform the decision whether to overrule a long-established precedent that has become integrated into the fabric of the law. Overruling precedent of that kind naturally may have consequences for "the ideal of the rule of law." In addition, such precedent is likely to have engendered substantial reliance, as was true in *Casey* itself. But in this case, as we have explained, we do not face a precedent of that kind, because *Metro Broadcasting* itself departed from our prior cases—and did so quite recently. By refusing to follow *Metro Broadcasting*, then, we do not depart from the fabric of the law; we restore it. . . .

Accordingly, the judgment of the Court of Appeals is vacated, and the case is remanded for further proceedings consistent with this opinion.

It is so ordered.

Justice SCALIA, concurring in part and concurring in the judgment.

. . . In my view, government can never have a "compelling interest" in discriminating on the basis of race in order to "make up" for past racial discrimination in the opposite direction. In the eyes of government, we are just one race here. It is American. . . .

Justice STEVENS, with whom Justice GINSBURG joins, dissenting.

. . . [I]n *Metro Broadcasting, Inc. v. FCC*, 497 U.S. 547 (1990), in which we upheld a federal program designed to foster racial diversity in broadcasting, we identified the special "institutional competence" of our National Legislature. "It is of overriding significance in these cases," we were careful to emphasize, "that the FCC's minority ownership programs have been specifically approved indeed, mandated—by Congress." We recalled the several opinions in *Fullilove* that admonished this Court to "'approach our task with appropriate deference to the Congress, a co-equal branch charged by the Constitution with the power to "provide for the . . . general Welfare of the United States" and "to enforce, by appropriate legislation," the equal protection guarantees of the Fourteenth Amendment.'" . . .

The majority in *Metro Broadcasting* and the plurality in *Fullilove* were not alone in relying upon a critical distinction between federal and state programs. . . .

In her plurality opinion in *Croson*, Justice O'Connor also emphasized the importance of this distinction when she responded to the City's argument that *Fullilove* was controlling. She wrote: "What appellant ignores is that Congress, unlike any State or political subdivision, has a specific constitutional mandate to enforce the dictates of the Fourteenth Amendment. The power to 'enforce' may at times also include the power to define situations which Congress determines threaten principles of equality and to adopt prophylactic rules to deal with those situations. The Civil War Amendments themselves worked a dramatic change in the balance between congressional and state power over matters of race."

An additional reason for giving greater deference to the National Legislature than to a local law-making body is that federal affirmative-action programs represent the will of our entire Nation's elected representatives, whereas a state or local program may have an impact on nonresident entities who played no part in the decision to enact it. Thus, in the state or local context, individuals who were unable to vote for the local representatives who enacted a race-conscious program may nonetheless feel the effects of that program. This difference recalls the goals of the Commerce Clause, which permits Congress to legislate on certain matters of national importance while denying power to the States in this area for fear of undue impact upon out-of-state residents.

Ironically, after all of the time, effort, and paper this Court has expended in differentiating between federal and state affirmative action, the majority today virtually ignores the issue. . . .

Our opinion in *Metro Broadcasting* relied on several constitutional provisions to justify the greater deference we owe to Congress when it acts with respect to private individuals. In the programs challenged in this case, Congress has acted both with respect to private individuals and, as in *Fullilove*, with respect to the States themselves. . . .

The Court's holding in *Fullilove* surely governs the result in this case. The Public Works Employment Act of 1977, which this Court upheld in *Fullilove*, is different in several critical respects from the portions of the Small Business Act (SBA), and the Surface Transportation and

Uniform Relocation Assistance Act of 1987 (STURAA) challenged in this case. Each of those differences makes the current program designed to provide assistance to disadvantaged business enterprises (DBE's) significantly less objectionable than the 1977 categorical grant of $400 million in exchange for a 10% set-aside in public contracts to "a class of investors defined solely by racial characteristics." *Fullilove*. In no meaningful respect is the current scheme more objectionable than the 1977 Act. Thus, if the 1977 Act was constitutional, then so must be the SBA and STURAA. Indeed, even if my dissenting views in *Fullilove* had prevailed, this program would be valid.

Unlike the 1977 Act, the present statutory scheme does not make race the sole criterion of eligibility for participation in the program. Race does give rise to a rebuttable presumption of social disadvantage which, at least under STURAA, gives rise to a second rebuttable presumption of economic disadvantage. But a small business may qualify as a DBE, by showing that it is both socially and economically disadvantaged, even if it receives neither of these presumptions. Thus, the current preference is more inclusive than the 1977 Act because it does not make race a necessary qualification.

More importantly, race is not a sufficient qualification. Whereas a millionaire with a long history of financial successes, who was a member of numerous social clubs and trade associations, would have qualified for a preference under the 1977 Act merely because he was an Asian American or an African American, neither the SBA nor STURAA creates any such anomaly. The DBE program excludes members of minority races who are not, in fact, socially or economically disadvantaged. . . .

My skeptical scrutiny of the Court's opinion leaves me in dissent. The majority's concept of "consistency" ignores a difference, fundamental to the idea of equal protection, between oppression and assistance. The majority's concept of "congruence" ignores a difference, fundamental to our constitutional system, between the Federal Government and the States. And the majority's concept of *stare decisis* ignores the force of binding precedent. I would affirm the judgment of the Court of Appeals.

Case 4.6

Grutter v. Bollinger
539 U.S. 306, 123 S.Ct. 2325 (2003)

The University of Michigan School of Law is one of the nation's prestigious public law schools. It was not surprising that Barbara

Grutter, a white Michigan resident, wanted to attend. When she applied in 1996, she had earned a high undergraduate 3.8 Grade Point Average, and she had scored 161 on the Law School Admission Test (LSAT), placing her in the 90th percentile. Her record made her an attractive candidate for most law school admissions committees. The Michigan law school initially offered her a place on the waiting list, but when it ultimately found that the class was filled, it rejected her application.

In December, 1997, Grutter filed suit in United States district court for the Eastern District of Michigan against the following defendants: the law school, the Regents of the University of Michigan, Lee Bollinger (who was dean of the school from 1987 to 1994, and then president of the university from 1996 to 2002), Jeffrey Lehman (Bollinger's successor as dean), and Dennis Shields (the then-director of law school admissions). She argued that they had discriminated against her on the basis of her race in violation of the Equal Protection Clause of the Fourteenth Amendment and Title VI of the Civil Rights Act of 1964.

She also stated that her application was rejected because the law school had used race as a "predominant" factor, giving applicants who belong to certain minority groups "a significantly greater chance of admission than students with similar credentials from disfavored racial groups." She alleged that respondents "had no compelling interest to justify their use of race in the admissions process." Her suit demanded three outcomes: compensatory and punitive damages, an order requiring the school to offer her admission, and an injunction prohibiting the school from continuing to discriminate on the basis of race.

In response, the University of Michigan argued that its law school admission policies were based in part on its desire to achieve a diverse student body which was constitutionally accepted in *Regents of University of California v. Bakke*, 438 U.S. 265 (1978). The admissions committee focused on several factors in determining whether an applicant would be an appropriate and qualified candidate for its freshman law school class. First, it assessed their talents, experiences, and potential by evaluating all of the material the applicant submitted, including a grade point average, LSAT score, a personal statement, letters of recommendation, an essay describing how the applicant will contribute to law school life and diversity.

In addition, committee members looked beyond grades and scores to so-called "soft variables," such as recommenders' enthusiasm, the quality of the undergraduate institution and the applicant's essay, and the areas and difficulty of undergraduate major and course selection. Nowhere did the policy define diversity solely in terms of racial and ethnic status nor did it restrict the types of diversity contributions eligible for "substantial weight." On the other hand, it reaffirmed the school's commitment to diversity with special reference to the inclusion of African-American, Hispanic, and Native-American students who otherwise might not be represented in the student body in *meaningful numbers*. By enrolling a *critical mass* of underrepresented minority students, the policy sought to ensure their ability to contribute to the law school's character and to the legal profession. (The law school used the words in italic.)

At trial in federal district court, the then-admissions director, Dennis Shields, testified he did not direct his staff to admit a particular percentage or number of minority students, but only to consider an applicant's race along with all other factors. His goal, along with members of the staff and the admission committee, was to ensure that a *critical mass* of underrepresented minority students would be reached so as to realize the educational benefits of a diverse student body. He was careful to include the statement that he never once sought to admit any particular number or percentage of underrepresented minority students. In other words, there were no quotas.

His successor, Erica Munzel, defined what the law school meant when it used the terms that *critical mass, meaningful numbers*, and *meaningful representation*. They all referred to a number that encourages underrepresented minority students to participate in the classroom and not feel isolated. While there was no number, percentage, or range of numbers or percentages that constituted a critical mass, it was clear to the admissions staff that it had to consider the race and ethnicity of applicants: a critical mass of underrepresented minority students would not be enrolled if admissions decisions were based solely or even primarily on undergraduate GPAs and LSAT scores.

The district court held that law school's use of race as an admissions factor was unlawful. The university appealed, and the Court of Appeals for the Sixth Circuit reversed, holding that Justice Powell's opinion in *Bakke* was binding precedent establishing diversity as a compelling state interest. It also found that the school's use of race was narrowly tailored because race was merely a "potential 'plus' factor" and because the law school's program was virtually identical to the Harvard admissions program described approvingly by Justice Powell and appended to his *Bakke* opinion. Grutter appealed the appellate court's decision to the Supreme Court, which sustained the ruling by a vote of five to four.

There were six opinions. Justice Sandra O'Connor delivered the opinion of the court, which was joined by Justices John Paul Stevens, David H. Souter, Ruth Bader Ginsburg, and Stephen G. Breyer. Justice Ginsburg filed a concurring opinion in which Justice Breyer joined. Justice Antonin Scalia filed an opinion concurring in part and dissenting in part, in which Justice Clarence Thomas joined, and Justice Thomas filed an opinion concurring in part and dissenting in part, in which Justice Scalia joined as to Parts I-VII. Chief Justice William H. Rehnquist filed a dissenting opinion, in which Justices Scalia, Thomas, and Anthony M. Kennedy joined, and Justice Kennedy filed a separate dissenting opinion.

On the same day, by a six to three vote, the Court overturned the University of Michigan's undergraduate admissions program. Chief Justice William H. Rehnquist ruled that the program constituted a quota system because it automatically awarded twenty additional points to applicants were from underrepresented minorities or socio-economically disadvantaged families (*Gratz v. Bollinger*, 539 U.S. 244).

Justice O'CONNOR delivered the opinion of the Court.

. . . We have held that all racial classifications imposed by government "must be analyzed by a reviewing court under strict scrutiny." This means that such classifications are constitutional only if they are narrowly tailored to further compelling governmental interests. "Absent searching judicial inquiry into the justification for such race-based measures," we have no way to determine what "classifications are 'benign' or 'remedial' and what classifications are in fact motivated by illegitimate notions of racial inferiority or simple racial politics." [*City of*] *Richmond v. J. A. Croson Co.*, 488 U.S. 469 (1989) (plurality opinion). We apply strict scrutiny to all racial classifications to " 'smoke out' illegitimate uses of race by assuring that [government] is pursuing a goal important enough to warrant use of a highly suspect tool."

Strict scrutiny is not "strict in theory, but fatal in fact." *Adarand Constructors, Inc. v. Pena*, 515 U.S. 200 (1995). Although all governmental uses of race are subject to strict scrutiny, not all are invalidated by it. As we have explained, "whenever the government treats any person unequally because of his or her race, that person has suffered an injury that falls squarely within the language and spirit of the Constitution's guarantee of equal protection." But that observation "says nothing about the ultimate validity of any particular law; that determination is the job of the court applying strict scrutiny." When race-based action is necessary to further a compelling governmental interest, such action does not violate the constitutional guarantee of equal protection so long as the narrow-tailoring requirement is also satisfied.

Context matters when reviewing race-based governmental action under the Equal Protection Clause.... In *Adarand Constructors, Inc. v. Pena*, we made clear that strict scrutiny must take " 'relevant differences' into account." Indeed, as we explained, that is its "fundamental purpose." Not every decision influenced by race is equally objectionable and strict scrutiny is designed to provide a framework for carefully examining the importance and the sincerity of the reasons advanced by the governmental decisionmaker for the use of race in that particular context....

With these principles in mind, we turn to the question whether the Law School's use of race is justified by a compelling state interest. Before this Court, as they have throughout this litigation, respondents assert only one justification for their use of race in the admissions process: obtaining "the educational benefits that flow from a diverse student body." In other words, the Law School asks us to recognize, in the context of higher education, a compelling state interest in student body diversity.

We first wish to dispel the notion that the Law School's argument has been foreclosed, either expressly or implicitly, by our affirmative-action cases decided since [*Regents of University of California v.*] *Bakke* [438 U.S. 265 (1978)]. It is true that some language in those opinions might be read to suggest that remedying past discrimination is the only permissible justification for race-based governmental action. But we have never held that the only governmental use of race that can survive strict scrutiny is remedying past discrimination. Nor, since *Bakke*, have we directly addressed the use of race in the context of public higher education. Today, we hold that the Law School has a compelling interest in attaining a diverse student body....

In order to cultivate a set of leaders with legitimacy in the eyes of the citizenry, it is necessary that the path to leadership be visibly open to talented and qualified individuals of every race and ethnicity. All members of our heterogeneous society must have confidence in the openness and integrity of the educational institutions that provide this training. As we have recognized, law schools "cannot be effective in isolation from the individuals and institutions with which the law interacts." Access to legal education (and thus the legal profession) must be inclusive of talented and qualified individuals of every race and ethnicity, so that all members of our heterogeneous society may participate in the educational institutions that provide the training and education necessary to succeed in America.

The Law School does not premise its need for critical mass on "any belief that minority students always (or even consistently) express some characteristic minority viewpoint on any issue." To the contrary, diminishing the force of such stereotypes is both a crucial part of the Law

School's mission, and one that it cannot accomplish with only token numbers of minority students. . . . The Law School has determined, based on its experience and expertise, that a "critical mass" of underrepresented minorities is necessary to further its compelling interest in securing the educational benefits of a diverse student body.

Even in the limited circumstance when drawing racial distinctions is permissible to further a compelling state interest, government is still "constrained in how it may pursue that end: The means chosen to accomplish the [government's] asserted purpose must be specifically and narrowly framed to accomplish that purpose." *Shaw v. Hunt*, 517 U.S. 899 (1996). The purpose of the narrow tailoring requirement is to ensure that "the means chosen 'fit' . . . the compelling goal so closely that there is little or no possibility that the motive for the classification was illegitimate racial prejudice or stereotype." *Richmond v. J. A. Croson Co.* . . .

To be narrowly tailored, a race-conscious admissions program cannot use a quota system—it cannot "insulate each category of applicants with certain desired qualifications from competition with all other applicants." Instead, a university may consider race or ethnicity only as a " 'plus' in a particular applicant's file," without "insulating the individual from comparison with all other candidates for the available seats." In other words, an admissions program must be "flexible enough to consider all pertinent elements of diversity in light of the particular qualifications of each applicant, and to place them on the same footing for consideration, although not necessarily according them the same weight."

We find that the Law School's admissions program bears the hallmarks of a narrowly tailored plan. . . . We are satisfied that the Law School's admissions program, like the Harvard plan described by Justice Powell, does not operate as a quota. Properly understood, a "quota" is a program in which a certain fixed number or proportion of opportunities are "reserved exclusively for certain minority groups." Quotas " 'impose a fixed number or percentage which must be attained, or which cannot be exceeded,' and "insulate the individual from comparison with all other candidates for the available seats." In contrast, "a permissible goal . . . requires only a good-faith effort . . . to come within a range demarcated by the goal itself," and permits consideration of race as a "plus" factor in any given case while still ensuring that each candidate "competes with all other qualified applicants" [*Bakke*]. . . .

Here, the Law School engages in a highly individualized, holistic review of each applicant's file, giving serious consideration to all the ways an applicant might contribute to a diverse educational environment. The Law School affords this individualized consideration to applicants of all races. There is no policy, either *de jure* or *de facto*, of automatic acceptance or rejection based on any single "soft" variable.

Unlike the program at issue in *Gratz v. Bollinger* [539 U.S.244 (2003)], the Law School awards no mechanical, predetermined diversity "bonuses" based on race or ethnicity. Like the Harvard plan, the Law School's admissions policy "is flexible enough to consider all pertinent elements of diversity in light of the particular qualifications of each applicant, and to place them on the same footing for consideration, although not necessarily according them the same weight."

We also find that, like the Harvard plan Justice Powell referenced in *Bakke*, the Law School's race-conscious admissions program adequately ensures that all factors that may contribute to student body diversity are meaningfully considered alongside race in admissions decisions. With respect to the use of race itself, all underrepresented minority students admitted by the Law School have been deemed qualified. . . .

What is more, the Law School actually gives substantial weight to diversity factors besides race. The Law School frequently accepts nonminority applicants with grades and test scores lower than underrepresented minority applicants (and other nonminority applicants) who are rejected. This shows that the Law School seriously weighs many other diversity factors besides race that can make a real and dispositive difference for nonminority applicants as well. . . .

We acknowledge that "there are serious problems of justice connected with the idea of preference itself." *Bakke*. Narrow tailoring, therefore, requires that a race-conscious admissions program not unduly harm members of any racial group. Even remedial race-based governmental action generally "remains subject to continuing oversight to assure that it will work the least harm possible to other innocent persons competing for the benefit." To be narrowly tailored, a race-conscious admissions program must not "unduly burden individuals who are not members of the favored racial and ethnic groups." *Metro Broadcasting, Inc. v. FCC*, 497 U.S. 547 (1990) (Justice O'Connor, dissenting).

We are satisfied that the Law School's admissions program does not. Because the Law School considers "all pertinent elements of diversity," it can (and does) select nonminority applicants who have greater potential to enhance student body diversity over underrepresented minority applicants. As Justice Powell recognized in *Bakke*, so long as a race-conscious admissions program uses race as a "plus" factor in the context of individualized consideration, a rejected applicant "will not have been foreclosed from all consideration for that seat simply because he was not the right color or had the wrong surname. . . .

In summary, the Equal Protection Clause does not prohibit the Law School's narrowly tailored use of race in admissions decisions to further a compelling interest in obtaining the educational benefits that flow from a diverse student body. Consequently, petitioner's statutory claims based on Title VI and 42 USC Section 1981 also fail. The judgment of the Court of Appeals for the Sixth Circuit, accordingly, is affirmed.

It is so ordered.

Chief Justice REHNQUIST, with whom Justices SCALIA, KENNEDY, and THOMAS join, dissenting.

... The Law School claims it must take the steps it does to achieve a " 'critical mass' " of underrepresented minority students. But its actual program bears no relation to this asserted goal. Stripped of its "critical mass" veil, the Law School's program is revealed as a naked effort to achieve racial balancing.

As we have explained many times, "any preference based on racial or ethnic criteria must necessarily receive a most searching examination." *Adarand Constructors, Inc. v. Pena* [515 U.S. 200 (1995)]. Our cases establish that, in order to withstand this demanding inquiry, respondents must demonstrate that their methods of using race "fit" a compelling state interest "with greater precision than any alternative means."

Before the Court's decision today, we consistently applied the same strict scrutiny analysis regardless of the government's purported reason for using race and regardless of the setting in which race was being used. We rejected calls to use more lenient review in the face of claims that race was being used in "good faith" because " 'more than good motives should be required when government seeks to allocate its resources by way of an explicit racial classification system.' " We likewise rejected calls to apply more lenient review based on the particular setting in which race is being used. Indeed, even in the specific context of higher education, we emphasized that "constitutional limitations protecting individual rights may not be disregarded."

Although the Court recites the language of our strict scrutiny analysis, its application of that review is unprecedented in its deference. Respondents' asserted justification for the Law School's use of race in the admissions process is "obtaining 'the educational benefits that flow from a diverse student body.' " They contend that a "critical mass" of underrepresented minorities is necessary to further that interest. Respondents and school administrators explain generally that "critical mass" means a sufficient number of underrepresented minority students to achieve several objectives: To ensure that these minority students do not feel isolated or like spokespersons for their race; to provide adequate opportunities for the type of interaction upon which the educational benefits of diversity depend; and to challenge all students to think critically and reexamine stereotypes. These objectives indicate that "critical mass" relates to the size of the student body. Respondents further claim that the Law School is achieving "critical mass."

In practice, the Law School's program bears little or no relation to its asserted goal of achieving "critical mass." Respondents explain that the Law School seeks to accumulate a "critical mass" of *each* underrepresented minority group. But the record demonstrates that the Law School's admissions practices with respect to these groups differ dramatically and cannot be defended under any consistent use of the term "critical mass."

From 1995 through 2000, the Law School admitted between 1,130 and 1,310 students. Of those, between 13 and 19 were Native American, between 91 and 108 were African-Americans, and between 47 and 56 were Hispanic. If the Law School is admitting between 91 and 108 African-Americans in order to achieve "critical mass," thereby preventing African-American students from feeling "isolated or like spokespersons for their race," one would think that a number of the same order of magnitude would be necessary to accomplish the same purpose for Hispanics and Native Americans. Similarly, even if all of the Native American applicants admitted in a given year matriculate, which the record demonstrates is not at all the case, how can this possibly constitute a "critical mass" of Native Americans in a class of over 350 students? In order for this pattern of admission to be consistent with the Law School's explanation of "critical mass," one would have to believe that the objectives of "critical mass" offered by respondents are achieved with only half the number of Hispanics and one-sixth the number of Native Americans as compared to African-Americans. But respondents offer no race-specific reasons for such disparities. Instead, they simply emphasize the importance of achieving "critical mass," without any explanation of why that concept is applied differently among the three underrepresented minority groups.

These different numbers, moreover, come only as a result of substantially different treatment among the three underrepresented minority groups, as is apparent in an example offered by the Law School and highlighted by the Court: The school asserts that it "frequently accepts nonminority applicants with grades and test scores lower than underrepresented minority applicants (and other nonminority applicants) who are rejected." Specifically, the Law School states that "sixty-nine minority applicants were rejected between 1995 and 2000 with at least a 3.5 Grade Point Average (GPA) and a [score of] 159 or higher on the [Law School Admissions Test (LSAT)]" while a number of Caucasian and Asian-American applicants with similar or lower scores were admitted.

Review of the record reveals only 67 such individuals. Of these 67 individuals, 56 were Hispanic, while only 6 were African-American, and only 5 were Native American. This discrepancy reflects a consistent practice. For example, in 2000, 12 Hispanics who scored between a 159-160 on the LSAT and earned a GPA of 3.00 or higher applied for admission and only 2 were admitted. Meanwhile, 12 African-Americans in the same range of qualifications applied for admission and all 12 were admitted. Likewise, that same year, 16 Hispanics who scored between a 151-153 on the LSAT and earned a 3.00 or higher applied for admission and only 1 of those applicants was admitted. Twenty-three similarly qualified African-Americans applied for admission and 14 were admitted.

These statistics have a significant bearing on petitioner's case. Respondents have *never* offered any race-specific arguments explaining why significantly more individuals from one underrepresented minority group are needed in order to achieve "critical mass" or further student body diversity. They certainly have not explained why Hispanics, who they have said are among "the groups most isolated by racial barriers in our country," should have their admission capped out in this manner. . . .

I do not believe that the Constitution gives the Law School such free rein in the use of race. The Law School has offered no explanation for its actual admissions practices and, unexplained, we are bound to conclude that the Law School has managed its admissions program, not to achieve a "critical mass," but to extend offers of admission to members of selected minority groups in proportion to their statistical representation in the applicant pool. But this is precisely the type of racial balancing that the Court itself calls "patently unconstitutional." . . .

Rulings in Context

Affirmative Action and Race

U.S. v. Paradise, 480 U.S. 149 (1987)   5-4

In applying the strict scrutiny test, the Court found a compelling government interest in upholding a federal court order demanding that half of all new Alabama state trooper promotions must be reserved to blacks because none of the current black troopers held officer rank. The Court argued that the quota was narrowly tailored to achieve the order's goal.

Johnson v. Transportation Agency, Santa Clara, Calif.,
480 U.S. 616 (1987)   6-3

The Court ruled that the agency's program to ensure the promotion of qualified women and minorities in historically segregated occupations did not constitute a quota because no specific number of women or minorities was set aside. Gender or minority status was only one factor among many.

City of Richmond v. J. A. Croson, 488 U.S. 469 (1989)   6-3

The Court overturned Richmond's set aside program for hiring minority-owned contractors because the city failed to demonstrate that the program achieved a compelling interest, and the program failed to be narrowly tailored to achieve that purpose with the least restrictive means.

Gratz v. Bollinger, 539 U.S. 244 (2003)   6-3

The companion to *Grutter v. Bollinger*, the Court ruled in an opinion by Chief Justice Rehnquist that the undergraduate admissions office at the University of Michigan used an unconstitutional quota by awarding twenty points to applicants from "underrepresented minorities."

Fisher v. University of Texas, 570 U.S. _____ (2013)   7-1

In its admissions program, the University of Texas uses the "Top Ten Percent Plan" to achieve a diverse student body. Under the plan, the top 10 percent of the graduates of all Texas high schools are automatically admitted to one of the nine campuses in the university system. Around 80 percent of the freshman class at the University of Texas at Austin is admitted under this plan. For the remaining seats, admissions officials review several factors, including grades, test scores, race, and ethnicity. Abigail Fisher did not graduate in the top 10 percent of her class. After she was not admitted to the Austin campus, she challenged the use of race as a violation of the equal protection of the laws. Justice Anthony Kennedy, writing for the Court, ruled that the United States Court of Appeals for the Fifth Circuit had not determined, under the strict scrutiny test, whether the University had a race-neutral way to achieve a diverse student body. He remanded the case to the lower court to determine whether the admissions program satisfied the strict scrutiny test. Justice Elena Kagan took no part in the case.

Sex Discrimination: Case

The case that follows asked whether the government may discriminate on the basis of sex, specifically whether the Commonwealth of Virginia may constitutionally discriminate against women by denying them admission to a single-sex public institution of higher education.

Case 4.7

United States v. Virginia
518 U.S. 515, 116 S.Ct. 2264 (1996)

The Virginia Military Institute (VMI), founded in 1839, is the only single-sex public university in the state. Its mission is to train its students to become "citizen-soldiers" who will be future leaders during their military service and later in their civilian careers. The training is crucial to achieving this goal. Students must experience the institution's "adversative" educational method by gaining vigorous mental and physical discipline as the school imparts to them its strong moral code. The program emphasizes physical rigor and mental stress as well as the absolute equality of treatment, the absence of privacy, and the minute regulation of behavior. As a rigorous and challenging educational experience, it is designed to give its graduates a sense of achievement after they have completed it.

While nothing in the course of study is unsuitable for women students, VMI has always chosen to maintain its all-male status. In 1990 the Justice Department, during the administration of President George H. W. Bush, challenged its single-sex status as a violation of the Equal Protection Clause of the Fourteenth Amendment. Although the federal district court heard from experts that many young women wanted to attend the school and were capable of completing the program, it ruled in favor of VMI, noting that *Mississippi University for Women v. Hogan*, 458 U.S. 718 (1982), had upheld the single-sex status of that institution. It also noted that intermediate scrutiny of the program indicated that Virginia had an important governmental interest in maintaining an all-male institution. Moreover, the rigor of the program enhanced the diversity of educational opportunity because no other institution provided the same experience to its students. The court concluded that because a single-sex education is an important governmental objective, the only means to achieve it is to exclude women from VMI.

Although the Court of Appeals for the Fourth Circuit agreed in the usefulness of VMI's program, it added that the Fourteenth Amendment required that the institution had to admit women or the state of Virginia had to produce a comparable program for women elsewhere. Virginia responded by creating a military-oriented program—the Virginia Women's Institute for Leadership or VWIL—at Mary Baldwin College. This program did not possess the same "adversative" or harsh methods of training as those at VMI. When Virginia returned to the district court to ask for approval of the new remedial program, the district court said the plan met the requirements of the Equal Protection Clause, and the Court of Appeals agreed.

The Justice Department then appealed to the Supreme Court. In overruling the Fourth Circuit's decision, the Court voted seven to one, with Justice Clarence Thomas not participating in the decision because his son was a VMI student. Justice Ruth Bader Ginsburg wrote the judgment of the Court in an opinion joined by Justices John Paul Stevens, Sandra Day O'Connor, Anthony M. Kennedy, David H. Souter, and Stephen G. Breyer. Chief Justice William H. Rehnquist wrote a concurring opinion, and Justice Antonin Scalia filed a dissent.

Justice GINSBURG delivered the opinion of the Court.

. . . The heightened review standard our precedent establishes does not make sex a proscribed classification. Supposed "inherent differences" are no longer accepted as a ground for race or national origin classifications. Physical differences between men and women, however, are enduring: "The two sexes are not fungible; a community made up exclusively of one [sex] is different from a community composed of both." *Ballard v. United States*, 329 U.S. 187 (1946).

"Inherent differences" between men and women, we have come to appreciate, remain cause for celebration, but not for denigration of the members of either sex or for artificial constraints on an individual's opportunity. Sex classifications may be used to compensate women "for particular economic disabilities [they have] suffered," *Califano* [*v. Goldfarb*, 430 U.S. 199 (1977)], to "promote equal employment opportunity," see *California Federal Savings & Loan Assn. v. Guerra*, 479 U.S. 272 (1987), to advance full development of the talent and capacities of our Nation's people. But such classifications may not be used, as they once were, to create or perpetuate the legal, social, and economic inferiority of women.

Measuring the record in this case against the review standard just described, we conclude that Virginia has shown no "exceedingly persuasive justification" for excluding all women from the citizen-soldier training afforded by VMI. We therefore affirm the Fourth Circuit's initial judgment, which held that Virginia had violated the Fourteenth Amendment's Equal Protection Clause. Because the remedy proffered by Virginia—the Mary Baldwin VWIL program—does not cure the constitutional violation, i.e., it does not provide equal opportunity, we reverse the Fourth Circuit's final judgment in this case. Virginia . . . argues that VMI's adversative method of training provides educational benefits that cannot be made available, unmodified, to women. Alterations to accommodate women would necessarily be "radical," so "drastic," Virginia asserts, as to transform, indeed "destroy," VMI's program. Neither sex would be favored by the transformation, Virginia maintains: Men would be deprived of the unique opportunity currently available to them; women would not gain that opportunity because their participation would "eliminate the very aspects of [the] program that distinguish [VMI] from . . . other institutions of higher education in Virginia." . . .

Women's successful entry into the federal military academies, and their participation in the Nation's military forces, indicate that Virginia's fears for the future of VMI may not be solidly grounded. The State's justification for excluding all women from "citizen-soldier" training for which some are qualified, in any event, cannot rank as "exceedingly persuasive," as we have explained and applied that standard.

Virginia and VMI trained their argument on "means" rather than "end," and thus misperceived our precedent. Single-sex education at VMI serves an "important governmental objective," they maintained, and exclusion of women is not only "substantially related," it is essential to that objective. By this notably circular argument, the "straightforward" test *Mississippi University for Women* [*v. Hogan*, 458 U.S. 718 (1982)] described, was bent and bowed . . . .

In the second phase of the litigation, Virginia presented its remedial plan—maintain VMI as a male-only college and create VWIL as a separate program for women. The plan met District Court approval. The Fourth Circuit, in turn, deferentially reviewed the State's proposal and decided that the two single-sex programs directly served Virginia's reasserted purposes: single-gender education, and "achieving the results of an adversative method in a military environment." . . . The United States challenges this "remedial" ruling as pervasively misguided.

VWIL affords women no opportunity to experience the rigorous military training for which VMI is famed. Instead, the VWIL program "deemphasizes" military education and uses a "cooperative method" of education "which reinforces self-esteem." . . .

Virginia maintains that these methodological differences are "justified pedagogically," based on "important differences between men and women in learning and developmental needs," "psychological and sociological differences" Virginia describes as "real" and "not stereotypes." . . . As earlier stated, generalizations about "the way women are," estimates of what is appropriate for most women, no longer justify denying opportunity to women whose talent and capacity place them outside the average description. Notably, Virginia never asserted that VMI's method of education suits most men. It is also revealing that Virginia ac-

counted for its failure to make the VWIL experience "the entirely militaristic experience of VMI" on the ground that VWIL "is planned for
women who do not necessarily expect to pursue military careers." By
that reasoning, VMI's "entirely militaristic" program would be inappropriate for men in general or as a group, for "only about 15% of VMI ca-
dets enter career military service." . . .

Virginia, in sum, while maintaining VMI for men only, has failed to
provide any "comparable single-gender women's institution." Instead,
the Commonwealth has created a VWIL program fairly appraised as a
"pale shadow" of VMI in terms of the range of curricular choices and
faculty stature, funding, prestige, alumni support and influence.

Virginia's VWIL solution is reminiscent of the remedy Texas
proposed 50 years ago, in response to a state trial court's 1946 ruling
that, given the equal protection guarantee, African Americans could not
be denied a legal education at a state facility. See *Sweatt v. Painter*, 339
U.S. 629 (1950). . . .

The Fourth Circuit plainly erred in exposing Virginia's VWIL plan
to a deferential analysis, for "all gender-based classifications today" warrant "heightened scrutiny." Valuable as VWIL may prove for students
who seek the program offered, Virginia's remedy affords no cure at all
for the opportunities and advantages withheld from women who want a
VMI education and can make the grade. In sum, Virginia's remedy does
not match the constitutional violation; the State has shown no "exceedingly persuasive justification" for withholding from women qualified for
the experience premier training of the kind VMI affords. . . .

For the reasons stated, the initial judgment of the Court of Appeals is
affirmed, the final judgment of the Court of Appeals is reversed, and the
case is remanded for further proceedings consistent with this opinion.

It is so ordered.

Justice SCALIA, dissenting.

. . . I shall devote most of my analysis to evaluating the Court's opinion
on the basis of our current equal-protection jurisprudence, which regards this Court as free to evaluate everything under the sun by applying
one of three tests: "rational basis" scrutiny, intermediate scrutiny, or
strict scrutiny. These tests are no more scientific than their names suggest, and a further element of randomness is added by the fact that it is
largely up to us which test will be applied in each case. Strict scrutiny, we
have said, is reserved for state "classifications based on race or national
origin and classifications affecting fundamental rights," *Clark v. Jeter*, 486
U.S. 456 (1988). It is my position that the term "fundamental rights"
should be limited to "interests traditionally protected by our society,"

Michael H. v. Gerald D., 491 U.S. 110 (1989) (plurality opinion of Justice Scalia); but the Court has not accepted that view, so that strict scrutiny will be applied to the deprivation of whatever sort of right we consider "fundamental." We have no established criterion for "intermediate scrutiny" either, but essentially apply it when it seems like a good idea to load the dice. So far it has been applied to content-neutral restrictions that place an incidental burden on speech, to disabilities attendant to illegitimacy, and to discrimination on the basis of sex.

I have no problem with a system of abstract tests such as rational-basis, intermediate, and strict scrutiny (though I think we can do better than applying strict scrutiny and intermediate scrutiny whenever we feel like it). Such formulas are essential to evaluating whether the new restrictions that a changing society constantly imposes upon private conduct comport with that "equal protection" our society has always accorded in the past. But in my view the function of this Court is to preserve our society's values regarding (among other things) equal protection, not to revise them; to prevent backsliding from the degree of restriction the Constitution imposed upon democratic government, not to prescribe, on our own authority, progressively higher degrees. For that reason it is my view that, whatever abstract tests we may choose to devise, they cannot supersede—and indeed ought to be crafted so as to reflect—those constant and unbroken national traditions that embody the people's understanding of ambiguous constitutional texts. More specifically, it is my view that "when a practice not expressly prohibited by the text of the Bill of Rights bears the endorsement of a long tradition of open, widespread, and unchallenged use that dates back to the beginning of the Republic, we have no proper basis for striking it down." *Rutan v. Republican Party of Ill.*, 497 U.S. 62 (1990) (Justice Scalia, dissenting). The same applies, *mutatis mutandis*, to a practice asserted to be in violation of the post-Civil War Fourteenth Amendment.

The all-male constitution of VMI comes squarely within such a governing tradition. Founded by the Commonwealth of Virginia in 1839 and continuously maintained by it since, VMI has always admitted only men. . . . In other words, the tradition of having government-funded military schools for men is as well rooted in the traditions of this country as the tradition of sending only men into military combat. The people may decide to change the one tradition, like the other, through democratic processes; but the assertion that either tradition has been unconstitutional through the centuries is not law, but politics-smuggled-into-law . . . .

. . . The potential of today's decision for widespread disruption of existing institutions lies in its application to private single-sex education. Government support is immensely important to private educational institutions. Mary Baldwin College—which designed and runs VWIL—

notes that private institutions of higher education in the 1990-1991 school year derived approximately 19 percent of their budgets from federal, state, and local government funds, not including financial aid to students. Charitable status under the tax laws is also highly significant for private educational institutions, and it is certainly not beyond the Court that rendered today's decision to hold that a donation to a single-sex college should be deemed contrary to public policy and therefore not deductible if the college discriminates on the basis of sex. See also *Bob Jones University v. United States*, 461 U.S. 574 (1983)....

The only hope for state-assisted single-sex private schools is that the Court will not apply in the future the principles of law it has applied today. That is a substantial hope, I am happy and ashamed to say. After all, did not the Court today abandon the principles of law it has applied in our earlier sex-classification cases? And does not the Court positively invite private colleges to rely upon our ad-hocery by assuring them this case is "unique"? I would not advise the foundation of any new single-sex college (especially an all-male one) with the expectation of being allowed to receive any government support; but it is too soon to abandon in despair those single-sex colleges already in existence. It will certainly be possible for this Court to write a future opinion that ignores the broad principles of law set forth today, and that characterizes as utterly dispositive the opinion's perceptions that VMI was a uniquely prestigious all-male institution, conceived in chauvinism, etc., etc. I will not join that opinion....

Rulings in Context

Non-Racial Classifications

Frontiero v. Richardson, 411 U.S. 677 (1973)   8-1

The Court ruled that the United States Department of Defense violated the Equal Protection component of the Fifth Amendment's Due Process Clause by denying benefits to female Air Force officers while granting them to their male counterparts. Four justices, led by Justice Brennan, argued that gender discrimination should be subject to the strict scrutiny test, while four others, led by Justice Powell, argued that gender discrimination should be subject to rational basis review in light of the then-recent passage by Congress of the Equal Rights Amendment, which failed to gain ratification.

Craig v. Boren, 429 U.S. 190 (1976)   7-2

On equal rights grounds, the Court overturned an Oklahoma law that prohibited young men from purchasing 3.2 or low-alcohol beer until they were 21 years old, but allowed young women to purchase it at age 18. Justice Brennan, for the first time, applied the heightened scrutiny test to matters of gender discrimination over Justice Rehnquist's dissent.

San Antonio School District v. Rodriguez, 411 U.S. 1 (1973)   5-4

In a case involving Texas's unequal financial support of public school districts, where wealthier areas received more funding than poorer ones, the Court ruled that the Constitution's Equal Protection Clause did not extend to wealth. The Court also held that education is not a fundamental right.

CHAPTER **5**

Due Process of Law and
Rights of the Accused

In an attempt to limit and guide interpretation of the [Due Process] Clause, we have insisted not merely that the interest denominated as a "liberty" be "fundamental" (a concept that, in isolation, is hard to objectify), but also that it be an interest traditionally protected by our society. As we have put it, the Due Process Clause affords only those protections "so rooted in the traditions and conscience of our people as to be ranked as fundamental."
—Justice Antonin Scalia, *Michael H. v. Gerald D.*, 491 U.S. 110 (1989), quoting *Snyder v. Massachusetts*, 291 U.S. 97 (1934)

The phrase *due process of law* may sometimes seem confusing because the way it has evolved over the years. Both the Fifth and Fourteenth Amendments provide for due process: the former binds the federal government as of 1791; the latter, the states as of 1868.

Its most basic meaning is encompassed in wording used in the Magna Carta in 1215, namely the phrase *the law of the land*, when the English barons and churchmen at Runnymede forced a reluctant King John to agree to recognize their rights. It was one of the first attempts to force a king to abide by the law, or in other words, for him to say that he, as they were, was also under the law. Its most powerful passage reads, "No free man shall be taken or imprisoned or deprived of his freehold or of his liberties or free customs, or outlawed, or exiled, or in any manner destroyed, nor shall we go upon him, nor shall we send upon him, except by a legal judgment of his peers or by *the law of the land*" (emphasis added).

Although the king agreed to the document, unsurprisingly he ignored it until his death the following year. While its main import was reactionary in the sense that it reinforced baronial feudal rights and was not a statement of fundamental human rights, it was still a major step toward English constitutionalism. The king for the first time officially recognized that those other than himself and members of the royal family possessed certain rights, privileges, and liberties.

Procedural Due Process

Due process of law, as it developed in the seventeenth and eighteenth centuries in the Anglo-American legal tradition, gradually became understood as procedural due process, as the Magna Carta specified. In theory, due process means that the government could no longer legally deprive any persons of life, freedom, or property—and note, the amendments do not specify "citizens" or "free men"—unless they first have access to courts of law and all the essential safeguards that courts offer.

The government may not, for example, execute, imprison, or fine criminal defendants, that is, deprive them of life, liberty, or property, until it provides them with the guarantees embodied in the Fourth, Fifth, Sixth, and Seventh Amendments:

1. The people must not be subjected to unreasonable searches and seizures (the Fourth Amendment).

2. Law enforcement officers must present good reasons before the government issues a warrant to undertake a search (the Fourth Amendment).

3. Defendants must have access to legal counsel (the Sixth Amendment).

4. They must have a speedy and public trial by jury (for criminal cases, Article III and the Sixth Amendment; for civil cases, the Seventh Amendment).

5. They must not be subjected to double jeopardy, that is, people must not have to stand trial a second time for the same crime

after a court has found them not guilty the first time (the Fifth Amendment).

6. They must be allowed to confront the witnesses against them (the Sixth Amendment).

These protections were not originally binding on the state governments. Only over time have most of them gradually become incorporated into the Due Process Clause of the Fourteenth Amendment and made applicable to the states. They underscore the importance of procedural due process: the government must guarantee to those accused of crimes certain legal remedies, procedures, and protections that are fair, equitable, and just.

Substantive Due Process

In the meantime, by the end of the nineteenth century, the idea of due process embodying legal procedures began to expand. This expansion came during the Industrial Revolution when the United States developed into an economic and world power. Soon, the Court gradually viewed the denial of due process as a denial of certain substantive rights. The Due Process Clause, the Court concluded, also protects substantive rights like civil and economic rights. (This chapter will focus on civil, not economic rights.)

We can think of substantive due process as more than the legal safeguards that we have highlighted above. We have seen how this works when we addressed the equal protection cases, and we will see it again when we deal with the right to privacy. The easiest way to think of it is in terms of the Civil Rights Movement in the 1950s and 60s.

Many people argued at that time, as many still do today, that the government deprives a person, in this case a child, of liberty when a law establishes a segregated school system. In 1954, the Supreme Court ruled that laws prohibiting African-American children the freedom to attend a school with white children denied to them their Fifth and Fourteenth Amendments' guarantee of due process of law. *Brown v. Board of Education of Topeka, Kan.*, 347 U.S. 483 (Case 4.2), and *Bolling v. Sharpe*, 347 U.S. 497, had virtually nothing to do with legal *procedures* designed to protect criminal defendants. They had much to do with providing "substance"—in this case, the freedom to attend any public school—to the government's guarantee of due process.

Another "substantive due process" example may be found in the right to privacy (chapter six). Such a right is nowhere explicitly guaranteed in any provision or amendment of the Constitution. In 1965, the

Court discovered a right of privacy embedded in several of amendments, and applied the right to the states through the liberty component of the Due Process Clause of the Fourteenth Amendment (*Griswold v. Connecticut*, 381 U.S. 481) (Case 1.4). From this initial discovery of a right to privacy, the Court has considered a variety of other substantive privacy rights with varying degrees of acceptance or rejection:

> A woman's right to an abortion, sustained in 1973 in *Roe v. Wade*, 410 U.S. 113 (Case 6.1)

> A terminally ill person's right to deliberately refuse life-saving care, upheld in 1990 in *Cruzan by Cruzan v. Director, Missouri Department of Health*, 497 U.S. 261

> A terminally ill person's right to assisted suicide, upheld in 2006 in *Gonzales v. Oregon*, 546 U.S. 243 (Case 6.4)

> The right of gay men and lesbians to engage in consensual sexual activity in the privacy of their home, upheld in 2003 in *Lawrence v. Texas*, 539 U.S. 558 (Case 6.5)

Due Process: Cases

In the cases that follow in this chapter, we will examine how the Court has used substantive and procedural due process to review laws and state actions that appear to violate the Due Process Clauses of the Fifth or Fourteenth Amendments. The first case is a classic example of substantive due process of law. It demonstrates how the justices create new judicial theories, in this case the doctrine of the liberty of contract, in terms of the relationship between employers and workers. The next two cases involve procedural due process. They both focus on the fundamental rights of criminal defendants. The first asks whether a defendant, even one who did not face a felony charge or the death penalty, has the right to have a lawyer represent him. Clarence Gideon's ordeal has become a classic example of a prisoner who tenaciously and successfully fought to secure his right to counsel. In the third case, Ernesto Miranda did not understand all of his rights after he was arrested and felt coerced to confess to a crime. The Court ruled that law enforcement officers had a duty to inform him of his rights before he offered any information to them.

Case 5.1

Lochner v. New York
198 U.S. 45, 25 S. Ct. 539 (1905)

In the second week of April, 1901, Joseph Lochner was doing what any self-respecting baker thought he should be doing. He was providing products that he thought his customers wanted and making a living doing it. Life in Utica, New York, in the heart of the Mohawk Valley at the dawn of the twentieth century was difficult, but not unpleasant. His shop produced many good things his customers needed and enjoyed: biscuits, breads, cake, and confections. Most workers, typical of the time, worked by the day, not the hour, so it was often impossible to determine what constituted a day's work. At the end of the Civil War, the standard that many progressive social reformers and fledgling union organizers sought was the eight-hour day, but it was long time coming into reality. In an unusual twist, Lochner's workers were hired to work by the hour, and when Lochner allowed them to stay on the job, some at their request, for more than 10 hours a day that April morning in 1901, he found himself in trouble.

Six years earlier, in 1895, the state legislature of New York passed a law forbidding an employer from requiring or permitting any employee from working more than 10 hours a day or 60 hours a week. The law also set forth various sanitation standards. As for the first of these, the part that Lochner violated, the law was in many respects a response to the eight-hour day crusade. Industrialization throughout the nineteenth century had brought into being a new economic order, one based on the factory system and the increasing use of machine technology.

Adherents of the Progressive Movement, who fought for the eight-hour day, often cited bakeries as among the worst working environments. Unlike the factory system, bakeries were typically small in physical size and in terms of the number of men who worked in them, usually around four or five, under the supervision of master or "boss" bakers. They were highly labor intensive. The major piece of equipment was an oven. The rest of the business required storage space for flour and other ingredients, some utensils, and labor to mix, knead, and bake the dough.

In New York City, bakeries were often relegated to damp, smelly basements, which were underground cellars where the sewers of the tenements drained offal and other materials that the tenants disposed of or threw away. The sewers often leaked, and because they were unvented, they smelled horribly from the foul odors emanating from the sewer drain. Some drains were simply encased in wood on top of which the bakers placed racks in order to store baked bread. If ventilation was poor, so was the lighting since the bakeries were underground, some with very low ceilings hardly measuring six feet.

The bakers hired to work in these establishments suffered not only from these features, but also from the flour floating constantly in the air and into their lungs. The cellars were hardly ever cleaned, and even worse, the bakers themselves rarely washed their hands before work. Wasting, or lung diseases, especially tuberculosis, were common among them, causing them to have continuous coughing spells, to spit up blood, and to experience fatigue and have a general sense of malaise. It is not clear whether Lochner's small bakery in Upstate New York, paralleled these conditions: a photograph taken years later showed an airy, first-floor bakeshop, but there is no record of what his establishment looked like six years earlier. The baking industry, with new inventions and mechanisms, was rapidly changing in these years.

The Progressive Movement began in the last decades of the nineteenth century. The essential principle underlying it was that government must intervene to solve social problems whenever and wherever they appeared. The demand for an eight-hour day was part of this movement. In the case of bakeshops, this meant that laws should regulate hours of operation and developing standards of cleanliness and sanitation. Enter the Bakeshop Act of 1895, which included both of these provisions.

Joseph Lochner was found guilty of violating the hours of operation restrictions and fined $50: he had a choice. Pay the fine or go to jail for 50 days. He appealed his case to the appellate division of the New York Supreme Court, and when he lost, he appealed to the New York Court of Appeals, the state's highest tribunal. That court again found his conviction to be constitutional. He then appealed to the United States Supreme Court, and by a five-to-four decision, he won.

The Court's decision in overturning the New York law was five to four. Justice Rufus Peckham wrote the majority opinion. Dissents were entered by Justices Oliver Wendell Holmes and John Marshall Harlan.

Justice PECKHAM delivered the opinion of the court.

The statute necessarily interferes with the right of contract between the employer and employees concerning the number of hours in which the latter may labor in the bakery of the employer. The general right to make a contract in relation to his business is part of the liberty of the individual protected by the Fourteenth Amendment of the Federal Constitution. *Allgeyer v. Louisiana*, 165 U.S. 578 (1897). Under that provision, no State can deprive any person of life, liberty or property without due process of law. The right to purchase or to sell labor is part of the liberty protected by this amendment unless there are circumstances which exclude the right. There are, however, certain powers, existing in the sovereignty of each State in the Union, somewhat vaguely termed police powers, the exact description and limitation of which have not been attempted by the courts. Those powers . . . relate to the safety, health, morals and general welfare of the public. Both property and liberty are held on such reasonable conditions as may be imposed by the governing power of the State in the exercise of those powers, and with such conditions the Fourteenth Amendment was not designed to interfere.

The State therefore has power to prevent the individual from making certain kinds of contracts. . . . Contracts in violation of a statute, either of the Federal or state government, or a contract to let one's property for immoral purposes, or to do any other unlawful act, could obtain no protection from the Federal Constitution as coming under the liberty of person or of free contract. Therefore, when the State, by its legislature, in the assumed exercise of its police powers, has passed an act which seriously limits the right to labor or the right of contract in regard to their means of livelihood between persons . . . it becomes of great importance to determine which shall prevail—the right of the individual to labor for such time as he may choose or the right of the State to prevent the individual from laboring or from entering into any contract to labor beyond a certain time prescribed by the State.

This court has recognized the existence and upheld the exercise of the police powers of the States in many cases. . . .

It must, of course, be conceded that there is a limit to the valid exercise of the police power by the State. . . . Otherwise the Fourteenth Amendment would have no efficacy, and the legislatures of the States would have unbounded power, and it would be enough to say that any piece of legislation was enacted to conserve the morals, the health or the safety of the people. . . . The claim of the police power would be a mere pretext—become another and delusive name for the supreme sovereignty of the State to be exercised free from constitutional restraint. . . . In every case that comes before this court, therefore, where legislation of this character is concerned and where the protection of the Federal Constitution is sought, the question necessarily arises: is this a fair, reasonable and appropriate exercise of the police power of the State? . . . Of course, the liberty of contract relating to labor includes both parties to it. The one has as much right to purchase as the other to sell labor.

This is not a question of substituting the judgment of the court for that of the legislature. If the act be within the power of the State, it is valid although the judgment of the court might be totally opposed to the enactment of such a law. But the question would still remain: is it within the police power of the State?, and that question must be answered by the court. . . .

There is no reasonable ground for interfering with the liberty of person or the right of free contract by determining the hours of labor in the occupation of a baker. There is no contention that bakers as a class are not equal in intelligence and capacity to men in other trades or manual occupations, or that they are able to assert their rights and care for themselves without the protecting arm of the State, interfering with their independence of judgment and of action. They are in no sense wards of the State. Viewed in the light of a purely labor law, with no reference whatever to the question of health, we think that a law like the one before us involves neither the safety, the morals, nor the welfare of the public, and that the interest of the public is not in the slightest degree affected by such an act. The law must be upheld, if at all, as a law pertaining to the health of the individual engaged in the occupation of a baker. . . . Clean and wholesome bread does not depend upon whether the baker works but ten hours per day or only sixty hours a week. The limitation of the hours of labor does not come within the police power on that ground. . . .

We think that there can be no fair doubt that the trade of a baker, in and of itself, is not an unhealthy one to that degree which would authorize the legislature to interfere with the right to labor, and with the right of free contract on the part of the individual, either as employer or employee. . . . It might be safely affirmed that almost all occupations more or less affect the health. . . . But are we all, on that account, at the mercy of legislative majorities? A printer, a tinsmith, a locksmith, a carpenter, a cabinetmaker, a dry goods clerk, a bank's, a lawyer's or a physician's clerk, or a clerk in almost any kind of business, would all come under the power of the legislature on this assumption. No trade, no occupation, no mode of earning one's living could escape this all-pervading power, and the acts of the legislature in limiting the hours of labor in all employments would be valid although such limitation might seriously cripple the ability of the laborer to support himself and his family. . . .

It is also urged . . . that it is to the interest of the State that its population should be strong and robust, and therefore any legislation which may be said to tend to make people healthy must be valid as health laws, enacted under the police power. If this be a valid argument . . . it follows that the protection of the Federal Constitution from undue interference with liberty of person and freedom of contract is visionary. . . . Scarcely any law but might find shelter under such assumptions. . . . Not only the hours of employees, but the hours of employers, could be regulated, and doctors, lawyers, scientists, all professional men, as well as athletes and artisans, could be forbidden to fatigue their brains and bodies by prolonged hours of exercise. . . . We do not believe in the soundness of the views which uphold this law. On the contrary, we think that such a law as this, although passed in the assumed exercise of the police power, and as relating to the public health, or the health of the employees named, is not within that power, and is invalid. The act is . . . an illegal interference with the rights of individuals, both employers and employees, to make contracts regarding labor upon such terms as they may think best. . . . Statutes of the nature of that under review . . . are mere meddlesome interferences with the rights of the individual. . . .

It is manifest to us that . . . the real object and purpose were simply to regulate the hours of labor between the master and his employees . . . in a private business, not dangerous in any degree to morals or in any real and substantial degree to the health of the employees. Under such circumstances, the freedom of master and employee to contract with each other in relation to their employment, and in defining the same, cannot be prohibited or interfered with without violating the Federal Constitution. . . . Reversed.

Justice HOLMES, dissenting.

. . . This case is decided upon an economic theory which a large part of the country does not entertain. If it were a question whether I agreed with that theory, I should desire to study it further and long before making up my mind. But I do not conceive that to be my duty, because I strongly believe that my agreement or disagreement has nothing to do with the right of a majority to embody their opinions in law. It is settled by various decisions of this court that state constitutions and state laws may regulate life in many ways which we, as legislators, might think as injudicious, or, if you like, as tyrannical, as this, and which, equally with this, interfere with the liberty to contract. Sunday laws and usury laws are ancient examples. . . . The liberty of the citizen to do as he likes so long as he does not interfere with the liberty of others to do the same, which has been a shibboleth for some well known writers, is interfered with by school laws, by the Post Office, by every state or municipal institution which takes his money for purposes thought desirable, whether he likes it or not. The Fourteenth Amendment does not enact Mr. Herbert Spencer's Social Statics. The other day, we sustained the Massachusetts vaccination law. *Jacobson v. Massachusetts*, 197 U.S. 11 (1905). . . . United States and state statutes and decisions cutting down the liberty to contract by way of combination are familiar to this court. . . . Two years ago, we upheld the prohibition of sales of stock on margins or for future delivery in the constitution of California. . . . The decision sustaining an eight hour law for miners is still recent. . . . Some of these laws embody convictions or prejudices which judges are likely to share. Some may not. But a constitution is not intended to embody a particular economic theory, whether of paternalism and the organic relation of the citizen to the State or of *laissez faire*. It is made for people of fundamentally differing views, and the accident of our finding certain opinions natural and familiar or novel and even shocking ought not to conclude our judgment upon the question whether statutes embodying them conflict with the Constitution of the United States.

Case 5.2

Gideon v. Wainwright
372 U.S. 335, 83 S.Ct. 792 (1963)

Clarence Earl Gideon, a middle-aged drifter, was in and out jail for minor crimes when police accused him with breaking and entering a pool hall in Panama City, Florida. When he asked the trial court judge for a public defender because he was too poor to hire a lawyer, the judge informed him that Florida law permitted the appointment of counsel for indigent defendants only in capital cases. Gideon conducted his own defense as well as he could, but he was convicted and sentenced to prison. On appeal, the state supreme court denied relief.

While serving time in jail, he asked a prison guard for plain, lined paper on which he prepared a hand-written petition to the U.S. Supreme Court. While he was unaware of precedents, he was asking the Court to declare that he had a fundamental right to a fair trial with counsel, implying that his trial and conviction without the assistance of counsel violated the Sixth and Fourteenth Amendments. In 1942, the Court had dealt with this right and held that it only applied in state court proceeding when there were special circumstances (*Betts v. Brady*, 316 U.S. 455). Ten years earlier, the Court ruled in *Powell v. Alabama*, 287 U.S. 45, that nine black youths had deserved counsel after their trial for allegedly raping two white girls had ended in conviction and death sentences, but Gideon was neither young ignorant, surrounded by hostile forces, nor black, and there were no seemingly "special circumstances."

By the time Gideon appealed to the Supreme Court, the *Betts* majority had disappeared as a result of new appointees. Of the three dissenters, Justices William O. Douglas and Hugo Black remained, and only Justice Felix Frankfurter, who was in the majority, remained. But Frankfurter was ill and had retired in 1962, and the seven justices who had joined the Court since 1942 were sympathetic to the issue of more widely requiring counsel in state courts: Chief Justice Earl Warren and Justices Tom Clark, John Marshall Harlan (II), Potter Stewart, Byron White, and Arthur Goldberg who succeeded Frankfurter. The Court's decision was unanimous in Gideon's favor.

Justice BLACK delivered the opinion of the Court.

Since 1942, when *Betts v. Brady* was decided by a divided Court, the problem of a defendant's federal constitutional right to counsel in a state court has been a continuing source of controversy and litigation in both state and federal courts. To give this problem another review here, we granted *certiorari*. Since Gideon was proceeding *in forma pauperis*, we appointed counsel to represent him and requested both sides to discuss in their briefs and oral arguments the following: "Should this Court's holding in *Betts v. Brady* be reconsidered?"

The facts upon which Betts claimed that he had been unconstitutionally denied the right to have counsel appointed to assist him are strikingly like the facts upon which Gideon here bases his federal constitutional claim. . . . Treating due process as "a concept less rigid and more fluid than those envisaged in other specific and particular provisions of the Bill of Rights," the Court held that refusal to appoint counsel under the particular facts and circumstances in the Betts case was not so "offensive to the common and fundamental ideas of fairness" as to amount to a denial of due process. Since the facts and circumstances of the two cases are so nearly indistinguishable, we think the *Betts v. Brady* holding if left standing would require us to reject Gideon's claim that the Constitution guarantees him the assistance of counsel. Upon full reconsideration we conclude that Betts v. Brady should be overruled. . . .

We accept *Betts v. Brady's* assumption, based as it was on our prior cases, that a provision of the Bill of Rights which is "fundamental and essential to a fair trial" is made obligatory upon the States by the Fourteenth Amendment. We think the Court in *Betts* was wrong, however, in concluding that the Sixth Amendment's guarantee of counsel is not one of these fundamental rights. Ten years before *Betts v. Brady*, this Court, after full consideration of all the historical data examined in *Betts*, had unequivocally declared that "the right to the aid of counsel is of this fundamental character." *Powell v. Alabama*, 287 U.S. 45 (1932). While the Court at the close of its *Powell* opinion did by its language, as this Court frequently does, limit its holding to the particular facts and circumstances of that case, its conclusions about the fundamental nature of the right to counsel are unmistakable. . . .

In light of these and many other prior decisions of this Court, it is not surprising that the *Betts* Court, when faced with the contention that "one charged with crime, who is unable to obtain counsel, must be furnished counsel by the State," conceded that "expressions in the opinions of this court lend color to the argument . . . ." The fact is that in deciding as it did—that "appointment of counsel is not a fundamental right, essential to a fair trial"—the Court in *Betts v. Brady* made an abrupt break with its own well-considered precedents. In returning to these old precedents, sounder we believe than the new, we but restore constitutional principles established to achieve a fair system of justice. Not only these precedents but also reason and reflection require us to recognize that in our adversary system of criminal justice, any person haled into court, who is too poor to hire a lawyer, cannot be assured a fair trial unless counsel is provided for him. This seems to us to be an obvious truth. Governments, both state and federal, quite properly spend vast sums of money to establish machinery to try defendants accused of crime. Lawyers to prosecute are everywhere deemed essential to protect the public's interest in an orderly society. Similarly, there are few defendants charged with crime, few indeed, who fail to hire the best lawyers they can get to prepare and present their defenses. That government hires lawyers to prosecute and defendants who have the money hire lawyers to defend are the strongest indications of the widespread belief that lawyers in criminal courts are necessities, not luxuries. The right of one charged with crime to counsel may not be deemed fundamental and essential to fair trials in some countries, but it is in ours. From the very beginning, our state and national constitutions and laws have laid great emphasis on procedural and substantive safeguards designed to assure fair trials before impartial tribunals in which every defendant stands equal before the law. This noble ideal cannot be realized if the poor man charged with crime has to face his accusers without a lawyer to assist him. . . .

The Court in *Betts v. Brady* departed from the sound wisdom upon which the Court's holding in *Powell v. Alabama* rested. Florida, supported by two other States, has asked that *Betts v. Brady* be left intact. Twenty-two States, as friends of the Court, argue that *Betts* was "an anachronism when handed down" and that it should now be overruled. We agree.

Case 5.3

Miranda v. Arizona
384 U.S. 436, 86 S.Ct. 1602 (1966)

The use of confessions in criminal trials has long been a topic of controversy, given an array of circumstances that might lead a suspect to confess to a crime. Faulty police work, physical violence, and psychological trickery are only a few problems involved. This landmark case set forth the procedures that federal, state, and local law enforcement officers must follow after a suspect has been taken into custody. It began in March of 1963 when an eighteen-year old young woman was kidnapped and raped in a Phoenix, Arizona, suburb. A week and a half later, itinerant, unemployed Ernesto Miranda was arrested. While a psychological examination showed he was mildly schizophrenic, he was declared competent to stand trial.

After the young woman picked him out of a lineup as her attacker, police officers interrogated him. He confessed to the crime, signed a statement describing what happened, and was convicted. He then appealed on the grounds that the police had forced him to confess, and thus violated the prohibition in the Fifth Amendment, which applied to the states through the Due Process Clause of the Fourteenth Amendment, to be a witness against himself: his right to remain silent.

The Supreme Court heard this case along with three others concerning coerced police confessions. The decision overturning Miranda's conviction was five and one-half to three and one-half. Chief Justice Earl Warren wrote the majority opinion, and another opinion, concurring and dissenting in part, was prepared by Justice Tom Clark. Dissenting were Justices John Marshall Harlan (II), Byron White, and Potter Stewart.

Chief Justice WARREN delivered the opinion of the Court.

The cases before us raise questions which go to the roots of our concepts of American criminal jurisprudence: the restraints society must observe consistent with the Federal Constitution in prosecuting individuals for crime. More specifically, we deal with the admissibility of statements obtained from an individual who is subjected to custodial police interrogation and the necessity for procedures which assure that the individual is accorded his privilege under the Fifth Amendment to the Constitution not to be compelled to incriminate himself.

We dealt with certain phases of this problem recently in *Escobedo v. Illinois*, 378 U.S. 478 (1964). There, as in the four cases before us, law enforcement officials took the defendant into custody and interrogated him in a police station for the purpose of obtaining a confession. The police did not effectively advise him of his right to remain silent or of his right to consult with his attorney. Rather, they confronted him with an alleged accomplice who accused him of having perpetrated a murder. When the defendant denied the accusation and said "I didn't shoot Manuel, you did it," they handcuffed him and took him to an interrogation room. There, while handcuffed and standing, he was questioned for four hours until he confessed. During this interrogation, the police denied his request to speak to his attorney, and they prevented his retained attorney, who had come to the police station, from consulting with him. At his trial, the State, over his objection, introduced the confession against him. We held that the statements thus made were constitutionally inadmissible. . . .

The constitutional issue we decide in each of these cases is the admissibility of statements obtained from a defendant questioned while in custody or otherwise deprived of his freedom of action in any significant way. In each, the defendant was questioned by police officers, detectives, or a prosecuting attorney in a room in which he was cut off from the outside world. In none of these cases was the defendant given a full and effective warning of his rights at the outset of the interrogation process. In all the cases, the questioning elicited oral admissions, and in three of them, signed statements as well which were admitted at their trials. They all thus share salient features—incommunicado interrogation of individuals in a police—dominated atmosphere, resulting in self-incriminating statements without full warnings of constitutional rights.

An understanding of the nature and setting of this in-custody interrogation is essential to our decisions today. The difficulty in depicting what transpires at such interrogations stems from the fact that in this country they have largely taken place incommunicado. From extensive factual studies undertaken in the early 1930's, including the famous Wickersham Report to Congress by a Presidential Commission, it is clear that police violence and the "third degree" flourished at that time. In a series of cases decided by this Court long after these studies, the police resorted to physical brutality—beating, hanging, whipping—and to sustained and protracted questioning incommunicado in order to extort confessions. The Commission on Civil Rights in 1961 found much evidence to indicate that "some policemen still resort to physical force to obtain confessions.". . .

[W]e stress that the modern practice of in-custody interrogation is psychologically rather than physically oriented. . . . A valuable source of information about present police practices . . . may be found in various police manuals and texts which document procedures employed with success in the past, and which recommend various other effective tactics. These texts are used by law enforcement agencies themselves as guides. . . .

[T]he setting prescribed by the manuals and observed in practice [is] clear. In essence, it is this: To be alone with the subject is essential to prevent distraction and to deprive him of any outside support. The aura of confidence in his guilt undermines his will to resist. He merely confirms the preconceived story the police seek to have him describe. Patience and persistence, at times relentless questioning, are employed. To obtain a confession, the interrogator must "patiently maneuver himself or his quarry into a position from which the desired objective may be attained." When normal procedures fail to produce the needed result, the police may resort to deceptive stratagems such as giving false legal advice. It is important to keep the subject off balance, for example, by trading on his insecurity about himself or his surroundings. The police then persuade, trick, or cajole him out of exercising his constitutional rights.

Today . . . there can be no doubt that the Fifth Amendment privilege is available outside of criminal court proceedings and serves to protect persons in all settings in which their freedom of action is curtailed in any significant way from being compelled to incriminate themselves. We have concluded that without proper safeguards the process of in-custody interrogation of persons suspected or accused of crime contains inherently compelling pressures which work to undermine the individual's will to resist and to compel him to speak where he would not otherwise do so freely. In order to combat these pressures and to permit a full opportunity to exercise the privilege against self-incrimination, the accused must be adequately and effectively apprised of his rights and the exercise of those rights must be fully honored. . . .

Accordingly we hold that an individual held for interrogation must be clearly informed that he has the right to consult with a lawyer and to have the lawyer with him during interrogation under the system for protecting the privilege we delineate today. As with the warnings of the right to remain silent and that anything stated can be used in evidence against him, this warning is an absolute prerequisite to interrogation. No amount of circumstantial evidence that the person may have been aware of this right will suffice to stand in its stead: Only through such a warning is there ascertainable assurance that the accused was aware of this right. . . .

In dealing with statements obtained through interrogation, we do not purport to find all confessions inadmissible. Confessions remain a proper element in law enforcement. Any statement given freely and voluntarily without any compelling influences is, of course, admissible in evidence. The fundamental import of the privilege while an individual is in custody is not whether he is allowed to talk to the police without the benefit of warnings and counsel, but whether he can be interrogated. There is no requirement that police stop a person who enters a police station and states that he wishes to confess to a crime, or a person who calls the police to offer a confession or any other statement he desires to make. Volunteered statements of any kind are not barred by the Fifth Amendment and their admissibility is not affected by our holding today.

To summarize, we hold that when an individual is taken into custody or otherwise deprived of his freedom by the authorities in any significant way and is subjected to questioning, the privilege against self-incrimination is jeopardized. Procedural safeguards must be employed to protect the privilege, and unless other fully effective means are adopted to notify the person of his right of silence and to assure that the exercise of the right will be scrupulously honored, the following measures are required. He must be warned prior to any questioning that he has the right to remain silent, that anything he says can be used against him in a court of law, that he has the right to the presence of an attorney, and that if he cannot afford an attorney one will be appointed for him prior to any questioning if he so desires. Opportunity to exercise these rights must be afforded to him throughout the interrogation. After such warnings have been given, and such opportunity afforded him, the individual may knowingly and intelligently waive these rights and agree to answer questions or make a statement. But unless and until such warnings and waiver are demonstrated by the prosecution at trial, no evidence obtained as a result of interrogation can be used against him. . . .

In announcing these principles, we are not unmindful of the burdens which law enforcement officials must bear, often under trying circumstances. We also fully recognize the obligation of all citizens to aid in enforcing the criminal laws. This Court, while protecting individual rights, has always given ample latitude to law enforcement agencies in the legitimate exercise of their duties. The limits we have placed on the interrogation process should not constitute an undue interference with a proper system of law enforcement. . . .

Because of the nature of the problem and because of its recurrent significance in numerous cases, we have to this point discussed the relationship of the Fifth Amendment privilege to police interrogation without specific concentration on the facts of the cases before us. . . . In each instance, we have concluded that statements were obtained from the defendant under circumstances that did not meet constitutional standards for protection of the privilege. It is so ordered.

Justice WHITE, dissenting.

The rule announced today will measurably weaken the ability of the criminal law to perform [several] tasks. It is a deliberate calculus to prevent interrogations, to reduce the incidence of confessions and pleas of guilty and to increase the number of trials. Criminal trials, no matter how efficient the police are, are not sure bets for the prosecution, nor should they be if the evidence is not forthcoming. Under the present law, the prosecution fails to prove its case in about 30 percent of the criminal cases actually tried in the federal courts. But it is something else again to remove from the ordinary criminal case all those confessions which heretofore have been held to be free and voluntary acts of the accused and to thus establish a new constitutional barrier to the ascertainment of truth by the judicial process. There is, in my view, every reason to believe that a good many criminal defendants who otherwise would have been convicted on what this Court has previously thought to be the most satisfactory kind of evidence will now, under this new version of the Fifth Amendment, either not be tried at all or will be acquitted if the State's evidence, minus the confession, is put to the test of litigation. . . .

At the same time, the Court's *per se* approach may not be justified on the ground that it provides a "bright line" permitting the authorities to judge in advance whether interrogation may safely be pursued without jeopardizing the admissibility of any information obtained as a consequence. Nor can it be claimed that judicial time and effort, assuming that is a relevant consideration, will be conserved because of the ease of application of the new rule. Today's decision leaves open such questions as whether the accused was in custody, whether his statements were spontaneous or the product of interrogation, whether the accused has effectively waived his rights, and whether nontestimonial evidence introduced at trial is the fruit of statements made during a prohibited interrogation, all of which are certain to prove productive of uncertainty during investigation and litigation during prosecution. For all these reasons, if further restrictions on police interrogation are desirable at this time, a more flexible approach makes much more sense than the Court's constitutional straitjacket. . . .

Case 5.4

Kyllo v. United States
533 U.S. 27, 121 S.Ct. 2038 (2001)

Danny Kyllo was growing marijuana in his triplex residence on Rhododendron Drive in Florence, Oregon, when suspicious federal agents from the Department of the Interior decided to target an Agema Thermovision 210 thermal-imager at his home. They knew that indoor marijuana growth required high intensity lamps and thus gave off a great deal of heat. The imager the agents used could detect infrared radiation that all objects emitted, though with varying degrees of intensity.

The imager indicates the degree of heat being generated by color: white is hot, black is cool, and various shades of gray indicate the relative difference between the two extremes. After the agents scanned Kyllo's home, they noted an unusual amount of heat coming from the roof over the garage and along a sidewall of the building. The heat was far more intensive than what his neighbors' homes were generating. With this information, along with the utility bills of the premises and tips from informants, the agents asked a federal magistrate for a search warrant, which they received. During the subsequent search, they found that Kyllo was growing over 100 marijuana plants under an elaborate system of plant lights. He was indicted on one count of manufacturing the illegal plant in violation of federal law.

Kyllo first moved to suppress the evidence because, he argued, the initial search via the thermal-imager violated the Fourth Amendment prohibition against unreasonable searches and seizures. When that failed, he entered a conditional plea of guilty. On appeal, the U.S. Court of Appeals for the Ninth Circuit remanded the case to the district court for more rulings on the use of the thermal-imager. The district court upheld the validity of the original warrant because, the court said, the imager did not violate Kyllo's reasonable expectation of privacy: the agents could not see what he was doing or hear what he was saying. They did not witness any intimate activities in his home.

On appeal yet again, the Ninth Circuit was divided. It initially reversed, but the opinion was withdrawn, and a new panel drawn, which then affirmed Kyllo's conviction. The court ruled that Kyllo had no expectation of privacy because he had not attempted to conceal the heat emanating from his home. Even had he taken that precaution to hide the heat, the court went on, the imager did not interfere with his privacy because it did not expose any intimate details of his life. As the court put it, the imager only revealed "amorphous 'hot spots' on the roof and exterior wall." Kyllo appealed to the Supreme Court.

Voting five to four, the Court overturned his conviction as a violation of the Fourth Amendment. Justice Antonin Scalia delivered the opinion of the Court, which was joined by Justices David H. Souter, Clarence Thomas, Ruth Bader Ginsburg, and Stephen G. Breyer. Justice John Paul Stevens filed a dissenting opinion, in which the Chief Justice and Justices Sandra Day O'Connor and Anthony M. Kennedy joined.

Justice SCALIA delivered the opinion of the Court.

. . . "At the very core" of the Fourth Amendment "stands the right of a man to retreat into his own home and there be free from unreasonable governmental intrusion." *Silverman v. United States*, 365 U.S. 505 (1961). With few exceptions, the question whether a warrantless search of a home is reasonable and hence constitutional must be answered no.

On the other hand, the antecedent question of whether or not a Fourth Amendment "search" has occurred is not so simple under our precedent. The permissibility of ordinary visual surveillance of a home used to be clear because, well into the 20th century, our Fourth Amendment jurisprudence was tied to common-law trespass. Visual surveillance was unquestionably lawful because "'the eye cannot by the laws of England be guilty of a trespass.'" *Boyd v. United States*, 116 U.S. 616 (1886) (quoting *Entick v. Carrington*, 19 How. St. Tr. 1029, 95 Eng. Rep. 807 [K.B. 1765]). We have since decoupled violation of a person's Fourth Amendment rights from trespassory violation of his property, but the lawfulness of warrantless visual surveillance of a home has still been preserved. As we observed in *California v. Ciraolo*, 476 U.S. 207 (1986), "the Fourth Amendment protection of the home has never been extended to require law enforcement officers to shield their eyes when passing by a home on public thoroughfares." . . .

In assessing when a search is not a search, we have applied somewhat in reverse the principle first enunciated in *Katz v. United States*, 389 U.S. 347 (1967). *Katz* involved eavesdropping by means of an electronic listening device placed on the outside of a telephone booth—a location not within the catalog ("persons, houses, papers, and effects") that the Fourth Amendment protects against unreasonable searches. We held that the Fourth Amendment nonetheless protected Katz from the warrantless eavesdropping because he "justifiably relied" upon the privacy of the telephone booth. As Justice Harlan's oft-quoted concurrence described it, a Fourth Amendment search occurs when the government violates a subjective expectation of privacy that society recognizes as reasonable. We have subsequently applied this principle to hold that a Fourth Amendment search does *not* occur—even when the explicitly protected location of a *house* is concerned—unless "the individual manifested a subjective expectation of privacy in the object of the challenged search," and "society [is] willing to recognize that expectation as reasonable." *Ciraolo.* . . .

The present case involves officers on a public street engaged in more than naked-eye surveillance of a home. We have previously reserved judgment as to how much technological enhancement of ordinary perception from such a vantage point, if any, is too much. While we upheld enhanced aerial photography of an industrial complex in *Dow Chemical* [*v. United States*, 476 U.S. 227 (1986)], we noted that we found "it important that this is *not* an area immediately adjacent to a private home, where privacy expectations are most heightened."

It would be foolish to contend that the degree of privacy secured to citizens by the Fourth Amendment has been entirely unaffected by the advance of technology. . . . The question we confront today is what limits there are upon this power of technology to shrink the realm of guaranteed privacy. . . .

. . . We think that obtaining by sense-enhancing technology any information regarding the interior of the home that could not otherwise have been obtained without physical "intrusion into a constitutionally protected area," *Silverman*, constitutes a search—at least where (as here) the technology in question is not in general public use. This assures preservation of that degree of privacy against government that existed when the Fourth Amendment was adopted. On the basis of this criterion, the information obtained by the thermal imager in this case was the product of a search.

The Government maintains, however, that the thermal imaging must be upheld because it detected "only heat radiating from the external surface of the house." The dissent makes this its leading point, contending that there is a fundamental difference between what it calls "off-the-wall" observations and "through-the-wall surveillance." But just as a thermal imager captures only heat emanating from a house, so also a powerful directional microphone picks up only sound emanating from a house—and a satellite capable of scanning from many miles away would pick up only visible light emanating from a house. We rejected such a mechanical interpretation of the Fourth Amendment in *Katz*, where the eavesdropping device picked up only sound waves that reached the exterior of the phone booth. Reversing that approach would leave the homeowner at the mercy of advancing technology— including imaging technology that could discern all human activity in the home. . . .

The Government also contends that the thermal imaging was constitutional because it did not "detect private activities occurring in private areas." . . . The Fourth Amendment's protection of the home has never been tied to measurement of the quality or quantity of information obtained. . . .

Limiting the prohibition of thermal imaging to "intimate details" would not only be wrong in principle; it would be impractical in application, failing to provide "a workable accommodation between the needs of law enforcement and the interests protected by the Fourth Amendment." To begin with, there is no necessary connection between the sophistication of the surveillance equipment and the "intimacy" of the details that it observes—which means that one cannot say (and the police cannot be assured) that use of the relatively crude equipment at issue here will always be lawful. The Agema Thermovision 210 might disclose, for example, at what hour each night the lady of the house takes her daily sauna and bath—a detail that many would consider "intimate"; and a much more sophisticated system might detect nothing more intimate than the fact that someone left a closet light on. We could not, in other words, develop a rule approving only that through-the-wall surveillance which identifies objects no smaller than 36 by 36 inches, but would have to develop a jurisprudence specifying which home activities are "intimate" and which are not. And even when (if ever) that jurisprudence were fully developed, no police officer would be able to know *in advance* whether his through-the-wall surveillance picks up "intimate" details—and thus would be unable to know in advance whether it is constitutional. . . .

We have said that the Fourth Amendment draws "a firm line at the entrance to the house," *Payton* [*v. New York*, 445 U.S. 573 (1980)]. That line, we think, must be not only firm but also bright—which requires clear specification of those methods of surveillance that require a warrant. While it is certainly possible to conclude from the videotape of the thermal imaging that occurred in this case that no "significant" compromise of the homeowner's privacy has occurred, we must take the long view, from the original meaning of the Fourth Amendment forward. "The Fourth Amendment is to be construed in the light of what was deemed an unreasonable search and seizure when it was adopted, and in a manner which will conserve public interests as well as the interests and rights of individual citizens." *Carroll v. United States*, 267 U.S. 132 (1925).

Where, as here, the Government uses a device that is not in general public use, to explore details of the home that would previously have been unknowable without physical intrusion, the surveillance is a "search" and is presumptively unreasonable without a warrant. . . .

Justice STEVENS, with whom the Chief Justice [REHNQUIST] and Justices O'CONNOR and KENNEDY join, dissenting.

. . . [T]his case involves nothing more than off-the-wall surveillance by law enforcement officers to gather information exposed to the general public from the outside of petitioner's home. All that the infrared camera did in this case was passively measure heat emitted from the exterior surfaces of petitioner's home; all that those measurements showed were relative differences in emission levels, vaguely indicating that some areas of the roof and outside walls were warmer than others. As still images from the infrared scans show, no details regarding the interior of petitioner's home were revealed. . . .

[T]he notion that heat emissions from the outside of a dwelling is a private matter implicating the protections of the Fourth Amendment [the text of which guarantees the right of people "to be secure *in* their . . . houses" against unreasonable searches and seizures (emphasis added)] is not only unprecedented but also quite difficult to take seriously. Heat waves, like aromas that are generated in a kitchen, or in a laboratory or opium den, enter the public domain if and when they leave a building. A subjective expectation that they would remain private is not only implausible but also surely not "one that society is prepared to recognize as 'reasonable.'" *Katz* [*v. United States*, 389 U.S. 347 (1967)], (Justice Harlan, concurring).

To be sure, the homeowner has a reasonable expectation of privacy concerning what takes place within the home, and the Fourth Amendment's protection against physical invasions of the home should apply to their functional equivalent. But the equipment in this case did not penetrate the walls of petitioner's home, and while it did pick up "details of the home" that were exposed to the public, it did not obtain "any information regarding the *interior* of the home," (emphasis added). . . .

Since what was involved in this case was nothing more than drawing inferences from off-the-wall surveillance, rather than any "through-the-wall" surveillance, the officers' conduct did not amount to a search and was perfectly reasonable. . . .

Capital Punishment: Cases

The two following cases focus on due process rights and capital punishment. The first addresses the issue of whether the intellectually challenged, formerly known as those judged to be "mentally retarded," are responsible for crimes they commit, including cold-blooded murder. The second inquires into whether the state should hold an adolescent responsible for that same crime. In both cases, the justices focused on whether a national consensus, determined by the number of state legislatures, permitted or banned executions for the intellectually disabled and adolescents.

Case 5.5

Atkins v. Virginia
526 U.S. 304 (2002)

Daryl Atkins and a friend, William Jones, spent the day drinking and then smoking marijuana in Virginia when they ran out of alcohol. They went to a convenience store only to find that they did not have enough money to replenish their liquor supply so they decided to rob a customer. They abducted an airman by the name of Eric Nesbitt, who was stationed at Langley Air Force Base, and forced him to withdraw $200 from an ATM. They then drove him to a secluded area where they shot him to death. The two were soon arrested, and in a plea deal, Jones turned testimony against Atkins in exchange for a reduced sentence: a defendant in Virginia is not eligible for the death penalty when he pleads guilty. Atkins however faced capital punishment.

At trial, both men claimed that the other one had shot and killed Nesbitt. The jury believed Jones, and Atkins was sentenced to death. The Virginia Supreme Court upheld the convictions, but overturned the penalty because the lower court had used the wrong verdict form. In the second penalty phase, the court heard testimony from a psychologist that Atkins had an I.Q. of 59—that of a 9 to 12 year old boy—and had difficulty interacting with the social environment around him. The prosecution's psychologist, in turn, argued that while Atkins exhibited anti-social behavior at times, he was a man of average intelligence and could tell the difference between right and wrong. The jury also learned that Atkins had had 16 previous felony convictions, ranging from robbery to maiming. He was again sentenced to death.

On appeal, Atkins's lawyer asked the Virginia Supreme Court to reduce his sentence to life in prison because of his intellectual disability. The court declined to do so, relying on *Penry v. Lynaugh*, 492 U.S. 302 (1989), which held that it was constitutional to execute a person who is intellectually challenged. In that case, Justice Sandra Day O'Connor noted that only one state banned executions of the intellectually disabled, which she termed "mentally retarded," and concluded that there was a national consensus that appeared to favor the practice. By the time *Atkins* reached the Court, however, seventeen additional states had banned executions of intellectually challenged people. The Supreme Court then accepted the *Atkins* case to reconsider *Penry*, which it overruled six to three. The opinion of the Court was written by Justice John Paul Stevens. Chief Justice William H. Rehnquist dissented as did Justice Antonin Scalia.

Justice STEVENS delivered the opinion of the Court.

Those mentally retarded persons who meet the law's requirements for criminal responsibility should be tried and punished when they commit crimes. Because of their disabilities in areas of reasoning, judgment, and control of their impulses, however, they do not act with the level of moral culpability that characterizes the most serious adult criminal conduct. Moreover, their impairments can jeopardize the reliability and fairness of capital proceedings against mentally retarded defendants. Presumably for these reasons, in the 13 years since we decided *Penry v. Lynaugh*, (1989), the American public, legislators, scholars, and judges have deliberated over the question whether the death penalty should ever be imposed on a mentally retarded criminal. The consensus reflected in those deliberations informs our answer to the question presented by this case: whether such executions are "cruel and unusual punishments" prohibited by the Eighth Amendment to the Federal Constitution. . . .

The Eighth Amendment succinctly prohibits "excessive" sanctions. . . . A claim that punishment is excessive is judged not by the standards that prevailed in 1685 when Lord Jeffreys presided over the "Bloody Assizes" or when the Bill of Rights was adopted, but rather by those that currently prevail. As Chief Justice Warren explained in his opinion in *Trop v. Dulles*, 356 U. S. 86 (1958): "The basic concept underlying the Eighth Amendment is nothing less than the dignity of man. . . . The

Amendment must draw its meaning from the evolving standards of decency that mark the progress of a maturing society."

Proportionality review under those evolving standards should be informed by " 'objective factors to the maximum possible extent.' " We have pinpointed that the "clearest and most reliable objective evidence of contemporary values is the legislation enacted by the country's legislatures." *Penry.* Relying in part on such legislative evidence, we have held that death is an impermissibly excessive punishment for the rape of an adult woman, *Coker v. Georgia,* 433 U. S. 584 (1977), or for a defendant who neither took life, attempted to take life, nor intended to take life, *Enmund v. Florida,* 458 U. S. 782 (1982). In *Coker,* we focused primarily on the then-recent legislation that had been enacted in response to our decision 10 years earlier in *Furman v. Georgia,* 408 U. S. 238 (1972), to support the conclusion that the "current judgment," though "not wholly unanimous," weighed very heavily on the side of rejecting capital punishment as a "suitable penalty for raping an adult woman." *Coker.* The current legislative judgment" relevant to our decision in *Enmund* was less clear than in *Coker* but "nevertheless weighed on the side of rejecting capital punishment for the crime at issue." *Enmund.* . . .

Guided by our approach in these cases, we shall first review the judgment of legislatures that have addressed the suitability of imposing the death penalty on the mentally retarded and then consider reasons for agreeing or disagreeing with their judgment. . . .

Much has changed since [*Penry* was decided]. Responding to the national attention received by the Bowden execution and our decision in *Penry,* state legislatures across the country began to address the issue. In 1990 Kentucky and Tennessee enacted statutes similar to those in Georgia and Maryland, as did New Mexico in 1991, and Arkansas, Colorado, Washington, Indiana, and Kansas in 1993 and 1994. In 1995, when New York reinstated its death penalty, it emulated the Federal Government by expressly exempting the mentally retarded. Nebraska followed suit in 1998. There appear to have been no similar enactments during the next two years, but in 2000 and 2001 six more States—South Dakota, Arizona, Connecticut, Florida, Missouri, and North Carolina—joined the procession. The Texas Legislature unanimously adopted a similar bill, and bills have passed at least one house in other States, including Virginia and Nevada.

It is not so much the number of these States that is significant, but the consistency of the direction of change. Given the well-known fact that anticrime legislation is far more popular than legislation providing protections for persons guilty of violent crime, the large number of States prohibiting the execution of mentally retarded persons (and the complete absence of States passing legislation reinstating the power to conduct such executions) provides powerful evidence that today our society views mentally retarded offenders as categorically less culpable than the average criminal. . . .

To the extent there is serious disagreement about the execution of mentally retarded offenders, it is in determining which offenders are in fact retarded. In this case, for instance, the Commonwealth of Virginia disputes that Atkins suffers from mental retardation. Not all people who claim to be mentally retarded will be so impaired as to fall within the range of mentally retarded offenders about whom there is a national consensus. As was our approach in *Ford v. Wainwright,* with regard to insanity, "we leave to the State[s] the task of developing appropriate ways to enforce the constitutional restriction upon its execution of sentences.". . .

Our death penalty jurisprudence provides two reasons consistent with the legislative consensus that the mentally retarded should be categorically excluded from execution. First, there is a serious question as to whether either justification that we have recognized as a basis for the death penalty applies to mentally retarded offenders. *Gregg v. Georgia,* 428 U. S. 153 (1976), identified "retribution and deterrence of capital crimes by prospective offenders" as the social purposes served by the death penalty. Unless the imposition of the death penalty on a mentally retarded person "measurably contributes to one or both of these goals, it 'is nothing more than the purposeless and needless imposition of pain and suffering,' and hence an unconstitutional punishment." *Enmund.* . . .

With respect to retribution—the interest in seeing that the offender gets his "just deserts"—the severity of the appropriate punishment necessarily depends on the culpability of the offender. Since *Gregg,* our jurisprudence has consistently confined the imposition of the death penalty to a narrow category of the most serious crimes. For example, in *Godfrey v. Georgia,* 446 U. S. 420 (1980), we set aside a death sentence because the petitioner's crimes did not reflect "a consciousness materially more 'depraved' than that of any person guilty of murder." If the culpability of the average murderer is insufficient to justify the most extreme sanction available to the State, the lesser culpability of the mentally retarded offender surely does not merit that form of retribution. Thus, pursuant to our narrowing jurisprudence, which seeks to ensure that only the most deserving of execution are put to death, an exclusion for the mentally retarded is appropriate.

With respect to deterrence—the interest in preventing capital crimes by prospective offenders—"it seems likely that 'capital punishment can serve as a deterrent only when murder is the result of premeditation and deliberation,'" *Enmund.* Exempting the mentally retarded from that punishment will not affect the "cold calculus that precedes the decision" of other potential murderers. *Gregg.* Indeed, that sort of calculus is at the opposite end of the spectrum from behavior of mentally retarded offenders. The theory of deterrence in capital sentencing is predicated upon the notion that the increased severity of the punishment will inhibit criminal actors from carrying out murderous conduct. Yet it is the same cognitive and behavioral impairments that make these defendants less morally culpable—for example, the diminished ability to understand and process information, to learn from experience, to engage in logical reasoning, or to control impulses—that also make it less likely that they can process the information of the possibility of execution as a penalty and, as a result, control their conduct based upon that information. Nor will exempting the mentally retarded from execution lessen the deterrent effect of the death penalty with respect to offenders who are not mentally retarded. Such individuals are unprotected by the exemption and will continue to face the threat of execution. Thus, executing the mentally retarded will not measurably further the goal of deterrence. . . .

The judgment of the Virginia Supreme Court is reversed and the case is remanded for further proceedings not inconsistent with this opinion.

Justice SCALIA, dissenting.

Today's decision is the pinnacle of our Eighth Amendment death-is-different jurisprudence. Not only does it, like all of that jurisprudence, find no support in the text or history of the Eighth Amendment; it does not even have support in current social attitudes regarding the conditions that render an otherwise just death penalty inappropriate. Seldom has an opinion of this Court rested so obviously upon nothing but the personal views of its members. . . .

I begin with a brief restatement of facts that are abridged by the Court but important to understanding this case. After spending the day drinking alcohol and smoking marijuana, petitioner Daryl Renard Atkins and a partner in crime drove to a convenience store, intending to rob a customer. Their victim was Eric Nesbitt, an airman from Langley Air Force Base, whom they abducted, drove to a nearby automated teller machine, and forced to withdraw $200. They then drove him to a deserted area, ignoring his pleas to leave him unharmed. According to the co-conspirator, whose testimony the jury evidently credited, Atkins ordered Nesbitt out of the vehicle and, after he had taken only a few steps, shot him one, two, three, four, five, six, seven, eight times in the thorax, chest, abdomen, arms, and legs. . . .

The Court is left to argue, therefore, that execution of the mildly retarded is inconsistent with the "evolving standards of decency that mark the progress of a maturing society." *Trop v. Dulles.* Before today, our opinions consistently emphasized that Eighth Amendment judgments regarding the existence of social "standards" "should be informed by objective factors to the maximum possible extent" and "should not be, or appear to be, merely the subjective views of individual Justices." *Coker v. Georgia.* . . .

The Court pays lipservice to these precedents as it miraculously extracts a "national consensus" forbidding execution of the mentally retarded, from the fact that 18 States—less than *half* (47%) of the 38 States that permit capital punishment (for whom the issue exists)—have very recently enacted legislation barring execution of the mentally retarded. Even that 47% figure is a distorted one. If one is to say, as the Court does today, that all executions of the mentally retarded are so morally repugnant as to violate our national "standards of decency," surely the "consensus" it points to must be one that has set its righteous face against all such executions. Not 18 States, but only seven—18% of death penalty jurisdictions—have legislation of that scope. Eleven of those that the Court counts enacted statutes prohibiting execution of mentally retarded defendants *convicted after,* or *convicted of crimes committed after, the effective date* of the legislation; those already on death row, or consigned there before the statute's effective date, or even (in those States using the date of the crime as the criterion of retroactivity) tried in the future for murders committed many years ago, could be put to death. That is not a statement of absolute moral repugnance, but one of current preference between two tolerable approaches. . . .

But let us accept, for the sake of argument, the Court's faulty count. That bare number of States alone—18—should be enough to convince any reasonable person that no "national consensus" exists. How is it possible that agreement among 47% of the death penalty jurisdictions amounts to "consensus?" Our prior cases have generally required a much higher degree of agreement before finding a punishment cruel and unusual on "evolving standards" grounds. . . .

The Court's thrashing about for evidence of "consensus" includes reliance upon the *margins* by which state legislatures have enacted bans on execution of the retarded. Presumably, in applying our Eighth Amendment "evolving-standards-of-decency" jurisprudence, we will henceforth weigh not only how many States have agreed, but how many States have agreed *by how much.* Of course if the percentage of legislators voting for the bill is significant, surely the number of people *represented* by the legislators voting for the bill is also significant: the fact that 49% of the legislators in a State with a population of 60 million voted against the bill should be more impressive than the fact that 90% of the legislators in a state with a population of 2 million voted *for* it. (By the way, the population of the death penalty States that exclude the mentally retarded is only 44% of the population of all death penalty States.) This is quite absurd. What we have looked for in the past to "evolve" the Eighth Amendment is a consensus of the same sort as the consensus that *adopted* the Eighth Amendment: a consensus of the sovereign States that form the Union, not a nose count of Americans for and against. . . .

But the Prize for the Court's Most Feeble Effort to fabricate "national consensus" must go to its appeal (deservedly relegated to a footnote) to the views of assorted professional and religious organizations, members of the so-called "world community," and respondents to opinion polls. I agree with the Chief Justice, (dissenting opinion), that the views of professional and religious organizations and the results of opinion polls are irrelevant. Equally irrelevant are the practices of the "world community," whose notions of justice are (thankfully) not always those of our people. . . .

Today's opinion adds one more to the long list of substantive and procedural requirements impeding imposition of the death penalty imposed under this Court's assumed power to invent a death-is-different jurisprudence. None of those requirements existed when the Eighth Amendment was adopted, and some of them were not even supported by current moral consensus. . . . This newest invention promises to be more effective than any of the others in turning the process of capital trial into a game. One need only read the definitions of mental retardation adopted by the American Association of Mental Retardation and the American Psychiatric Association to realize that the symptoms of this condition can readily be feigned. And whereas the capital defendant who feigns insanity risks commitment to a mental institution until he can be cured (and then tried and executed), the capital defendant who feigns mental retardation risks nothing at all. The mere pendency of the present case has brought us petitions by death row inmates claiming for the first time, after multiple *habeas* petitions, that they are retarded. . . . I respectfully dissent.

Case 5.6

Roper v. Simmons
125 S.Ct. 1183 (2005)

Christopher Simmons was 18 years old when he was convicted of capital murder in Missouri and sentenced to death for a crime he had committed in 1993 when he was a 17-year old junior in high school. Simmons and two friends planned to burglarize a house and kill its occupant by throwing the victim from a bridge. Simmons told his friends that he knew they could "get away with it" because they were minors.

On the night of the murder, one young man decided not to participate. (He later testified against Simmons when the state promised to drop all charges against him). Simmons and the other friend went to the home of Shirley Crook where they were able to unlock a door through an open window. After they turned on a hall light, Crook, whose husband was away, awakened and confronted the young men. Simmons recognized her as a woman with whom he had earlier been involved in an automobile accident. He admitted that this factor confirmed his decision to kill her.

After covering her eyes with duct tape, they drove her to the Meramec River where they reinforced the tape, covered her head with a towel, and bound her hands and feet with electrical wire. Then from a railroad trestle they dropped her into the river where she drowned. A few days later, fishermen called police after they found her body. Meantime, on the same day, Mr. Crook returned from his trip, found his house in disarray, and reported her missing. By this time, Simmons was bragging to his friends about his "achievement" and was continuing to claim he could get away with it because he was a juvenile. The police soon heard of his boasting, arrested him, and after waiving his Miranda rights, he confessed. He was charged with murder in the first degree, kidnapping, burglary, and robbery.

The state tried Simmons as an adult, and brought to the court his confession and his reenactment of the murder as well as his bragging about the crime. The defense put on no witnesses. Simmons was found guilty. The jury in the penalty phase delivered a verdict of capital punishment because Missouri allowed for the death penalty for juveniles as young as 16 years old who committed capital crimes. After the Missouri Supreme Court upheld the verdict, a federal district court denied his appeal.

Then in 2002, the United States Supreme Court ruled in *Atkins v. Virginia*, 536 U.S. 304, that the Eighth and Fourteenth Amendments prohibited the execution of intellectually challenged persons on the grounds that a majority of states either simply did not provide for capital punishment or no longer permitted the death penalty for those who committed capital crimes when they were intellectually disabled. The Court's reasoning was based on the changing understanding of the terms "cruel and unusual punishment" by considering history, tradition, and precedent as well as the place of the death penalty in the constitutional design. The key precedent the Court cited was *Trop v. Dulles*, 356 U.S. 86 (1958): there, the majority held that "the evolving standards of decency that mark the progress of a maturing society" must determine which punishments are so disproportionate as to be "cruel and unusual."

Now armed with the results of the *Atkins* decision, Simmons once again appealed to the Missouri Supreme Court, which this time agreed that the reasoning in *Atkins* concerning the intellectually challenged applied to juveniles facing capital punishment. The Missouri court claimed that *Atkins* effectively superseded the Supreme Court's decision in *Stanford v. Kentucky*, 492 U.S. 361 (1989), which had held that juveniles who committed capital crimes when they were 16 or older may be subject to the death penalty. Simmons was re-sentenced to life imprisonment without parole or probation. The state of Missouri appealed to the Supreme Court, which granted *certiorari*.

The Court's decision in upholding the Missouri Supreme Court was five to four. Justice Anthony Kennedy delivered the opinion of the Court, in which Justices John Paul Stevens, David Souter, Ruth Bader Ginsburg, and Stephen Breyer joined. Justice Stevens filed a concurring opinion, in which Justice Ginsburg joined. Justice Sandra Day O'Connor filed a dissenting opinion, as did Justice Antonin Scalia, who was joined by Chief Justice William H. Rehnquist, and Justice Clarence Thomas.

Justice KENNEDY delivered the opinion of the Court.

. . . The prohibition against "cruel and unusual punishments," like other expansive language in the Constitution, must be interpreted according to its text, by considering history, tradition, and precedent, and with due regard for its purpose and function in the constitutional design. To implement this framework we have established the propriety and affirmed the necessity of referring to "the evolving standards of decency that mark the progress of a maturing society" to determine which punishments are so disproportionate as to be cruel and unusual. *Trop v. Dulles*, 356 U.S. 86 (1958).

In *Thompson v. Oklahoma*, 487 U.S. 815 (1988), a plurality of the Court determined that our standards of decency do not permit the execution of any offender under the age of 16 at the time of the crime. . . .

The next year, in *Stanford v. Kentucky*, 492 U.S. 361 (1989), the Court, over a dissenting opinion joined by four Justices, referred to contemporary standards of decency in this country and concluded the

Eighth and Fourteenth Amendments did not proscribe the execution of juvenile offenders over 15 but under 18. . . .

The same day the Court decided *Stanford*, it held that the Eighth Amendment did not mandate a categorical exemption from the death penalty for the mentally retarded. *Penry v. Lynaugh*, 492 U.S. 302 (1989). In reaching this conclusion it stressed that only two States had enacted laws banning the imposition of the death penalty on a mentally retarded person convicted of a capital offense. According to the Court, "the two state statutes prohibiting execution of the mentally retarded, even when added to the 14 States that have rejected capital punishment completely, [did] not provide sufficient evidence at present of a national consensus."

Three terms ago the subject was reconsidered in *Atkins*. We held that standards of decency have evolved since *Penry* and now demonstrate that the execution of the mentally retarded is cruel and unusual punishment. The Court noted objective indicia of society's standards, as expressed in legislative enactments and state practice with respect to executions of the mentally retarded. When *Atkins* was decided only a minority of States permitted the practice, and even in those States it was rare. On the basis of these indicia the Court determined that executing mentally retarded offenders "has become truly unusual, and it is fair to say that a national consensus has developed against it." . . .

Just as the *Atkins* Court reconsidered the issue decided in *Penry*, we now reconsider the issue decided in *Stanford*. . . .

The evidence of national consensus against the death penalty for juveniles is similar, and in some respects parallel, to the evidence *Atkins* held sufficient to demonstrate a national consensus against the death penalty for the mentally retarded. . . . In the present case, too, even in the 20 States without a formal prohibition on executing juveniles, the practice is infrequent. Since *Stanford*, six States have executed prisoners for crimes committed as juveniles. In December 2003 the Governor of Kentucky decided to spare the life of Kevin Stanford, and commuted his sentence to one of life imprisonment without parole, with the declaration that " 'we ought not be executing people who, legally, were children.' " By this act the Governor ensured Kentucky would not add itself to the list of States that have executed juveniles within the last 10 years even by the execution of the very defendant whose death sentence the Court had upheld in *Stanford v. Kentucky*. . . .

A majority of States have rejected the imposition of the death penalty on juvenile offenders under 18, and we now hold this is required by the Eighth Amendment.

Because the death penalty is the most severe punishment, the Eighth Amendment applies to it with special force. . . . Three general differences between juveniles under 18 and adults demonstrate that juvenile offenders cannot with reliability be classified among the worst offenders. First, as any parent knows and as the scientific and sociological studies respondent and his *amici* cite tend to confirm, "a lack of maturity and an underdeveloped sense of responsibility are found in youth more often than in adults and are more understandable among the young. These qualities often result in impetuous and ill-considered actions and decisions." It has been noted that "adolescents are overrepresented statistically in virtually every category of reckless behavior." In recognition of the comparative immaturity and irresponsibility of juveniles, almost every State prohibits those under 18 years of age from voting, serving on juries, or marrying without parental consent.

The second area of difference is that juveniles are more vulnerable or susceptible to negative influences and outside pressures, including peer pressure. This is explained in part by the prevailing circumstance that juveniles have less control, or less experience with control, over their own environment.

The third broad difference is that the character of a juvenile is not as well formed as that of an adult. The personality traits of juveniles are more transitory, less fixed. . . .

Once the diminished culpability of juveniles is recognized, it is evident that the penological justifications for the death penalty apply to them with lesser force than to adults. We have held there are two distinct social purposes served by the death penalty: "'retribution and deterrence of capital crimes by prospective offenders.'" *Atkins* [quoting *Gregg v. Georgia*, 428 U.S. 153 (1976).] As for retribution, we remarked in *Atkins* that "if the culpability of the average murderer is insufficient to justify the most extreme sanction available to the State, the lesser culpability of the mentally retarded offender surely does not merit that form of retribution." The same conclusions follow from the lesser culpability of the juvenile offender. Whether viewed as an attempt to express the community's moral outrage or as an attempt to right the balance for the wrong to the victim, the case for retribution is not as strong with a minor as with an adult. Retribution is not proportional if the law's most severe penalty is imposed on one whose culpability or blameworthiness is diminished, to a substantial degree, by reason of youth and immaturity.

As for deterrence, it is unclear whether the death penalty has a significant or even measurable deterrent effect on juveniles, as counsel for the petitioner acknowledged at oral argument. In general we leave to legislatures the assessment of the efficacy of various criminal penalty schemes. Here, however, the absence of evidence of deterrent effect is of special concern because the same characteristics that render juveniles less culpable than adults suggest as well that juveniles will be less susceptible to deterrence. In particular, as the plurality observed in *Thompson*, "the likelihood that the teenage offender has made the kind of cost-benefit analysis that attaches any weight to the possibility of execution is so remote as to be virtually nonexistent." To the extent the juvenile death penalty might have residual deterrent effect, it is worth noting that the punishment of life imprisonment without the possibility of parole is itself a severe sanction, in particular for a young person.

In concluding that neither retribution nor deterrence provides adequate justification for imposing the death penalty on juvenile offenders, we cannot deny or overlook the brutal crimes too many juvenile offenders have committed. Certainly it can be argued, although we by no means concede the point, that a rare case might arise in which a juvenile offender has sufficient psychological maturity, and at the same time demonstrates sufficient depravity, to merit a sentence of death. . . .

These considerations mean *Stanford v. Kentucky* should be deemed no longer controlling on this issue. . . .

Our determination that the death penalty is disproportionate punishment for offenders under 18 finds confirmation in the stark reality that the United States is the only country in the world that continues to give official sanction to the juvenile death penalty. This reality does not become controlling, for the task of interpreting the Eighth Amendment remains our responsibility. Yet at least from the time of the Court's decision in *Trop*, the Court has referred to the laws of other countries and to international authorities as instructive for its interpretation of the Eighth Amendment's prohibition of "cruel and unusual punishments."

As respondent and a number of *amici* emphasize, Article 37 of the United Nations Convention on the Rights of the Child, which every country in the world has ratified save for the United States and Somalia, contains an express prohibition on capital punishment for crimes committed by juveniles under 18. No ratifying country has entered a reservation to the provision prohibiting the execution of juvenile offenders. Parallel prohibitions are contained in other significant international covenants.

Respondent and his *amici* have submitted, and petitioner does not contest, that only seven countries other than the United States have executed juvenile offenders since 1990: Iran, Pakistan, Saudi Arabia, Yemen, Nigeria, the Democratic Republic of Congo, and China. Since then each of these countries has either abolished capital punishment for juveniles or made public disavowal of the practice. In sum, it is fair to say that the United States now stands alone in a world that has turned its face against the juvenile death penalty.

Though the international covenants prohibiting the juvenile death penalty are of more recent date, it is instructive to note that the United Kingdom abolished the juvenile death penalty before these covenants came into being. . . .

The Eighth and Fourteenth Amendments forbid imposition of the death penalty on offenders who were under the age of 18 when their crimes were committed. The judgment of the Missouri Supreme Court setting aside the sentence of death imposed upon Christopher Simmons is affirmed.

It is so ordered.

Justice SCALIA, with whom the Chief Justice [REHNQUIST] and Justice THOMAS join, dissenting.

In urging approval of a constitution that gave life-tenured judges the power to nullify laws enacted by the people's representatives, Alexander Hamilton assured the citizens of New York that there was little risk in this, since "the judiciary . . . has neither FORCE nor WILL but merely judgment." The *Federalist* No. 78. But Hamilton had in mind a traditional judiciary, "bound down by strict rules and precedents which serve to define and point out their duty in every particular case that comes before them." Bound down, indeed. What a mockery today's opinion makes of Hamilton's expectation, announcing the Court's conclusion that the meaning of our Constitution has changed over the past 15 years—not, mind you, that this Court's decision 15 years ago was wrong, but that the Constitution has changed. The Court reaches this implausible result by purporting to advert, not to the original meaning of the Eighth Amendment, but to "the evolving standards of decency" of our national society. It then finds, on the flimsiest of grounds, that a national consensus which could not be perceived in our people's laws barely 15 years ago now solidly exists. . . . The Court thus proclaims itself sole arbiter of our Nation's moral standards—and in the course of discharging that awesome responsibility purports to take guidance from the views of foreign courts and legislatures. Because I do not believe that the meaning of our Eighth Amendment, any more than the meaning of other provisions of our Constitution, should be determined by the subjective views of five Members of this Court and like-minded foreigners, I dissent.

In determining that capital punishment of offenders who committed murder before age 18 is "cruel and unusual" under the Eighth Amendment, the Court first considers, in accordance with our modern (though in my view mistaken) jurisprudence, whether there is a "national consensus" that laws allowing such executions contravene our modern "standards of decency," *Trop v. Dulles*, 356 U.S. 86 (1958). We have held that this determination should be based on "objective indicia that reflect the public attitude toward a given sanction"—namely, "statutes passed by society's elected representatives." *Stanford v. Kentucky*, 492 U.S. 361 (1989). As in *Atkins v. Virginia*, 536 U.S. 304 (2002), the Court dutifully recites this test and claims halfheartedly that a national consensus has emerged since our decision in *Stanford*, because 18 States—or 47% of States that permit capital punishment—now have legislation prohibiting the execution of offenders under 18, and because all of four States have adopted such legislation since *Stanford*.

Words have no meaning if the views of less than 50% of death penalty States can constitute a national consensus. Our previous cases have required overwhelming opposition to a challenged practice, generally over a long period of time. . . . By contrast, agreement among 42% of death penalty States in *Stanford*, which the Court appears to believe was correctly decided at the time, was insufficient to show a national consensus.

In an attempt to keep afloat its implausible assertion of national consensus, the Court throws overboard a proposition well established in our Eighth Amendment jurisprudence. "It should be observed," the Court says, "that the *Stanford* Court should have considered those States that had abandoned the death penalty altogether as part of the consensus against the juvenile death penalty . . . ; a State's decision to bar the death penalty altogether of necessity demonstrates a judgment that the death penalty is inappropriate for all offenders, including juveniles." . . . Consulting States that bar the death penalty concerning the necessity of making an exception to the penalty for offenders under 18 is rather like including old-order Amishmen in a consumer-preference poll on the electric car. Of course they don't like it, but that sheds no light whatever on the point at issue. That 12 States favor no executions says something about consensus against the death penalty, but nothing—absolutely nothing—about consensus that offenders under 18 deserve special immunity from such a penalty. In repealing the death penalty, those 12 States considered none of the factors that the Court puts forth as determinative of the issue before us today—lower culpability of the young, inherent recklessness, lack of capacity for considered judgment, etc. What might be relevant, perhaps, is how many of those States permit 16- and 17-year-old offenders to be treated as adults with respect to noncapital offenses. (They all do; indeed, some even require that juveniles as young as 14 be tried as adults if they are charged with murder.) The attempt by the Court to turn its remarkable minority consensus into a faux majority by counting Amishmen is an act of nomological desperation. . . .

Of course, the real force driving today's decision is not the actions of four state legislatures, but the Court's "own judgment" that murderers younger than 18 can never be as morally culpable as older counterparts. The Court claims that this usurpation of the role of moral arbiter is simply a "return to the rule established in decisions predating *Stanford*." That supposed rule—which is reflected solely in dicta and never once in a holding that purports to supplant the consensus of the American people with the Justices' views—was repudiated in *Stanford* for the very good reason that it has no foundation in law or logic. If the Eighth Amendment set forth an ordinary rule of law, it would indeed be the role of this Court to say what the law is. But the Court having pronounced that the Eighth Amendment is an ever-changing reflection of "the evolving standards of decency" of our society, it makes no sense for the Justices then to prescribe those standards rather than discern them from the practices of our people. On the evolving-standards hypothesis, the only legitimate function of this Court is to identify a moral consensus of the American people. By what conceivable warrant can nine lawyers presume to be the authoritative conscience of the Nation? . . .

We need not look far to find studies contradicting the Court's conclusions. . . .

Though the views of our own citizens are essentially irrelevant to the Court's decision today, the views of other countries and the so-called international community take center stage. . . .

More fundamentally . . . the basic premise of the Court's argument—that American law should conform to the laws of the rest of the world—ought to be rejected out of hand. In fact the Court itself does not believe it. In many significant respects the laws of most other countries differ from our law—including not only such explicit provisions of our Constitution as the right to jury trial and grand jury indictment, but even many interpretations of the Constitution prescribed by this Court itself. . . .

The Court's special reliance on the laws of the United Kingdom is perhaps the most indefensible part of its opinion. It is of course true that we share a common history with the United Kingdom, and that we often consult English sources when asked to discern the meaning of a constitutional text written against the backdrop of 18th-century English law and legal thought. If we applied that approach today, our task would be an easy one. . . . The Court has, however—I think wrongly—long rejected a purely originalist approach to our Eighth Amendment, and that is certainly not the approach the Court takes today. Instead, the Court undertakes the majestic task of determining (and thereby prescribing) our Nation's current standards of decency. . . .

The Court should either profess its willingness to reconsider all these matters in light of the views of foreigners, or else it should cease putting forth foreigners' views as part of the reasoned basis of its decisions. To invoke alien law when it agrees with one's own thinking, and ignore it otherwise, is not reasoned decisionmaking, but sophistry. . . .

To add insult to injury, the Court affirms the Missouri Supreme Court without even admonishing that court for its flagrant disregard of our precedent in *Stanford*. Until today, we have always held that "it is this Court's prerogative alone to overrule one of its precedents." *State Oil Co. v. Khan*, 522 U.S. 3 (1997). . . . Today, however, the Court silently ap-

proves a state-court decision that blatantly rejected controlling precedent. . . .

Allowing lower courts to reinterpret the Eighth Amendment whenever they decide enough time has passed for a new snapshot leaves this
Court's decisions without any force—especially since the "evolution" of
our Eighth Amendment is no longer determined by objective criteria. To
allow lower courts to behave as we do, "updating" the Eighth Amendment as needed, destroys stability and makes our case law an unreliable
basis for the designing of laws by citizens and their representatives, and
for action by public officials. The result will be to crown arbitrariness
with chaos.

The Right to Bear Arms: Case

The Court has rarely reviewed the right to bear arms, which is rooted in
the Constitution's Second Amendment. In 2008, however, the Court for
the first time concluded arms possession and ownership were an individual right, and two years later, it decided that the right also applied to
the states as it was incorporated into the liberty component of the Fourteenth Amendment's Due Process Clause.

Case 5.7

McDonald v. City Of Chicago, Illinois
561 U.S. 3025, 130 S.Ct. 3020 (2010)

In 2008, the Supreme Court ruled that the Second Amendment
protected an individual's right to keep and bear arms for the purpose of self-defense. In *District of Columbia v. Heller*, it struck down a
District of Columbia law that banned the possession of handguns
in the home. The ruling only limited the federal—the District of
Columbia being a federal jurisdiction—and not state governments. Chicago and the village of Oak Park, a Chicago suburb,

had laws effectively banning handgun possession by almost all private citizens. After *Heller*, Otis McDonald and three other petitioners filed suit against Chicago, which was consolidated with two related actions, alleging that the handgun ban has left them vulnerable to criminals.

McDonald sought a declaration that the ban and several related City ordinances violate the Second and Fourteenth Amendments. Rejecting petitioners' argument that the ordinances were unconstitutional, the U.S. district court noted that the U.S. Court of Appeals for the Seventh Circuit previously had upheld the constitutionality of a handgun ban, that *Heller* had explicitly refrained from deciding whether the Second Amendment applied to the states, and that the court had a duty to follow established Circuit precedent. The Seventh Circuit affirmed, relying on three 19th-century cases—*United States v. Cruikshank* (1876), *Presser v. Illinois* (1886), and *Miller v. Texas* (1894)—which affirmed that the Second Amendment's right to bear arms applied only to Acts of Congress [*United States v. Cruikshank*, 92 U.S. 542 (1876), *Presser v. Illinois*, 116 U.S. 252 (1886), and *Miller v. Texas*, 153 U.S. 535 (1894)].

In a five to four decision, the U.S. Supreme Court reversed the judgment of the Seventh Circuit. The Court's opinion was written by Justice Samuel Alito, joined by Chief Justice Roberts and Justices Scalia, Thomas, and Kennedy. Dissenting was Justice John Paul Stevens as well as Justices Breyer, Ginsburg, and Sotomayor.

Justice ALITO delivered the opinion of the Court.

Two years ago, in *District of Columbia v. Heller* [554 U.S. 570] (2008), we held that the Second Amendment protects the right to keep and bear arms for the purpose of self-defense, and we struck down a District of Columbia law that banned the possession of handguns in the home. The city of Chicago (City) and the village of Oak Park, a Chicago suburb, have laws that are similar to the District of Columbia's, but Chicago and Oak Park argue that their laws are constitutional because the Second Amendment has no application to the States. We have previously held that most of the provisions of the Bill of Rights apply with full force to both the Federal Government and the States. Applying the standard that is well established in our case law, we hold that the Second Amendment right is fully applicable to the States. . . .

Petitioners argue that the Chicago and Oak Park laws violate the right to keep and bear arms for two reasons. Petitioners' primary submission is that this right is among the "privileges or immunities of citizens of the United States" and that the narrow interpretation of the Privileges or Immunities Clause adopted in the *Slaughter-House Cases* should now be rejected.

As a secondary argument, petitioners contend that the Fourteenth Amendment's Due Process Clause "incorporates" the Second Amendment right. . . .

The constitutional Amendments adopted in the aftermath of the Civil War fundamentally altered our country's federal system. The provision at issue in this case, Section 1 of the Fourteenth Amendment, provides, among other things, that a State may not abridge "the privileges or immunities of citizens of the United States" or deprive "any person of life, liberty, or property, without due process of law."

Four years after the adoption of the Fourteenth Amendment, this Court was asked to interpret the Amendment's reference to "the privileges or immunities of citizens of the United States." The *Slaughter-House Cases* involved challenges to a Louisiana law permitting the creation of a state-sanctioned monopoly on the butchering of animals within the city of New Orleans. Justice Samuel Miller's opinion for the Court concluded that the Privileges or Immunities Clause protects only those rights "which owe their existence to the Federal government, its National character, its Constitution, or its laws." The Court held that other fundamental rights—rights that predated the creation of the Federal Government and that "the State governments were created to establish and secure"—were not protected by the Clause.

In drawing a sharp distinction between the rights of federal and state citizenship, the Court relied on two principal arguments. First, the Court emphasized that the Fourteenth Amendment's Privileges or Immunities Clause spoke of "the privileges or immunities of *citizens of the United States*," and the Court contrasted this phrasing with the wording in the first sentence of the Fourteenth Amendment and in the Privileges and Immunities Clause of Article IV, both of which refer to state citizenship. Second, the Court stated that a contrary reading would "radically change the whole theory of the relations of the State and Federal governments to each other and of both these governments to the people," and the Court refused to conclude that such a change had been made "in the absence of language which expresses such a purpose too clearly to admit of doubt." Finding the phrase "privileges or immunities of citizens of the United States" lacking by this high standard, the Court reasoned that the phrase must mean something more limited.

Under the Court's narrow reading, the Privileges or Immunities Clause protects such things as the right "to come to the seat of government to assert any claim [a citizen] may have upon that government, to transact any business he may have with it, to seek its protection, to share its offices, to engage in administering its functions . . . [and to] become a citizen of any State of the Union by a *bona fide* residence therein, with the same rights as other citizens of that State."

Finding no constitutional protection against state intrusion of the kind envisioned by the Louisiana statute, the Court upheld the statute. . . .

Three years after the decision in the *Slaughter-House Cases*, the Court decided *Cruikshank*, the first of the three 19th-century cases on which the Seventh Circuit relied. In that case, the Court reviewed convictions stemming from the infamous Colfax Massacre in Louisiana on Easter Sunday 1873. Dozens of blacks, many unarmed, were slaughtered by a rival band of armed white men. Cruikshank himself allegedly marched unarmed African-American prisoners through the streets and then had them summarily executed. Ninety-seven men were indicted for participating in the massacre, but only nine went to trial. Six of the nine were acquitted of all charges; the remaining three were acquitted of murder but convicted under the Enforcement Act of 1870 for banding and conspiring together to deprive their victims of various constitutional rights, including the right to bear arms.

The Court reversed all of the convictions, including those relating to the deprivation of the victims' right to bear arms. The Court wrote that the right of bearing arms for a lawful purpose "is not a right granted by the Constitution" and is not "in any manner dependent upon that instrument for its existence." "The second amendment," the Court continued, "declares that it shall not be infringed; but this . . . means no more than that it shall not be infringed by Congress." "Our later decisions in *Presser v. Illinois* (1886) and *Miller v. Texas* (1894) reaffirmed that the Second Amendment applies only to the Federal Government." . . .

As previously noted, the Seventh Circuit concluded that *Cruikshank*, *Presser*, and *Miller* doomed petitioners' claims at the Court of Appeals level. Petitioners argue, however, that we should overrule those decisions and hold that the right to keep and bear arms is one of the "privileges or immunities of citizens of the United States." . . . We see no need to reconsider that interpretation here. For many decades, the question of the rights protected by the Fourteenth Amendment against state infringement has been analyzed under the Due Process Clause of that Amendment and not under the Privileges or Immunities Clause. We therefore decline to disturb the *Slaughter-House* holding.

At the same time, however, this Court's decisions in *Cruikshank*, *Presser*, and *Miller* do not preclude us from considering whether the Due Process Clause of the Fourteenth Amendment makes the Second Amendment right binding on the States. . . . *Cruikshank*, *Presser*, and *Miller* all preceded the era in which the Court began the process of "selective incorporation" under the Due Process Clause, and we have never previously addressed the question whether the right to keep and bear arms applies to the States under that theory.

In the late 19th century, the Court began to consider whether the Due Process Clause prohibits the States from infringing rights set out in the Bill of Rights. . . . The Court began to hold that the Due Process Clause fully incorporates particular rights contained in the first eight Amendments. . . . We must decide whether the right to keep and bear arms is fundamental to our scheme of ordered liberty, or as we have said in a related context, whether this right is "deeply rooted in this Nation's history and tradition."

Our decision in *Heller* points unmistakably to the answer. Self-defense is a basic right, recognized by many legal systems from ancient times to the present day, and in *Heller*, we held that individual self-defense is "the *central component*" of the Second Amendment right. Explaining that "the need for defense of self, family, and property is most acute" in the home, we found that this right applies to handguns because they are "the most preferred firearm in the nation to 'keep' and use for protection of one's home and family." Thus, we concluded, citizens must be permitted "to use handguns for the core lawful purpose of self-defense."

Heller makes it clear that this right is "deeply rooted in this Nation's history and tradition." *Heller* explored the right's origins, noting that the 1689 English Bill of Rights explicitly protected a right to keep arms for self-defense. Blackstone's assessment was shared by the American colonists. As we noted in *Heller*, King George III's attempt to disarm the colonists in the 1760's and 1770's "provoked polemical reactions by Americans invoking their rights as Englishmen to keep arms." . . .

Municipal respondents' main argument is nothing less than a plea to disregard 50 years of incorporation precedent and return (presumably for this case only) to a bygone era. Municipal respondents submit that the Due Process Clause protects only those rights " 'recognized by all temperate and civilized governments, from a deep and universal sense of [their] justice.' " According to municipal respondents, if it is possible to imagine *any* civilized legal system that does not recognize a particular right, then the Due Process Clause does not make that right binding on the States. Therefore, the municipal respondents continue, because such countries as England, Canada, Australia, Japan, Denmark, Finland, Luxembourg, and New Zealand either ban or severely limit handgun ownership, it must follow that no right to possess such weapons is protected by the Fourteenth Amendment.

This line of argument is, of course, inconsistent with the long-established standard we apply in incorporation cases. And the present-day implications of municipal respondents' argument are stunning. For example, many of the rights that our Bill of Rights provides for persons accused of criminal offenses are virtually unique to this country. If *our*

understanding of the right to a jury trial, the right against self-incrimination, and the right to counsel were necessary attributes of *any* civilized
country, it would follow that the United States is the only civilized Nation
in the world. . . .

Municipal respondents maintain that the Second Amendment differs from all of the other provisions of the Bill of Rights because it concerns the right to possess a deadly implement and thus has implications
for public safety. And they note that there is intense disagreement on the
question whether the private possession of guns in the home increases or
decreases gun deaths and injuries. . . .

In *Heller*, we held that the Second Amendment protects the right to
possess a handgun in the home for the purpose of self-defense. Unless
considerations of *stare decisis* counsel otherwise, a provision of the Bill of
Rights that protects a right that is fundamental from an American perspective applies equally to the Federal Government and the States. We
therefore hold that the Due Process Clause of the Fourteenth Amendment incorporates the Second Amendment right recognized in *Heller*.
The judgment of the Court of Appeals is reversed, and the case is remanded for further proceedings.

Justice STEVENS, dissenting.

. . . Across the Nation, States and localities vary significantly in the patterns and problems of gun violence they face, as well as in the traditions
and cultures of lawful gun use they claim. The city of Chicago, for example, faces a pressing challenge in combating criminal street gangs. Most
rural areas do not. The city of Chicago has a high population density,
which increases the potential for a gunman to inflict mass terror and
casualties. Most rural areas do not. The city of Chicago offers little in
the way of hunting opportunities. Residents of rural communities are,
one presumes, much more likely to stock the dinner table with game
they have personally felled.

Given that relevant background conditions diverge so much across
jurisdictions, the Court ought to pay particular heed to state and local
legislatures' "right to experiment." *New State Ice,* (1928). So long as the
regulatory measures they have chosen are not "arbitrary, capricious, or
unreasonable," we should be allowing them to "try novel social and economic" policies. It "is more in keeping . . . with our federal system," under these circumstances, "to avoid imposing a single solution . . . from
the top down." . . .

Chicago's handgun ban, in itself, has divided researchers. Of course,
on some matters the Constitution requires that we ignore such pragmatic
considerations. But the Constitution's text, history, and structure are not

so clear on the matter before us—as evidenced by the groundbreaking nature of today's fractured decision—and this Court lacks both the technical capacity and the localized expertise to assess "the wisdom, need, and propriety" of most gun-control measures.

Nor will the Court's intervention bring any clarity to this enormously complex area of law. Quite to the contrary, today's decision invites an avalanche of litigation that could mire the federal courts in fine-grained determinations about which state and local regulations comport with the *Heller* right—the precise contours of which are far from pellucid—under a standard of review we have not even established. The plurality's "assurance" that "incorporation does not imperil every law regulating firearms" provides only modest comfort. For it is also an admission of just how many different types of regulations are potentially implicated by today's ruling, and of just how ad hoc the Court's initial attempt to draw distinctions among them was in *Heller*. The practical significance of the proposition that "the Second Amendment right is fully applicable to the States" remains to be worked out by this Court over many, many years.

Furthermore, and critically, the Court's imposition of a national standard is still more unwise because the elected branches have shown themselves to be perfectly capable of safeguarding the interest in keeping and bearing arms. . . . Neither petitioners nor those most zealously committed to their views represent a group or a claim that is liable to receive unfair treatment at the hands of the majority. On the contrary, petitioners' views are supported by powerful participants in the legislative process. Petitioners have given us no reason to believe that the interest in keeping and bearing arms entails any special need for judicial lawmaking, or that federal judges are more qualified to craft appropriate rules than the people's elected representatives. Having failed to show why their asserted interest is intrinsic to the concept of ordered liberty or vulnerable to maltreatment in the political arena, they have failed to show why "the word liberty in the Fourteenth Amendment" should be "held to prevent the natural outcome of a dominant opinion" about how to deal with the problem of handgun violence in the city of Chicago. . . .

The fact that the right to keep and bear arms appears in the Constitution should not obscure the novelty of the Court's decision to enforce that right against the States. By its terms, the Second Amendment does not apply to the States; read properly, it does not even apply to individuals outside of the militia context. The Second Amendment was adopted to protect the States from federal encroachment. And the Fourteenth Amendment has never been understood by the Court to have "incorporated" the entire Bill of Rights. There was nothing foreordained about today's outcome.

Although the Court's decision in this case might be seen as a mere adjunct to its decision in *Heller*, the consequences could prove far more destructive—quite literally—to our Nation's communities and to our constitutional structure. Thankfully, the Second Amendment right identified in *Heller* and its newly minted Fourteenth Amendment analogue are limited, at least for now, to the home. But neither the "assurances" provided by the plurality nor the many historical sources cited in its opinion should obscure the reality that today's ruling marks a dramatic change in our law—or that the Justices who have joined it have brought to bear an awesome amount of discretion in resolving the legal question presented by this case.

I would proceed more cautiously. For the reasons set out at length above, I cannot accept either the methodology the Court employs or the conclusions it draws. Although impressively argued, the majority's decision to overturn more than a century of Supreme Court precedent and to unsettle a much longer tradition of state practice is not, in my judgment, built "upon respect for the teachings of history, solid recognition of the basic values that underlie our society, and wise appreciation of the great roles that the doctrines of federalism and separation of powers have played in establishing and preserving American freedoms." Accordingly, I respectfully dissent.

Box 5.1

The USA PATRIOT Act of 2001

One month after the September 11, 2001, terrorist attacks in New York and Washington, D. C., Congress passed an act entitled Uniting and Strengthening America by Providing Appropriate Tools Required To Intercept and Obstruct Terrorism. The law, which overwhelmingly passed the Senate with one negative vote and the House with 66 negative votes, dramatically increased the investigative and law enforcement authority of the United States government, especially in the area of searches and seizures and the deportation or detention of suspected terrorists. The main features of the act include the following:

The observation and monitoring of international students

The expansion of wiretap authority, such as those involving the Internet, those that register each keystroke a person makes on a computer, and wiretaps on every telephone used by a suspected terrorist

"Sneak-and-peek" searches by law enforcement officers so that they may search private property without the permission of the owner and without a warrant

A relaxed standard for approval by a judge of wiretaps on telephones or electronic devices of a suspected terrorist

The authority of the Attorney General to label a domestic group a terrorist organization and to halt the entry into the U.S. of any individual suspected of terrorism or aligned to any terrorist group

The authority of the Central Intelligence Agency to investigate any American citizen suspected of terrorism or associated with a terrorist organization

The authority of the Federal Bureau of Investigation to seize a suspected terrorist's library and bookstore sales records without informing the person in advance

The authority of the Treasury Department to keep under surveillance banking and non-banking institutions and to seize medical and other electronic records of any individual

The detention and deportation of aliens living in the United States suspected of terrorism or suspected of having any association with terrorism

Sixteen provisions of the act were set to expire at the end of 2005. In the summer of that year, both the House of Representatives and the Senate renewed these provisions, although the House did so for ten years, while the Senate did so for four. In addition, the Senate version contained greater protections of civil liberties, such as the requirement that the government describe an unknown suspect with some "particularity" and that federal law enforcement officers would have to submit a report to the Foreign Intelligence Surveillance Act (FISA) court "after the fact" explaining why they believed a terrorist suspect was using a tapped phone or computer.

A special court established in 1978, the FISA court consists of seven federal judges appointed by the Chief Justice of the United States. Their duty is to issue search warrants involving the gathering of foreign intelligence by electronic surveillance. The PATRIOT Act modified FISA by creating a limited exception to the Fourth Amendment probable cause requirement: now, the only thing federal agents need do is show that the target of their investigation is an agent of a foreign power in order to obtain the warrant. Searches and seizures may be kept secret from the target of the investigation.

In addition, the act further expanded FISA to permit "roving wire-taps." These allow the interception of any communications made to or by an intelligence target without specifying the particular telephone line, computer, or other facility to be monitored. President Barack Obama signed an five-year extension of the act in 2011.

Rulings in Context

Due Process of Law and Rights of the Accused

Kansas v. Hendricks, 521 U.S. 346 (1997)   5-4

The Court held as constitutional a state law that allowed sex offenders whose mental state made them a danger to themselves or society to re-main in continued confinement in a mental hospital beyond the term of the original sentence of convicted.

Dickerson v. United States, 530 U.S.428 (2000)   7-2

The Court not only reaffirmed its holding in *Miranda,* but held that the warning is constitutionally required, and not merely a warning that police could voluntarily decide to use. Section 3501 of the U.S. Code, passed by Congress in 1968, attempted to overrule *Miranda* by asserting that if law enforcement officers decided against adopting the warning, they could. The opinion by Chief Justice Rehnquist stated that Congress may not leg-islatively supersede a Supreme Court decision.

Apprendi v. New Jersey, 530 U.S. 466 (2000)   5-4

The first of a series of similar cases, the Court invalidated New Jersey's hate-crime statute that allowed judges to enhance a sentence on their finding that the act was motivated by bias. The Court held that only juries may increase a penalty for a crime proved beyond a reasonable doubt. Later cases along these lines include *Ring v. Arizona,* 536 U.S. 584 (2002) and *Blakely v. Washington State,* 542 U.S. 296 (2004).

Connecticut Department of Public Safety v. Doe, 538 U.S. 1 (2003)   9-0

The Court held that the government does not violate a convicted sex of-fenders' due process rights when their names and addresses are posted on a Web site to warn neighbors about their backgrounds. The government need only base the posting on offenders' prior conviction, not on the level of danger they posed to the community.

Hamdi v. Rumsfeld, 542 U.S. 507 (2004)   8-1

President George W. Bush declared Yaser Hamdi, an American citizen born in Louisiana, an enemy combatant and ordered his detention in a Virginia naval brig. An Afghan militia, the Northern Alliance, had captured Hamdi after the September 11, 2001, terrorist attacks in the United States. The group turned him over to American forces fighting the Taliban, the former leaders of Afghanistan, and al Qaeda, the organization responsible for the attacks. With no charges against him and without counsel, Hamdi, through his father, filed suit for him to have a lawyer and a trial to determine the grounds of his detention. With Justice O'Connor writing for the Court, the ruling held that "a state of war is not a blank check for the President when it comes to the rights of the Nation's citizens." She determined that Hamdi must have the opportunity to rebut the government's charges before a neutral tribunal, either a civilian or military court. Hamdi was eventually released and sent to Saudi Arabia where he had spent most of his life.

Rasul v. Bush, 542 U.S. 466 (2004)   6-3

The Court ruled that foreigners detained by the United States on the American naval base in Guantanamo Bay, Cuba, must be accorded due process rights, such as an independent review of their claims, even if the President designates them as enemy combatants captured in a theatre of war.

Hamdan v. Rumsfeld, 542 U.S 507 (2006)   5-3

Following the *Hamdi* and *Rasul* decisions, Congress passed the Detainee Treatment Act so military officials could determine the basis for holding Guantanamo Bay detainees for the duration of the war on terrorism. Salim Ahmed Hamdan, the chauffeur of Osama bin Laden who was the al Qaeda leader, was detained in 2002 as an enemy combatant after he was turned over to American forces by an Afghan militia. Hamdan sought a writ of *habeas corpus* to expedite his release. The Court determined that his alleged conspiracy against the United States took place several years before the September 11, 2001, attacks, and ruled that he deserved *habeas corpus* rights while the United States held him: after a trial by military tribunal, he received a sentence of 66 months, and, having served 61 already, he was released in 2009.

Boumediene v. Bush, 551 U.S. 723 (2008)   5-4

Lakhdar Boumediene, an Algerian national detained in Bosnia, was accused of plotting to bomb the U.S. and British embassies. Transferred to Guantanamo in 2002, he argued that he possessed *habeas corpus* rights. The Military Commissions Act of 2006 stated, however, that no Guantanamo detainee had a right to *habeas corpus* in a federal court. The Supreme Court ruled that denying him *habeas corpus* was unconstitutional, and Boumediene was eventually tried and released.

Kennedy v. Louisiana, 554 U.S. 407 (2008)   5-4
The Court ruled that a man found guilty of the rape of a child was not subject to capital punishment under the Due Process Clause. In 1977, in *Coker v. Georgia*, 433 U.S. 584, the justices barred the use of the death penalty as punishment for the rape of an adult woman. Writing for the Court, Justice Kennedy noted that only six states permitted such a punishment for the crime of the rape of a child, in this case an eight-year old girl. He ruled that "based both on consensus and our own independent judgment, our holding is that a death sentence for one who raped but did not kill a child, and who did not intend to assist another in killing the child, is unconstitutional under the Eighth and Fourteenth Amendments."

United States v. Jones, 565 U.S. ___, 32 S.Ct. 945 (2012)   9-0
The Court ruled that federal law enforcement officers in the District of Columbia violated the Fourth Amendment when they investigated Antoine Jones for drug trafficking. They placed a GPS device on Jones' wife's car but only after the search warrant had expired and in the wrong jurisdiction, namely Maryland, and not the District of Columbia. The Court held that the search involved an illegal trespass onto private property without a legitimate search warrant.

Miller v. Alabama/Jackson v. Hobbs, 567 U.S. ___ (2012)   5-4
The Court ruled that mandatory life sentences without parole of juveniles convicted of any crime violated the Eighth Amendment's prohibition of cruel and unusual punishment. The majority held that juveniles, unlike adults, were often impetuous, immature, and unable "to appreciate risks and consequences." The case followed two earlier ones: *Roper v. Simmons*, 543 U.S. 551 (2003), which prohibited as an Eighth Amendment violation the execution of those who commit capital crimes when they were less than 18 years old; and *Graham v. Florida*, 560 U.S. ___ (2010), in which the Court forbid life sentences without parole for juveniles who committed crimes that did not involve a murder.

Maryland v. King, 569 U.S. _____ (2013)   5-4
The Court ruled that police may conduct DNA testing on anyone arrested for a violent crime or an attempted crime of violence and not only prisoners convicted of a felony. Justice Anthony Kennedy, writing for the majority, found that DNA testing was a reasonable law enforcement technique to identify suspects and no more intrusive than fingerprinting or photographing. Justice Scalia, writing on behalf of the dissent, argued that "the Court's assertion that DNA is being taken, not to solve crimes, but to *identify* those in the State's custody, taxes the credulity of the credulous." He declared that it was a suspicionless search disallowed by the Fourth Amendment.

CHAPTER 6

Privacy

The makers of our Constitution undertook to secure conditions favorable to the pursuit of happiness. . . . They sought to protect Americans in their beliefs, their thoughts, their emotions and their sensations. They conferred, as against the government, the right to be let alone—the most comprehensive of rights and the right most valued by civilized men (emphasis added).
—Justice Louis D. Brandeis, dissenting in
Olmstead v. United States,
277 U.S. 438 (1928)

The Constitution provides for no explicit right to privacy, but it has become part and parcel of substantive due process, as we indicated in the previous chapter. In fact, the word and all its synonyms and derivations—private, solitude, isolation, seclusion—do not appear anywhere in the document. Does this mean the framers had no concept of privacy? Or does it mean that they understood it so well that they took it for granted that we could enjoy private lives?

Louis D. Brandeis, who served on the Supreme Court from 1916 to 1939, addressed the right to privacy in 1890 when, as young lawyer, he and his law partner, Charles Warren, wrote an article, entitled "The Right of Privacy," for the *Harvard Law Review*. Almost forty years later, he used the eloquent words that appear in the above epigraph in a powerful dissent that mirrored his language in the earlier article. In 1928, a bare five to four majority upheld Roy Olmstead's conviction based on evidence that the FBI had obtained when agents wiretapped his telephone conversations concerning his illegal importation and sale of liquor during Prohibition. Brandeis thought the FBI agents' action was a violation of one of Americans' fundamental freedoms.

Nearly four decades later, in 1967, the Court overruled *Olmstead* when it held that a criminal suspect had a reasonable expectation of privacy when talking on the phone in a telephone booth. The FBI had wiretapped the phone, which he often used when he called his bookies to make illegal bets and wagers (*Katz v. U.S.*, 389 U.S. 347).

"Discovering" Privacy in the Constitution

Just two years earlier, the Court adopted the Brandeis philosophy when a majority "discovered" privacy in the Constitution. Writing for the Court in the birth control case of *Griswold v. Connecticut*, 381 U.S. 479 (Case 1.4), for a seven to two majority, Justice William O. Douglas found "penumbras," or shadows (hints, inklings) in the phrases within several amendments to the Constitution. That case involved a challenge by Planned Parenthood of Connecticut (Estelle Griswold was the executive director) of a state law forbidding the distribution of any information about or the use of contraceptive devices. In overturning the law, Douglas noted that the penumbras lurking in the Constitution amounted to protected zones of privacy.

In the First Amendment's right of free expression, especially as that expression had to do with expressing one's (private) opinion

In the Third Amendment's prohibition against the authority's placing troops in (private) homes

In the Fourth Amendment's prohibition against unreasonable searches and seizures of personal (and private) papers

In the all-encompassing Ninth Amendment

One such zone, he said, included the decisions married couples make concerning when and whether they will have children, and once the decision is made, how many they will have.

Justice Arthur J. Goldberg agreed with the Court's conclusion in *Griswold;* only he would have relied on the reach of the Ninth Amendment. Justice John Marshall Harlan (II), whose namesake grandfather wrote the famous dissent in *Plessy*, also thought the Constitution protected a general right to privacy in the Constitution. He preferred, however, to locate it in the liberty component of the Due Process Clause of the Fourteenth Amendment, which, he said, contained substantive rights, like privacy, and not merely procedural ones.

Two justices fiercely dissented. Justice Hugo Black, who would have liked to see the right explicitly laid out somewhere in the Constitution's text, simply said that the document, as written, did not protect privacy at all. As he famously put it, "I like my privacy as well as the next one, but I am nevertheless compelled to admit that government has a right to invade it unless prohibited by some specific constitutional provision." Justice Potter Stewart agreed with Black's conclusion. He reasoned that the Connecticut law forbidding the dissemination of information about and the use of contraceptive devices was "uncommonly silly," but he could find no reason why states could not have uncommonly silly laws if the people wanted them. If they do not, they should ask their legislators to repeal them or elect new ones who will.

Since *Griswold*, a majority of the Court has found other zones of privacy, but they are never absolutely protected. It is never legal, for example, for a group of people to conspire to commit a crime even in the privacy of a home.

Most well known and debated among the protected zones is a woman's right to choose to have an abortion. The Court held, for example in *Roe v. Wade*, 410 U.S. 113 (1973), that while she does enjoy this right, like all rights, it is limited (Case 6.1). States may regulate the procedure, the Court wrote in 1992 as long as the regulations do not place "an undue burden" on her choice: see *Planned Parenthood v. Casey*, 505 U.S. 833 (Case 6.2). A more controversial issue is whether a woman may choose to have a procedure known as a "late-term abortion," one that is performed nearly at the end of term, in order to preserve the life and health of the mother: see the 2006 case of *Gonzales v. Carhart*, 550 U.S. 124 (Case 6.3).

In another zone of privacy, the Court ruled in 1990 that terminally ill or incapacitated patients, if they plan in advance by making their sentiments known in signed, written documents, may choose to end their lives by having life-support systems removed, as the Court found in *Cruzan by Cruzan v. Director, Missouri Department of Health*, 497 U.S. 261. People who plan for this eventuality must write a legal living will or advance directive that explicitly gives instructions about what to do when they are so ill or incapacitated that they cannot decide for themselves. If the living will is properly prepared, the state may not interfere in order to extend their life.

In 2003, the Court in *Lawrence v. Texas*, 539 U.S. 558, upheld the right of gay men and lesbian women to have consensual sex in the privacy of their own homes (Case 6.5). Ten years later, in *United States v.*

Windsor, the Court ruled that the government may not deny federal benefits to same-sex married couples as long as it offers them to heterosexual ones (Case 6.6).

Since *Griswold*, the "discovery" by the Court of a right to privacy embedded in the corners of the Constitution has become a highly controversial public issue. During Senate confirmation hearings of federal judges, for example, including the justices of the Supreme Court, senators will often focus on the nominees' views of privacy in general and their assessment of past Supreme Court decisions. Both Justices Blackmun and Scalia alluded to this phenomenon in their vigorous opinions in *Planned Parenthood of Southeastern Pa. v. Casey*.

Some like Justices Ginsburg and Souter hold that without the Court's intervention in these areas, states may well undercut the rights of minorities (like gays and lesbians) or women seeking an abortion. It is therefore the responsibility of the Court to uphold individual rights as a matter of substantive due process insofar as the Court has determined that the Constitution protects a variety of zones of privacy. In 1997, Justice Souter acknowledged this in his concurrence in *Washington v. Glucksberg*, 521 U.S. 702, involving assisted suicide for terminally ill patients. He argued that the Court's responsibility is "to construe constitutional text and review legislation for conformity to that text."

Meantime, Justice Scalia has long argued that the public market place of ideas is where these issues belong. See his dissent in *Stenberg v. Carhart*, 530 U.S. 914 (2000), where he speaks of his colleagues as "unelected lawyers" overcoming "the judgment of thirty state legislatures." Referring to these issues as part of the ongoing "culture war" in American society, he has contended that the democratic process is the way in which they must be resolved. In this way, the outcome will reflect the "will of the people" rather than the will of a few unelected judges. In dissents in *Romer v. Evans*, 517 U.S. 620 (1996), and in *Lawrence v. Texas*, concerning homosexual rights, he again excoriated the Court for improperly engaging in the nation's culture wars. In *Lawrence*, he wrote that "it is clear . . . that the Court has taken sides in the culture war, departing from its role of assuring, as neutral observer, that the democratic rules of engagement are observed."

Because these decisions are all based on judge-made law rather than any specific provision of the Constitution, they are subject to being overruled at any time the personnel of the Court changes or at any time a few members of the Court change their minds. In 2003, for example, the Court overturned a 1986 decision when it reversed itself in the *Lawrence* decision by ruling in that adult homosexuals have a constitutional right to engage in private consensual sexual activity (the overruled case was *Bowers v. Hardwick*, 478 U.S. 186). On the other hand, just as the Court has upheld a woman's right to an abortion under certain circumstances, it could potentially overrule the *Roe v. Wade* decision when new justices join the Court. In the summer of 2005, after the death of Chief Justice Rehnquist, the Senate confirmed John G. Roberts Jr. to succeed him, so the composition of the Court was changing. Many changes have occurred since then.

Abortion: Cases

Few issues are as contentious and populated with so uncompromising parties as abortion. Since the Court's 1973 ruling in *Roe v. Wade*, establishing the constitutional guarantee, inherent in the liberty component of the Due Process Clause of the Fourteenth Amendment, that a woman had a right to choose an abortion under certain circumstances, adherents on both sides of the issue have looked to their state legislatures for resolutions that often end up in the courts. Here we look at three cases: the first is the landmark case, *Roe v. Wade*; the second involves a Pennsylvania law restricting abortion; the third involves a federal law banning late-term abortions.

Several states have passed new restrictive laws on abortion that may soon be challenged before the Supreme Court. These restrictions include: the requirement that all physicians practicing abortion must have nearby hospital privileges; the prohibition of abortion after a pregnancy of 20 weeks; the necessity of a woman seeking an abortion to have a sonogram of the fetus so she is knowledgeable about its development; the state recognition that a human life begins with the first heartbeat. In the October Term 2013, the Court heard arguments in *Cline v. Oklahoma Coalition for Reproductive Justice*. The case involves a state law regulating physicians' prescription of drugs that stimulate "medical abortions," so called because they do not require invasive surgical procedures.

Case 6.1

Roe v. Wade
410 U.S. 113, 93 S.Ct. 705 (1973)

Although she was divorced, Norma McCorvey, who lived in Texas, became pregnant in 1969. Initially claiming she had been raped, she admitted many years later that she had been involved in an affair out of wedlock. McCorvey had had, in fact, a very troubled childhood. At one point, she ran away from home and was then sent to a reform school. After she married at 16, she had a child that her mother raised. Following her divorce, she had another child but gave it up to the father. Now, once again finding herself pregnant, McCorvey decided that she not could afford to take care of a baby. When she decided to have an abortion, she found that Texas law prohibited abortions with only one exception, to save the woman's life. After she delivered her baby, she gave the child up for adoption. Through the lawyer who helped her with the adoption, she met two recent graduates of the University of Texas, Sarah Weddington and Linda Coffee, and the three of them agreed to challenge the Texas law. McCorvey filed suit in federal district court under the pseudonymous name "Jane Roe" against Henry Wade, the Dallas County district attorney.

A three-judge federal district court panel ruled the Texas law unconstitutional, but declined to enjoin or prevent enforcement of the law. Roe appealed to the Supreme Court, which heard the case first in 1971, but then asked for re-argument the following year. The Court, in an opinion by Justice Harry Blackmun, upheld the lower court's ruling in a seven to two decision. Justices William H. Rehnquist and Byron White dissented.

Justice BLACKMUN delivered the opinion of the Court.

The Texas statutes that concern us here make it a crime to "procure an abortion," as therein defined, or to attempt one, except with respect to "an abortion procured or attempted by medical advice for the purpose of saving the life of the mother." Similar statutes are in existence in a majority of the States. . . .

The principal thrust of appellant's attack on the Texas statutes is that they improperly invade a right, said to be possessed by the pregnant woman, to choose to terminate her pregnancy. Appellant would discover this right in the concept of personal "liberty" embodied in the Fourteenth Amendment's Due Process Clause; or in personal, marital, familial, and sexual privacy said to be protected by the Bill of Rights or its penumbras, see *Griswold v. Connecticut*, 381 U.S. 479 (1965); or among those rights reserved to the people by the Ninth Amendment, *Griswold*, (Goldberg, J., concurring). Before addressing this claim, we feel it desirable briefly to survey, in several aspects, the history of abortion, for such insight as that history may afford us, and then to examine the state purposes and interests behind the criminal abortion laws. . . .

It is undisputed that at common law, abortion performed before "quickening"—the first recognizable movement of the fetus in utero, appearing usually from the 16th to the 18th week of pregnancy—was not an indictable offense. . . . In this country, the law in effect in all but a few States until mid-19th century was the pre-existing English common law. Connecticut, the first State to enact abortion legislation, adopted in 1821 that part of Lord Ellenborough's Act that related to a woman "quick with child." The death penalty was not imposed. Abortion before quickening was made a crime in that State only in 1860. In 1828, New York enacted legislation that, in two respects, was to serve as a model for early anti-abortion statutes. First, while barring destruction of an unquickened fetus as well as a quick fetus, it made the former only a misdemeanor, but the latter second-degree manslaughter. Second, it incorporated a concept of therapeutic abortion by providing that an abortion was excused if it "shall have been necessary to preserve the life of such mother, or shall have been advised by two physicians to be necessary for such purpose." By 1840, when Texas had received the common law, only eight American States had statutes dealing with abortion. It was not until after the War Between the States that legislation began generally to replace the common law. Most of these initial statutes dealt severely with abortion after quickening but were lenient with it before quickening. . . .

Gradually, in the middle and late 19th century the quickening distinction disappeared from the statutory law of most States and the degree of the offense and the penalties were increased. By the end of the 1950's, a large majority of the jurisdictions banned abortion, however and whenever performed, unless done to save or preserve the life of the mother. . . .

It is thus apparent that at common law, at the time of the adoption of our Constitution, and throughout the major portion of the 19th century, abortion was viewed with less disfavor than under most American statutes currently in effect. Phrasing it another way, a woman enjoyed a substantially broader right to terminate a pregnancy than she does in most States today. . . .

Three reasons have been advanced to explain historically the enactment of criminal abortion laws in the 19th century and to justify their continued existence.

It has been argued occasionally that these laws were the product of a Victorian social concern to discourage illicit sexual conduct. Texas, however, does not advance this justification in the present case, and it appears that no court or commentator has taken the argument seriously. . . .

A second reason is concerned with abortion as a medical procedure. When most criminal abortion laws were first enacted, the procedure was a hazardous one for the woman. . . . Thus, it has been argued that a State's real concern in enacting a criminal abortion law was to protect the pregnant woman, that is, to restrain her from submitting to a procedure that placed her life in serious jeopardy.

Modern medical techniques have altered this situation. Appellants and various *amici* refer to medical data indicating that abortion in early pregnancy, that is, prior to the end of the first trimester, although not without its risk, is now relatively safe. Mortality rates for women undergoing early abortions, where the procedure is legal, appear to be as low as or lower than the rates for normal childbirth. Consequently, any interest of the State in protecting the woman from an inherently hazardous procedure, except when it would be equally dangerous for her to forgo it, has largely disappeared. Of course, important state interests in the areas of health and medical standards do remain. The State has a legitimate interest in seeing to it that abortion, like any other medical procedure, is performed under circumstances that insure maximum safety for the patient. . . .

The third reason is the State's interest—some phrase it in terms of duty—in protecting prenatal life. Some of the argument for this justification rests on the theory that a new human life is present from the moment of conception. The State's interest and general obligation to protect life then extends, it is argued, to prenatal life. Only when the life of the pregnant mother herself is at stake, balanced against the life she carries within her, should the interest of the embryo or fetus not prevail. Logically, of course, a legitimate state interest in this area need not stand or fall on acceptance of the belief that life begins at conception or at some other point prior to live birth. In assessing the State's interest, recognition may be given to the less rigid claim that as long as at least potential life is involved, the State may assert interests beyond the protection of the pregnant woman alone. . . .

The Constitution does not explicitly mention any right of privacy. In a line of decisions, however, . . . the Court has recognized that a right of personal privacy, or a guarantee of certain areas or zones of privacy, does exist under the Constitution. . . . This right of privacy, whether it be founded in the Fourteenth Amendment's concept of personal liberty and restrictions upon state action, as we feel it is, or, as the District Court determined, in the Ninth Amendment's reservation of rights to the people, is broad enough to encompass a woman's decision whether or not to terminate her pregnancy. The detriment that the State would impose upon the pregnant woman by denying this choice altogether is apparent. Specific and direct harm medically diagnosable even in early pregnancy may be involved. Maternity, or additional offspring, may force upon the woman a distressful life and future. Psychological harm may be imminent. Mental and physical health may be taxed by child care. There is also the distress, for all concerned, associated with the unwanted child, and there is the problem of bringing a child into a family already unable, psychologically and otherwise, to care for it. In other cases, as in this one, the additional difficulties and continuing stigma of unwed motherhood may be involved. All these are factors the woman and her responsible physician necessarily will consider in consultation. . . . The Court has refused to recognize an unlimited right of this kind in the past.

We, therefore, conclude that the right of personal privacy includes the abortion decision, but that this right is not unqualified and must be considered against important state interests in regulation.

The appellee and certain *amici* argue that the fetus is a "person" within the language and meaning of the Fourteenth Amendment. In support of this, they outline at length and in detail the well-known facts of fetal development. If this suggestion of personhood is established, the appellant's case, of course, collapses, for the fetus' right to life would then be guaranteed specifically by the Amendment. The appellant conceded as much on re-argument. On the other hand, the appellee conceded on re-argument that no case could be cited that holds that a fetus is a person within the meaning of the Fourteenth Amendment.

The Constitution does not define "person" in so many words. Section 1 of the Fourteenth Amendment contains three references to "person." The first, in defining "citizens," speaks of "persons born or naturalized in the United States." The word also appears both in the Due Process Clause and in the Equal Protection Clause. . . . But in nearly all these instances, the use of the word is such that it has application only postnatally. None indicates, with any assurance, that it has any possible pre-natal application.

All this, together with our observation that throughout the major portion of the 19th century prevailing legal abortion practices were far freer than they are today, persuades us that the word "person," as used in the Fourteenth Amendment, does not include the unborn. This conclusion, however, does not of itself fully answer the contentions raised by Texas, and we pass on to other considerations. . . .

The pregnant woman cannot be isolated in her privacy. She carries an embryo and, later, a fetus, if one accepts the medical definitions of the developing young in the human uterus. The situation therefore is inherently different from marital intimacy, or bedroom possession of obscene material, or marriage, or procreation, or education. As we have intimated above, it is reasonable and appropriate for a State to decide that at some point in time another interest, that of health of the mother or that of potential human life, becomes significantly involved. The woman's privacy is no longer sole and any right of privacy she possesses must be measured accordingly.

Texas urges that, apart from the Fourteenth Amendment, life begins at conception and is present throughout pregnancy, and that, therefore, the State has a compelling interest in protecting that life from and after conception. We need not resolve the difficult question of when life begins. When those trained in the respective disciplines of medicine, philosophy, and theology are unable to arrive at any consensus, the judiciary, at this point in the development of man's knowledge, is not in a position to speculate as to the answer.

It should be sufficient to note briefly the wide divergence of thinking on this most sensitive and difficult question. There has always been strong support for the view that life does not begin until live birth. This was the belief of the Stoics. It appears to be the predominant, though not the unanimous, attitude of the Jewish faith. It may be taken to represent also the position of a large segment of the Protestant community, insofar as that can be ascertained; organized groups that have taken a formal position on the abortion issue have generally regarded abortion as a matter for the conscience of the individual and her family. As we have noted, the common law found greater significance in quickening. Physicians and their scientific colleagues have regarded that event with less interest and have tended to focus either upon conception, upon live birth, or upon the interim point at which the fetus becomes "viable," that is, potentially able to live outside the mother's womb, albeit with artificial aid. Viability is usually placed at about seven months (28 weeks) but may occur earlier, even at 24 weeks. . . .

In areas other than criminal abortion, the law has been reluctant to endorse any theory that life, as we recognize it, begins before live birth or to accord legal rights to the unborn except in narrowly defined situations and except when the rights are contingent upon live birth. . . .

In view of all this, we do not agree that, by adopting one theory of life, Texas may override the rights of the pregnant woman that are at stake. We repeat, however, that the State does have an important and legitimate interest in preserving and protecting the health of the pregnant woman, whether she be a resident of the State or a nonresident who seeks medical consultation and treatment there, and that it has still another important and legitimate interest in protecting the potentiality of human life. These interests are separate and distinct. Each grows in substantiality as the woman approaches term and, at a point during pregnancy, each becomes "compelling."

With respect to the State's important and legitimate interest in the health of the mother, the "compelling" point, in the light of present medical knowledge, is at approximately the end of the first trimester. This is so because of the now-established medical fact that until the end of the first trimester mortality in abortion may be less than mortality in normal childbirth. It follows that, from and after this point, a State may regulate the abortion procedure to the extent that the regulation reasonably relates to the preservation and protection of maternal health. Examples of permissible state regulation in this area are requirements as to the qualifications of the person who is to perform the abortion; as to the licensure of that person; as to the facility in which the procedure is to be performed, that is, whether it must be a hospital or may be a clinic or some other place of less-than-hospital status; as to the licensing of the facility; and the like.

This means, on the other hand, that, for the period of pregnancy prior to this "compelling" point, the attending physician, in consultation with his patient, is free to determine, without regulation by the State, that, in his medical judgment, the patient's pregnancy should be terminated. If that decision is reached, the judgment may be effectuated by an abortion free of interference by the State.

With respect to the State's important and legitimate interest in potential life, the "compelling" point is at viability. This is so because the fetus then presumably has the capability of meaningful life outside the mother's womb. State regulation protective of fetal life after viability thus has both logical and biological justifications. If the State is interested in protecting fetal life after viability, it may go so far as to proscribe abortion during that period, except when it is necessary to preserve the life or health of the mother.

Measured against these standards, Art. 1196 of the Texas Penal Code . . . sweeps too broadly. The statute makes no distinction between abortions performed early in pregnancy and those performed later, and it limits to a single reason, "saving" the mother's life, the legal justification for the procedure. The statute, therefore, cannot survive the constitutional attack made upon it here. . . .

To summarize and to repeat:

A state criminal abortion statute of the current Texas type, that excepts from criminality only a life-saving procedure on behalf of the mother, without regard to pregnancy stage and without recognition of the other interests involved, is violative of the Due Process Clause of the Fourteenth Amendment.

    (a) For the stage prior to approximately the end of the first trimester, the abortion decision and its effectuation must be left to the medical judgment of the pregnant woman's attending physician.

    (b) For the stage subsequent to approximately the end of the first trimester, the State, in promoting its interest in the health of the mother, may, if it chooses, regulate the abortion procedure in ways that are reasonably related to maternal health.

    (c) For the stage subsequent to viability, the State in promoting its interest in the potentiality of human life may, if it chooses, regulate, and even proscribe, abortion except where it is necessary, in appropriate medical judgment, for the preservation of the life or health of the mother. . . .

This holding, we feel, is consistent with the relative weights of the respective interests involved, with the lessons and examples of medical and legal history, with the lenity of the common law, and with the demands of the profound problems of the present day.

Justice REHNQUIST, dissenting.

. . . I have difficulty in concluding, as the Court does, that the right of "privacy" is involved in this case. Texas, by the statute here challenged, bars the performance of a medical abortion by a licensed physician on a plaintiff such as Roe. A transaction resulting in an operation such as this is not "private" in the ordinary usage of that word. Nor is the "privacy" that the Court finds here even a distant relative of the freedom from searches and seizures protected by the Fourth Amendment to the Constitution, which the Court has referred to as embodying a right to privacy.

If the Court means by the term "privacy" no more than that the claim of a person to be free from unwanted state regulation of consensual transactions may be a form of "liberty" protected by the Fourteenth Amendment, there is no doubt that similar claims have been upheld in our earlier decisions on the basis of that liberty. . . . But that liberty is not guaranteed absolutely against deprivation, only against deprivation without due process of law. The test traditionally applied in the area of social and economic legislation is whether or not a law such as that challenged has a rational relation to a valid state objective. The Due Process Clause of the Fourteenth Amendment undoubtedly does place a limit, albeit a broad one, on legislative power to enact laws such as this. If the Texas statute were to prohibit an abortion even where the mother's life is in jeopardy, I have little doubt that such a statute would lack a rational relation to a valid state objective. . . . But the Court's sweeping invalidation of any restrictions on abortion during the first trimester is impossible to justify under that standard, and the conscious weighing of competing factors that the Court's opinion apparently substitutes for the established test is far more appropriate to a legislative judgment than to a judicial one. . . .

To reach its result, the Court necessarily has had to find within the scope of the Fourteenth Amendment a right that was apparently completely unknown to the drafters of the Amendment. As early as 1821, the first state law dealing directly with abortion was enacted by the Connecticut Legislature. By the time of the adoption of the Fourteenth Amendment in 1868, there were at least 36 laws enacted by state or territorial legislatures limiting abortion. . . .

The only conclusion possible from this history is that the drafters did not intend to have the Fourteenth Amendment withdraw from the States the power to legislate with respect to this matter.

Case 6.2

Planned Parenthood of Southeastern Pa. v. Casey
505 U.S. 833, 112 S.Ct. 2791 (1992)

After *Roe v. Wade,* several states began to seek ways to restrict, though not abolish, that right. In 1982, Pennsylvania enacted the Abortion Control Act that set forth five such restrictions.

The law required a woman seeking an abortion to give her informed consent before the procedure and to wait 24 hours before she actually had the abortion. She also had to obtain the consent of a parent or guardian if she were a minor, although the law provided for a "judicial bypass," that is, a judge could give her permission if she did not want to ask her parents. Moreover, a married woman had to sign a statement that she had informed her husband in advance of having the procedure. Finally, the law set forth what constituted a "medical emergency" that, if applicable to her, would have allowed her to waive these requirements. A medical emergency meant that a pregnant woman would risk death or a substantial and irreversible impairment unless she immediately had an abortion.

Before the provisions took effect, Planned Parenthood of Southeastern Pennsylvania challenged these provisions. After the district court ruled that all of them violated the Constitution, the U.S. Court of Appeals for the Third Circuit reversed in part by upholding all but the spousal notification provision. The Third Circuit based its decision on the principles that Justice O'Connor had laid out in a dissenting opinion in the 1983 case of *Akron v. Akron Center for Reproductive Health, Inc.,* 462 U.S. 416. She had argued that restrictions on abortion, as long as they do not undermine the right itself, were permissible as long as they did not cause an "undue burden" on the woman. The Court of Appeals ruled that restrictions placing a "substantial obstacle" before the woman who wants an abortion would be subject to the strict scrutiny test (see the judicial tests described in Box 4.1).

This meant that the Third Circuit considered the undue burden test a version of strict scrutiny. It also meant that the court treated restrictions that may create an undue burden in the same way it has in the other areas in which strict scrutiny is used, such as in cases involving suspect classifications and fundamental rights.

Specifically the court demanded the state to shoulder the burden of proof to demonstrate why the restriction was in the state's compelling interest. It also demanded the state to show how that restriction was narrowly tailored with the least restrictive means to achieve that compelling interest.

In the meantime, the court also determined whether all other restrictions, those not subject to an undue burden on the woman, had a rational basis. In this case, it concluded that the four provisions it upheld were rationally based, but that spousal notification placed an undue burden on the woman because she may then be subject to violence, abuse, or economic deprivation.

Both Planned Parenthood and the State of Pennsylvania appealed to the Supreme Court, which ruled five to four in upholding most of the provisions. Because of the controversial nature of each provision, the justices actually split three to four to two. Justices Sandra Day O'Connor, Anthony M. Kennedy, and David H. Souter announced the judgment of the Court and delivered the opinion of the Court in Parts I, II, III, V-A, V-C, and VI. Justices Harry A. Blackmun and John Paul Stevens wrote separate opinions, concurring with the Court's judgment, but dissenting from the Court's approval of some restrictions, such as the parental consent requirement. Chief Justice William H. Rehnquist and Justices Antonin Scalia, Clarence Thomas, and Byron R. White dissented. Note that Justice Scalia predicted that the Court's ruling would lead to greater strife in society over whether a woman possesses a constitutional right to abortion. He claims that such a sentiment is akin to the hope that the Peace of Westphalia ending the Thirty Years War in 1648 would end religious wars, which it did not, and that such a hope was no more than "Orwellian," a reference to George Orwell's famous utopian novel *1984*.

Justice O'CONNOR, Justice KENNEDY, and Justice SOUTER announced the judgment of the Court and delivered the opinion of the Court with respect to Parts I, II, III, V-A, V-C, and VI, an opinion with respect to Part V-E, in which Justice STEVENS joins, and an opinion with respect to Parts IV, V-B, and V-D.

After considering the fundamental constitutional questions resolved by *Roe* [*v. Wade*, 410 U.S. 113 (1973)] principles of institutional integrity, and the rule of *stare decisis*, we are led to conclude this: the essential holding of *Roe v. Wade* should be retained and once again reaffirmed....

... We conclude that the basic decision in *Roe* was based on a constitutional analysis which we cannot now repudiate. The woman's liberty is not so unlimited, however, that, from the outset, the State cannot show its concern for the life of the unborn and, at a later point in fetal development, the State's interest in life has sufficient force so that the right of the woman to terminate the pregnancy can be restricted.

That brings us, of course, to the point where much criticism has been directed at *Roe*, a criticism that always inheres when the Court draws a specific rule from what in the Constitution is but a general standard. We conclude, however, that the urgent claims of the woman to retain the ultimate control over her destiny and her body, claims implicit in the meaning of liberty, require us to perform that function. Liberty must not be extinguished for want of a line that is clear. And it falls to us to give some real substance to the woman's liberty to determine whether to carry her pregnancy to full term.

We conclude the line should be drawn at viability, so that, before that time, the woman has a right to choose to terminate her pregnancy. We adhere to this principle for two reasons. First, as we have said, is the doctrine of *stare decisis*. Any judicial act of line-drawing may seem somewhat arbitrary, but *Roe* was a reasoned statement, elaborated with great care. We have twice reaffirmed it in the face of great opposition. Although we must overrule those parts of *Thornburgh* [*v. American College of Obstetricians and Gynecologists*, 476 U.S. 747 (1986)] and *Akron I* [*Akron v. Akron Center for Reproductive Services*, 462 U.S. 416 (1983)], which, in our view, are inconsistent with *Roe*'s statement that the State has a legitimate interest in promoting the life or potential life of the unborn, the central premise of those cases represents an unbroken commitment by this Court to the essential holding of *Roe*. It is that premise which we reaffirm today.

The second reason is that the concept of viability, as we noted in *Roe*, is the time at which there is a realistic possibility of maintaining and nourishing a life outside the womb, so that the independent existence of the second life can, in reason and all fairness, be the object of state protection that now overrides the rights of the woman. Consistent with other constitutional norms, legislatures may draw lines which appear arbitrary without the necessity of offering a justification. But courts may not. We must justify the lines we draw. And there is no line other than viability which is more workable. . . .

. . . The fact that a law which serves a valid purpose, one not designed to strike at the right itself, has the incidental effect of making it more difficult or more expensive to procure an abortion cannot be enough to invalidate it. Only where state regulation imposes an undue burden on a woman's ability to make this decision does the power of the State reach into the heart of the liberty protected by the Due Process Clause. . . .

Because we set forth a standard of general application to which we intend to adhere, it is important to clarify what is meant by an undue burden. A finding of an undue burden is a shorthand for the conclusion that a state regulation has the purpose or effect of placing a substantial obstacle in the path of a woman seeking an abortion of a nonviable fetus. . . . We give this summary:

(a) To protect the central right recognized by *Roe v. Wade* while at the same time accommodating the State's profound interest in potential life, we will employ the undue burden analysis as explained in this opinion. An undue burden exists, and therefore a provision of law is invalid, if its purpose or effect is to place a substantial obstacle in the path of a woman seeking an abortion before the fetus attains viability.

(b) We reject the rigid trimester framework of *Roe v. Wade*. To promote the State's profound interest in potential life, throughout pregnancy, the State may take measures to ensure that the woman's choice is informed, and measures designed to advance this interest will not be invalidated as long as their purpose is to persuade the woman to choose childbirth over abortion. These measures must not be an undue burden on the right.

(c) As with any medical procedure, the State may enact regulations to further the health or safety of a woman seeking an abortion. Unnecessary health regulations that have the purpose or effect of presenting a substantial obstacle to a woman seeking an abortion impose an undue burden on the right.

(d) Our adoption of the undue burden analysis does not disturb the central holding of *Roe v. Wade*, and we reaffirm that holding. Regardless of whether exceptions are made for particular circumstances, a State may not prohibit any woman from making the ultimate decision to terminate her pregnancy before viability.

(e) We also reaffirm *Roe*'s holding that, "subsequent to viability, the State, in promoting its interest in the potentiality of human life, may, if it chooses, regulate, and even proscribe, abortion except where it is necessary, in appropriate medical judgment, for the preservation of the life or health of the mother."

These principles control our assessment of the Pennsylvania statute, and we now turn to the issue of the validity of its challenged provisions.

Because it is central to the operation of various other requirements, we begin with the statute's definition of medical emergency. Under the statute, a medical emergency is "that condition which, on the basis of the physician's good faith clinical judgment, so complicates the medical condition of a pregnant woman as to necessitate the immediate abortion of her pregnancy to avert her death or for which a delay will create serious risk of substantial and irreversible impairment of a major bodily function." . . .

We . . . conclude that, as construed by the Court of Appeals, the medical emergency definition imposes no undue burden on a woman's abortion right. . . .

We next consider the informed consent requirement. . . .

Our prior decisions establish that, as with any medical procedure, the State may require a woman to give her written informed consent to an abortion. In this respect, the statute is unexceptional. Petitioners challenge the statute's definition of informed consent because it includes the provision of specific information by the doctor and the mandatory 24-hour waiting period. The conclusions reached by a majority of the Justices in the separate opinions filed today and the undue burden standard adopted in this opinion require us to overrule in part some of the Court's past decisions, decisions driven by the trimester framework's prohibition of all pre-viability regulations designed to further the State's interest in fetal life. . . .

To the extent *Akron I* and *Thornburgh* find a constitutional violation when the government requires, as it does here, the giving of truthful, nonmisleading information about the nature of the procedure, the attendant health risks and those of childbirth, and the "probable gestational age" of the fetus, those cases go too far, are inconsistent with *Roe*'s acknowledgment of an important interest in potential life, and are overruled. . . .

Section 3209 of Pennsylvania's abortion law provides, except in cases of medical emergency, that no physician shall perform an abortion on a married woman without receiving a signed statement from the woman that she has notified her spouse that she is about to undergo an abortion. The woman has the option of providing an alternative signed statement certifying that her husband is not the man who impregnated her; that her husband could not be located; that the pregnancy is the result of spousal sexual assault which she has reported; or that the woman believes that notifying her husband will cause him or someone else to inflict bodily injury upon her. A physician who performs an abortion on a married woman without receiving the appropriate signed statement will have his or her license revoked, and is liable to the husband for damages. . . .

[T]here are millions of women in this country who are the victims of regular physical and psychological abuse at the hands of their husbands. Should these women become pregnant, they may have very good reasons for not wishing to inform their husbands of their decision to obtain an abortion. Many may have justifiable fears of physical abuse, but may be no less fearful of the consequences of reporting prior abuse to the Commonwealth of Pennsylvania. Many may have a reasonable fear that notifying their husbands will provoke further instances of child abuse; these women are not exempt from 3209's notification requirement. Many may fear devastating forms of psychological abuse from their husbands, including verbal harassment, threats of future violence, the destruction of possessions, physical confinement to the home, the withdrawal of financial support, or the disclosure of the abortion to family and friends. These methods of psychological abuse may act as even more of a deterrent to notification than the possibility of physical violence, but women who are the victims of the abuse are not exempt from 3209's notification requirement. And many women who are pregnant as a result of sexual assaults by their husbands will be unable to avail themselves of the exception for spousal sexual assault, because the exception requires that the woman have notified law enforcement authorities within 90 days of the assault, and her husband will be notified of her report once an investigation begins. . . .

The unfortunate yet persisting conditions we document above will mean that, in a large fraction of the cases in which 3209 is relevant, it will operate as a substantial obstacle to a woman's choice to undergo an abortion. It is an undue burden, and therefore invalid. . . .

We next consider the parental consent provision. Except in a medical emergency, an unemancipated young woman under 18 may not obtain an abortion unless she and one of her parents (or guardian) provides informed consent as defined above. If neither a parent nor a guardian provides consent, a court may authorize the performance of an abortion upon a determination that the young woman is mature and capable of giving informed consent and has, in fact, given her informed consent, or that an abortion would be in her best interests.

We have been over most of this ground before. Our cases establish, and we reaffirm today, that a State may require a minor seeking an abortion to obtain the consent of a parent or guardian, provided that there is an adequate judicial bypass procedure. Under these precedents, in our view, the one-parent consent requirement and judicial bypass procedure are constitutional. . . .

Under the recordkeeping and reporting requirements of the statute, every facility which performs abortions is required to file a report stating its name and address as well as the name and address of any related entity, such as a controlling or subsidiary organization. In the case of state-funded institutions, the information becomes public. . . .

. . . This provision in effect requires women, as a condition of obtaining an abortion, to provide the Commonwealth with the precise information we have already recognized that many women have pressing reasons not to reveal. Like the spousal notice requirement itself, this provision places an undue burden on a woman's choice, and must be invalidated for that reason.

Our Constitution is a covenant running from the first generation of

Americans to us, and then to future generations. It is a coherent succession. Each generation must learn anew that the Constitution's written terms embody ideas and aspirations that must survive more ages than one. We accept our responsibility not to retreat from interpreting the full meaning of the covenant in light of all of our precedents. We invoke it once again to define the freedom guaranteed by the Constitution's own promise, the promise of liberty.

Justice BLACKMUN, concurring in part, concurring in the judgment in part, and dissenting in part.

. . . In one sense, the Court's approach is worlds apart from that of the Chief Justice and Justice Scalia. And yet, in another sense, the distance between the two approaches is short—the distance is but a single vote.

I am 83 years old. I cannot remain on this Court forever, and when I do step down, the confirmation process for my successor well may focus on the issue before us today. That, I regret, may be exactly where the choice between the two worlds will be made.

Chief Justice REHNQUIST, with whom Justices WHITE, SCALIA, and THOMAS join, concurring in the judgment in part and dissenting in part.

The joint opinion, following its newly minted variation on *stare decisis*, retains the outer shell of *Roe v. Wade*, 410 U.S. 113 (1973), but beats a wholesale retreat from the substance of that case. We believe that *Roe* was wrongly decided, and that it can and should be overruled consistently with our traditional approach to *stare decisis* in constitutional cases. We would adopt the approach of the plurality in *Webster v. Reproductive Health Services*, 492 U.S. 490 (1989), and uphold the challenged provisions of the Pennsylvania statute in their entirety. . . .

The sum of the joint opinion's labors in the name of *stare decisis* and "legitimacy" is this: *Roe v. Wade* stands as a sort of judicial Potemkin Village, which may be pointed out to passers-by as a monument to the importance of adhering to precedent. But behind the facade, an entirely new method of analysis, without any roots in constitutional law, is imported to decide the constitutionality of state laws regulating abortion. Neither *stare decisis* nor "legitimacy" are truly served by such an effort. . . .

For the reasons stated, we therefore would hold that each of the challenged provisions of the Pennsylvania statute is consistent with the Constitution.

Justice SCALIA, with whom the Chief Justice [REHNQUIST] and Justices WHITE and THOMAS join, concurring in the judgment in part and dissenting in part.

... *Roe* created a vast new class of abortion consumers and abortion proponents by eliminating the moral opprobrium that had attached to the act. ("If the Constitution guarantees abortion, how can it be bad?"—not an accurate line of thought, but a natural one.) Many favor all of those developments, and it is not for me to say that they are wrong. But to portray *Roe* as the statesmanlike "settlement" of a divisive issue, a jurisprudential Peace of Westphalia that is worth preserving, is nothing less than Orwellian. *Roe* fanned into life an issue that has inflamed our national politics in general, and has obscured with its smoke the selection of Justices to this Court, in particular, ever since. And by keeping us in the abortion-umpiring business, it is the perpetuation of that disruption, rather than of any *Pax Roeana* that the Court's new majority decrees.

Case 6.3

Gonzales v. Carhart
550 U.S. 124, 127 S.Ct. 1610 (2007)

In light of the Court's holdings in *Roe v. Wade* in 1973 and *Planned Parenthood of Southeastern Pennsylvania v. Casey* in 1992 upholding a woman's right to an abortion, Nebraska enacted a law prohibiting late-stage abortions whereby a woman in the second or third trimester of her pregnancy required an abortion for health or lifesaving reasons. Typically in a first-trimester abortion, doctors employ a procedure known as Dilation and Evacuation (D&E) where they dilate the cervix and then insert surgical instruments into the uterus to grab the fetus and pull it back through the cervix and vagina. The fetus is usually ripped apart as it is removed, and the doctor may take 10 to 15 passes to remove it in its entirety. In late-stage abortions, doctors use a procedure known as intact D&E, sometimes called Dilation and Extraction and is the same as Dilation and Evacuation, where doctors extract the fetus intact or largely intact with only a few passes, pulling out its entire body instead of ripping it apart. In order to allow the head to pass through the cervix, doctors typically pierce or crush the skull.

In 2000, in *Stenberg v. Carhart*, or *Carhart I*, the Court held that Nebraska's late-stage abortion law violated the Constitution as the Court had interpreted it in *Roe* and *Casey* largely on the grounds that the act did not have a health exception for the mother. Three years later, the U.S. Congress passed the Partial-Birth Abortion Ban Act that proscribed intact D&E with no health exception. Once the statute was challenged, both the federal district and appellate courts enjoined enforcement of the act, and the Bush administration appealed to the Supreme Court.

By a vote of five to four, the Court overturned the Ninth Circuit's decision in an opinion by Justice Anthony Kennedy with a concurring opinion by Justice Clarence Thomas, which was joined by Justice Antonin Scalia. Justice Ruth Bader Ginsburg dissented, joined by Justices David Souter, John Paul Stevens, and Stephen Breyer.

Justice KENNEDY delivered the opinion of the Court.

These cases require us to consider the validity of the Partial-Birth Abortion Ban Act of 2003 (Act), a federal statute regulating abortion procedures. In recitations preceding its operative provisions the Act refers to the Court's opinion in *Stenberg v. Carhart* (2000), which also addressed the subject of abortion procedures used in the later stages of pregnancy. Compared to the state statute at issue in *Stenberg*, the Act is more specific concerning the instances to which it applies and in this respect more precise in its coverage. We conclude the Act should be sustained against the objections lodged by the broad, facial attack brought against it. . . .

The Act proscribes a particular manner of ending fetal life, so it is necessary here, as it was in *Stenberg*, to discuss abortion procedures in some detail. . . .

The Act responded to *Stenberg* in two ways. First, Congress made factual findings. Congress determined that this Court in *Stenberg* "was required to accept the very questionable findings issued by the district court judge," but that Congress was "not bound to accept the same factual findings." . . .

Second, and more relevant here, the Act's language differs from that of the Nebraska statute struck down in *Stenberg*. The operative provisions of the Act provide in relevant part: Any physician who, in or affecting interstate or foreign commerce, knowingly performs a partial-birth abortion and thereby kills a human fetus shall be fined under this title or imprisoned not more than two years, or both. This subsection does not apply to a partial-birth abortion that is necessary to save the life of a mother whose life is endangered by a physical disorder, physical illness, or physical injury, including a life-endangering physical condition caused by or arising from the pregnancy itself. . . .

The District Court in *Carhart* concluded the Act was unconstitutional for two reasons. First, it determined the Act was unconstitutional because it lacked an exception allowing the procedure where necessary for the health of the mother. Second, the District Court found the Act deficient because it covered not merely intact D&E but also certain other D&Es. . . .

The principles set forth in the joint opinion in *Planned Parenthood of Southeastern Pa. v. Casey* 505 U.S. 833 (1992) did not find support from all those who join the instant opinion. (Justices Scalia and Thomas). Whatever one's views concerning the *Casey* joint opinion, it is evident a premise central to its conclusion—that the government has a legitimate and substantial interest in preserving and promoting fetal life—would be repudiated were the Court now to affirm the judgments of the Courts of Appeals. . . .

. . . *Casey* rejected both *Roe*'s rigid trimester framework and the interpretation of *Roe* that considered all pre-viability regulations of abortion unwarranted. On this point *Casey* overruled the holdings in two cases because they undervalued the State's interest in potential life, overruling *Thornburgh v. American College of Obstetricians and Gynecologists*, 476 U.S. 747 (1986), and *Akron v. Akron Center for Reproductive Health, Inc.*, 462 U.S. 416 (1983).

We assume the following principles for the purposes of this opinion. Before viability, a State "may not prohibit any woman from making the ultimate decision to terminate her pregnancy." It also may not impose upon this right an undue burden, which exists if a regulation's "purpose or effect is to place a substantial obstacle in the path of a woman seeking an abortion before the fetus attains viability." On the other hand, "regulations which do no more than create a structural mechanism by which the State, or the parent or guardian of a minor, may express profound respect for the life of the unborn are permitted, if they are not a substantial obstacle to the woman's exercise of the right to choose." *Casey*, in short, struck a balance. The balance was central to its holding. We now apply its standard to the cases at bar.

We begin with a determination of the Act's operation and effect. A straightforward reading of the Act's text demonstrates its purpose and the scope of its provisions: It regulates and proscribes, with exceptions or qualifications to be discussed, performing the intact D&E procedure. . . .

Respondents . . . argue the Act is unconstitutionally vague on its face. "As generally stated, the void-for-vagueness doctrine requires that a penal statute define the criminal offense with sufficient definiteness that ordinary people can understand what conduct is prohibited and in a manner that does not encourage arbitrary and discriminatory enforcement." *Kolender v. Lawson*, 461 U.S. 352 (1983). The Act satisfies both requirements.

The Act provides doctors "of ordinary intelligence a reasonable opportunity to know what is prohibited." *Grayned v. City of Rockford*, 408 U.S. 104 (1972). . . .

Respondents likewise have failed to show that the Act should be invalidated on its face because it encourages arbitrary or discriminatory enforcement. Just as the Act's anatomical landmarks provide doctors with objective standards, they also "establish minimal guidelines to govern law enforcement." . . .

We next determine whether the Act imposes an undue burden, as a facial matter, because its restrictions on second-trimester abortions are too broad. A review of the statutory text discloses the limits of its reach. The Act prohibits intact D&E; and, notwithstanding respondents' arguments, it does not prohibit the D&E procedure in which the fetus is removed in parts. . . .

The Act's purposes are set forth in recitals preceding its operative provisions. A description of the prohibited abortion procedure demonstrates the rationale for the congressional enactment. The Act proscribes a method of abortion in which a fetus is killed just inches before completion of the birth process. Congress stated as follows: "Implicitly approving such a brutal and inhumane procedure by choosing not to prohibit it will further coarsen society to the humanity of not only newborns, but all vulnerable and innocent human life, making it increasingly difficult to protect such life." . . .

Casey reaffirmed these governmental objectives. The government may use its voice and its regulatory authority to show its profound respect for the life within the woman. A central premise of the opinion was that the Court's precedents after *Roe* had "undervalued the State's interest in potential life." . . .

The Act's ban on abortions that involve partial delivery of a living fetus furthers the Government's objectives. No one would dispute that, for many, D&E is a procedure itself laden with the power to devalue human life. Congress could nonetheless conclude that the type of abortion proscribed by the Act requires specific regulation because it implicates additional ethical and moral concerns that justify a special prohibition. Congress determined that the abortion methods it proscribed had a "disturbing similarity to the killing of a newborn infant," and thus it was concerned with "drawing a bright line that clearly distinguishes abortion and infanticide." . . .

Respect for human life finds an ultimate expression in the bond of love the mother has for her child. The Act recognizes this reality as well. Whether to have an abortion requires a difficult and painful moral decision. While we find no reliable data to measure the phenomenon, it seems unexceptionable to conclude some women come to regret their choice to abort the infant life they once created and sustained. Severe depression and loss of esteem can follow.

In a decision so fraught with emotional consequence some doctors may prefer not to disclose precise details of the means that will be used, confining themselves to the required statement of risks the procedure entails. From one standpoint this ought not to be surprising. Any number of patients facing imminent surgical procedures would prefer not to hear all details, lest the usual anxiety preceding invasive medical procedures become the more intense. This is likely the case with the abortion procedures here in issue.

It is, however, precisely this lack of information concerning the way in which the fetus will be killed that is of legitimate concern to the State. The State has an interest in ensuring so grave a choice is well informed. It is self-evident that a mother who comes to regret her choice to abort must struggle with grief more anguished and sorrow more profound when she learns, only after the event, what she once did not know: that she allowed a doctor to pierce the skull and vacuum the fast-developing brain of her unborn child, a child assuming the human form. . . .

The Act's furtherance of legitimate government interests bears upon, but does not resolve, the next question: whether the Act has the effect of imposing an unconstitutional burden on the abortion right because it does not allow use of the barred procedure where " 'necessary, in appropriate medical judgment, for the preservation of the . . . health of the mother.' " The prohibition in the Act would be unconstitutional, under precedents we here assume to be controlling, if it "subjected women to significant health risks." . . . [T]he parties agreed a health exception to the challenged parental-involvement statute was necessary "to avert serious and often irreversible damage to [a pregnant minor's] health." Here, by contrast, whether the Act creates significant health risks for women has been a contested factual question. . . .

The question becomes whether the Act can stand when this medical uncertainty persists. The Court's precedents instruct that the Act can survive this facial attack. The Court has given state and federal legislatures wide discretion to pass legislation in areas where there is medical and scientific uncertainty.

This traditional rule is consistent with *Casey*, which confirms the State's interest in promoting respect for human life at all stages in the pregnancy. Physicians are not entitled to ignore regulations that direct them to use reasonable alternative procedures. The law need not give abortion doctors unfettered choice in the course of their medical practice, nor should it elevate their status above other physicians in the medical community. . . .

Medical uncertainty does not foreclose the exercise of legislative power in the abortion context any more than it does in other contexts. The medical uncertainty over whether the Act's prohibition creates significant health risks provides a sufficient basis to conclude in this facial attack that the Act does not impose an undue burden.

The conclusion that the Act does not impose an undue burden is supported by other considerations. Alternatives are available to the prohibited procedure. As we have noted, the Act does not proscribe D&E. . . .

As the previous sections of this opinion explain, respondents have not demonstrated that the Act would be unconstitutional in a large fraction of relevant cases. We note that the statute here applies to all instances in which the doctor proposes to use the prohibited procedure, not merely those in which the woman suffers from medical complications. It is neither our obligation nor within our traditional institutional role to resolve questions of constitutionality with respect to each potential situation that might develop. . . .

The Act is open to a proper as-applied challenge in a discrete case. Respondents have not demonstrated that the Act, as a facial matter, is void for vagueness, or that it imposes an undue burden on a woman's right to abortion based on its overbreadth or lack of a health exception. For these reasons the judgments of the Courts of Appeals for the Eighth and Ninth Circuits are reversed.

Justice GINSBURG, with whom Justices STEVENS, SOUTER, and BREYER join, dissenting.

. . . Taking care to speak plainly, the *Casey* Court restated and reaffirmed *Roe*'s essential holding. First, the Court addressed the type of abortion regulation permissible prior to fetal viability. It recognized "the right of the woman to choose to have an abortion before viability and to obtain it without undue interference from the State." Second, the Court acknowledged "the State's power to restrict abortions after fetal viability, if the law contains exceptions for pregnancies which endanger the woman's life or health." Third, the Court confirmed that "the State has legitimate interests from the outset of the pregnancy in protecting the health of the woman and the life of the fetus that may become a child."

In reaffirming *Roe*, the *Casey* Court described the centrality of "the decision whether to bear . . . a child," *Eisenstadt v. Baird*, 405 U. S. 438 (1972), to a woman's "dignity and autonomy," her "personhood" and "destiny," her "conception of . . . her place in society." Of signal importance here, the *Casey* Court stated with unmistakable clarity that state regulation of access to abortion procedures, even after viability, must protect "the health of the woman."

Seven years ago, in *Stenberg v. Carhart*, 530 U.S. 914 (2000), the Court invalidated a Nebraska statute criminalizing the performance of a medical procedure that, in the political arena, has been dubbed "partial-birth abortion." With fidelity to the *Roe-Casey* line of precedent, the Court held the Nebraska statute unconstitutional in part because it lacked the requisite protection for the preservation of a woman's health.

Today's decision is alarming. It refuses to take *Casey* and *Stenberg* seriously. It tolerates, indeed applauds, federal intervention to ban nation-wide a procedure found necessary and proper in certain cases by the American College of Obstetricians and Gynecologists (ACOG). It blurs the line, firmly drawn in *Casey*, between pre-viability and post-viability abortions. And, for the first time since *Roe*, the Court blesses a prohibi-tion with no exception safeguarding a woman's health. . . .

As *Casey* comprehended, at stake in cases challenging abortion re-strictions is a woman's "control over her own destiny." "There was a time, not so long ago," when women were "regarded as the center of home and family life, with attendant special responsibilities that precluded full and independent legal status under the Constitution." Those views, this Court made clear in *Casey*, "are no longer consistent with our understanding of the family, the individual, or the Constitution." Women, it is now acknowl-edged, have the talent, capacity, and right "to participate equally in the economic and social life of the Nation." Their ability to realize their full potential, the Court recognized, is intimately connected to "their ability to control their reproductive lives." Thus, legal challenges to undue re-strictions on abortion procedures do not seek to vindicate some general-ized notion of privacy; rather, they center on a woman's autonomy to determine her life's course, and thus to enjoy equal citizenship stature.

In keeping with this comprehension of the right to reproductive choice, the Court has consistently required that laws regulating abortion, at any stage of pregnancy and in all cases, safeguard a woman's health.

We have thus ruled that a State must avoid subjecting women to health risks not only where the pregnancy itself creates danger, but also where state regulation forces women to resort to less safe methods of abortion. Indeed, we have applied the rule that abortion regulation must safeguard a woman's health to the particular procedure at issue here—intact dilation and evacuation (D&E).

In *Stenberg*, we expressly held that a statute banning intact D&E was unconstitutional in part because it lacked a health exception. We noted that there existed a "division of medical opinion" about the relative safety of intact D&E, but we made clear that as long as "substantial medical au-thority supports the proposition that banning a particular abortion proce-dure could endanger women's health," a health exception is required. . . .

During the District Court trials, "numerous" "extraordinarily accom-plished" and "very experienced" medical experts explained that, in cer-tain circumstances and for certain women, intact D&E is safer than alternative procedures and necessary to protect women's health. According to the expert testimony plaintiffs introduced, the safety advantages of intact D&E are marked for women with certain medical conditions, for example, uterine scarring, bleeding disorders, heart disease, or compromised immune systems. Further, plaintiffs' experts testified that intact D&E is significantly safer for women with certain pregnancy-related conditions . . . and for women carrying fetuses with certain abnormalities. . . .

The Court offers flimsy and transparent justifications for upholding a nationwide ban on intact D&E. . . .

Ultimately, the Court admits that "moral concerns" are at work, concerns that could yield prohibitions on any abortion. Notably, the concerns expressed are untethered to any ground genuinely serving the Government's interest in preserving life. By allowing such concerns to carry the day and case, overriding fundamental rights, the Court dishonors our precedent.

Revealing in this regard, the Court invokes an anti-abortion shibboleth for which it concededly has no reliable evidence: women who have abortions come to regret their choices, and consequently suffer from "severe depression and loss of esteem." Because of women's fragile emotional state and because of the "bond of love the mother has for her child," the Court worries, doctors may withhold information about the nature of the intact D&E procedure. The solution the Court approves, then, is not to require doctors to inform women, accurately and adequately, of the different procedures and their attendant risks. Instead, the Court deprives women of the right to make an autonomous choice, even at the expense of their safety.

This way of thinking reflects ancient notions about women's place in the family and under the Constitution—ideas that have long since been discredited. *Bradwell v. State*, 16 Wall. 130 (1873) (Bradley, J., concurring: "Man is, or should be, woman's protector and defender. The natural and proper timidity and delicacy which belongs to the female sex evidently unfits it for many of the occupations of civil life. . . . The paramount destiny and mission of woman are to fulfill the noble and benign offices of wife and mother.").

Though today's majority may regard women's feelings on the matter as "self-evident," this Court has repeatedly confirmed that "the destiny of the woman must be shaped . . . on her own conception of her spiritual imperatives and her place in society." *Casey*.

In cases on a "woman's liberty to determine whether to continue her pregnancy," this Court has identified viability as a critical consideration. "There is no line more workable than viability," the Court explained in *Casey*, for viability is "the time at which there is a realistic possibility of maintaining and nourishing a life outside the womb, so that the independent existence of the second life can in reason and all fairness be the object of state protection that now overrides the rights of the woman. . . . In some broad sense it might be said that a woman who fails to act before viability has consented to the State's intervention on behalf of the developing child." . . .

If there is anything at all redemptive to be said of today's opinion, it is that the Court is not willing to foreclose entirely a constitutional challenge to the Act. "The Act is open," the Court states, "to a proper as-applied challenge in a discrete case." But the Court offers no clue on what a "proper" lawsuit might look like. Nor does the Court explain why the injunctions ordered by the District Courts should not remain in place, trimmed only to exclude instances in which another procedure would safeguard a woman's health at least equally well. Surely the Court cannot mean that no suit may be brought until a woman's health is immediately jeopardized by the ban on intact D&E. A woman "suffering from medical complications" needs access to the medical procedure at once and cannot wait for the judicial process to unfold. . . .

In sum, the notion that the Partial-Birth Abortion Ban Act furthers any legitimate governmental interest is, quite simply, irrational. The Court's defense of the statute provides no saving explanation. In candor, the Act, and the Court's defense of it, cannot be understood as anything other than an effort to chip away at a right declared again and again by this Court—and with increasing comprehension of its centrality to women's lives. When "a statute burdens constitutional rights and all that can be said on its behalf is that it is the vehicle that legislators have chosen for expressing their hostility to those rights, the burden is undue."

For the reasons stated, I dissent from the Court's disposition and would affirm the judgments before us for review.

Rulings in Context

Abortion Rights

Eisenstadt v. Baird, 405 U.S. 438 (1972)   6-1
> In light of *Griswold v. Connecticut* (Case 1.3), the Court extended the right to privacy in the use of contraceptives to unmarried individuals.

Webster v. Reproductive Health Services, 492 U.S. 490 (1989)   5-4
> The Court, led by Chief Justice Rehnquist, upheld several Missouri restrictions on abortion. These included a declaration that life begins at conception, that physicians test a fetus's gestational age if a woman is 20 or more weeks pregnant, that no public employee perform an abortion unless the

woman's life was in danger, and that no public funds used to counsel a woman to have an abortion unless her life was in danger if the pregnancy were to continue.

Stenberg v. Carhart, 530 U.S. 914 (2000)   5-4

The Court ruled that a Nebraska law that provided for late-term abortions was void for vagueness and failed to provide an exception if the woman's health was in danger.

Right to Die: Case

The issue of the right to die, or more specifically, physician-assisted suicide for the terminally ill, has roiled American society since the case of *Cruzan v. Director, Missouri Department of Health,* 497 U.S. 261, was decided in 1990. The parents of twenty-five-year-old Nancy Cruzan had sought permission to remove her feeding tube after she was pronounced brain dead as a result of sustaining severe injuries in a 1983 automobile accident. After her doctors determined that with artificial support her body would remain alive in a vegetative state for nearly thirty years, the state of Missouri prohibited the doctors from removing the tube. The Supreme Court, in an opinion by Chief Justice Rehnquist, upheld the Missouri decision because Nancy had never written and signed a document indicating how her life should end: in short, there was no clear and convincing evidence of her end-of-life wishes. The case that follows involved Oregon's Death with Dignity Act, which the U.S. Attorney General challenged as a violation of the federal Controlled Substances Act of 1970. The Attorney General argued that physicians' use of drugs to help terminally ill patients commit suicide was medically improper.

Case 6.4

Gonzales v. Oregon
546 U.S. 243, 128 S.Ct. 904 (2006)

The Court has decided a few cases involving assisted suicide and the right to die for terminally ill patients, including *Cruzan* and

Glucksberg. In writing for the Court in the latter case, Chief Justice William Rehnquist noted that "throughout the Nation, Americans are engaged in an earnest and profound debate about the morality, legality, and practicality of physician-assisted suicide. Our holding permits this debate to continue, as it should a democratic society."

In 1994, Oregon became the first State to legalize assisted suicide when voters approved a ballot measure enacting the Oregon Death With Dignity Act (ODWDA). In the meantime, the Controlled Substances Act (CSA), a federal law in effect since 1970, was designed to combat drug abuse and control legitimate and illegitimate traffic in controlled substances or illegal drugs. In 2001, Attorney General John Ashcroft challenged the ODWDA as a violation of the CSA, especially drugs listed in Schedule II, which are generally available only by written prescription. Ashcroft issued an Interpretative Rule, declaring that using controlled substances to assist suicide was not a legitimate medical practice and that dispensing or prescribing them for this purpose was unlawful under the CSA.

The State of Oregon, a physician, a pharmacist, and some terminally ill state residents objected to Ashcroft's interpretation, and a federal district court agreed. On appeal, the U.S. Court of Appeals for the Ninth Circuit invalidated the Attorney General's Rule. It reasoned that by making a medical procedure authorized under Oregon law a federal offense, it altered the balance between the States and the Federal Government because the CSA did not authorize the Attorney General to intervene when a controlled drug was used for a medical purpose. Moreover, the Court held that his interpretation could not be squared with the CSA's plain language, which targets only conventional drug abuse and excludes the Attorney General from medical policy decisions. By the time the case reached the Supreme Court, Alberto Gonzales had succeeded John Ashcroft as U.S. Attorney General, and the case title reflected the change.

By a six to three vote upholding the Ninth Circuit, the Court ruled that the CSA does not allow the Attorney General to prohibit doctors from prescribing regulated drugs for use in physician-assisted suicide under state law permitting the procedure. Justice Anthony Kennedy delivered the opinion of the Court, in which Justices John Paul Stevens, Sandra Day O'Connor, David Souter, Ruth Bader Ginsburg, and Stephen Breyer joined. Justice Antonin Scalia filed a dissenting opinion, in which he was joined by Chief Justice John Roberts and Justice Clarence Thomas. Justice Thomas also filed a dissent.

Justice KENNEDY delivered the opinion of the Court.

The dispute before us is in part a product of this political and moral debate, but its resolution requires an inquiry familiar to the courts: interpreting a federal statute to determine whether Executive action is authorized by, or otherwise consistent with, the enactment. . . .

The Attorney General has rulemaking power to fulfill his duties under the CSA. The specific respects in which he is authorized to make rules, however, instruct us that he is not authorized to make a rule declaring illegitimate a medical standard for care and treatment of patients that is specifically authorized under state law.

The starting point for this inquiry is, of course, the language of the delegation provision itself. In many cases authority is clear because the statute gives an agency broad power to enforce all provisions of the statute. The CSA does not grant the Attorney General this broad authority to promulgate rules.

The CSA gives the Attorney General limited powers, to be exercised in specific ways. His rulemaking authority under the CSA is described in two provisions: (1) "The Attorney General is authorized to promulgate rules and regulations and to charge reasonable fees relating to the registration and control of the manufacture, distribution, and dispensing of controlled substances and to listed chemicals," and (2) "The Attorney General may promulgate and enforce any rules, regulations, and procedures which he may deem necessary and appropriate for the efficient execution of his functions under this subchapter." As is evident from these sections, Congress did not delegate to the Attorney General authority to carry out or effect all provisions of the CSA. Rather, he can promulgate rules relating only to "registration" and "control," and "for the efficient execution of his functions" under the statute.

Turning first to the Attorney General's authority to make regulations for the "control" of drugs, this delegation cannot sustain the Interpretive Rule's attempt to define standards of medical practice. Control is a term of art in the CSA. . . .

The authority desired by the Government is inconsistent with the design of the statute . . . . The Attorney General does not have the sole delegated authority under the CSA. He must instead share it with, and in some respects defer to, the Secretary [of Health and Human Services], whose functions are likewise delineated and confined by the statute. The CSA allocates decisionmaking powers among statutory actors so that medical judgments, if they are to be decided at the federal level and for the limited objects of the statute, are placed in the hands of the Secretary. In the scheduling context, for example, the Secretary's recommendations on scientific and medical matters bind the Attorney

General. The Attorney General cannot control a substance if the Secretary disagrees. . . .

The Government contends the Attorney General's decision here is a legal, not a medical, one. This generality, however, does not suffice. The Attorney General's Interpretive Rule, and the Office of Legal Counsel memo it incorporates, place extensive reliance on medical judgments and the views of the medical community in concluding that assisted suicide is not a "legitimate medical purpose." This confirms that the authority claimed by the Attorney General is both beyond his expertise and incongruous with the statutory purposes and design.

The idea that Congress gave the Attorney General such broad and unusual authority through an implicit delegation in the CSA's registration provision is not sustainable. "Congress, we have held, does not alter the fundamental details of a regulatory scheme in vague terms or ancillary provisions—it does not, one might say, hide elephants in mouseholes." *Whitman v. American Trucking Assns., Inc.,* 531 U. S. 457 (2001).

The importance of the issue of physician-assisted suicide, which has been the subject of an "earnest and profound debate" across the country, *Glucksberg,* makes the oblique form of the claimed delegation all the more suspect. Under the Government's theory, moreover, the medical judgments the Attorney General could make are not limited to physician-assisted suicide. Were this argument accepted, he could decide whether any particular drug may be used for any particular purpose, or indeed whether a physician who administers any controversial treatment could be deregistered. This would occur, under the Government's view, despite the statute's express limitation of the Attorney General's authority to registration and control, with attendant restrictions on each of those functions, and despite the statutory purposes to combat drug abuse and prevent illicit drug trafficking. . . .

Oregon's regime is an example of the state regulation of medical practice that the CSA presupposes. Rather than simply decriminalizing assisted suicide, ODWDA limits its exercise to the attending physicians of terminally ill patients, physicians who must be licensed by Oregon's Board of Medical Examiners. The statute gives attending physicians a central role, requiring them to provide prognoses and prescriptions, give information about palliative alternatives and counseling, and ensure patients are competent and acting voluntarily. Any eligible patient must also get a second opinion from another registered physician, and the statute's safeguards require physicians to keep and submit to inspection detailed records of their actions. . . .

The Government, in the end, maintains that the prescription requirement delegates to a single Executive officer the power to effect a radical shift of authority from the States to the Federal Government to define general standards of medical practice in every locality. The text and structure of the CSA show that Congress did not have this far-reaching intent to alter the federal-state balance and the congressional role in maintaining it. The judgment of the Court of Appeals is Affirmed.

Justice SCALIA, with whom Chief Justice ROBERTS and Justice THOMAS join, dissenting.

The Court concludes that the Attorney General lacked authority to declare assisted suicide illicit under the Controlled Substances Act (CSA), because the CSA is concerned only with "*illicit* drug dealing and trafficking." This question-begging conclusion is obscured by a flurry of arguments that distort the statute and disregard settled principles of our interpretive jurisprudence.

In sum, the Directive's first conclusion—namely that physician-assisted suicide is not a "legitimate medical purpose"—is supported both by the deference we owe to the agency's interpretation of its own regulations and by the deference we owe to its interpretation of the statute. The other two conclusions—(2) that prescribing controlled drugs to assist suicide violates the CSA, and (3) that such conduct is also "inconsistent with the public interest"—are inevitable consequences of that first conclusion. Moreover, the third conclusion, standing alone, is one that the Attorney General is authorized to make.

The Court's decision today is perhaps driven by a feeling that the subject of assisted suicide is none of the Federal Government's business. It is easy to sympathize with that position. The prohibition or deterrence of assisted suicide is certainly not among the enumerated powers conferred on the United States by the Constitution, and it is within the realm of public morality (*bonos mores*) traditionally addressed by the so-called police power of the States. But then, neither is prohibiting the recreational use of drugs or discouraging drug addiction among the enumerated powers. From an early time in our national history, the Federal Government has used its enumerated powers, such as its power to regulate interstate commerce, for the purpose of protecting public morality—for example, by banning the interstate shipment of lottery tickets, or the interstate transport of women for immoral purposes. See *Hoke v. United States*, 227 U. S. 308 (1913); *Lottery Case*, 188 U. S. 321 (1903). Unless we are to repudiate a long and well-established principle of our jurisprudence, using the federal commerce power to prevent assisted suicide is unquestionably permissible. The question before us is not whether Congress *can* do this, or even whether Congress *should* do this; but simply whether Congress *has* done this in the CSA. I think there is no doubt that it has. If the term "*legitimate* medical purpose" has any meaning, it surely excludes the prescription of drugs to produce death. For the above reasons, I respectfully dissent from the judgment of the Court.

Rulings in Context

Right to Die

Cruzan v. Director, Missouri Department of Health,
497 U.S. 261 (1990)   5-4

> Chief Justice Rehnquist held for a bare majority that a terminally ill person must provide clear and convincing evidence, by a written and signed document, of how their life should end, including a decision to remove all mechanical life-sustaining equipment, such as hydration and feeding tubes.

Washington v. Glucksberg, 521 U.S. 702 (1997)   9-0

> This case, along with another from New York State, involved Washington State's ban on physician-assisted suicide for terminally ill patients. The Court ruled that the ban was justified on the grounds that the practice violated the 1970 Controlled Substances Act and that terminally ill patients are especially vulnerable to manipulation by physicians and family members.

Gay and Lesbian Rights: Cases

The complicated and divisive issue of the right of adults of the same sex to engage in private consensual sexual conduct became especially controversial after the Supreme Court ruled in 1986 that a Georgia law prohibiting such conduct did not violate the Constitution's liberty component of the Due Process Clause (*Bowers v. Hardwick,* 478 U.S. 186). Since that time, other issues have focused on whether homosexuals have the right to marry or enter into civil unions. The case that follows narrowly overturned *Bowers,* and set the stage for the Court to continue to hear cases concerning gay rights.

In 2013, the Court announced opinions in two cases related to same-sex marriage, *Hollingsworth v. Perry* and *United States v. Windsor.* The first concerned a California initiative called Proposition 8, which passed in 2008 by popular vote after that state's highest court held that same-sex marriage was permissible under the state constitution. An initiative in the electoral process is when the people rather than lawmakers initiate a law and then petition it to the ballot so the total electorate may vote on it. Prop 8 amended the state constitution with the declaration that the state recognized a marriage only between one man and one woman. Although two same-sex couples challenged the amendment as a violation of the U.S. Constitution's Equal Protection Clause, the Court declined to rule as a jurisdictional matter after state officials decided not to defend Prop 8. The other case, *United States v. Windsor*, pertained to a provision of a 1996 federal law known as the Defense of Marriage Act—or DOMA—that denied federal benefits to same-sex married couples. A widow, Edith Windsor, had to pay over $363,000 in federal estate taxes after her same-sex spouse died whereas she would have owed nothing if her spouse had been a man. (Case 6.6).

Case 6.5

Lawrence v. Texas
539 U.S. 558, 123 S.Ct. 2472 (2003)

In Houston, Texas, officers of the Harris County Police Department entered a private residence after responding to reports of a weapons disturbance. They entered an apartment where they observed the resident, John Geddes Lawrence, and another man, Tyron Garner, engaging in private consensual sodomy. The two petitioners were eventually convicted of violating Texas Penal Code Section 21.06, which made it a crime to engage in "deviate sexual intercourse, namely anal sex, with a member of the same sex (man)." Specifically, the law defined "deviate sexual intercourse" as "any contact between any part of the genitals of one person and the mouth or anus of another person; or the penetration of the genitals or the anus of another person with an object."

Lawrence and Garner claimed the statute violated the Equal Protection Clause of the Fourteenth Amendment. After the court rejected their argument, it fined them each $200 and assessed court costs of $141.25. Lawrence and Garner appealed to the Texas Court of Appeals, which, sitting *en banc*, also rejected their federal constitutional arguments based both on the Equal Protection and Due Process Clauses of the Fourteenth Amendment and affirmed their convictions. That court's decision was based largely on the 1986 Supreme Court decision in *Bowers v. Hardwick*, 478 U.S. 186, which upheld Georgia's anti-sodomy law. Lawrence and Garner appealed to the Supreme Court, which granted *certiorari*.

The major questions before the Court were whether the police, in invading their privacy in the exercise of their liberty, violated the Due Process Clause of the Fourteenth Amendment and whether *Bowers* decision should be overturned. There were two additional questions for the Court: first, whether the law violated the Equal Protection Clause of the Fourteenth Amendment because it addressed the sexual relationship only between men, not between men and women; and second, whether it made a difference that many state legislatures had repealed their laws against sodomy since 1986 when *Bowers* was decided.

The Court decided in a six to three decision that the Texas law violated the Fourteenth Amendment. Five justices, with Justice Anthony M. Kennedy writing the opinion of the Court, ruled that the law unconstitutionally invaded Lawrence and Garner's privacy decisions, which is a form of liberty protected by the Due Process Clause. He also took the rare step of citing international law as a basis for his decision.

These five justices also held that because *Bowers* was mistakenly decided, it was thus overruled. Justice Sandra Day O'Connor concurred with the Court's decision, but focused on the law's singling out only homosexual, and not heterosexual, sodomy as a violation of the Fourteenth Amendment's Equal Protection Clause. Justice Antonin Scalia, along with Chief Justice William H. Rehnquist and Justice Clarence Thomas, dissented.

Cases like this one have become the source of much criticism, usually from political conservatives and the religious right, charging that the Court has overstepped its bounds to deal with an issue that ought to be left to the states to decide through legislation. And yet, for others, as Justice Kennedy notes in his opinion, the gay and lesbian community is but a minority in American society and thus it needs greater constitutional protection from the tyranny of the majority.

Justice KENNEDY delivered the opinion of the Court.

... The Court began its substantive discussion in *Bowers* [*v. Hardwick*, 478 U.S. 186 (1986)] as follows: "The issue presented is whether the Federal Constitution confers a fundamental right upon homosexuals to engage in sodomy and hence invalidates the laws of the many States that still make such conduct illegal and have done so for a very long time." That statement, we now conclude, discloses the Court's own failure to appreciate the extent of the liberty at stake. To say that the issue in *Bowers* was simply the right to engage in certain sexual conduct demeans the claim the individual put forward, just as it would demean a married couple were it to be said marriage is simply about the right to have sexual intercourse. The laws involved in *Bowers* and here are, to be sure, statutes that purport to do no more than prohibit a particular sexual act. Their penalties and purposes, though, have more far-reaching consequences, touching upon the most private human conduct, sexual behavior, and in the most private of places, the home. The statutes do seek to control a personal relationship that, whether or not entitled to formal recognition in the law, is within the liberty of persons to choose without being punished as criminals.

This, as a general rule, should counsel against attempts by the State, or a court, to define the meaning of the relationship or to set its boundaries absent injury to a person or abuse of an institution the law protects. It suffices for us to acknowledge that adults may choose to enter upon this relationship in the confines of their homes and their own private lives and still retain their dignity as free persons. When sexuality finds overt expression in intimate conduct with another person, the conduct can be but one element in a personal bond that is more enduring. The liberty protected by the Constitution allows homosexual persons the right to make this choice. . . .

Chief Justice Burger joined the opinion for the Court in *Bowers* and further explained his views as follows: "Decisions of individuals relating to homosexual conduct have been subject to state intervention throughout the history of Western civilization. Condemnation of those practices is firmly rooted in Judeao-Christian moral and ethical standards." . . . [S]cholarship casts some doubt on the sweeping nature of the statement by Chief Justice Burger as it pertains to private homosexual conduct between consenting adults. In all events we think that our laws and traditions in the past half century are of most relevance here. These references show an emerging awareness that liberty gives substantial protection to adult persons in deciding how to conduct their private lives in matters pertaining to sex. "History and tradition are the starting point but not in all cases the ending point of the substantive due process inquiry." *County of Sacramento v. Lewis,* 523 U.S. 833 (1998) (Justice Kennedy, concurring).

This emerging recognition should have been apparent when *Bowers* was decided. In 1955 the American Law Institute promulgated the Model Penal Code and made clear that it did not recommend or provide for "criminal penalties for consensual sexual relations conducted in private. It justified its decision on three grounds: (1) The prohibitions undermined respect for the law by penalizing conduct many people engaged in; (2) the statutes regulated private conduct not harmful to others; and (3) the laws were arbitrarily enforced and thus invited the danger of blackmail. In 1961 Illinois changed its laws to conform to the Model Penal Code. Other States soon followed.

In *Bowers* the Court referred to the fact that before 1961 all 50 States had outlawed sodomy, and that at the time of the Court's decision 24 States and the District of Columbia had sodomy laws. Justice Powell pointed out that these prohibitions often were being ignored, however. Georgia, for instance, had not sought to enforce its law for decades.

The sweeping references by Chief Justice Burger to the history of Western civilization and to Judeo-Christian moral and ethical standards did not take account of other authorities pointing in an opposite direction. A committee advising the British Parliament recommended in 1957 repeal of laws punishing homosexual conduct. The Wolfenden Report: Report of the Committee on Homosexual Offenses and Prostitution (1963). Parliament enacted the substance of those recommendations 10 years later.

Of even more importance, almost five years before *Bowers* was decided the European Court of Human Rights considered a case with parallels to *Bowers* and to today's case. . . . The court held that the laws proscribing the conduct were invalid under the European Convention on Human Rights. Authoritative in all countries that are members of the Council of Europe (21 nations then, 45 nations now), the decision is at odds with the premise in *Bowers* that the claim put forward was insubstantial in our Western civilization.

In our own constitutional system the deficiencies in *Bowers* became even more apparent in the years following its announcement. The 25 States with laws prohibiting the relevant conduct referenced in the *Bowers* decision are reduced now to 13, of which 4 enforce their laws only against homosexual conduct. In those States where sodomy is still proscribed, whether for same-sex or heterosexual conduct, there is a pattern of nonenforcement with respect to consenting adults acting in private. The State of Texas admitted in 1994 that as of that date it had not prosecuted anyone under those circumstances.

Two principal cases decided after *Bowers* cast its holding into even more doubt. In *Planned Parenthood of Southeastern Pa. v. Casey* [505 U.S. 833 (1992)], the Court reaffirmed the substantive force of the liberty protected by the Due Process Clause. . . . In explaining the respect the Constitution demands for the autonomy of the person in making these choices, we stated as follows: "These matters, involving the most intimate and personal choices a person may make in a lifetime, choices central to personal dignity and autonomy, are central to the liberty protected by the Fourteenth Amendment. At the heart of liberty is the right to define one's own concept of existence, of meaning, of the universe, and of the mystery of human life. Beliefs about these matters could not define the attributes of personhood were they formed under compulsion of the State." Persons in a homosexual relationship may seek autonomy for these purposes, just as heterosexual persons do. The decision in *Bowers* would deny them this right.

The second post-*Bowers* case of principal relevance is *Romer v. Evans*, 517 U.S. 620 (1996). There the Court struck down class-based legislation directed at homosexuals as a violation of the Equal Protection Clause. *Romer* invalidated an amendment to Colorado's constitution which named as a solitary class persons who were homosexuals, lesbians, or bisexual either by "orientation, conduct, practices or relationships," and deprived them of protection under state antidiscrimination laws. We concluded that the provision was "born of animosity toward the class of persons affected" and further that it had no rational relation to a legitimate governmental purpose.

As an alternative argument in this case, counsel for the petitioners and some *amici* contend that *Romer* provides the basis for declaring the Texas statute invalid under the Equal Protection Clause. That is a tenable argument, but we conclude the instant case requires us to address whether *Bowers* itself has continuing validity. Were we to hold the statute invalid under the Equal Protection Clause, some might question whether a prohibition would be valid if drawn differently, say, to prohibit the conduct both between same-sex and different-sex participants. . . .

The stigma this criminal statute imposes . . . is not trivial. The offense, to be sure, is but a class C misdemeanor, a minor offense in the Texas legal system. Still, it remains a criminal offense with all that imports for the dignity of the persons charged. The petitioners will bear on their record the history of their criminal convictions. Just this term we rejected various challenges to state laws requiring the registration of sex offenders. *Connecticut Department of Public Safety v. Doe*, 538 U.S. 1 (2003). We are advised that if Texas convicted an adult for private, consensual homosexual conduct under the statute here in question, the convicted person would come within the registration laws of a least four States were he or she to be subject to their jurisdiction. [Justice Kennedy cites Idaho, Louisiana, Mississippi, and South Carolina.] This underscores the consequential nature of the punishment and the state-sponsored condemnation attendant to the criminal prohibition. Furthermore, the Texas criminal conviction carries with it the other collateral consequences always following a conviction, such as notations on job application forms, to mention but one example.

The foundations of *Bowers* have sustained serious erosion from our recent decisions in *Casey* and *Romer*. When our precedent has been thus weakened, criticism from other sources is of greater significance. In the United States criticism of *Bowers* has been substantial and continuing, disapproving of its reasoning in all respects, not just as to its historical assumptions. See, for example, Charles Fried, *Order and Law: Arguing the Reagan Revolution—A Firsthand Account*, 81–84 (1991); Richard Posner, *Sex and Reason*, 341–350 (1992). The courts of five different States have declined to follow it in interpreting provisions in their own state constitutions parallel to the Due Process Clause of the Fourteenth Amendment [Justice Kennedy cites Arkansas, Georgia, Montana, Tennessee, and Kentucky]. . . .

Bowers was not correct when it was decided, and it is not correct today. It ought not to remain binding precedent. *Bowers v. Hardwick* should be and now is overruled.

The present case does not involve minors. It does not involve persons who might be injured or coerced or who are situated in relationships where consent might not easily be refused. It does not involve public conduct or prostitution. It does not involve whether the government must give formal recognition to any relationship that homosexual persons seek to enter. The case does involve two adults who, with full and mutual consent from each other, engaged in sexual practices common to a homosexual lifestyle. The petitioners are entitled to respect for their private lives. . . .

The judgment of the Court of Appeals for the Texas Fourteenth District is reversed, and the case is remanded for further proceedings not inconsistent with this opinion.

It is so ordered.

Justice O'CONNOR, concurring in the judgment.

. . . I agree with the Court that Texas' statute banning same-sex sodomy is unconstitutional. Rather than relying on the substantive component of the Fourteenth Amendment's Due Process Clause, as the Court does, I base my conclusion on the Fourteenth Amendment's Equal Protection Clause. . . .

The statute at issue here makes sodomy a crime only if a person "engages in deviate sexual intercourse with another individual of the same sex." Sodomy between opposite-sex partners, however, is not a crime in Texas. That is, Texas treats the same conduct differently based solely on the participants. Those harmed by this law are people who have a same-sex sexual orientation and thus are more likely to engage in behavior prohibited by Section 21.06 [of the Texas code]. . . .

Justice SCALIA, with whom the Chief Justice [REHNQUIST] and Justice THOMAS join, dissenting.

. . . I turn . . . to the ground on which the Court squarely rests its holding: the contention that there is no rational basis for the law here under attack. This proposition is so out of accord with our jurisprudence—indeed, with the jurisprudence of any society we know—that it requires little discussion.

The Texas statute undeniably seeks to further the belief of its citizens that certain forms of sexual behavior are "immoral and unacceptable," *Bowers* [*v. Hardwick*, 478 U.S. 186 (1986)—the same interest furthered by criminal laws against fornication, bigamy, adultery, adult incest, bestiality, and obscenity. *Bowers* held that this was a legitimate state interest. The Court today reaches the opposite conclusion. The Texas statute, it says, "furthers *no legitimate state interest* which can justify its intrusion into the personal and private life of the individual" (emphasis added). The Court embraces instead Justice Stevens' declaration in his *Bowers* dissent, that "the fact that the governing majority in a State has traditionally viewed a particular practice as immoral is not a sufficient reason for upholding a law prohibiting the practice." This effectively decrees the end of all morals legislation. If, as the Court asserts, the promotion of majoritarian sexual morality is not even a legitimate state interest, none of the above-mentioned laws can survive rational-basis review. . . .

Today's opinion is the product of a Court, which is the product of a law-profession culture, that has largely signed on to the so-called homosexual agenda, by which I mean the agenda promoted by some homosexual activists directed at eliminating the moral opprobrium that has traditionally attached to homosexual conduct. I noted in an earlier opinion the fact that the American Association of Law Schools (to which any reputable law school must seek to belong) excludes from membership any school that refuses to ban from its job-interview facilities a law firm (no matter how small) that does not wish to hire as a prospective partner a person who openly engages in homosexual conduct. See *Romer* [*v. Evans*, 517 U.S. 620 (1996)].

One of the most revealing statements in today's opinion is the Court's grim warning that the criminalization of homosexual conduct is "an invitation to subject homosexual persons to discrimination both in the public and in the private spheres." It is clear from this that the Court has taken sides in the culture war, departing from its role of assuring, as neutral observer, that the democratic rules of engagement are observed. Many Americans do not want persons who openly engage in homosexual conduct as partners in their business, as scoutmasters for their children, as teachers in their children's schools, or as boarders in their home. They view this as protecting themselves and their families from a lifestyle that they believe to be immoral and destructive. The Court views it as "discrimination" which it is the function of our judgments to deter. So imbued is the Court with the law profession's anti-anti-homosexual culture, that it is seemingly unaware that the attitudes of that culture are not obviously "mainstream"; that in most States what the Court calls "discrimination" against those who engage in homosexual acts is perfectly legal; that proposals to ban such "discrimination" under Title VII have repeatedly been rejected by Congress; that in some cases such "discrimination" is mandated by federal statute; and that in some cases such "discrimination" is a constitutional right, see *Boy Scouts of America v. Dale*, 530 U.S. 640 (2000).

Let me be clear that I have nothing against homosexuals, or any other group, promoting their agenda through normal democratic means. Social perceptions of sexual and other morality change over time, and every group has the right to persuade its fellow citizens that its view of such matters is the best. That homosexuals have achieved some success in that enterprise is attested to by the fact that Texas is one of the few remaining States that criminalize private, consensual homosexual acts. But persuading one's fellow citizens is one thing, and imposing one's views in absence of democratic majority will is something else. I would no more require a State to criminalize homosexual acts—or, for that matter, display any moral disapprobation of them—than I would forbid it to do so. What Texas has chosen to do is well within the range of traditional democratic action, and its hand should not be stayed through the invention of a brand-new "constitutional right" by a Court that is impatient of democratic change. It is indeed true that "later generations can see that laws once thought necessary and proper in fact serve only to oppress;" and when that happens, later generations can repeal those laws. But it is the premise of our system that those judgments are to be made by the people, and not imposed by a governing caste that knows best.

One of the benefits of leaving regulation of this matter to the people rather than to the courts is that the people, unlike judges, need not carry things to their logical conclusion. The people may feel that their disapprobation of homosexual conduct is strong enough to disallow homosexual marriage, but not strong enough to criminalize private homosexual acts—and may legislate accordingly. The Court today pretends that it possesses a similar freedom of action, so that that we need not fear judicial imposition of homosexual marriage, as has recently occurred in Canada. At the end of its opinion—after having laid waste the foundations of our rational-basis jurisprudence—the Court says that the present case "does not involve whether the government must give formal recognition to any relationship that homosexual persons seek to enter." Do not believe it. . . .

Case **6.6**

United States v. Windsor
570 U.S. _____ (2013)

Justice Scalia's dissenting opinion in *Lawrence* noted that the majority argued that the Court would not have to deal with "any relationship that homosexual persons seek to enter.'" He ended with this warning, "Do not believe it." He was right in one sense: in 2013, the issue of same-sex marriage reached the Court in two cases, one involving a federal law, known as the Defense of Marriage Act or DOMA, the other an amendment to the California constitution stating that the state recognized only marriages between one man and one woman.

In 1996, Congress passed DOMA that also recognized marriage as the union of one man and one woman. DOMA was an amendment to the "Dictionary Act," a measure that identified over 1,000 federal programs, including social security survivors' benefits, filing joint tax returns, and non-payment of estate taxes for a surviving spouse. Section 3 of DOMA denied all these federal benefits to same-sex couples. President Barack Obama supported it until 2011 when he announced that the Department of Justice would no longer defend it in court but would continue to enforce it.

In 2007, Edith Windsor and Thea Clara Spyer were married in Ontario, Canada. Two years later, Spyer died, leaving her entire estate to Windsor who was, because of DOMA, faced with a federal inheritance tax bill of over $363,000. A surviving spouse in an opposite-sex marriage would not have had to pay any tax. The Internal Revenue Service rejected Windsor's exemption claim.

In 2011, New York State legalized same-sex marriages and Windsor filed suit in federal district court against the IRS demanding a refund. That court overturned DOMA on grounds that it violated the equal protection of the laws as incorporated into the Due Process Clause of the Fifth Amendment. See *Bolling v. Sharpe* (1954) and *Adarand Constructors, Inc. v. Pena,* above, when the Court created and used the principle of "reverse incorporation:" the Due Process Clause of the Fifteenth Amendment incorporates the Equal Protection Clause of the Fourteenth Amendment and applies it to the United States.

Because the Obama administration declined to defend the

law, the Republican leadership of the House of Representatives, the Bipartisan Legal Advisory Group or BLAG, intervened. Five leaders of House Republicans led by Speaker of the House John Boehner argued the case for DOMA. The United States Court of Appeals for the Second Circuit affirmed the lower court decision to overturn the act. At this point, even with the law overturned at the circuit court level, the Justice Department appealed to the Supreme Court, arguing that the final decision on the law must come from the nation's highest court, which granted *certiorari*.

In its decision, the Supreme Court focused only on Section 3's denial of federal benefits to same-sex couples. It specifically did not deal with another section of the law that allowed the states to refuse to recognize the marriages of these spouses. Nor did it deal with the level of scrutiny required in cases involving gay and lesbian rights: Windsor and the United States asked the Court to employ heightened scrutiny standard, as it does in sex discrimination cases, rather than the rational basis test. See Box 4.1 above, "Three Judicial Tests."

In a five to four ruling, Justice Anthony Kennedy, writing for the Court, held that BLAG had standing because the Second Circuit required the IRS to issue a refund with interest: the United States thus suffered "a real and immediate economic injury." He then ruled that the denial of federal benefits to same-sex married couples violated the Due Process Clause of the Fifth Amendment as it incorporated the equal protection of the laws. The federal government must therefore offer all benefits to same-sex married couples in those states that recognized such marriages just as it does to opposite-sex ones.

Joined by Justices Ginsburg, Breyer, Sotomayor, and Kagan, Kennedy declined to rule that same-sex marriage was a fundamental right under the Constitution. Nor did he rule on the standard that courts should use in gay and lesbian rights cases. Chief Justice Roberts and Justices Scalia, Thomas, and Alito dissented.

Justice KENNEDY delivered the opinion of the Court.

By history and tradition the definition and regulation of marriage . . . has been treated as being within the authority and realm of the separate States. Yet it is further established that Congress, in enacting discrete statutes, can make determinations that bear on marital rights and privileges. . . . DOMA has a far greater reach; for it enacts a directive applicable to over 1,000 federal statutes and the whole realm of federal regulations. And its operation is directed to a class of persons that the laws of New York, and of 11 other States, have sought to protect.

In order to assess the validity of that intervention it is necessary to discuss the extent of the state power and authority over marriage as a matter of history and tradition. State laws defining and regulating marriage, of course, must respect the constitutional rights of persons, see, e.g., *Loving v. Virginia*, 388 U.S. 1 (1967); but, subject to those guarantees, "regulation of domestic relations" is "an area that has long been regarded as a virtually exclusive province of the States." *Sosna v. Iowa*, 419 U.S. 393 (1975). . . .

Against this background DOMA rejects the long-established precept that the incidents, benefits, and obligations of marriage are uniform for all married couples within each State, though they may vary, subject to constitutional guarantees, from one State to the next. Despite these considerations, it is unnecessary to decide whether this federal intrusion on state power is a violation of the Constitution because it disrupts the federal balance. The State's power in defining the marital relation is of central relevance in this case quite apart from principles of federalism. Here the State's decision to give this class of persons the right to marry conferred upon them a dignity and status of immense import. When the State used its historic and essential authority to define the marital relation in this way, its role and its power in making the decision enhanced the recognition, dignity, and protection of the class in their own community. DOMA, because of its reach and extent, departs from this history and tradition of reliance on state law to define marriage. . . .

The Federal Government uses this state-defined class for the opposite purpose—to impose restrictions and disabilities. That result requires this Court now to address whether the resulting injury and indignity is a deprivation of an essential part of the liberty protected by the Fifth Amendment. What the State of New York treats as alike the federal law deems unlike by a law designed to injure the same class the State seeks to protect. . . .

DOMA seeks to injure the very class New York seeks to protect. By doing so it violates basic due process and equal protection principles applicable to the Federal Government. See U. S. Const., Amdt. 5; *Bolling v. Sharpe*, 347 U.S. 497 (1954). . . . DOMA cannot survive under these principles. . . . DOMA's unusual deviation from the usual tradition of recognizing and accepting state definitions of marriage here operates to deprive same-sex couples of the benefits and responsibilities that come with the federal recognition of their marriages. This is strong evidence of a law having the purpose and effect of disapproval of that class. The avowed purpose and practical effect of the law here in question are to impose a disadvantage, a separate status, and so a stigma upon all who

enter into same-sex marriages made lawful by the unquestioned authority of the States.

The history of DOMA's enactment and its own text demonstrate
that interference with the equal dignity of same-sex marriages, a dignity
conferred by the States in the exercise of their sovereign power, was
more than an incidental effect of the federal statute. It was its essence. . . .

DOMA writes inequality into the entire United States Code. The
particular case at hand concerns the estate tax, but DOMA is more than
a simple determination of what should or should not be allowed as an
estate tax refund. Among the over 1,000 statutes and numerous federal
regulations that DOMA controls are laws pertaining to Social Security,
housing, taxes, criminal sanctions, copyright, and veterans' benefits.

DOMA's principal effect is to identify a subset of state-sanctioned
marriages and make them unequal. The principal purpose is to impose
inequality, not for other reasons like governmental efficiency. Responsibilities, as well as rights, enhance the dignity and integrity of the person.
And DOMA contrives to deprive some couples married under the laws
of their State, but not other couples, of both rights and responsibilities.
By creating two contradictory marriage regimes within the same State,
DOMA forces same-sex couples to live as married for the purpose of
state law but unmarried for the purpose of federal law, thus diminishing
the stability and predictability of basic personal relations the State has
found it proper to acknowledge and protect.

By this dynamic DOMA undermines both the public and private
significance of state-sanctioned same-sex marriages; for it tells those
couples, and all the world, that their otherwise valid marriages are unworthy of federal recognition. This places same-sex couples in an unsta-
ble position of being in a second-tier marriage. . . .

The power the Constitution grants it also restrains. And though
Congress has great authority to design laws to fit its own conception of
sound national policy, it cannot deny the liberty protected by the Due
Process Clause of the Fifth Amendment.

What has been explained to this point should more than suffice to
establish that the principal purpose and the necessary effect of this law
are to demean those persons who are in a lawful same-sex marriage.
This requires the Court to hold, as it now does, that DOMA is unconstitutional as a deprivation of the liberty of the person protected by the
Fifth Amendment of the Constitution.

The liberty protected by the Fifth Amendment's Due Process
Clause contains within it the prohibition against denying to any person
the equal protection of the laws. See *Bolling; Adarand Constructors, Inc.*
While the Fifth Amendment itself withdraws from Government the
power to degrade or demean in the way this law does, the equal protection guarantee of the Fourteenth Amendment makes that Fifth Amend-

ment right all the more specific and all the better understood and preserved.

The class to which DOMA directs its restrictions and restraints are those persons who are joined in same-sex marriages made lawful by the State. DOMA singles out a class of persons deemed by a State entitled to recognition and protection to enhance their own liberty. It imposes a disability on the class by refusing to acknowledge a status the State finds to be dignified and proper. DOMA instructs all federal officials, and indeed all persons with whom same-sex couples interact, including their own children, that their marriage is less worthy than the marriages of others.

The federal statute is invalid, for no legitimate purpose overcomes the purpose and effect to disparage and to injure those whom the State, by its marriage laws, sought to protect in personhood and dignity. By seeking to displace this protection and treating those persons as living in marriages less respected than others, the federal statute is in violation of the Fifth Amendment. This opinion and its holding are confined to those lawful marriages. The judgment of the Court of Appeals for the Second Circuit is affirmed. It is so ordered.

Justice SCALIA, with whom, the Chief Justice [Roberts] and Justice THOMAS join, dissenting.

This case is about power in several respects. It is about the power of our people to govern themselves, and the power of this Court to pronounce the law. Today's opinion aggrandizes the latter, with the predictable consequence of diminishing the former. We have no power to decide this case. And even if we did, we have no power under the Constitution to invalidate this democratically adopted legislation. The Court's errors on both points spring forth from the same diseased root: an exalted conception of the role of this institution in America.

The Court is eager—*hungry*—to tell everyone its view of the legal question at the heart of this case. Standing in the way is an obstacle, a technicality of little interest to anyone but the people of We the People, who created it as a barrier against judges' intrusion into their lives. They gave judges, in Article III, only the "judicial Power," a power to decide not abstract questions but real, concrete "Cases" and "Controversies." Yet the plaintiff and the Government agree entirely on what should happen in this lawsuit. They agree that the court below got it right; and they agreed in the court below that the court below that one got it right as well. What, then, are we *doing* here?

The answer lies at the heart of the jurisdictional portion of today's opinion, where a single sentence lays bare the majority's vision of our role. The Court says that we have the power to decide this case because if we did not, then our "primary role in determining the constitutionality of a law" (at least one that "has inflicted real injury on a plaintiff") would "become only secondary to the President's." But wait, the reader wonders—Windsor won below, and so *cured* her injury, and the President was glad to see it. True, says the majority, but judicial review must march on regardless, lest we "undermine the clear dictate of the separation-of-powers principle that when an Act of Congress is alleged to conflict with the Constitution, it is emphatically the province and duty of the judicial department to say what the law is."

That is jaw-dropping. It is an assertion of judicial supremacy over the people's Representatives in Congress and the Executive. It envisions a Supreme Court standing (or rather enthroned) at the apex of government, empowered to decide all constitutional questions, always and everywhere "primary" in its role.

This image of the Court would have been unrecognizable to those who wrote and ratified our national charter. They knew well the dangers of "primary" power, and so created branches of government that would be "perfectly co-ordinate by the terms of their common commission," none of which branches could "pretend to an exclusive or superior right of settling the boundaries between their respective powers." The Federalist, No. 49, p. 314 (C. Rossiter ed. 1961) (J. Madison). . . .

In the more than two centuries that this Court has existed as an institution, we have never suggested that we have the power to decide a question when every party agrees with both its nominal opponent *and the court below* on that question's answer. The United States reluctantly conceded that at oral argument. . . .

This suit saw the light of day only because the President enforced the Act (and thus gave Windsor standing to sue) even though he believed it unconstitutional. He could have equally chosen (more appropriately, some would say) neither to enforce nor to defend the statute he believed to be unconstitutional—in which event Windsor would not have been injured, the District Court could not have refereed this friendly scrimmage, and the Executive's determination of unconstitutionality would have escaped this Court's desire to blurt out its view of the law. The matter would have been left, as so many matters ought to be left, to a tug of war between the President and the Congress, which has innumerable means (up to and including impeachment) of compelling the President to enforce the laws it has written. . . .

The opinion does not resolve and indeed does not even mention what had been the central question in this litigation: whether, under the Equal Protection Clause, laws restricting marriage to a man and a woman are reviewed for more than mere rationality. That is the issue that divided the parties and the court below. In accord with my previously expressed skepticism about the Court's "tiers of scrutiny" approach, I would review this classification only for its rationality. [*United States v. Virginia*, 518 U.S. 515 (1996).] As nearly as I can tell, the Court agrees with that; its opinion does not apply strict scrutiny, and its central propositions are taken from rational-basis cases. . . .

Some might conclude that this loaf could have used a while longer in the oven. But that would be wrong; it is already overcooked. The most expert care in preparation cannot redeem a bad recipe. The sum of all the Court's nonspecific hand-waving is that this law is invalid (maybe on equal-protection grounds, maybe on substantive-due-process grounds, and perhaps with some amorphous federalism component playing a role) because it is motivated by a " 'bare . . . desire to harm' " couples in same-sex marriages. . . .

When the Court declared a constitutional right to homosexual sodomy, we were assured that the case had nothing, nothing at all to do with "whether the government must give formal recognition to any relationship that homosexual persons seek to enter." *Lawrence* [*v. Texas*, 539 U.S. 558 (2003)]. Now we are told that DOMA is invalid because it "demeans the couple, whose moral and sexual choices the Constitution protects"—with an accompanying citation of *Lawrence*. It takes real cheek for today's majority to assure us, as it is going out the door, that a constitutional requirement to give formal recognition to same-sex marriage is not at issue here—when what has preceded that assurance is a lecture on how superior the majority's moral judgment in favor of same-sex marriage is to the Congress's hateful moral judgment against it. I promise you this: The only thing that will "confine" the Court's holding is its sense of what it can get away with. . . .

As I have said, the real rationale of today's opinion, whatever disappearing trail of its legalistic argle-bargle one chooses to follow, is that DOMA is motivated by " 'bare . . . desire to harm' " couples in same-sex marriages. How easy it is, indeed how inevitable, to reach the same conclusion with regard to state laws denying same-sex couples marital status. . . .

By formally declaring anyone opposed to same-sex marriage an enemy of human decency, the majority arms well every challenger to a state law restricting marriage to its traditional definition. Henceforth those challengers will lead with this Court's declaration that there is "no legitimate purpose" served by such a law, and will claim that the traditional definition has "the purpose and effect to disparage and to injure" the "personhood and dignity" of same-sex couples. The majority's limiting assurance will be meaningless in the face of language like that, as the majority well knows. That is why the language is there. The result will be a judicial distortion of our society's debate over marriage—a debate that can seem in need of our clumsy "help" only to a member of this institution. . . .

In the majority's telling, this story is black-and-white: Hate your neighbor or come along with us. The truth is more complicated. It is hard to admit that one's political opponents are not monsters, especially in a struggle like this one, and the challenge in the end proves more than today's Court can handle. Too bad. A reminder that disagreement over something so fundamental as marriage can still be politically legitimate would have been a fit task for what in earlier times was called the judicial temperament. We might have covered ourselves with honor today, by promising all sides of this debate that it was theirs to settle and that we would respect their resolution. We might have let the People decide.

But that the majority will not do. Some will rejoice in today's decision, and some will despair at it; that is the nature of a controversy that matters so much to so many. But the Court has cheated both sides, robbing the winners of an honest victory, and the losers of the peace that comes from a fair defeat. We owed both of them better. I dissent.

Rulings in Context

Gay and Lesbian Rights

Hurley v. Irish-American Gay, Lesbian, and Bisexual Group of Boston,
515 U.S. 557 (1995)   9-0

> The Court unanimously reversed a Massachusetts state court decision that veterans who organized a St. Patrick's Day parade could not exclude participants who were gay, lesbian, or bisexual. The Court ruled that the veterans were protected by the First Amendment's guarantee of the right of association and that the gay, lesbian, and bisexual participants could plan their own parade.

Romer v. Evans, 517 U.S. 620 (1996)   6-3

> The Court ruled that an amendment to the Colorado constitution violated the Equal Protection Clause of the Fourteenth Amendment. The amendment prohibited municipal and county subdivisions from passing laws that protected gays against discrimination in the workplace and places of public accommodation.

Boy Scouts of America v. Dale, 530 U.S. 640 (2000)   5-4

> The Court ruled that the Boy Scouts of America may constitutionally bar James Dale as a scoutmaster because he was gay. The Court said that the

First Amendment guarantees of free speech and free association allowed the organization to determine its membership.

Hollingsworth v. Perry   5-4

The Court declined to rule on the constitutionality of Proposition 8, the amendment to the California constitution that passed in 2008 by popular vote officially recognizing marriage as only between one man and one woman. After Governor Jerry Brown decided not to defend the amendment because he believed it violated the Equal Protection Clause, the initial proponents of Prop 8 led by Dennis Hollingsworth intervened. Chief Justice John Roberts ruled that Hollingsworth and other proponents had no standing after the state withdrew. "We have never before upheld the standing of a private party to defend the constitutionality of a state statute when state officials have chosen not to. We decline to do so for the first time here." He vacated the Ninth Circuit's ruling, which shortly thereafter lifted its stay on the injunction that a federal district court judge had placed on the amendment. Same-sex marriages began immediately in California.

The United States Constitution

We the People of the United States, in Order to form a more perfect Union, establish Justice, insure domestic Tranquility, provide for the common defence, promote the general Welfare, and secure the Blessings of Liberty to ourselves and our Posterity, do ordain and establish this Constitution for the United States of America.

Article I.

Section 1.   All legislative Powers herein granted shall be vested in a Congress of the United States, which shall consist of a Senate and House of Representatives.

Section 2.   The House of Representatives shall be composed of Members chosen every second Year by the People of the several States, and the Electors in each State shall have the Qualifications requisite for Electors of the most numerous Branch of the State Legislature.

No Person shall be a Representative who shall not have attained to the Age of twenty five Years, and been seven Years a Citizen of the United States, and who shall not, when elected, be an Inhabitant of that State in which he shall be chosen.

Representatives and direct Taxes shall be apportioned among the several States which may be included within this Union, according to their respective Numbers, which shall be determined by adding to the whole Number of free Persons, including those bound to Service for a Term of Years, and excluding Indians not taxed, three fifths of all other Persons. *(See Note 1)* The actual Enumeration shall be made within three Years after the first Meeting of the Congress of the United States, and within every subsequent Term of ten Years, in such Manner as they shall by Law direct. The Number of Representatives shall not exceed one for every thirty Thousand, but each State shall have at Least one Representative; and until such enumeration shall be made, the State of New Hampshire shall be entitled to chuse three, Massachusetts eight, Rhode-Island and Providence Plantations one, Connecticut five, New-York six, New Jersey four, Pennsylvania eight, Delaware one, Maryland six, Virginia ten, North Carolina five, South Carolina five, and Georgia three.

When vacancies happen in the Representation from any State, the Executive Authority thereof shall issue Writs of Election to fill such Vacancies.

The House of Representatives shall chuse their Speaker and other Officers; and shall have the sole Power of Impeachment.

Section 3.   The Senate of the United States shall be composed of two Senators from each State, chosen by the Legislature thereof, *(See Note 2)* for six Years; and each Senator shall have one Vote.

Immediately after they shall be assembled in Consequence of the first Election, they shall be divided as equally as may be into three Classes. The Seats of the Senators of the first Class shall be vacated at the Expiration of the second Year, of the second Class at the Expiration of the fourth Year, and of the third Class at the Expiration of the sixth Year, so that one third may be chosen every second Year; and if Vacancies happen by Resignation, or otherwise, during the Recess of the Legislature of any State, the Executive thereof may make temporary Appointments until the next Meeting of the Legislature, which shall then fill such Vacancies. *(See Note 3)*

No Person shall be a Senator who shall not have attained to the Age of thirty Years, and been nine Years a Citizen of the United States, and who shall not, when elected, be an Inhabitant of that State for which he shall be chosen.

The Vice President of the United States shall be President of the Senate, but shall have no Vote, unless they be equally divided.

The Senate shall chuse their other Officers, and also a President pro tempore, in the Absence of the Vice President, or when he shall exercise the Office of President of the United States.

The Senate shall have the sole Power to try all Impeachments. When sitting for that Purpose, they shall be on Oath or Affirmation. When the President of the United States is tried, the Chief Justice shall preside: And no Person shall be convicted without the Concurrence of two thirds of the Members present.

Judgment in Cases of Impeachment shall not extend further than to removal from Office, and disqualification to hold and enjoy any Office of honor, Trust or Profit under the United States: but the Party convicted shall nevertheless be liable and subject to Indictment, Trial, Judgment and Punishment, according to Law.

Section 4.   The Times, Places and Manner of holding Elections for Senators and Representatives, shall be prescribed in each State by the Legislature thereof; but the Congress may at any time by Law make or alter such Regulations, except as to the Places of chusing Senators.

The Congress shall assemble at least once in every Year, and such Meeting shall be on the first Monday in December, *(See Note 4)* unless they shall by Law appoint a different Day.

Section 5.   Each House shall be the Judge of the Elections, Returns and Qualifications of its own Members, and a Majority of each shall constitute a Quorum to do Business; but a smaller Number may adjourn from day to day, and may be authorized to compel the Attendance of absent Members, in such Manner, and under such Penalties as each House may provide.

Each House may determine the Rules of its Proceedings, punish its Members for disorderly Behaviour, and, with the Concurrence of two thirds, expel a Member.

Each House shall keep a Journal of its Proceedings, and from time to time publish the same, excepting such Parts as may in their Judgment require Secrecy; and the Yeas and Nays of the Members of either House on any question shall, at the Desire of one fifth of those Present, be entered on the Journal.

Neither House, during the Session of Congress, shall, without the Consent of the other, adjourn for more than three days, nor to any other Place than that in which the two Houses shall be sitting.

Section 6.   The Senators and Representatives shall receive a Compensation for their Services, to be ascertained by Law, and paid out of the Treasury of the United States. *(See Note 5)* They shall in all Cases, except Treason, Felony and Breach of the Peace, beprivileged from Arrest during their Attendance at the Session of their respective Houses, and in going to and returning from the same; and for any Speech or Debate in either House, they shall not be questioned in any other Place.

No Senator or Representative shall, during the Time for which he was elected, be appointed to any civil Office under the Authority of the United States, which shall have been created, or the Emoluments whereof shall have been encreased during such time; and no Person holding any Office under the United States, shall be a Member of either House during his Continuance in Office.

Section 7.   All Bills for raising Revenue shall originate in the House of Representatives; but the Senate may propose or concur with Amendments as on other Bills.

Every Bill which shall have passed the House of Representatives and the Senate, shall, before it become a Law, be presented to the President of the United States; If he approve he shall sign it, but if not he shall return it, with his Objections to that House in which it shall have originated, who shall enter the Objections at large on their Journal, and proceed to reconsider it. If after such Reconsideration two thirds of that House shall agree to pass the Bill, it shall be sent, together with the Objections, to the other House, by which it shall likewise be reconsidered, and if approved by two thirds of that House, it shall become a Law. But in all such Cases the Votes of both Houses shall be determined by yeas and Nays, and the Names of the Persons voting for and against the Bill shall be entered on the Journal of each House respectively. If any Bill shall not be returned by the President within ten Days (Sundays excepted) after it shall have been presented to him, the Same shall be a Law, in like Manner as if he had signed it, unless the Congress by their Adjournment prevent its Return, in which Case it shall not be a Law.

Every Order, Resolution, or Vote to which the Concurrence of the Senate and House of Representatives may be necessary (except on a question of Adjournment) shall be presented to the President of the United States; and before the Same shall take Effect, shall be approved by him, or being disapproved by him, shall be repassed by two thirds of the Senate and House of Representatives, according to the Rules and Limitations prescribed in the Case of a Bill.

Section 8.   The Congress shall have Power To lay and collect Taxes, Duties, Imposts and Excises, to pay the Debts and provide for the common Defence and general Welfare of the United States; but all Duties, Imposts and Excises shall be uniform throughout the United States;

To borrow Money on the credit of the United States;

To regulate Commerce with foreign Nations, and among the several States, and with the Indian Tribes;

To establish an uniform Rule of Naturalization, and uniform Laws on the subject of Bankruptcies throughout the United States;

To coin Money, regulate the Value thereof, and of foreign Coin, and fix the Standard of Weights and Measures;

To provide for the Punishment of counterfeiting the Securities and current Coin of the United States;

To establish Post Offices and post Roads;

To promote the Progress of Science and useful Arts, by securing for limited Tmes to Authors and Inventors the exclusive Right to their respective Writings and Discoveries;

To constitute Tribunals inferior to the supreme Court;

To define and punish Piracies and Felonies committed on the high Seas, and Offences against the Law of Nations;

To declare War, grant Letters of Marque and Reprisal, and make Rules concerning Captures on Land and Water;

To raise and support Armies, but no Appropriation of Money to that Use shall be for a longer Term than two Years;

To provide and maintain a Navy;

To make Rules for the Government and Regulation of the land and naval Forces;

To provide for calling forth the Militia to execute the Laws of the Union, suppress Insurrections and repel Invasions;

To provide for organizing, arming, and disciplining, the Militia, and for governing such Part of them as may be employed in the Service of the United States, reserving to the States respectively, the Appointment of the Officers, and the Authority of training the Militia according to the discipline prescribed by Congress;

To exercise exclusive Legislation in all Cases whatsoever, over such District (not exceeding ten Miles square) as may, by Cession of particular States, and the Acceptance of Congress, become the Seat of the Government of the United States, and to exercise like Authority over all Places purchased by the Consent of the Legislature of the State in which the Same shall be, for the Erection of Forts, Magazines, Arsenals, dock-Yards, and other needful Buildings;—And

To make all Laws which shall be necessary and proper for carrying into Execution the foregoing Powers, and all other Powers vested by this Constitution in the Government of the United States, or in any Department or Officer thereof.

Section 9. The Migration or Importation of such Persons as any of the States now existing shall think proper to admit, shall not be prohibited by the Congress prior to the Year one thousand eight hundred and eight, but a Tax or duty may be imposed on such Importation, not exceeding ten dollars for each Person.

The Privilege of the Writ of Habeas Corpus shall not be suspended, unless when in Cases of Rebellion or Invasion the public Safety may require it.

No Bill of Attainder or ex post facto Law shall be passed.

No Capitation, or other direct, Tax shall be laid, unless in Proportion to the Census or Enumeration herein before directed to be taken. *(See Note 6)*

No Tax or Duty shall be laid on Articles exported from any State.

No Preference shall be given by any Regulation of Commerce or Revenue to the Ports of one State over those of another: nor shall Vessels bound to, or from, one State, be obliged to enter, clear, or pay Duties in another.

No Money shall be drawn from the Treasury, but in Consequence of Appropriations made by Law; and a regular Statement and Account of the Receipts and Expenditures of all public Money shall be published from time to time.

No Title of Nobility shall be granted by the United States: And no Person holding any Office of Profit or Trust under them, shall, without the Consent of the Congress, accept of any present, Emolument, Office, or Title, of any kind whatever, from any King, Prince, or foreign State.

Section 10.   No State shall enter into any Treaty, Alliance, or Confederation; grant Letters of Marque and Reprisal; coin Money; emit Bills of Credit; make any Thing but gold and silver Coin a Tender in Payment of Debts; pass any Bill of Attainder, ex post facto Law, or Law impairing the Obligation of Contracts, or grant any Title of Nobility.

No State shall, without the Consent of the Congress, lay any Imposts or Duties on Imports or Exports, except what may be absolutely necessary for executing it's inspection Laws: and the net Produce of all Duties and Imposts, laid by any State on Imports or Exports, shall be for the Use of the Treasury of the United States; and all such Laws shall be subject to the Revision and Controul of the Congress.

No State shall, without the Consent of Congress, lay any Duty of Tonnage, keep Troops, or Ships of War in time of Peace, enter into any Agreement or Compact with another State, or with a foreign Power, or engage in War, unless actually invaded, or in such imminent Danger as will not admit of delay.

Article II.

Section 1.   The executive Power shall be vested in a President of the United States of America. He shall hold his Office during the Term of four Years, and, together with the Vice President, chosen for the same Term, be elected, as follows

Each State shall appoint, in such Manner as the Legislature thereof may direct, a Number of Electors, equal to the whole Number of Senators and Representatives to which the State may be entitled in the Congress: but no Senator or Representative, or Person holding an Office of Trust or Profit under the United States, shall be appointed an Elector.

The Electors shall meet in their respective States, and vote by Ballot for two Persons, of whom one at least shall not be an Inhabitant of the same State with themselves. And they shall make a List of all the Persons voted for, and of the Number of Votes for each; which List they shall sign and certify, and transmit sealed to the Seat of the Government of the United States, directed to the President of the Senate. The President of the Senate shall, in the Presence of the Senate and House of Representatives, open all the Certificates, and the Votes shall then be counted. The Person having the greatest Number of Votes shall be the President, if such Number be a Majority of the whole Number of Electors appointed; and if there be more than one who have such Majority, and have an equal Number of Votes, then the House of Representatives shall immediately chuse by Ballot one of them for President; and if no Person have a Majority, then from the five highest on the List the said House shall in like Manner chuse the President. But in chusing the President, the Votes shall be taken by States, the Representation from each State having one Vote; A quorum for this Purpose shall consist of a Member or Members from two thirds of the States, and a Majority of all the States shall be necessary to a Choice. In every Case, after the Choice of the President, the Person having the greatest Number of Votes of the Electors shall be the Vice President. But if there should remain two or more who have equal Votes, the Senate shall chuse from them by Ballot the Vice President. *(See Note 7)*

The Congress may determine the Time of chusing the Electors, and the Day on which they shall give their Votes; which Day shall be the same throughout the United States.

No Person except a natural born Citizen, or a Citizen of the United States, at the time of the Adoption of this Constitution, shall be eligible to the Office of President; neither shall any Person be eligible to that Office who shall not have attained to the Age of thirty five Years, and been fourteen Years a Resident within the United States.

In Case of the Removal of the President from Office, or of his Death, Resignation, or Inability to discharge the Powers and Duties of the said Office, *(See Note 8)* the Same shall devolve on the Vice President, and the Congress may by Law provide for the Case of Removal, Death, Resignation or Inability, both of the President and Vice President, declaring what Officer shall then act as President, and such Officer shall act accordingly, until the Disability be removed, or a President shall be elected.

The President shall, at stated Times, receive for his Services, a Compensation, which shall neither be encreased nor diminished during the Period for which he shall have been elected, and he shall not receive within that Period any other Emolument from the United States, or any of them.

Before he enter on the Execution of his Office, he shall take the following Oath or Affirmation:—"I do solemnly swear (or affirm) that

I will faithfully execute the Office of President of the United States, and will to the best of my Ability, preserve, protect and defend the Constitution of the United States."

Section 2.   The President shall be Commander in Chief of the Army and Navy of the United States, and of the Militia of the several States, when called into the actual Service of the United States; he may require the Opinion, in writing, of the principal Officer in each of the executive Departments, upon any Subject relating to the Duties of their respective Offices, and he shall have Power to grant Reprieves and Pardons for Offences against the United States, except in Cases of Impeachment.

He shall have Power, by and with the Advice and Consent of the Senate, to make Treaties, provided two thirds of the Senators present concur; and he shall nominate, and by and with the Advice and Consent of the Senate, shall appoint Ambassadors, other public Ministers and Consuls, Judges of the supreme Court, and all other Officers of the United States, whose Appointments are not herein otherwise provided for, and which shall be established by Law: but the Congress may by Law vest the Appointment of such inferior Officers, as they think proper, in the President alone, in the Courts of Law, or in the Heads of Departments.

The President shall have Power to fill up all Vacancies that may happen during the Recess of the Senate, by granting Commissions which shall expire at the End of their next Session.

Section 3.   He shall from time to time give to the Congress Information of the State of the Union, and recommend to their Consideration such Measures as he shall judge necessary and expedient; he may, on extraordinary Occasions, convene both Houses, or either of them, and in Case of Disagreement between them, with Respect to the Time of Adjournment, he may adjourn them to such Time as he shall think proper; he shall receive Ambassadors and other public Ministers; he shall take Care that the Laws be faithfully executed, and shall Commission all the Officers of the United States.

Section 4.   The President, Vice President and all civil Officers of the United States, shall be removed from Office on Impeachment for, and Conviction of, Treason, Bribery, or other high Crimes and Misdemeanors.

Article III.

Section 1.   The judicial Power of the United States, shall be vested in one supreme Court, and in such inferior Courts as the Congress may from time to time ordain and establish. The Judges, both of the supreme and inferior Courts, shall hold their Offices during good Behaviour, and shall, at stated Times, receive for their Services, a Compensation, which shall not be diminished during their Continuance in Office.

Section 2.   The judicial Power shall extend to all Cases, in Law and Equity, arising under this Constitution, the Laws of the United States, and Treaties made, or which shall be made, under their Authority;—to all Cases affecting Ambassadors, other public Ministers and Consuls;—to all Cases of admiralty and maritime Jurisdiction;—to Controversies to which the United States shall be a Party;—to Controversies between two or more States;—between a State and Citizens of another State; *(See Note 9)*—between Citizens of different States,—between Citizens of the same State claiming Lands under Grants of different States, and between a State, or the Citizens thereof, and foreign States, Citizens or Subjects.

In all Cases affecting Ambassadors, other public Ministers and Consuls, and those in which a State shall be Party, the supreme Court shall have original Jurisdiction. In all the other Cases before mentioned, the supreme Court shall have appellate Jurisdiction, both as to Law and Fact, with such Exceptions, and under such Regulations as the Congress shall make.

The Trial of all Crimes, except in Cases of Impeachment, shall be by Jury; and such Trial shall be held in the State where the said Crimes shall have been committed; but when not committed within any State, the Trial shall be at such Place or Places as the Congress may by Law have directed.

Section 3.   Treason against the United States, shall consist only in levying War against them, or in adhering to their Enemies, giving them Aid and Comfort. No Person shall be convicted of Treason unless on the Testimony of two Witnesses to the same overt Act, or on Confession in open Court.

The Congress shall have Power to declare the Punishment of Treason, but no Attainder of Treason shall work Corruption of Blood, or Forfeiture except during the Life of the Person attainted.

Article IV.

Section 1.   Full Faith and Credit shall be given in each State to the public Acts, Records, and judicial Proceedings of every other State. And the Congress may by general Laws prescribe the Manner in which such Acts, Records and Proceedings shall be proved, and the Effect thereof.

Section 2.   The Citizens of each State shall be entitled to all Privileges and Immunities of Citizens in the several States.

A Person charged in any State with Treason, Felony, or other Crime, who shall flee from Justice, and be found in another State, shall on Demand of the executive Authority of the State from which he fled, be delivered up, to be removed to the State having Jurisdiction of the Crime.

No Person held to Service or Labour in one State, under the Laws thereof, escaping into another, shall, in Consequence of any Law or Regulation therein, be discharged from such Service or Labour, but shall be delivered up on Claim of the Party to whom such Service or Labour may be due. *(See Note 10)*

Section 3.   New States may be admitted by the Congress into this Union; but no new State shall be formed or erected within the Jurisdiction of any other State; nor any State be formed by the Junction of two or more States, or Parts of States, without the Consent of the Legislatures of the States concerned as well as of the Congress.

The Congress shall have Power to dispose of and make all needful Rules and Regulations respecting the Territory or other Property belonging to the United States; and nothing in this Constitution shall be so construed as to Prejudice any Claims of the United States, or of any particular State.

Section 4.   The United States shall guarantee to every State in this Union a Republican Form of Government, and shall protect each of them against Invasion; and on Application of the Legislature, or of the Executive (when the Legislature cannot be convened) against domestic Violence.

Article V.

The Congress, whenever two thirds of both Houses shall deem it necessary, shall propose Amendments to this Constitution, or, on the Application of the Legislatures of two thirds of the several States, shall call a Convention for proposing Amendments, which, in either Case, shall be valid to all Intents and Purposes, as Part of this Constitution, when ratified by the Legislatures of three fourths of the several States, or by Conventions in three fourths thereof, as the one or the other Mode of Ratification may be proposed by the Congress; Provided that no Amendment which may be made prior to the Year One thousand eight hundred and eight shall in any Manner affect the first and fourth Clauses in the Ninth Section of the first Article; and that no State, without its Consent, shall be deprived of its equal Suffrage in the Senate.

Article VI.

All Debts contracted and Engagements entered into, before the Adoption of this Constitution, shall be as valid against the United States under this Constitution, as under the Confederation.

This Constitution, and the Laws of the United States which shall be made in Pursuance thereof; and all Treaties made, or which shall be made, under the Authority of the United States, shall be the supreme Law of the Land; and the Judges in every State shall be bound thereby, any Thing in the Constitution or Laws of any State to the Contrary notwithstanding.

The Senators and Representatives before mentioned, and the Members of the several State Legislatures, and all executive and judicial Officers, both of the United States and of the several States, shall be bound by Oath or Affirmation, to support this Constitution; but no religious Test shall ever be required as a Qualification to any Office or public Trust under the United States.

Article VII.

The Ratification of the Conventions of nine States, shall be sufficient for the Establishment of this Constitution between the States so ratifying the Same.

Done in Convention by the Unanimous Consent of the States present the Seventeenth Day of September in the Year of our Lord one thousand seven hundred and Eighty seven and of the Independence of the United States of America the Twelfth In witness whereof We have hereunto subscribed our Names, George Washington—President and deputy from Virginia

[Signed also by the deputies of twelve States.]

Delaware: George Read, Gunning Bedford Jr., John Dickinson, Richard Bassett, Jacob Broom; Maryland: James McHenry, Dan of St. Thomas Jenifer, Daniel Carroll; Virginia: John Blair, James Madison Jr.; North Carolina: William Blount, Richard Dobbs Spaight, Hugh Williamson; South Carolina: John Rutledge, Charles Cotesworth Pinckney, Charles Pinckney, Pierce Butler; Georgia: William Few, Abraham Baldwin; New Hampshire: John Langdon, Nicholas Gilman; Massachusetts: Nathaniel Gorham, Rufus King; Connecticut: William Samuel Johnson, Roger Sherman; New York: Alexander Hamilton; New Jersey: William Livingston, David Brearley, William Paterson, Jonathan Dayton; Pennsylvania: Benjamin Franklin, Thomas Mifflin, Robert Morris, George Clymer, Thomas FitzSimons, Jared Ingersoll, James Wilson, Gouverneur Morris

Attest William Jackson Secretary

NOTES

Note 1: The part of this Clause relating to the mode of apportionment of representatives among the several States has been affected by Section 2 of Amendment XIV, and as to taxes on incomes without apportionment by amendment XVI.

Note 2: This Clause has been affected by Clause 1 of Amendment XVII.

Note 3: This Clause has been affected by Clause 2 of Amendment XVIII.

Note 4: This Clause has been affected by Amendment XX.

Note 5: This Clause has been affected by Amendment XXVII.

Note 6: This Clause has been affected by Amendment XVI.

Note 7: This Clause has been superseded by Amendment XII.

Note 8: This Clause has been affected by Amendment XXV.

Note 9: This Clause has been affected by Amendment XI.

Note 10: This Clause has been affected by Amendment XIII.

Note 14: This sentence has been superseded by section 3 of Amendment XX.

Note 15: See amendment XIX and section 1 of Amendment XXVI.

Note 16: Repealed by section 1 of Amendment XXI.

The first ten amendments were ratified on December 15, 1791.

Amendment I

Congress shall make no law respecting an establishment of religion, or prohibiting the free exercise thereof; or abridging the freedom of speech, or of the press; or the right of the people peaceably to assemble, and to petition the Government for a redress of grievances.

Amendment II

A well regulated Militia, being necessary to the security of a free State, the right of the people to keep and bear Arms, shall not be infringed.

Amendment III

No Soldier shall, in time of peace be quartered in any house, without the consent of the Owner, nor in time of war, but in a manner to be prescribed by law.

Amendment IV

The right of the people to be secure in their persons, houses, papers, and effects, against unreasonable searches and seizures, shall not be violated, and no Warrants shall issue, but upon probable cause, supported by Oath or affirmation, and particularly describing the place to be searched, and the persons or things to be seized.

Amendment V

No person shall be held to answer for a capital, or otherwise infamous crime, unless on a presentment or indictment of a Grand Jury, except in cases arising in the land or naval forces, or in the Militia, when in actual service in time of War or public danger; nor shall any person be subject for the same offence to be twice put in jeopardy of life or limb; nor shall be compelled in any criminal case to be a witness against himself, nor be deprived of life, liberty, or property, without due process of law; nor shall private property be taken for public use, without just compensation.

Amendment VI

In all criminal prosecutions, the accused shall enjoy the right to a speedy and public trial, by an impartial jury of the State and district wherein the crime shall have been committed, which district shall have been previously ascertained by law, and to be informed of the nature and cause of the accusation; to be confronted with the witnesses against him; to have compulsory process for obtaining witnesses in his favor, and to have the Assistance of Counsel for his defence.

Amendment VII

In suits at common law, where the value in controversy shall exceed twenty dollars, the right of trial by jury shall be preserved, and no fact tried by a jury, shall be otherwise reexamined in any Court of the United States, than according to the rules of the common law.

Amendment VIII

Excessive bail shall not be required, nor excessive fines imposed, nor cruel and unusual punishments inflicted.

Amendment IX

The enumeration in the Constitution, of certain rights, shall not be construed to deny or disparage others retained by the people.

Amendment X

The powers not delegated to the United States by the Constitution, nor prohibited by it to the States, are reserved to the States respectively, or to the people.

Amendment XI

(*Passed by Congress March 4, 1794. Ratified February 7, 1795.*)

NOTE: Article III, section 2, of the Constitution was modified by amendment 11.

The Judicial power of the United States shall not be construed to extend to any suit in law or equity, commenced or prosecuted against one of the United States by Citizens of another State, or by Citizens or Subjects of any Foreign State.

Amendment XII

(*Passed by Congress December 9, 1803. Ratified June 15, 1804.*)

NOTE: A portion of Article II, section 1 of the Constitution was superseded by the 12th amendment.

The Electors shall meet in their respective states and vote by ballot for President and Vice-President, one of whom, at least, shall not be an inhabitant of the same state with themselves; they shall name in their ballots the person voted for as President, and in distinct ballots the person voted for as Vice-President, and they shall make distinct lists of all persons voted for as President, and of all persons voted for as Vice-President, and of the number of votes for each, which lists they shall sign and certify, and transmit sealed to the seat of the government of the United States, directed to the President of the Senate;—the President of the Senate shall, in the presence of the Senate and House of Representatives, open all the certificates and the votes shall then be counted;—The person having the greatest number of votes for President, shall be the President, if such number be a majority of the whole number of Electors appointed; and if no person have such majority, then from the persons having the highest numbers not exceeding three on the list of those voted for as President, the House of Representatives shall choose immediately, by ballot, the President. But in choosing the President, the votes shall be taken by states, the representation from each state having one vote; a quorum for this purpose shall consist of a member or members from two-thirds of the states, and a majority of all the states shall be necessary to a choice. [And if the House of Representatives shall not choose a President whenever the right of choice shall devolve upon them, before the fourth day of March next following, then the Vice-President shall act as President, as in case of the death or other constitutional disability of the President.—]* The person having the greatest number of votes as Vice-President, shall be the Vice-President, if such number be a majority of the whole number of Electors appointed, and if no person have a majority, then from the two highest numbers on the list, the Senate shall choose the Vice-President; a quorum for the purpose shall consist of two-thirds of the whole number of Senators, and a majority of the whole number shall be necessary to a choice. But no person constitutionally ineligible to the office of President shall be eligible to that of Vice-President of the United States.

*Superseded by section 3 of the 20th amendment.

Amendment XIII

(*Passed by Congress January 31, 1865. Ratified December 6, 1865.*)

NOTE: A portion of Article IV, section 2, of the Constitution was superseded by the 13th Amendment.

Section 1. Neither slavery nor involuntary servitude, except as a punishment for crime whereof the party shall have been duly convicted, shall exist within the United States, or any place subject to their jurisdiction.

Section 2. Congress shall have power to enforce this article by appropriate legislation.

Amendment XIV

(*Passed by Congress June 13, 1866. Ratified July 9, 1868.*)

NOTE: Article I, section 2, of the Constitution was modified by section 2 of the 14th amendment.

Section 1.   All persons born or naturalized in the United States, and subject to the jurisdiction thereof, are citizens of the United States and of the State wherein they reside. No State shall make or enforce any law which shall abridge the privileges or immunities of citizens of the United States; nor shall any State deprive any person of life, liberty, or property, without due process of law; nor deny to any person within its jurisdiction the equal protection of the laws.

Section 2.   Representatives shall be apportioned among the several States according to their respective numbers, counting the whole number of persons in each State, excluding Indians not taxed. But when the right to vote at any election for the choice of electors for President and Vice-President of the United States, Representatives in Congress, the Executive and Judicial officers of a State, or the members of the Legislature thereof, is denied to any of the male inhabitants of such State, being twenty-one years of age,* and citizens of the United States, or in any way abridged, except for participation in rebellion, or other crime, the basis of representation therein shall be reduced in the proportion which the number of such male citizens shall bear to the whole number of male citizens twenty-one years of age in such State.

Section 3.   No person shall be a Senator or Representative in Congress, or elector of President and Vice-President, or hold any office, civil or military, under the United States, or under any State, who, having previously taken an oath, as a member of Congress, or as an officer of the United States, or as a member of any State legislature, or as an executive or judicial officer of any State, to support the Constitution of the United States, shall have engaged in insurrection or rebellion against the same, or given aid or comfort to the enemies thereof. But Congress may by a vote of two-thirds of each House, remove such disability.

Section 4.   The validity of the public debt of the United States, authorized by law, including debts incurred for payment of pensions and bounties for services in suppressing insurrection or rebellion, shall not be questioned. But neither the United States nor any State shall assume or pay any debt or obligation incurred in aid of insurrection or rebellion against the United States, or any claim for the loss or emancipation of any slave; but all such debts, obligations and claims shall be held illegal and void.

Section 5.   The Congress shall have the power to enforce, by appropriate legislation, the provisions of this article.

Changed by section 1 of the 26th amendment.

Amendment XV

(Passed by Congress February 26, 1869. Ratified February 3, 1870.)

Section 1.   The right of citizens of the United States to vote shall not be denied or abridged by the United States or by any State on account of race, color, or previous condition of servitude.

Section 2.   The Congress shall have the power to enforce this article by appropriate legislation.

Amendment XVI

(Passed by Congress July 2, 1909. Ratified February 3, 1913.)

NOTE: Article I, section 9, of the Constitution was modified by amendment 16.

The Congress shall have power to lay and collect taxes on incomes, from whatever source derived, without apportionment among the several States, and without regard to any census or enumeration.

Amendment XVII

(Passed by Congress May 13, 1912. Ratified April 8, 1913.)

NOTE: Article I, section 3, of the Constitution was modified by the 17th amendment.

The Senate of the United States shall be composed of two Senators from each State, elected by the people thereof, for six years; and each Senator shall have one vote. The electors in each State shall have the qualifications requisite for electors of the most numerous branch of the State legislatures.

When vacancies happen in the representation of any State in the Senate, the executive authority of such State shall issue writs of election to fill such vacancies: Provided, That the legislature of any State may empower the executive thereof to make temporary appointments until the people fill the vacancies by election as the legislature may direct.

This amendment shall not be so construed as to affect the election or term of any Senator chosen before it becomes valid as part of the Constitution.

Amendment XVIII

(Passed by Congress December 18, 1917. Ratified January 16, 1919 and repealed by amendment 21.)

Section 1.   After one year from the ratification of this article the manufacture, sale, or transportation of intoxicating liquors within, the importation thereof into, or the exportation thereof from the United States and all territory subject to the jurisdiction thereof for beverage purposes is hereby prohibited.

Section 2.   The Congress and the several States shall have concurrent power to enforce this article by appropriate legislation.

Section 3.   This article shall be inoperative unless it shall have been ratified as an amendment to the Constitution by the legislatures of the several States, as provided in the Constitution, within seven years from the date of the submission hereof to the States by the Congress.

Amendment XIX

(Passed by Congress June 4, 1919. Ratified August 18, 1920.)

The right of citizens of the United States to vote shall not be denied or abridged by the United States or by any State on account of sex.

Congress shall have power to enforce this article by appropriate legislation.

Amendment XX

(Passed by Congress March 2, 1932. Ratified January 23, 1933.)

NOTE: Article I, section 4, of the Constitution was modified by section 2 of this amendment. In addition, a portion of the 12th amendment was superseded by section 3.

Section 1.   The terms of the President and the Vice President shall end at noon on the 20th day of January, and the terms of Senators and Representatives at noon on the 3d day of January, of the years in which such terms would have ended if this article had not been ratified; and the terms of their successors shall then begin.

Section 2.   The Congress shall assemble at least once in every year, and such meeting shall begin at noon on the 3d day of January, unless they shall by law appoint a different day.

Section 3.   If, at the time fixed for the beginning of the term of the President, the President elect shall have died, the Vice President elect shall become President. If a President shall not have been chosen before the time fixed for the beginning of his term, or if the President elect shall have failed to qualify, then the Vice President elect shall act as President until a President shall have qualified; and the Congress may by law provide for the case wherein neither a President elect nor a Vice President shall have qualified, declaring who shall then act as President, or the manner in which one who is to act shall be selected, and such person shall act accordingly until a President or Vice President shall have qualified.

Section 4.   The Congress may by law provide for the case of the death of any of the persons from whom the House of Representatives may choose a President whenever the right of choice shall have devolved upon them, and for the case of the death of any of the persons from whom the Senate may choose a Vice President whenever the right of choice shall have devolved upon them.

Section 5.   Sections 1 and 2 shall take effect on the 15th day of October following the ratification of this article.

Section 6.   This article shall be inoperative unless it shall have been ratified as an amendment to the Constitution by the legislatures of three-fourths of the several States within seven years from the date of its submission.

Amendment XXI

(Passed by Congress February 20, 1933. Ratified December 5, 1933.)

Section 1.   The eighteenth article of amendment to the Constitution of the United States is hereby repealed.

Section 2.   The transportation or importation into any State, Territory, or Possession of the United States for delivery or use therein of intoxicating liquors, in violation of the laws thereof, is hereby prohibited.

Section 3.   This article shall be inoperative unless it shall have been ratified as an amendment to the Constitution by conventions in the several States, as provided in the Constitution, within seven years from the date of the submission hereof to the States by the Congress.

Amendment XXII

(Passed by Congress March 21, 1947. Ratified February 27, 1951.)

Section 1.   No person shall be elected to the office of the President more than twice, and no person who has held the office of President, or acted as President, for more than two years of a term to which some other person was elected President shall be elected to the office of President more than once. But this Article shall not apply to any person holding the office of President when this Article was proposed by Congress, and shall not prevent any person who may be holding the office of President, or acting as President, during the term within which this Article becomes operative from holding the office of President or acting as President during the remainder of such term.

Section 2.   This article shall be inoperative unless it shall have been ratified as an amendment to the Constitution by the legislatures of three-fourths of the several States within seven years from the date of its submission to the States by the Congress.

Amendment XXIII

(Passed by Congress June 16, 1960. Ratified March 29, 1961.)

Section 1.   The District constituting the seat of Government of the United States shall appoint in such manner as Congress may direct: A number of electors of President and Vice President equal to the whole number of Senators and Representatives in Congress to which the District would be entitled if it were a State, but in no event more than the least populous State; they shall be in addition to those appointed by the States, but they shall be considered, for the purposes of the election of President and Vice President, to be electors appointed by a State; and they shall meet in the District and perform such duties as provided by the twelfth article of amendment.

Section 2.   The Congress shall have power to enforce this article by appropriate legislation.

Amendment XXIV

(*Passed by Congress August 27, 1962. Ratified January 23, 1964.*)

Section 1. The right of citizens of the United States to vote in any primary or other election for President or Vice President, for electors for President or Vice President, or for Senator or Representative in Congress, shall not be denied or abridged by the United States or any State by reason of failure to pay poll tax or other tax.

Section 2. The Congress shall have power to enforce this article by appropriate legislation.

Amendment XXV

(*Passed by Congress July 6, 1965. Ratified February 10, 1967.*)

NOTE: Article II, section 1, of the Constitution was affected by the 25th amendment.

Section 1. In case of the removal of the President from office or of his death or resignation, the Vice President shall become President.

Section 2. Whenever there is a vacancy in the office of the Vice President, the President shall nominate a Vice President who shall take office upon confirmation by a majority vote of both Houses of Congress.

Section 3. Whenever the President transmits to the President pro tempore of the Senate and the Speaker of the House of Representatives his written declaration that he is unable to discharge the powers and duties of his office, and until he transmits to them a written declaration to the contrary, such powers and duties shall be discharged by the Vice President as Acting President.

Section 4. Whenever the Vice President and a majority of either the principal officers of the executive departments or of such other body as Congress may by law provide, transmit to the President pro tempore of the Senate and the Speaker of the House of Representatives their written declaration that the President is unable to discharge the powers and duties of his office, the Vice President shall immediately assume the powers and duties of the office as Acting President.

Thereafter, when the President transmits to the President pro tempore of the Senate and the Speaker of the House of Representatives his written declaration that no inability exists, he shall resume the powers and duties of his office unless the Vice President and a majority of either the principal officers of the executive department or of such other body as Congress may by law provide, transmit within four days to the President pro tempore of the Senate and the Speaker of the House of Representatives their written declaration that the President is unable to discharge the powers and duties of his office. Thereupon Congress shall decide the issue, assembling within forty-eight hours for that purpose if not in session. If the Congress, within twenty-one days after receipt of the latter written declaration, or, if Congress is not in session, within twenty-one days after Congress is required to assemble, determines by two-thirds vote of both Houses that the President is unable to discharge the powers and duties of his office, the Vice President shall continue to discharge the same as Acting President; otherwise, the President shall resume the powers and duties of his office.

Amendment XXVI

(*Passed by Congress March 23, 1971. Ratified July 1, 1971.*)

NOTE: Amendment 14, section 2, of the Constitution was modified by section 1 of the 26th amendment.

Section 1.   The right of citizens of the United States, who are eighteen years of age or older, to vote shall not be denied or abridged by the United States or by any State on account of age.

Section 2.   The Congress shall have power to enforce this article by appropriate legislation.

Amendment XXVII

(*Originally proposed Sept. 25, 1789. Ratified May 7, 1992.*)

No law, varying the compensation for the services of the Senators and Representatives, shall take effect, until an election of representatives shall have intervened.